ÉMINENCE

Cardinal Richelieu and the Rise of France

ÉMINENCE

Cardinal Richelieu and the Rise of France

JEAN-VINCENT BLANCHARD

Walker & Company

New York

Published by Walker Publishing Company, Inc., New York

A Division of Bloomsbury Publishing

All papers used by Walker & Company are natural, recyclable products made from wood grown in well-managed forests. The manufacturing processes conform to the environmental regulations of the country of origin.

LIBRARY OF CONGRESS CATALOGING-IN-PUBLICATION DATA HAS BEEN APPLIED FOR.

ISBN: 978-0-8027-1704-7

Visit Walker & Company's Web site at www.walkerbooks.com

First U.S. edition 2011

1 3 5 7 9 10 8 6 4 2

Typeset by Westchester Book Group
Printed in the U.S.A. by Quad/Graphics, Fairfield, Pennsylvania

CONTENTS

Il m'a fait trop de bien pour en dire du mal
Il m'a fait trop de mal pour en dire du bien

—PIERRE CORNEILLE

Introduction

TAKE A LOOK AT his portrait. See the poised authority of the statesman, the gaze that stares back with lucid intelligence, and maybe a touch of bemused irony, as if he had just been asked a question ignorant of the magnitude of his responsibilities, the immense task of making France a powerful and prestigious land. Notice the blue ribbon and cross of the Order of the Holy Ghost, elegant gesture of the hand, the studied theatricality of the décor.

These are not just effects born under the flattering paintbrush of the painter Philippe de Champaigne. Armand-Jean du Plessis—Cardinal Richelieu's full name—was a leader of the government of France, a chief of diplomacy, and a war commander. Born in 1585, he became a cardinal of the Catholic Church in 1622, and then Duc de Richelieu in 1631, in recognition of his outstanding service as principal minister to King Louis XIII, the father of the Sun King, Louis XIV. Among the many exploits that earned Richelieu elevation and fame was the 1628 siege of La Rochelle, where he subdued those French Protestants who threatened the political unity of the kingdom. His career at the service of the French king continued for many years, during which he untangled the intrigues of the high nobility, and fought the hegemonic ambitions of the Spanish and Austrian Habsburgs. For generations, the French have learned that the cardinal strengthened the monarchy, shaped the character of their nation, and was a crucial actor in a chaotic conflict, the Thirty Years' War, out of which modern Europe emerged.

"Few statesmen can claim a greater impact on history. Richelieu was the father of the modern state system," asserts Henry Kissinger in his opus, *Diplomacy*.[1] The cardinal was a pragmatist who thought rational political decisions and "natural right" were reconcilable with God's designs. This was in marked contrast with the thinking of most other European rulers, including the Habsburgs, to whom religious orthodoxy and dogma were the foundations of politics. Richelieu wrote: "The natural light of thought makes it obvious to anyone that man, having been created reasonable, is bound to act using this power. Otherwise, he would act against his own nature and consequently offend his Creator."[2] Even though he defeated the French Protestants—or, as they were often called, the Huguenots—at La Rochelle, the cardinal was content merely to obtain their loyalty to Louis XIII, and he did not seek to eradicate their religion. He sought alliances with German Protestant princes and the King of Sweden, Gustavus Adolphus, to counter the ambitions of Holy Roman emperors Ferdinand II and Ferdinand III during the Thirty Years' War. Thereby, it is argued, Richelieu created a balance of power in Europe and contributed to the rise of nationalism. Richelieu was to statesmanship what Machiavelli was to political theory, Galileo to science, or Descartes to philosophy, with the caveat that his greater aim still remained the triumph of Catholicism. "The kingdom of God," he wrote, "is the principle of government, and, indeed, it is such a necessity that without this foundation, no prince can ever reign well and no state can be happy."[3]

Such was his daring statesmanship. Then there was Richelieu's style. One contemporary observed: "In all fairness, this man had great qualities. He carried himself with high poise and in the manner of a grand sire, he spoke agreeably and with amazing ease, his mind was focused and worked with subtle ease, his general manner was noble, his ability to handle business inconceivably adroit, and finally he put a grace in what he did and said that ravished everyone."[4] The cardinal personified politics with what his countrymen call *le grand goût* (the grand taste). Richelieu was a brilliant orator, and his persuasive talents were valuable aids to his governance. He lived in superb palaces, patronized the theater, and founded the Académie Française with a mission to perfect the French language. This style is why, like Colbert, Napoléon, and Général de Gaulle after him, Richelieu is understood to have influenced not only the history of his country but also its civilization.[5]

Nevertheless, any reader who is familiar with Alexandre Dumas's epic *The*

Three Musketeers might ask about another side of the man: the disquieting Richelieu for whom the ends justified the means. To his detractors, indeed, the cardinal's realpolitik appeared to be a betrayal of higher ideals of justice, French tradition, and morality. They decried his network of spies and secret police, viewed his trials as political shams, and lamented how his administrators in the kingdom's provinces enacted his iron will with no concern for local tradition. The punishments Richelieu meted out against those whom he considered threats to the power of the king were often violent, and many thought that this rigor represented brutality more than justice and exemplarity. Other critics argued that the cardinal took advantage of Louis XIII's feeble nature and quashed any dissent in a relentless quest for personal power. The man would show no mercy toward enemies of the state, and the state's enemies were his own. Richelieu seemed high-strung, harsh, and vindictive. A diplomat described his fits of wrath as "canine." Cardinal de Retz, another priest-politician of his time, put it bluntly: "He struck down humans like lightning rather than governing them."[6] The scandal, of course, was even worse when these critics thought he used his moral authority to cover political and personal crimes. Guy Patin, one of Richelieu's contemporaries, called him the "red tyrant": the scarlet color of the cardinal's robe, instead of signaling that he stood ready to shed his blood for the love of humanity, had come to represent the blood of his victims.

How did Cardinal Richelieu govern with a principle of human rationality, a "reason of state," while still thinking that he was doing God's work? Did character influence his decisions, and were his personal ambitions truly limitless? The historian who wishes to answer these questions faces many challenges. Because Richelieu promised Louis XIII early on that he would "use all the resources necessary, and the authority that he would care to give [him], to ruin the Huguenots' party, to humble the high nobility, to bring all the subjects to know their duty, and to raise his name in all the foreign nations up to where it should be," nineteenth-century and early twentieth-century French historians often readily recognized a sense of purpose throughout his career.[7] To be a republican and nationalist hero, Richelieu needed to be a clairvoyant political genius: "Richelieu was one of the greatest politicians of modern times, and one of those who did the most for France's grandeur and unity," said the *Dictionnaire Universel.*[8] It is always crucial, however, to beware of hindsight in writing a biography, especially in the case of a man who always took great care of how his own life and legacy would be perceived by posterity.

Richelieu died in 1642. Consider, then, that it took six years of skillful diplomacy for his successor, Giulio Mazarini, to ratify the Treaties of Westphalia that terminated the Thirty Years' War (1648), and eleven years of military action to sign the Treaty of the Pyrenees that brought a satisfying conclusion to France's war with Spain (1659). Consider, last but not least, that France was roiled from 1648 to 1652 by a civil war known as the Fronde. How is it that we consider Richelieu's political action to have been so decisive, and having laid such firm foundations for French power? Even those contemporaries of the cardinal who did not hate him with a passion could still hold a surprising, if not dim, view on the real outcomes of his ministerial career. Surely they were less susceptible to hindsight than we are. The memoirist Claude de Bourdeille de Montrésor squarely attributed the few successes he was willing to recognize in Richelieu's endeavors to sheer luck: "Cardinal Richelieu's enterprises owed much more to good fortune than the state owed to his counsel and prudence."[9] One can marvel at how many times fate helped Richelieu, when, for example, Gustavus Adolphus lost his life at the Battle of Lützen, just as the Swedish king was turning out to be an unreliable ally, and even a threat to the cardinal's grand design for a European balance of power. At the very least, telling the life of Richelieu is to find out what political genius really is. It could well be, as expected, a superlative sense of prudence, doubling with an ability to manipulate emotions, notably by deft management of appearances. Or could it be something entirely different, a force whose nature makes it difficult to capture the essence of Richelieu's action and legacy?

In any case, the problem warrants consideration into the life of Richelieu the man. When it comes to character, the historian ventures on even more daunting terrain. The cardinal was born more than four hundred years ago, and, as just noted, he carefully crafted his public image. Yet historians do pay attention to the life of the cardinal as a private individual. That is because seventeenth-century Frenchmen did not dissociate politics from the personal, and to understand what they said about the cardinal one must consider this emotional and ethical life of the statesman. Central to Richelieu's action was his complex and oftentimes tense relation with the dark and enigmatic King Louis XIII. "The six square feet of the king's private study gave him more worries than all of Europe," wrote a contemporary historian.[10] Persons who feature prominently in Richelieu's life are the choleric and stubborn queen mother, Marie de' Medici; the seductive and at times disloyal consort, Queen Anne of Austria; the happy-go-lucky and lethal brother, Gaston d'Orléans. These French royals spent their lives betraying each other, with consequences for both domestic and international politics. Richelieu's existence, as it turns out, was a constant fight for survival. No wonder he fascinated writers of the French romantic period, like Alexandre Dumas and Victor Hugo.

What makes a comprehensive and faithful portrait of Richelieu possible is the wealth of primary sources that have survived. His correspondence is available, partly in print editions, partly still as manuscripts.[11] To produce a general history of Louis's reign and his career, and for the general purpose of constituting an archive, the cardinal asked his clerks to file all sorts of materials, including interrogation and trial proceedings, reports from spies and agents, and even simple memos where he summed up a particular situation for future reference; we still have this history of Louis XIII—a long tradition refers to it as the *Mémoires* of the cardinal—and many of those supporting documents.[12] The records of the cardinal's operatives and state secretaries are also extensive. Of great interest are the dispatches sent by diplomatic envoys at the court of France to their own governments. I made extensive use of those diplomatic sources because, although not entirely devoid of bias, they offer an alternative view to French official sources and to Richelieu's oftentimes self-serving narrative of his ministry. Seeing the court of Louis XIII through the keen Italian prose of the Venetian ambassadors, or of the papal nuncios, is fascinating. The correspondences of the time also give us a good sense of the French mood in general, especially in the capital, Paris. Then there are the memoirs written by contemporaries, stories that are sometimes a little too fancy or self-involved to be entirely reliable, but that can give rich details. Preference is given to eyewitness testimonies and those least suspect of political bias. One of the first newspapers ever printed, the *Gazette de France*, as well as many pamphlets and chronicles, provides descriptions of key events. Last but not least, the works of other historians, particularly those early scholars of Richelieu who interviewed his contemporaries, or accessed documents that have since disappeared, were valuable sources of information.

Some readers, in the end, might find the image of Richelieu that I propose to be quite different from those solemn portraits of Philippe de Champaigne, where the cardinal calmly embodies reason, prudence, and French grandeur. But notice again how, in those portraits, Richelieu stares with piercing intelligence and irony. Or is it melancholy? This gaze, I argue, is that of a man who had the task of making France a powerful and prestigious land, and for that, he had to contemplate the essential, often shockingly violent truth of politics. This gaze reflects how a certain aura of *francité* manifested itself personally and humanly, too. Richelieu's life was a passion for politics in many different ways.

PART I

The Rise

CHAPTER 1

Toward a Coup d'État (1617)

WITH ITS CENTRAL LOCATION near the Palais du Louvre and wide sidewalks leading to the Île de la Cité, the Pont-Neuf, or "New Bridge," had been a popular meeting place ever since King Henri IV finished it and opened it to the public in 1607. Until then, there was actually little space within the moats and walls surrounding Paris. The capital of France still looked like a dense city of the Middle Ages, a maze of narrow winding streets, some of them barely six feet wide, where about 250,000 inhabitants lived in a formidable concentration of humanity. Parisians eagerly went to the new bridge to take a breath of fresh air or learn the latest news.

On the morning of April 25, 1617, the crowd on the bridge was bigger and noisier than usual. From all corners of the city, Parisians had gathered to hear about a coup d'état: a day earlier, sixteen-year-old King Louis XIII had terminated the regency of his mother, Marie de' Medici, and had her favorite, the Italian Concino Concini, shot dead at the gate of the Louvre. For a majority of Parisians there could not have been better news. They held Concini responsible for the political turmoil that engulfed the kingdom since the death of Louis's father in 1610. Also, the coup d'état revealed to Parisians that they now had a true sovereign. Louis XIII was an awkward youngster, and until then he had widely been considered to be completely subject to his mother's authority. Louis's coup surely had not ended the upheavals of Marie's regency. The high nobles threatened the monarchy with demands for more power. French Protestants gave signs of rebellion. More than ever, the Spanish and

Austrian houses of the Habsburgs nurtured ambitions to rule over more of Europe, which the French saw as a mortal threat. Still, on that sunny April 25, 1617, the news indicated to the crowd on the Pont-Neuf that France's dark days were over.

But Concini's killing had not satisfied all Parisians. Around ten o'clock, a clamor arose, from Saint-Germain-l'Auxerrois, a church near the Louvre where Concini's few remaining friends had hastily buried his body in the middle of the night. Hundreds of men, women, and children erupted from the narrow streets that surrounded the palace and ran toward the Pont-Neuf. Those on the bridge discerned they were dragging Concini's naked cadaver, pulled with a rope. When the crowd carrying Concini's body reached the bridge, they strung him up by his feet. Someone cut off his nose, his ears, and gouged his eyes out. A man tore off his genitals.[1] Another one managed to rip out the corpse's heart and licked his fingers with mad delight. Soon the heart was cooked over charcoal, offered in bits, and eaten in a communion of revenge. The mob stopped the few carriages that ventured onto the bridge and asked the passengers to express their loyalty to King Louis XIII. Those who did not shout "Vive le roi!" with enough enthusiasm were pulled from their coaches and beaten with sticks.

One of those carriages carried a slim, dark-haired man in his midthirties, with an aquiline nose and an intelligent gaze. This man caught on the Pont-Neuf was Richelieu.* At the time of the coup, he was a bishop who had risen to become a minister in the regency of Marie de' Medici, dependent on the very man whose naked and mutilated corpse was exposed to the insults and rage of Paris. As Richelieu told it in a vivid page of his memoirs, the danger of his situation on the Pont-Neuf was immediately apparent. The howling mob could have lynched him next to Concini's mangled cadaver: "I sensed the great peril in which I had fallen, for if one had shouted that I was a partisan of [Concini], their rage could have led them against those who, having liked him, had accepted his actions, as if they had approved of these."[2] His coachman tried to clear a passage by shouting to those who blocked his way. These

---

*Armand-Jean du Plessis did not hold the title "de Richelieu" before he could inherit the family estate from his brother Henri, who passed away in 1619. We shall already name him Richelieu for the sake of clarity.

efforts attracted the attention of a few men in the mob, who turned toward the carriage. Instinctively, Richelieu leaned through the window of his carriage and urged his men to shout: "Vive le roi! Vive le roi!"

The crowd opened to let the carriage go. The mob carried on its festival of revenge by parading the corpse of Concini throughout Paris. Until sunset, the city resounded with screams and insults, from the Bastille in the east to the Faubourg Saint-Germain in the west. What was left of the body at the end of the tour was brought back to the Pont-Neuf and burned, the ashes and bones thrown into the Seine.

Armand-Jean du Plessis was born in Paris on September 9, 1585. His father, François, was a good nobleman from Richelieu, a hamlet in the mid-Atlantic region of the Poitou in western France. Because he was an officer of the royal court, François also kept a residence in Paris to lodge his family. It was the birthplace of Armand-Jean, his third son.[3] Armand-Jean's mother, Suzanne de La Porte, whom du Plessis married in 1569, was not of noble lineage. She was the daughter of a prominent lawyer of the Paris Parlement, the kingdom's principal sovereign court on the Île de la Cité, and could give to the house of Richelieu what many aristocrats held as sufficient reason to betray the rules of their social order: a generous dowry. The Richelieu clan was not rich. As with the greater part of the French nobility, their pride in being warriors for their king was much of all they had for a long time.

The France in which Armand-Jean du Plessis was born was a sad country. During the last four decades of the sixteenth century, the Wars of Religion pitted French Catholics against French Calvinists, of whom there were about a million in a country of sixteen million subjects. These were times of destructive military campaigns, mob massacres, and abominable crimes, times when fanaticism dissolved all social bonds and left the country ravaged. The reigning kings of the Valois dynasty could not pacify their subjects. A figure stood out in this mayhem, the Italian-born Queen Catherine de' Medici, the widow of Henri II who saw three of her children become French monarchs: François II, Charles IX, and Henri III. Catherine held some of the power her son the king had at any time, and she oscillated between tolerance and Machiavellianism. Historians hold her responsible for the most infamous bloodbath of the wars, the Saint-Barthélemy, when, on August 24, 1572, mobs of Parisians murdered thousands of Protestants who were celebrating the wedding of Henri de

Navarre—the future Henri IV—with his first wife, Marguerite, Catherine's own daughter. When Catherine de' Medici died, the religious wars were still raging.

The Richelieu name gained stature when François du Plessis showed distinction in warfare and the art of negotiation, and became a figure in the administration of Henri III. He was Prévost de l'Hôtel du Roi and Grand Prévost de France. The sixteenth-century French kings lived a nomadic existence, traveling from one royal house to another, from the Louvre in Paris to the castles that dotted the Loire Valley. As provost, du Plessis was responsible for planning the voyage of thousands of persons several times a year, organizing everyday life once they settled, keeping the law, and administering justice in the royal domain. When an extremist assassinated Henri III, and Henri de Navarre became the first king of the French Bourbon dynasty, François du Plessis remained at the service of the Crown, even though many other royal officers refused to recognize the new king because of his Protestant faith. The royal army settled in Gonesse to lay siege to Paris, the Catholic dissidents' stronghold. There, du Plessis caught a fever and died on June 10, 1590.

Like many other high-ranking officials at court, François had used his privileged political position to borrow and lend money, but with the kingdom at war, this was not a good time for financial ventures.[4] He also risked money in overseas commercial enterprises. François, it appears, was in considerable debt when he passed away. One contemporary chronicler says that the provost left his household "in a furious jumble."[5] Suzanne de La Porte and her five children—Françoise, Henri, Alphonse, Armand-Jean, and Nicole—were in Richelieu, having left Paris to distance themselves from the religious troubles.[6] Eventually, Suzanne restored stability to her family. She sold the Parisian townhouse where Armand-Jean was born, while managing to keep the house at Richelieu in the family's possession. Armand-Jean grew up in the Poitou province within a close circle of women: his mother, Suzanne; an aunt, Françoise de Marconnay; and his grandmother and godmother, Françoise de Rochechouart. At the time, the family estate was a modest *seigneurie*, by no means remarkable. To call Richelieu a "place of wealth," as an exact translation would have it, was a contradiction.[7] It lay away from major thoroughfares, in the middle of a charming but altogether monotonous countryside. Only a small river, the Mable, flows through it.

In 1594, Armand-Jean left Richelieu to reunite with his brother Henri. The elder du Plessis was a page at the court of Henri IV, who had converted to Catholicism a year earlier and was reaffirming his sovereign authority over all Frenchmen. Tradition has it that a family of clerks related to Armand-Jean's maternal grandfather, the Bouthilliers, agreed to take care of him while he went to school in the capital. He undertook the classical *cursus* in the humanities at the Collège de Navarre on the Left Bank, the place of many schools and private academies, and studied classical letters and the art of rhetoric. Because he was a third male child, Armand-Jean's prospects were not promising. To avoid breaking up the family line's possessions, the eldest son of a noble family traditionally inherited everything. The second son could hope for an ecclesiastical career. After the Collège de Navarre, Richelieu went to the academy of Antoine de Pluvinel, the place of choice to perfect skills in horseback riding, the handling of arms, and dancing, all skills necessary to be a proper noble. The young man likely prepared for a career in the army. But an unexpected event changed the course of his life forever.[8]

Since 1584, the du Plessis family held the rights to appoint the bishop in Luçon, a city on the Atlantic coast, and this privilege allowed them to draw steady revenues from the bishopric. Henri (the eldest son) and his mother destined Alphonse (the second son) to this seat. Suddenly, in 1602, Alphonse announced that he wanted to be a monk instead, and he joined the Grande Chartreuse monastery, set deep in the Alps near Grenoble. The duty fell naturally to Armand-Jean, who began a course of religious studies. A theology degree was not necessary to become a bishop, but pursuing advanced studies placed him in a better position to secure his family's source of revenue—his nomination was contingent on the king's final approval. Armand-Jean left the Pluvinel academy to follow a course on the canons of Aristotle's philosophical teachings, which allowed him to join the Collège de Sorbonne, one of Europe's most prestigious schools of theology. By all accounts the younger Richelieu was a fine student, perhaps not the intellectual wonder that his later apologists described, but certainly a diligent and capable scholar. His elder brother Henri, at the same time, was making a name for himself at court through his military skills. At the end of the year 1606, King Henri named Armand-Jean du Plessis, aged twenty-one, Bishop of Luçon.

Richelieu traveled to Rome to obtain a special permission from the pope because he was not yet twenty-six, the minimum age to be a bishop. In Rome, he was first made a priest, and then consecrated a bishop by Pope Paul V, after winning the esteem of many with his intelligence and piety. The spiritual center of Catholicism basked in the enthusiasm and militant spirit generated by the Council of Trent (1545–1563), the ecumenical conference by which the Church had responded to the Protestant challenge. The Catholic Reformation was also very much an enterprise to win over souls by means of artistic propaganda. The temporal splendors of Rome, such as those grand baroque churches built by the new order of the Jesuits, or the sumptuous palaces that cardinals from the Roman aristocratic families built for themselves, no doubt showed Richelieu that religion is as much a matter of politics and appearances as of creed and faith.

Upon returning to Paris, Richelieu studied for a few more months, though the new bishop never obtained a doctorate in theology, probably because he had to leave for Luçon in 1608.[9] The bishopric at Luçon could mean more than merely fulfilling familial duties. Under the firm rule of Henri IV and his minister Maximilien de Béthune, Duc de Sully, peace was restored all over France. Agriculture, commerce, and even manufacturing developed, thanks to a new infrastructure of roads and canals. This new wealth also benefited the Church. France, like most other countries in Europe, had been for centuries a land of religious ignorance, superstition, and clerical illiteracy and corruption, making it a fertile ground for the Reformation. But in the wake of the Council of Trent, spiritual effervescence, apostolic zeal, and Catholic reform were the order of the day. Figures such as François de Sales and Jeanne de Chantal encouraged forms of devotion designed to attract new followers. They also envisioned the founding of new religious orders. The Jesuits were establishing an admirable network of schools to educate the ruling classes. Overseeing the diocese of Luçon presented Richelieu with a chance to participate in that budding renewal. Through his administrative duties, he had an opportunity to develop the talents of a leader and improve his material life. Richelieu was not rich. He even had to borrow a coach and four horses to reach his new home.

Yet departing for a provincial bishopric also took Richelieu far away from a fascinating capital. Richelieu always described himself as a true Parisian. He was born there, and it had been a place of learning and formative experiences, including his first, and possibly last, sexual relations with women.[10] When he left, in 1608, Paris shined again as a beacon of intellectual life. Henri had initiated grand projects for his capital and made it a worthy setting for cultural renewal. A town square in the Marais, and a whole urban ensemble at the tip of the Île de la Cité, including the Pont-Neuf, were nearing completion.

Upon his arrival in Luçon, in 1608, the twenty-three-year-old Richelieu discovered a small coastal town of about three thousand inhabitants, a town which he infamously described in a letter as "the ugliest, most dirty and most unpleasant bishopric in France."[11] There, the effects of Henri's rule were not felt yet. Because it lay in the midst of swamps, mudflows menaced Luçon constantly. Disease-carrying mosquitoes infested its air. The Wars of Religion had left many of its structures in ruin, including the cathedral and the bishop's official residence. The clergy of the diocese was in urgent need of motivation and training. The surrounding countryside, where most of the population of the diocese lived, was poor and bleak. Finally, the new bishop had to contend with the strong Protestant power in the region. The Duc de Sully, Henri IV's minister and a Protestant himself, governed the Poitou, and La Rochelle, an important port city nearby, was a Protestant stronghold.

Undaunted by the tasks ahead, the new bishop took to his duties. He preached to his flock in and around Luçon, gave advice, and administered the religious business of clergy training. He organized the repairs to the cathedral and the dredging of the canal that linked the town to the ocean. He prevented the Protestants from building a place of worship near the Catholic church, spied on them for the benefit of the royal council in Paris, and used his spare time to study matters of controversy. Richelieu's zeal to oppose the Reformed faith and to convert the Protestants, nonetheless, never went as far as violating the Edict of Nantes, Henri IV's 1598 royal declaration that guaranteed his subjects freedom of conscience and civil liberties.

Documents needed to retrace Richelieu's personality are naturally scarce at this early stage in his life, when he was a simple provincial bishop. His *Instruction du chrétien*, a catechism published in 1618 but written years earlier in Luçon, indicates an authoritarian outlook. In this book, the bishop extends the meanings of the Fourth Commandment—"Honor your father and your mother"—to ground the power of religious authority: "By that name of father, one should not only understand the fathers and mothers who gave us birth, but also all the prelates of the Church who deserve that name, on account of their spiritual authority and the holy teachings by which they lead us towards a better life."[12] Undoubtedly, as with most of his peers, Richelieu's sense of authority also came from a firm belief that nobles were natural rulers. By the same token, he was very loyal to the monarchy, a belief he expressed in the few sermons that have survived from that period.[13] Some have observed that his capacity and tenacity were rooted in his mother's strong bourgeois work ethic.

Richelieu's remaining correspondence from Luçon shows that he felt the modesty of his material means. Once he paid out revenues due to Henri as head of the family, little was left from the bishopric's income to restore buildings and sustain the lifestyle he found appropriate for his rank. Nevertheless, Richelieu found a suitable house near the cathedral, then purchased a few pieces of silverware to further improve his status. Later he delighted in recruiting a maître d'hôtel who had served the Montpensiers, a prestigious aristocratic family to whom his family was pledged in the Poitou. But seeing his maître d'hôtel serve him with silverware was a meager satisfaction when he dreamed of having a pied-à-terre in the capital: "Since I am a bit glorious, I wouldn't mind showing off more, but for that I would need a lodging [in Paris] where I could be more at ease. What a pity to be a poor noble," he wrote.[14]

No matter how deep his religiosity when Alphonse gave him the bishopric, Richelieu revealed true commitment to the Catholic Church and was a fore-runner of France's Catholic Reformation. His preoccupation to keep his status was not unusual for his times. The only things that could take him away from his duties were recurring migraines and the fevers he caught in the bishopric's unhealthy climate. The diocese's ecclesiastics warmed up to their new bishop and even admired him. Besides his hard work, they surely appreciated the good political connections he maintained with Paris. After 1610 and the death of Henri IV, Richelieu's episcopal dignity allowed him to visit the court on several occasions, even for months at a time. He counted on loyal friends to further his diocese's interests and stay well informed of political news. In 1611, while reorganizing a convent's administration, he met François-Joseph Le Clerc du Tremblay, a Capuchin friar born in 1577 and who became known as Father Joseph, the "Gray Eminence."[15] In 1612, Richelieu preached before Marie de' Medici, Henri's second wife and regent of the kingdom after her husband's death, in the church of Saint-André-des-Arts, in Paris. The Bishop of Luçon stated his admiration for Cardinal du Perron, a prelate-diplomat who also had a reputation for being an outstanding orator. Perhaps this is the kind of larger profile that he aimed for. In truth, it is impossible to determine what was the exact scope of his aspirations at the time, and what purpose there was to his good relations with the regent queen, except that he wanted to be a respectable bishop of the French Catholic Reformation.

By the time Richelieu preached before the royal family, he had found enough money to rent a lodging in the capital. The expense required careful budgeting; his correspondence shows him wondering whether he should not send cheaper wine from Luçon to avoid dealing with expensive Parisian merchants. Still, taking the pied-à-terre turned out to be a good investment. In 1614, six years after Richelieu arrived in the bishopric at Luçon, and while Queen Marie de' Medici contended with increasing difficulties in her regency, a unique opportunity presented itself.

After the madman François Ravaillac assassinated her husband, Henri, in 1610, Marie de' Medici had to lead France until her son Louis reached the age of majority. A robust blond figure with majestic deportment, she had the physique to play the part. Man of war, royal officer, and diplomat of the time, François Duval de Fontenay-Mareuil wrote in his memoirs that when she came to power, "nothing could rival the queen, who without doubt was more beautiful than in the late king's time, as if her blood had renewed when she found herself in that position of authority."[16] The daughter of the Grand Duke of Tuscany, she had been born and raised in Florence, where politics was a home-grown specialty. Once the sovereign court of justice in Paris pronounced her regent, she retained the ministers who had served Henri, maintaining stability in the royal council. Soon after, she organized Louis's coronation, to confirm his legitimacy.[17] Four years after she acceded to power, however, Marie's political liabilities caused her to face serious opposition.

At issue was the peace that existed between French Catholics and Protestants, and the role of France in European confessional and political relations. Henri's marriage with Marie de' Medici had pleased French Catholics and ensured good relations with both the Catholic Habsburg dynasty and Pope Paul V. Ever since the rise to power in 1519 of Holy Roman Emperor Charles V of Habsburg, and even after the 1555–1556 split of his empire in two parts, one ruled by the Spanish branch of the family, one by the Austrian branch, French monarchs and the Habsburgs had often been at war or embroiled in diplomatic disputes. The French were convinced that the Habsburgs nurtured projects of a universal monarchy at their expense. The Spanish king Philip III reigned over what was considered the "elder," richer, and most important branch of the dynasty. His territories comprised the Spanish Netherlands—an area roughly corresponding to Belgium today and which was left after the Dutch United Provinces had seceded—a sizable part of northern and southern Italy, and the vast territories of the Americas.[18] His cousin Emperor Matthias ruled Austria, Hungary, Bohemia, Germany, Lorraine, and a myriad of other states. Some of these possessions were hereditary or elective to the emperor. The Germanic part of the Habsburg empire included the powerful Catholic principality of Bavaria, and many Protestant states large and small, the result of complex religious compromises made necessary after the Reformation. Facing the Habsburgs were England and the Dutch provinces, rich nations rising as maritime powers, and Protestant Denmark and Sweden, kingdoms that gave signs that they would soon affirm their own standing.

Although the Habsburgs' power was immense, there were also dangerous underlying weaknesses to their might. Spain was in urgent need of social reforms because its revenues from the Americas were declining. The diet, a representative assembly that the Holy Roman Emperor needed to consult on some important matters, was a weak institution. Germany lacked any sentiment of political unity, torn as it was not only between Catholics and Protestants, but also between Lutherans and a growing number of Calvinists.

When Spain actively supported France's ultra-Catholics during the Wars of Religion, Henri had declared open hostilities, a conflict eventually resolved with the Treaty of Vervins, on April 13, 1598. Henri's second marriage with a woman who was a descendant of Charles V was a conciliatory political gesture. Pope Paul V could finally hope that the Catholic powers of Europe would show a united front against the Reformation. Yet promoting good relations with the Habsburgs did not make Henri forget that he had been a Protestant. His Edict of Nantes protected the French Protestants from judicial discrimination, allowed them to hold public offices, and even gave them fortified towns. Henri also maintained a benevolent position toward the princes of Reformed Europe. Many subjects, known as the Good Frenchmen, revered their king for these pro-French and nonpartisan politics. At the same time, Henri's sensible balancing act still left the stauncher Catholic Zealots, or the Devouts, hoping that his union with Marie would steer the French toward a more pro-Catholic religious and political stance. In turn, this gave rise to the widely held suspicion that the queen was an agent of dissent, reinforced by unpleasant memories of her distant cousin Catherine's reign and the French Marie spoke with a thick Italian accent.

Such was the situation when Marie de' Medici made a crucial decision: on January 26, 1612, the Crown announced that Louis would marry Anne, the Spanish king Philip III's daughter, and that Louis's sister Élisabeth would take the future Philip IV as her husband. For the regent's disgruntled subjects, the Spanish marriage project was proof of her disregard for the political integrity of the kingdom, even if right after her ascent to power, she had opposed Habsburg imperial influence in Jülich-Clèves-Berg, a strategic territory in the Rhineland. They still held the Habsburgs as a whole to be a formidable threat. Henri II de Bourbon, Prince de Condé, a man who stood second in line as heir to the French throne, expressed his fierce opposition to Marie's policies. His followers included the Ducs de Vendôme, de Longueville, de Bouillon, and de Nevers, all high nobles, many of them quite young. Traditionally, these nobles advised the French sovereign, a role that Henri IV had accepted while maintaining a firm hold on his scepter. They could participate in the royal council, the traditional gathering of the highest officers, where the French monarch—or the regent—sought advice, deliberated, and made his decisions. With the king gone and an Italian woman in charge, Condé and the dukes saw themselves as fighting to free Louis from bad counsel. Notwithstanding their self-proclaimed duty to aid the monarchy, much of their cause had to do with personal gain, because the queen had found it necessary to reduce their stipends, to balance the Crown's budget.

The princes' anger and resentment gradually turned toward Marie de' Medici's principal confidants, Concino Concini and his wife, Leonora Galigaï. The thirty-one-year-old Italian was a pleasant-looking man, "tall and straight, well proportioned," with graceful manners and taste for gambling.[19] He had come to France as part of Marie's expatriate entourage. Initially she employed him as her maître d'hôtel, to manage her household; then he became her equerry, the master of her horse. While Concini had noble origins, his wife, who also came from Tuscany, was a commoner.[20] Yet because the queen cherished her for having been her childhood companion at the Pitti Palace in Florence, she wielded even more power than he did. In charge of the queen's finery, the small, frail, and dark Leonora resided at the Louvre, in a luxuriously appointed apartment that stood above the queen's own. Concini and Leonora lived separately and often fought. But they had two children, and Concini took care of his wife when she had to be exorcised for suffering from a mysterious psycho-somatic condition.[21] The true cement of their union was ambition and greed, and they quickly rose in the ranks of French society after Henri's death. Marie made Concini the king's lieutenant general in the region of Picardy and gave her two protégés the titles Marquis and Marquise d'Ancre. It did little to quiet the xenophobia of the French nobles. She then offered Concini even more distinctions, including the titles of counsel to the state and marshal of the army. The rank of marshal was typically the reward for outstanding service, yet Concini had absolutely no military experience. To further irritate the nobles, the Concinis did what royal favorites did in those days: they peddled their influence and trafficked public charges to amass a fortune.

In early 1614, one by one, Condé and the other malcontents left Paris to arm themselves in their provinces. The prince wrote a manifesto on February 19 to voice his grievances. Marie de' Medici could have opted to nip this revolt in the bud. Instead, she appeased the rebels with a peace treaty. Besides granting money to the princes and postponing the Spanish marriages until at least the king would reach the age of legal majority at thirteen, the treaty called for con-vening the Estates General, an emergency meeting of the three major divisions of society: the clergy, the nobility, and the so-called Third Estate, which repre-sented the bulk of France's population. Throughout the kingdom, local au-thorities began to organize the election of delegates for each of these three constituencies. To call for the Estates General was not an ordinary decision; while they had convened a few times during the Wars of Religion, they would only meet twice again, during the period of civil disturbances known as the Fronde, and then at the great revolution of 1789.

During the princes' revolt, the Bishop of Luçon wrote a submissive letter to Concini to express his loyalty to him and to the Crown: "I can only implore you to believe that my promises will always be followed by effects, and that as long as you will honor me with your consideration, I will always serve you with dignity."[22] His position gave him a role to play from the early stages of con-ference organization, when officials called him to poll the clergy of his diocese. Then he joined other church dignitaries to elect two representatives for the Poitou's First Estate, the clergy. On October 27, 1614, the Estates General's 474 delegates first gathered at the Petit-Bourbon Hall in Paris for weeks of meetings. In the crowd was Richelieu, who, after winning the election with the support of an influential church prelate—La Rocheposay, Bishop of Poitiers—had traveled to his native city to be right in the middle of political action.

The Estates were a microcosm of France's highly segmented and hierarchical society, and its discussions contentious from the beginning. The Third Estate comprised the overwhelming majority of the French population, yet no peasants or artisans were to be seen among the delegates. Rather, a privileged order of civil servants represented the Third, most often emerging from the small urban bourgeoisie that made its money from commerce. Many of these officers had posts in the fiscal and judicial administration. Others came from institutions known as parlements. These parlements—there were eight of them in 1614, including the most powerful and prestigious one in Paris—functioned both as courts of appeal and as bodies that had a prerogative, albeit in a non-binding way, to validate the laws enacted by the king, according to settled law or custom.[23]

In this context, one particular issue stood out. The rise of these elite servants of the Third was founded on their capacity to buy the right of employment, which the Crown had been selling for profit. The nobles, who held themselves as socially superior, denounced the monarchy's selling of administrative offices, to counterbalance the rise of the Third Estate and, perhaps, because the practice rewarded money instead of talent.[24] The clergy seconded this motion. The Third lamented the increasing poverty in the kingdom, argued for a reduction in taxes, and complained about the high pensions paid by the Crown to the high nobility. Also, it demanded that a fundamental principle be adopted as the law of the kingdom: "The king is sovereign in France, he holds his crown from God only, and there is no power on earth, let it be spiritual or temporal, that can have any right on his kingdom." The proposed law was intended to ward off papal authority and contain the influence of the Jesuits, the militant religious order that many Frenchmen saw as uninterested in indigenous traditions of religious and political independence from Rome. The French clergy, no matter how much it valued that independence, could not accept this law at a time when it argued that the principles of the Council of Trent should be formally accepted as the law of the kingdom.[25]

Richelieu conducted some useful mediation between the nobility and the Third Estate and had a prominent role in the fight against the Third's article. As historian Françoise Hildesheimer remarks, he did not stand in the way of his more established colleagues such as Jacques Davy, Cardinal du Perron, nor did he appear as too partisan, and this moderation might explain why the clergy chose him to pronounce its final speech at the close of the Estates General.[26] On February 23, 1615, almost four months after the beginning of the conference, all delegates gathered for the last time at the Petit-Bourbon near the Louvre, under the vaults of an immense hall gilt with a motif of royal lilies. This event drew such a crowd of fashionable Parisians that cardinals, bishops, nobles, and bourgeois alike were jostled about. The royal family, dressed in ceremonial attire, made its entrance, but the commotion continued. When Marie de' Medici threatened to leave, calm finally prevailed, and thirty-year-old Richelieu took the floor. The bishop spoke about several problems then troubling to his Estate, including the costs of the high nobility's pensions and the selling of charges to the Third Estate. The king only answers to God in the end, said Richelieu, and he might ready himself for the task by admitting prelates to his council.[27] His speech also admonished provocations from the Protestants: "a prince could not tell his subjects to disregard his powers in a better way than by tolerating any harm to the great God that gave him his own powers."[28] Finally, after an hour, the bishop concluded with adroit flattery at Marie de' Medici, whose particular wisdom, he argued, allowed the kingdom to navigate treacherous waters. Followed by an attendant who held a book detailing the wishes of the clergy, Richelieu then approached King Louis, kneeled respectfully, and presented him with the manuscript. The public lauded the distinguished air of his performance: his arguments were stitched together with such art that they seemed inspired as much by divine truth as by reason. After hearing the representatives of the nobility and the Third Estate pronounce their own speeches, Louis XIII thanked all the speakers and promised to consider the wishes of his subjects with great care.

The Estates General led to no tangible results. It merely placated the princes for a while and gave the regency of Marie de' Medici some respite. But for Richelieu's career, it was an important stepping-stone. The queen promoted him when in spite of the princes' continuing opposition, she decided to go through with the Spanish marriages because Louis had reached majority at the age of thirteen.

In August 1615, a convoy of coaches and carriages left Paris in the stifling heat of the hottest summer in memory and headed toward Bordeaux, where wedding ceremonies were to be held. A large army protected it. In Poitiers, Princess Élisabeth, who was promised to the Spanish prince, fell ill from smallpox. The queen asked Richelieu, who had come to visit the court, to care for her daughter while the convoy kept on. After a few weeks, once Élisabeth caught up with the court and reached Bordeaux, the rewards of good service materialized: the Bishop of Luçon was named chaplain to Queen Anne of Austria.[29]

More rewards for good service came after that. Following the royal marriages, the princes led by Condé made Concini their open target of criticism in flurries of pamphlets and threw the kingdom in yet more turmoil by roaming around with troops and forming alliances with both Protestants and members of the Paris Parlement. The Crown agreed to another peace treaty, signed in Loudun in May 1616. This time, the agreement boiled down to additional payments to the princes and a place for Condé in the royal council. For Concini and Leonora, it was time to secure their political power. Leonora persuaded the queen to dismiss the old guard of her ministers, and to replace them with men she trusted. A protégé named Claude Barbin was put in charge of finances. Marie de' Medici also readily agreed to name Richelieu Conseiller d'État, an official adviser to the Crown.

Richelieu settled for good in Paris, this time in the kind of Parisian pied-à-terre he had wanted for so long. The influence of his brother Henri, who commanded in the army and often showed up at court, and the backing of the clergy, not just in France but also in Rome, who were keen to have the talented Richelieu rise, had aided his advancement.[30] Mostly, the Bishop of Luçon owed his rise to the Concinis, the royal favorites, and he continued to write the two Italians the most obsequious letters to assure them of his dedication.[31]

Dauphin Louis was born on September 27, 1601, and he had lived with his parents at the Louvre for only a year when his father was assassinated in 1610. Before then he was raised at the royal Château de Saint-Germain-en-Laye, about twelve miles west of Paris, alongside his five siblings and the legitimized children of Henri's mistresses. Thanks to Louis's personal physician, Jean Héroard, the first three decades in the French king's life are known in extraordinary detail. Héroard tirelessly kept a journal that grew to thousands of pages, painstakingly noting his observations on the king's health, state of mind, and activities.[32] The heir to the throne was quite healthy in his youth. His mood swung between cheerfulness—"gai," Jean Héroard would then write in his daily journal—and a somber and stubborn disposition, "opiniâtre." Fierce tantrums brought the child close to seizure, and his parents would then order a guard to whip him forcefully. His father, Henri, who remained at the Louvre with his queen, could be at once an affectionate and a terrifying father figure. Marie, while not the cold-hearted mother that some historians have depicted, seems to have lacked a nurturing touch.[33] To make matters worse for Louis, she developed a preference for Gaston, her second-born son who had a more appealing physique and personality.

His humiliations notwithstanding, Louis had a keen awareness of his royal status and was a stickler for protocol from his very early years. Once, when the boy was two, Concini came to visit while he played with a small carriage, housing dolls in the likeness of his mother and other nobles. Concini asked Louis where his wife, a commoner, would have to sit. "Gurgling 'Ga' [the king] pointed to a spot backing the rear of the carriage," wrote the physician Héroard, who witnessed the scene.[34] As he grew up, Louis ruled over his band of siblings, setting up a tiny court and organizing elaborate games of soldiery. The Venetian ambassador reported that he was "proud, ardent and agile, he loves already and with predilection arms and horses, and speaks often of wars, of captains, soldiers, and fortresses."[35]

When his father died at the knife of François Ravaillac, the eight-year-old Louis declared himself angry and chagrined. Nightmares tormented him for a long time. Over time he grew into an awkward and introverted teenager. A strong stutter made it difficult for him to communicate. This king did not care for fashion, except when he wore elaborate attire during court ceremonies. His interest in crafts such as gardening, carpentry, and ironwork appeared unbecoming. The liberal arts left him indifferent, but he had an excellent ear for music, played the guitar, and had a talent for sketching. Marie de' Medici, who liked power, took advantage of the fact that many at court doubted her son's fitness for the throne. When Louis reached the age of majority, she maneuvered to become chief of the royal council and maintained her hold on power. Another Venetian ambassador reported that the queen and her two Italian confidants played on the king's nature and gave him mediocre courtiers, to thwart his intellectual development.[36] One day in April 1615, Louis arrived unannounced at a meeting of the royal council. Marie de' Medici took him by the arm and unceremoniously threw him out. "Go frolic somewhere else," she shouted to the blushing thirteen-year-old.[37]

It is easy to speculate that Louis's general awkwardness was the effect of an emotional wound, perhaps due to the beatings sustained in his younger years, his mother's emotional detachment, or, as his most recent biographer, Jean-Christian Petitfils, has argued, his father's death. Contemporaries recognized that Louis's personality was determined by a keen awareness of his inalienable authority and a deep lack of self-esteem.[38]

Whatever the roots of this ambivalent sense of selfhood, Louis grew up to pursue a series of relationships in which he sought the exclusive attention of an attractive man. The passion he had at an early age for Charles d'Albert de Luynes, a handsome Provençal gentleman whom Henri had hired for the royal hunting staff, is one early example. Louis's physician, Héroard, reported in his journal that the boy royal dreamed of his hunting mentor and called his name in his sleep. Day after day, month after month, Louis and Luynes spent much time together. Luynes practiced the art of fowling, which Louis loved with a passion. An expert from a very young age, the boy had an aviary that counted up to 140 birds of prey of different species, with tens of servants attending. His preference went to merlins, a species of small falcons. Luynes was in charge of kites with a support staff of six, for that specific part of the royal aviary only.

After Henri's death, Luynes became master of the king's birds. Years passed. When Louis reached the age of majority, Luynes was still his favorite companion. Eventually, the Concinis took full measure of Luynes's influence on the young sovereign, but they let him stay in his entourage. They did not think that Luynes could pose a threat to their power. Louis did see that the Concinis strengthened their hold over the regency of Marie de' Medici. As the months following the Estates General of 1614 and the wedding went by, and the longer his mother and her clique ignored him while trouble roiled his kingdom, he became even more reclusive and detached, letting out once in a while a caustic remark. Memoirists who got to know the king right at that time concur: only a very keen observer could have discerned that growing exasperation lay behind the king's rare expressions of displeasure.[39] Louis remained outwardly respectful to his mother, and even feared her, but resentment simmered. If we trust the memoirist Paul de Pontchartrain, a royal officer close to the center of power, the Concinis did not grasp this change and even showed outright disdain for the king.[40]

In spite of the peace signed after the marriages, Condé did not return to Paris and stubbornly remained in the province he governed, the Berry. Prompted by Marie de' Medici, Richelieu went to meet him. His diplomacy proved efficient, and, at the end of July, the queen finally saw Condé back to court. The prince made a point of showing up at every session of the council and seemed to finally have quieted. During the month of August, however, Condé banqueted around town with a cohort of brash nobles and toasted the demise of the ruling Bourbon branch and the death of the Italian couple. Concini prudently retreated to one of his strongholds. The queen decided to neutralize Condé by locking him up at the Bastille. Richelieu's role in this decision remains unclear, but quite possibly his forceful temper had some effect. A prince's arrest was a highly sensitive action that needed careful planning and the collaboration of many actors to avoid unnecessary violence. The queen regent informed Louis and asked him to help in the capture of his cousin. The young king agreed. On September 1, 1616, as Condé entered the Louvre for a meeting of the council, the men of his entourage alerted the prince to some suspicious comings and goings around the palace, but Condé proceeded toward Marie de' Medici's apartment. Upon entering the antechamber, the prince saw Louis leaning against the wall near a window, plucking on his guitar. The king greeted Condé warmly and asked him if he would like to join him in a hunting party. The invitation reassured the prince. Louis left the room, and a few moments later a group of armed men arrived to arrest the prince.

The arrest of Condé scandalized the other princes, even those who were not allied with him. It was a grave violation of the unwritten code of hospitality and an attack on a royal prince, the second in line to the throne. In the city, the tension grew to a sudden and violent reaction. Public opinion had been highly unfavorable to the Italian couple. Since the last revolt, and after some skirmishes between Concini and the local powers of Picardy, the princes' relentless printed propaganda had given Marie's favorites a negative reputation, calling them thieves and foreign agents of trouble. Growls of resentment had also been heard ever since the Italian's guard had beaten and left for dead a member of the city's militia. The man, a shoemaker called Picard, had dared to ask for Concini's passport as he left Paris to reach one of his properties. In addition, many Parisians appreciated that Condé often mingled with them casually. After the arrest, an infuriated mob converged on the Hôtel d'Ancre, Concini's residence, and sacked it while one of the mobsters rang the bells at the nearby church of Saint-Sulpice.

Charles III, Duc de Nevers, taking over Condé's role as chief malcontent, left the court and gave signs of unrest from his strongholds in the northeast. Richelieu went to quiet Nevers, but with little success this time. Once back in Paris, he learned of the passing of his mother, Suzanne de La Porte, but chose not to travel to the Poitou to pay his last respects.[41] A few days later, on September 24, the queen shuffled her staff and named new officers to the council. Next to financial officer Claude Barbin, Richelieu was put in charge of foreign affairs as secretary of state, and, a little later, in November, of military affairs. He had no experience in these domains, but the queen was desperate for fresh talent, ideas, and loyalty. At thirty-one, Richelieu now operated much closer to power. The pope agreed that a member of the clergy could be responsible for military affairs. In deference to his title, the bishop demanded priority to speak during royal council meetings; seasoned officers found him quite arrogant. Though his new responsibilities were more significant, he was still not the most influential figure in the government.[42] One person for whom he showed due respect was Leonora: "Above everything I desire the honor of remaining in your thoughts, and you have given me that [with your gratification]. Thus I have contracted such a debt, that I can thank you for it, but I will never be able to rightly acknowledge that favor, a favor that I hold in such high esteem, all the more so that it comes from a fair lady in a time of continuing misfortune [the passing of his mother, which had come after that of his sister Françoise]."[43]

Richelieu held fast in this time of turmoil. The former minister in charge of foreign affairs, Nicolas de Neufville, Sieur de Villeroy, had kept all his diplomatic papers to himself to express his adversity to the current government, requiring double work and making the task even more difficult for a young man with no experience.[44] Richelieu sent missives to diplomats in every corner of France and Europe and made his first attempts at international diplomacy. For the last few years the Venetians, the Habsburgs, and the Dukes of Mantua and of Savoy had clashed over territorial disputes and security matters in northern Italy; particularly contested was the strategic principality of the Monferrato, south of the Piedmont. Belying the ambassadors who thought that as a clergyman he had to represent the Catholic pro-Habsburg party within the council, Richelieu followed the audacious and neutral diplomatic path of Henri IV: his plan was to convene a peace conference in Paris and broker an accord.[45] But this was too ambitious a plan for the newly appointed foreign minister of a troubled regime, and he saw his initiative flounder when

Spain and Rome took matters into their own hands to settle the disputes. This was not the last Richelieu would hear of the Monferrato. In another move, he sent diplomats to Protestant princes all over Europe, to reassure those who had trusted Henri IV that intolerant Catholic views did not guide French policy. The instruction carried by the envoy to Germany, Henri de Schomberg, could not have been clearer: "To say that we are so Roman and Spanish that we would embrace those interests of Rome, or Spain, with prejudice to our former alliances and to ourselves, meaning also to the French Protestants and anyone else who hates Spain and thus professes to be a *good Frenchman*, is pure defamation."[46]

But midway into his trip, the envoy received an urgent letter. Richelieu needed him to raise troops because, suddenly, the princes had risen in yet another armed insurgency, centered in the northeast. On January 18, Marie's minister drafted a royal declaration that sternly admonished Nevers and others to terminate their rebellion and disband their troops. The litany of the rebels' complaints in their own manifesto of February 4 was the same: the usurping of power by the Italian foreigners, the mismanagement of finances, and the lack of action on the Estates General's requests. In a marked contrast with previous actions of the government, Marie de' Medici steadfastly refused to let the princes get away with yet another benign peace treaty. Richelieu's military response was assertive, even though he claimed to be overwhelmed by his duties: he took care of arming the army, mobilized the nobles who remained faithful to the Crown, and raised regiments. Among the commanders of the army he set up was his own brother Henri.

Meanwhile, Concini was taking bolder actions to secure his power, provoking wider discontent in the population. "I want to see how far Fortune can carry a man," he is reported to have said.[47] After Marie formally admitted him to the king's council, his demands to the government's staff, including Richelieu, became erratic and even more imperious. Marie's favorite acquired strongholds on the Seine that could block access to Paris by the river. Outside the royal palace, opposition grew even louder. In response, he increased police surveillance and raised gallows all over the city, including on the Pont-Neuf. Stress began to take its toll on Concini, especially after his daughter died early in January. Leonora, who was also greatly saddened by the loss of her child, spoke frequently of returning to Italy, as if the risks her husband took scared her. The papal nuncio Guido Bentivoglio saw a catastrophe looming over the court of France: "This violence cannot last!" he exclaimed in his reports to Rome.

Marie de' Medici offered Louis her withdrawal from the affairs of the state. The reasons for this move remain unclear. Had the queen sensed a threat to her power after all these years of ignoring her son? Some anonymous letters had warned her that the Concini couple was highly disliked in her son's close circle. Yet Louis also assured her of his trust and kept to his daily occupations. Richelieu also foresaw danger. After unsuccessfully offering his resignation to the queen, he contacted Luynes, Louis's confidant, and proposed to keep the king abreast of all the dealings in the council. Marie de' Medici and Concini had planned to send Louis to his armies in Champagne to motivate the troops that fought the rebels led by Nevers. They postponed this trip many times and eventually canceled it. Even though the army had the upper hand, they feared that the king's presence among the troops might motivate the rise of a second fractious party within the army itself.

Since October 1616, Louis had been suffering from a debilitating intestinal ailment with bouts of infectious dysentery. Pontchartrain interpreted it as a psychosomatic manifestation.[48] Louis named his falconer Luynes captain of the Louvre guard, which allowed him to live at the palace and take care of him. During the malady the new captain slept in the king's bedroom, on a camp bed. Queen Anne's sentiment on this particular relationship is unknown, but given the prominent role that favorites played at the Spanish court, one can surmise that she accepted it as long as Louis visited every day for protocol. Then, as Louis recovered from his illness, both he and Luynes met late at night, in his apartment at the Louvre, with other gentlemen of the court, including Luynes's two brothers. They spoke of Concini's provocations. One day, for example, Concini entered the Grande Galerie at the Louvre with more than one hundred courtiers, and, though he knew that Louis stood nearby, alone with just a few servants, he did not bother to acknowledge his presence. Louis left the gallery with "his heart full of displeasure," noted the physician Héroard in his journal. Real provocation or not, the Italian's gesture caused a great scandal. On another occasion, Concini offered Louis to raise troops at his own expense, an offer that angered the king, who knew perfectly well that the Italian's money came from his own coffers.

The period before Lent was always a time of joyful celebration at the court of France, and for the magnificent Marie de' Medici, not putting on a show would have sent the wrong signal to the Crown's enemies. As the Carnival of 1617 approached, court poets started working on a production known as the *Ballet de la délivrance de Renaud*. Meanwhile, Louis and his acolytes spent their days devising elaborate choreographies and rehearsing them. The story was based on Torquato Tasso's epic poem, *Gerusalemme Liberata*, which weaves chivalric virtue, magic, and romance in the context of the First Crusade led by Godfrey of Bouillon. In the episode chosen for the French spectacle, Renaud is ensnared by the beautiful sorceress Armide and kept under a spell on a magic island to enjoy her amorous delights. His companions-in-arms then break the charm by placing him in front of a diamond mirror.

The performance took place on January 29, late into the night, and before a crowd so thick that Louis himself could barely get into the Louvre's torch-lit Great Hall. When the first scene opened on a dreamy set of rocky mountains and forests hosting more than a hundred musicians and chorus singers, one saw Luynes playing the part of Renaud. He lay in front of the hills, resting on a bed of grass and flowers. All around danced the demons sent by the sorceress Armide to guard and entertain the prisoner. Fifteen-year-old Louis stepped on stage wearing a mask and a gleaming costume covered in gold lamé flames. He was Fire, watching over the rapture of Renaud. After he danced alone around Luynes for a while, other masked demons joined him, Messieurs de Vendôme, de Bassompierre, de Montpouillan, and many others, until there were fourteen of them dancing on stage. Four theatrical sets followed, all spectacular. At the end of the show, the machinery turned the stage around to reveal one last magical piece of scenery. It featured Louis again, playing the role of a majestic Godfrey of Bouillon. He sat under a golden canopy, with all the knights paying homage around him.

CHAPTER 2

Wars of a Mother and a Son (1617–1620)

I T WAS ALMOST THREE MONTHS after the performance of the *Ballet de la délivrance de Renaud*, on April 24, 1617, on a gray and humid Parisian morning, when gunfire resounded in the courtyard of the Louvre. The Marquis de Vitry, a man who had joined the king's secret meetings a few weeks earlier, shot and killed Concino Concini, Marquis and Maréchal d'Ancre.

Concini had rushed back from his provincial strongholds in Normandy to meet with the queen mother. Perhaps he had heard rumors of a coup attempt, or he had come back to assist the council at a time when the rebels gave signs that they would soon surrender. A faithful reconstruction of this day and its aftermaths is possible thanks to many documents. Chief among these is a detailed description produced by one of Luynes's brothers, which other sources corroborate.

On that fateful morning, Concini left his Paris home, which stood near the southeast corner of the Louvre, on the Seine, and proceeded to walk along the Rue d'Autriche toward the palace. The Louvre of those days bears little resemblance to its current state. Except for two Renaissance galleries built along the Seine, it was still a medieval fortress, surrounded by a moat, set amid tortuous alleys, and accessible by a heavy and gloomy gate. The Italian, followed by his entourage of orange-, black-, and gold-clad gentlemen, read a letter while he headed for that entrance. A week of rain had left the street muddy. When Concini reached the gate and took the bridge across the moat, the doors suddenly shut, leaving most of his retinue in the street. He was trapped on the other side of the closed gate. Vitry, who had waited in the courtyard, came forward and said to the Italian, "The king told me to arrest you."

"Me?" asked a startled Concini.

He then put his hand on his sword's pommel. At once, Vitry's men pulled their pistols and shot him several times in the head. Concini died instantly.

The king was playing billiards while waiting in the Galerie. He leaned through a window on the courtyard and shouted to the crowd that cheered him from below. "Thank you! Thank you! I am really the king now!"

Marie de' Medici was in her apartments. An order from Louis told her to stay put, after which his guards replaced her own. The day after the coup, workers came to wall up the passageway between her quarters and her son's apartment. Louis refused to speak to his mother in spite of several requests.

Richelieu heard the news while he was visiting a Sorbonne dignitary. He immediately went to join the other ministers. His first reaction, as revealed by the journal of Robert Arnauld d'Andilly, a government official, was baffling. He told his colleagues with a content face that with Concini gone, they were now "safe and protected." Perhaps he had legitimately acted to keep his earnest role of servant of the Crown by hedging his bets with Luynes, and thought this made him safe. In any case, Claude Barbin, who understood the consequences of the queen's fall, quickly dampened this optimism.[1] Richelieu then went to the Louvre. He found the king in the Galerie. In a wild and jubilant atmosphere, surrounded by all the princes—save for Condé, still held at the Bastille—Louis stood, elated, on a billiard table, above everyone. The sovereign entertained the crowd with stories of other attempts to liquidate Concini, and how miraculously the secret had been kept. Richelieu approached, intending to declare himself a loyal servant. As he knew well from experience, times of turmoil are when power is up for grabs.

But Louis called out to him loudly and brutally, in front of everyone. "Well, Luçon, finally I am free from your tyranny!"[2]

The king then told his mother's protégé to decamp from the Louvre.

In contrast to two trustworthy testimonies, Richelieu himself gave a different version of this humiliating episode. He claimed that the king welcomed him warmly and told him that he knew of his earlier approaches. It seems more likely, however, that it is Luynes who remembered Richelieu's overtures. Indeed, Pontchartrain states that the king's companion told Richelieu shortly after the scene in the Galerie that he could come to the next council meeting, though not in his capacity as secretary.[3] Richelieu showed up at the meeting, but at the council's door, Villeroy, the minister Richelieu had supplanted after the November cabinet shuffle and whom Louis had reinstated with the coup, ignored him. The bishop spent the entire meeting waiting in vain for a sign of goodwill from Luynes or another and then left alone. A day after the coup d'état, Richelieu boarded his carriage and went to seek advice from the papal envoy, ending up stuck in the mob scene on the Pont-Neuf.

In the aftermath of the coup, Louis, Luynes, and his royal council were still left with quite a problem: what to do with Marie de' Medici, still kept under tight surveillance in her Louvre apartment. The queen mother had to be sent away in a fashion befitting her rank. Undaunted by his earlier setback, Richelieu spotted an opportunity. With the queen's own consent, a good word from Nuncio Guido Bentivoglio, and despite Louis's animosity, he convinced the new rulers that he could mediate the situation. By negotiating an arrangement that was satisfactory to both sides, he saved his political career. Marie de' Medici was to leave for the Château de Blois, a royal residence on the Loire, about one hundred miles from Paris. As part of the deal, she kept her pensions, titles, and even the governorship of Normandy. Richelieu became chief of the queen's council and administrator of her household. Before the queen could leave for exile with her bishop, however, one last detail needed to be arranged: how would the widow of Henri IV bid adieu to her son? Richelieu consulted with Luynes, and on May 3, 1617, eleven days after the coup d'état, everything was ready for courtly theatrics.

It was yet another gray and wet Parisian day. Marie, looking sad and depressed, waited in her chambers, until a pale Louis appeared with Luynes at around half past two. The two men held hands. Close by were Luynes's brothers. Outside the royal family's private quarters, the crowd was huge, filling the corridors, staterooms, and courtyard of the palace. Marie de' Medici led Louis toward one of the windows that overlooked the palace's gardens and the Seine. She told him that she had tried her best and that she was sorry that things had not turned out the way he wanted. Then she went off-script and asked for the freedom of Barbin, who did not have Richelieu's luck and had been jailed. Louis remained silent. The queen asked again, and, facing more silence, she begged, "Maybe this is the last thing that I will ever ask you."

The king said nothing and took a few steps back. When Marie de' Medici, in a last resort, turned toward his confidant, he objected: "Luynes! Luynes! Luynes!"

Marie watched her son the king leave the room with his companion. As soon as they were out she leaned on the wall between the two windows and wept bitterly. Then came the struggle to make it to her carriage. The crowd that jammed the Louvre was in a frenzy. The queen sat with four *dames d'honneur*. Richelieu was in the last carriage of the convoy, together with another church-man. The coachmen gave the signal. It rained, and, in the general confusion, the carriages jammed at that narrow bridge where Vitry had assassinated Concini. Finally, the vehicles and horses disentangled themselves and went on their way. Louis observed the slow and chaotic departure from above the courtyard, standing on a balcony outside Anne's apartment. Then he ran to the Petite Galerie and watched the long convoy cross the Pont-Neuf and disappear.[4]

During Marie de' Medici's first days in Blois, everyone had a chance to calm down. Marie's new residence overlooked the Loire River that gently flows toward Tours, Angers, and Nantes, bathing a region known as the "garden" of France. The queen spent time doing home improvements. She planted her garden with orange trees and jasmine, and ordered the building of an extension to house her wardrobe. Richelieu wrote the royal council a letter dripping with submission, as soon as he arrived at this destination, assuring that he would keep the Louvre abreast of the latest in Blois: "I swear to inform the king, at the price of my own head, of any conspiracy, or plotting."[5] It was a strange move for a man who, in the course of his short career, had presumed of his political skills and given ample evidence that he was an opportunist. This new game made him look disloyal to Marie de' Medici once more in both the king's council and at Marie's court, and generally of suspicious character. "What they feared in me was not a lack of sincerity; rather their crime tormented them and they feared most the little wit that God gave me," he explained in his memoirs, as if Louis, Luynes, and the former ministers who had taken their places back in the council distrusted him for no reason.[6]

The government's diffidence foreshadowed more trouble. No hunting party, visiting musicians, or theater troupe would make Marie de' Medici forget that she was out of the circle of power. In the cohort of schemers the queen had brought with her was a fashionable abbot called Luigi Rucellai. The man shuttled between Blois and Paris, devoting himself to his mistress's fortune with zeal and hoping for advancement wherever he could. The watchful eyes of the royal council at the Louvre tracked the agitation at Blois with increasing worry. Eventually, Richelieu received a panic-stricken letter from his brother Henri. His sibling had heard that the royal council had deliberated on sending the bishop away from Marie's court. The bishop did not wait for the order to come. On the morning of June 11, 1617, he left, first to go to Luçon and then to settle nearby in Coussay, a country manor he owned. The rumor that had sent Richelieu running was a false alarm, but the royal council was pleased with the results. On June 15, Louis wrote him an ironic letter, approving of his decision to settle in Coussay and firmly telling him to stay put. Marie de' Medici insisted on having Richelieu back. Every seditious movement detected in Blois again drew suspicions of him. In October, Louis forbade him to stay in Coussay, which he deemed too close to his mother's court, and relegated him to Luçon and its episcopal duties. Richelieu put a brave face on it and said he was happy spending time with his books. He dedicated himself to theological struggles with the Protestants and wrote *A Defense of the Principal Articles of the Catholic Faith*, a book wherein he preached that the duty of all Christians is to obey their king.[7]

Meanwhile, Luynes consolidated his power at the court. The king ordered a special jury to deliberate on whether Leonora had committed crimes of lèse-majesté—literally, of behavior harmful to the king's majesty. The plotters of the coup needed a death sentence to justify, retroactively, the expeditious methods used to get rid of Concini.[8] Also, the king had promised Luynes all of Leonora Galigaï's possessions, but Luynes faced legal complications to get them. According to one contemporary, Luynes assured the most reticent judges that if they sentenced Leonora to death, the king would pardon her.[9] The judges condemned Leonora Galigaï to beheading on July 8, 1617. Rather than condemning her for lèse-majesté, they based their verdict on flimsy charges of sorcery, which Richelieu in his memoirs found to be ridiculous.[10] No message of mercy came when Leonora reached the scaffold, where the executioner waited with his sword. His task accomplished, the executioner had to burn the body of the woman on the spot, as prescribed by the sentence.[11]

For Luynes, this death of Leonora had even more advantages than just material gain. It allowed him to maintain discord between Marie de' Medici and her son, and keep her at bay. To further ensure that any rapprochement between

mother and son would not happen, Luynes and his men went as far as lying to
the king by assuring him that Marie wanted him dead.[12] The young king did
want to assert himself as a good monarch, and he wished to be called "Louis
the Just." Piety, secrecy, and good judgment made this entirely possible. His
actions belied his good intent, however. The Venetian ambassador reported that
during his council sessions Louis smiled and whispered to himself again and
again, "I am really the king now!" The young man still spent his days hunting, building a mock fort in the Tuileries garden, or moving light pieces of
artillery with mules.

Luynes's ambition benefited much from Louis's complete disinterest for his
wife, Anne of Austria. The queen was charming, with curled blond hair and fine
complexion. Her hands and arms had a marblelike beauty famous throughout
Europe, and one contemporary deemed her lips "the perfect accomplices in all
the torments that her eyes could inflict."[13] She said that she found Louis's dark
physique and melancholic allure attractive. Alas, the prospect of engaging in
anything more than a courteous conversation with his wife sent the French
king into a panic. Not even the thought that he needed to secure the future of
the French Bourbon dynasty could warm up his interest. The crowd of Spanish ladies who lived with Anne looked at Louis derisively and made dubious
comments about his sexual capacities when he entered his wife's apartment.

Thus Louis relied entirely on his smooth, kind, and handsome companion
Luynes, a man who understood him and spoke on his behalf when his stutter
manifested itself too strongly. Contemporaries, including his mother, deemed
the king's sentiment for his falconer a true passion. As a reward for the com-
panionship, he offered Luynes more titles, showered him with largesse, and
supported his marriage to a rich, beautiful, and perky young heiress, Marie de
Rohan, whom he eventually made principal of Anne of Austria's household.
From this close proximity to the royal couple, the circles of Luynes and his
two brothers' favor grew greater and greater, to the point where any of their
distant cousins arriving from Provence led a rich lifestyle in Paris. Public
opinion mocked the Luynes siblings as having risen overnight "as fast as
three pumpkins." No matter how great his influence on the king was, however, Luynes did not govern by himself; until now, he had been the king's bird
keeper. His inexperience made the old ministers of Henri IV, chief among
them Chancellier Noël Brûlart de Sillery, indispensable in both domestic and
foreign matters of state at a time of increasing unrest.

Emperor Matthias of Austria was making moves to consolidate the power of the Habsburgs. The crown of the Holy Roman Empire, which Matthias held since 1612, actually did not belong to the Habsburgs. A vote by German princely electors, the Bishops of Mainz, of Cologne, of Trier, the rulers of Palatinate, of Brandenburg, and of Saxony—respectively, Frederick V, George William, and John George I—bestowed it upon him. The Habsburgs, however, had an advantage. The Estates of Bohemia traditionally elected them as kings, and because that title also came with that of elector, they could vote for themselves in the imperial election, a valuable advantage in their pursuit of a lasting dominance in Europe. In June of 1617, knowing that he would soon die without a direct heir, Matthias had his cousin Ferdinand of Styria crowned King of Bohemia in Prague, thus giving him a chance to become emperor. This concerned all other powers in Europe, and especially the Protestant communities whom France assured of its protection. The Catholic Ferdinand was known to be an affable man, but as the ruler of Styria he had relentlessly eradicated those he considered heretics.[14]

Political, religious, and fiscal challenges were even more pressing on the domestic front. In the southern region of the Béarn, Protestants balked at complying with the terms of a long-standing agreement that they should return possessions seized from Catholics during the religious wars. Moreover, the royal treasury was left empty after the turmoil of the regency. Because the complaints and reform proposals formulated at the Estates General of 1614 had not vanished, the Crown organized a conference at the end of 1617 to gauge the state of the kingdom and to enact some much-awaited social reforms. As with the Estates General of 1614, the assembly amounted to fruitless bickering, and public opinion began decrying the "reign" of Luynes—since 1618, the king's companion had been chief of the royal council.

All this mounting political tension in the government had a direct effect on Richelieu. Even though he kept a low profile in the Poitou, wild rumors were still swirling around him. He even had to defend himself against accusations that he had put on a disguise and visited Marie de' Medici. On April 7, 1618, a little more than five months after Louis had relegated him to the Poitou, Richelieu sank even lower. He received a letter from the king ordering him to retire to the city of Avignon, which stood in a papal enclave in the Rhône Valley. The order also concerned his brother Henri and his brother-in-law François de Pontcourlay, husband of his late sister Françoise.

Once in Avignon, Richelieu rented a house and devoted himself to the cat-echism book he had begun in Luçon. Informants kept a close watch on the movements of the du Plessis brothers, while in Paris, clerks scoured the files of the regency's administration to find incriminating documents. All they found were Richelieu's obsequious letters to Concini, not enough to seriously en-danger a bishop of the Catholic Church, but sufficient to keep him in Avignon for a long time. As Richelieu wrote, "The virtues of a man in favor are his vices in disgrace."[15] Rome, through Nuncio Guido Bentivoglio, expressed concern about this treatment of a bishop. The Louvre ignored the protest. As if his life could not get worse, Richelieu's brother Henri's wife died in labor in October of 1618, and her child survived for only two months.

In a letter dated February 8, 1619, Richelieu told the cathedral's ecclesias-tics in Luçon where he wanted to be buried, and what they should do with the silverware and tapestries that decorated his private chapels in Coussay and Luçon. The letter contained a dramatic injunction: "Put forth before your eyes that this world is a realm of deception, and that there is no contentment nor profit but in serving God, who would never betray those who love him."[16] The exact depth of Richelieu's despair at that moment is hard to measure. At the time when he wrote the sad letter to his diocese's ecclesiastics, he canceled the lease of the house he occupied. Definitely, the future seemed bleak enough to contemplate death eye to eye.

In June of 1618, a few months after Richelieu retired to Avignon, Luynes re-vealed to the royal council that he had discovered a secret correspondence between Marie de' Medici and Claude Barbin, her ex-minister locked at the Bastille. They were plotting her escape out of Blois. Actually, Luynes had been spying on the queen and Barbin's exchanges for quite a while. The time to re-veal the information came when Louis showed signs of easing the pressure on his mother. Upon hearing of the plot, the king went into a fury and sent more troops around Blois.[17] The king's confessor, the Jesuit Arnoux, attempted me-diation between the two camps. He extracted from Marie de' Medici a humili-ating declaration in which she swore not to carry out any seditious enterprise and not to return to Paris without her son's written consent.[18] Public opinion decried what it viewed as Luynes's harsh treatment of the queen.

Marie de' Medici, for her part, did not wait for the public's support before taking fate into her own hands. She acted with help from an old acquaintance,

Jean-Louis de Nogaret de La Valette, Duc d'Épernon. A companion of her late husband, Henri, the duke had showed his loyalty when he had strong-armed the parlement to confirm the queen's regency in 1610. D'Épernon hailed from Gascony and was the rough colonel general revered by the army. Luynes had denied one of his two sons, the Archbishop of Toulouse, a promotion. For that, d'Épernon had a quarrel to settle with the king's confidant. The plot to free Marie de' Medici began when Rucellai, the ebullient Italian abbot at the center of the situation now that Richelieu was exiled, put on a disguise, trav-eled incognito to Metz, and solicited d'Épernon for the queen.

The duke left Metz, a city in the northeast of the kingdom, in the early weeks of 1619. "I am going to make the boldest coup that I have ever made," he de-clared while the doors of Metz closed behind him and an escort of about one hundred men.

The gates remained shut for three days, so that no one would leave to warn the court of the duke's disappearance. The council had asked d'Épernon to stay in the northeast to mind the volatile situation in Germany. Once at a rea-sonable distance from the city, the duke wrote the king he had decided to check on the Huguenots in western France, for nothing happened on the German front.[19] His real destination was the Loire Valley.

The early hours of February 22, 1619, were cold and quiet in Blois. One of d'Épernon's men climbed the walls of the château on a rope ladder. He knocked on a window. Inside was Marie de' Medici. She grabbed her jewel case, hoisted her skirt, and went out into the winter night. Exercise was not the queen's forte. The heavyset woman struggled to reach the terrace of the château, still up above the town of Blois. When she saw a second ladder lead-ing from the terrace to the ground, about a hundred feet below, the thought of dangling once more in the void scared her so much that she balked. Marie had resourceful servants, explained d'Épernon's secretary, Guillaume Girard, who heard the story from good sources and told it in the duke's memoirs. After spotting a section of the terrace where the retaining wall had crumbled and was under repairs, her men tied ropes to a coat to improvise a sling, and they lowered the queen mother of France down the steep dirt incline toward the bottom of the moat. The landing was dry. Marie then walked briskly along Blois's streets with her servants. A few officers of the guard appeared. They saw a woman led by men without even a torch; it prompted a few lewd shouts. They then went on their way. "They think I am one of those *generous*

ladies!" declared Marie, giggling as she realized that the men were confusing
her for a woman of the night. At last, the troop reached the bridge over the
Loire, crossed the river, and boarded a coach.[20] When day broke over the Loire,
Marie de' Medici's equipage was still speeding through the countryside. There
was a quick change of carriages and horses, more speeding, until the fugitives
finally reached the Château de Loches, where d'Épernon waited.

When the news of Marie's escape arrived at the court, on the twenty-third,
the royal family was at the Château de Saint-Germain-en-Laye to celebrate
the wedding of Louis's sister Christine to the son of Charles Emmanuel I of
Savoy, Victor Amadeus. Panic immediately took over. A Venetian ambassador at the scene, Simeone Contarini, wrote: "The hunting parties, the games,
the laughter, the dances, all that was happening in shared joy suddenly turned
into anxiety and very dark thoughts, in the mind of Luynes more than any
other. Everyone has fled to Paris, and I use the word fleeing advisedly because
that sudden, disorganized, and fearful decamping resembled more flight than
departure."[21] Many recognized that this crisis could easily degenerate into
a devastating civil war, given the considerable strength and political capital
held by the queen and d'Épernon, and how little it would take for other princes
to partake in their cause. For the restless young nobles of the French court,
things had been rather quiet since the death of the Italians, and it was surely
hard to forget the intoxicating taste of revolt. The royal council met for six
hours to put out a response and devise a strategy. The queen's message that
came in from Angoulême, where both she and the duke had retreated, could
not have been clearer: she had to escape and arm because, as she argued,
Luynes and his cohort threatened her safety and were perils to the king's well-
being. In other words, she implied that her son was irresponsible, and that he
needed his mother back.

Her assertions stung Louis. To prove he had a mind of his own, he held back,
chose a mediator, and made sure merely that an army would be ready if the
conflict escalated. The king had no interest in seeing her back—yet. Luynes,
on the other hand, now needed to see mother and son reunited, because the
public scandal over his ever-growing influence hurt him.

Daringly, Richelieu signaled himself to the court from Avignon. The king's
favorite, Luynes, as it turns out, was not the fiercest of enemies, and he argued
against the ministers that the bishop could bring some reason into the queen's

entourage. In March 1619, less than a year after arriving in Avignon, the Bishop of Luçon received an official letter from the royal council inviting him to rejoin Marie de' Medici's court. It took him just a few hours to leave the papal city of Avignon. Because the king's new disposition toward him had not yet been made public, a dutiful royal officer arrested him in Vienne, thinking Richelieu was still persona non grata in the kingdom, a fugitive. The incident was quickly resolved.

When, on March 27, Richelieu arrived in Angoulême, Marie de' Medici's relations with her son were taking a turn for the worse. Mediators had failed, and troops had moved even closer. The queen proclaimed that she feared for her safety, and once again blamed Luynes for manipulating her son, which in turn added to the tension. The king fired back: "Madame, I can tell from your last letters that you are not capable of speaking your mind anymore about the governance of my state. You know that one cannot decry this governance without having the blame befall upon me. This is why I refuse to believe that you would take the glory of reigning away from me by suggesting that someone dominates my actions."[22]

After barely escaping political annihilation, Richelieu might have wanted to display his loyalty to the king and his confidant as soon as possible and push the queen into a quick bargain. Yet he had to take into consideration that other courtiers such as Rucellai were giving much more combative advice to the queen. Remembering how his double play at Blois had brought him down, Richelieu advised the queen not to rush into an inferior deal. The strategy consisted first in holding back, asking for safe havens and for the pardon of d'Épernon, and then taking time to calmly finalize a peace deal. It took courage to do so, because Louis was losing patience. He wrote to his mother: "War does not worry me nor does it scare me. The handling of arms is not only fitting for my age, but it also suits my disposition. Should I not find war close by I shall seek it afar, and I firmly believe that the large number of my enemies will only be a motive and an enhancement of my glory."[23] Following these fighting words, the royal army moved even closer to Angoulême.

Happily, calmer sentiments prevailed. Louis and his council acceded to the demand for safe havens, and, after some final diplomatic exchanges where Richelieu asserted himself as the key player, the king gave his mother the strongholds of Angers, Les Ponts-de-Cé, and Chinon. The king pardoned d'Épernon,

who had aided in the queen's escape. In a final concession to the queen, the
matter of her return to Paris was set aside. On April 30, 1619, Marie signed the
Peace of Angoulême.

Marie de' Medici's courtiers, including Rucellai, seethed at the sight of
Richelieu. Not only had he regained the trust of the queen and had superseded
them in importance, but he was also placing his close relatives in the highest
posts of the new administration. Provocation, gossip, and ill-chosen words began to target the Richelieu clan publicly. One day, Richelieu's brother Henri
and the Marquis de Thémines, another of Marie's disgruntled courtiers, met
face-to-face in a duel on one of Angers's medieval streets. It was a fast fight.
Henri died on the spot, a sword plunged through his body on July 8. Richelieu's grief was immense. He wrote movingly: "I cannot represent the state
this event threw me in, and the extreme sorrow it caused. Such it is that my quill
won't describe it. It almost drove me out would it not have been for the interests
of the queen."[24] Not only had he lost a crucial ally for his career, but this senseless death terminated the lineage on the male side.

Life and politics had to go on. The pressing matter on Richelieu's desk was
the actual reconciliation between Louis and his mother, which ended up demanding four additional months of careful negotiating. At long last, Marie de'
Medici, followed by Richelieu, left Angoulême after giving the Duc d'Épernon
a huge diamond.[25] They reached the château of Couzières near Tours on September 5, 1619. Louis, who was stationed nearby since early May, arrived at
around half past eleven that day. The meeting took place in the garden of the
château in front of an enormous crowd. Mother and son first saw each other in
an allée. Two years and four months had passed since the coup d'état. The
Venetian ambassador reported that Marie de' Medici looked tired and over-
weight, even with all her jewels and her grand air.[26] Her son appeared taller
and stronger. The dark shadow of a growing beard contrasted with his skin.
According to the official description of the event, which was published soon after the reunion to signal the end of the conflict, Marie de' Medici came forward
first, kissed him, and cried a little. Then she said: "Monsieur my son, you've
grown a lot since I've last seen you."

"Madame, I've grown to be at your service," replied Louis.

The crowd in the garden cheered. Louis graciously told his mother that she
looked the same, and Luynes, who had been made a duke and a peer a month

earlier, was equally charming. But even on such a historic day, Louis chose to hunt, so he left his mother in the care of her daughter-in-law Anne, who had arrived by that time at the château. Always a daughter of haughty Spain, and feeling emboldened because Louis had finally overcome his lack of enthusiasm for sexual relations, Anne insisted on preceding the queen mother in protocol. Proverbial animosity between mother and daughter-in-law threatened to sour the royal family's reunion. Eager to please his mother, Louis gave her precedence over his wife, and before she left he ordered magnificent festivities for the solemn entry into her new capital of Angers.

No doubt, Richelieu consoled himself with the sight of this reunion, even if he still grieved for his brother. He had regained his post as the queen's house superintendent, and the king and Luynes made it clear to him that the queen's return by the king's side could translate into many rewards.[27] But the queen was still reserved, and it was obvious that returning to court was not a guarantee of regaining her influence. At Couzières and in the following months, from Luçon where he had returned to tend to his episcopal duties, Richelieu advocated that she should go back to the court, but he must have also realized that staying away with her ensured his status. Interestingly, Fontenay-Mareuil wrote that Richelieu and Luynes parted as distrustful of each other from Couzières as they were eager to settle when they had arrived at Louis and Marie's historic reconciliation.[28]

Since his arrest at the Louvre in 1616, Condé had been in prison at the Bastille and then at Vincennes. Luynes feared that this prince of the blood would constitute yet another political party. But after the reconciliation at Couzières, with the queen having regained some political influence, her longtime enemy Condé was more useful to Luynes as a free man. Luynes secured the prince's release, and on October 17, 1619, Condé went straight to Chantilly to see Louis. He asked forgiveness on his knees.

"Let us forget the past," responded the king.

This event startled the queen mother in Angers. Adding to the situation, the council made a gaffe by publishing an official declaration that discharged Condé of any wrongdoings during the regency. It said that Condé had acted in earnest to "save" the monarchy from peril, that is, from Marie de' Medici's government. In one final insult, Luynes made Condé his witness when Louis promoted him as Chevalier du Saint-Esprit, the most prestigious chivalric order of the kingdom. Marie later discovered that many of the new chevaliers awarded promotion had contributed to Concini's elimination.

After returning by the queen's side in Angers, Richelieu continued to dispense moderating advice, but soon he found himself in yet another imbroglio. In a growing network of alliances that tended to dislodge Luynes, throngs of princes pledged alliance to Marie de' Medici in the winter of 1619 and spring of 1620. One of the leading characters, the Comtesse de Soissons, fought so that her teenage son, the cousin of Condé and third in the line of succession to the throne, could gain prominence. Louis continued corresponding with his mother and assured her that tension was just the result of a misunderstanding, but his tone became more anxious as he sensed that trouble simmered again.[29] No wonder that Nuncio Bentivoglio, in one of his daily briefings to the Holy See, lamented that France "just cannot be without excitement about some novelty."[30] To complicate matters for the king and his men, an ever-changing foreign and domestic political situation loomed over Marie de' Medici's threat of rebellion.

In Prague, the Thirty Years' War had begun in earnest with a revolution. Ferdinand of Styria, who had sat on the throne of Bohemia since June of 1617, provoked wide disapproval in the Protestant communities of his new kingdom. When Emperor Matthias declined to intervene on behalf of the Protestants, the result was the infamous Defenestration of Prague.[31] On May 23, 1618, angry Czech nobles went up to the Hrdcany Castle and hurled two of the most virulent men representing the new Austrian ruler out the window. Falling nearly fifty feet, they landed on a pile of garbage and survived. This triggered a catastrophic chain of events. The revolutionaries created a governing council and kicked the Jesuits out of Bohemia. More dramatic developments followed when Matthias died on March 20, 1619. As planned, a majority of imperial electors chose Ferdinand as the sovereign of the Holy Roman Empire, on August 28, to perpetuate the hold of the Habsburgs on that Crown. A few days earlier, however, the revolutionaries of Bohemia had deposed the same Ferdinand as King of Bohemia and chosen Frederick V—the German Calvinist prince, imperial elector, and son-in-law of the English king James I— to replace him.[32]

France became involved on December 5, when Louis XIII, surrounded by his chief officers, formally received an imperial ambassador arriving from Vienna. Would the French monarch send troops to support the emperor, a clear signal that he did not condone Protestant revolts, or would he choose not to stir up things at home? Their brethren's suffering in Bohemia frightened the Huguenots at a time when some of them contended with the Crown in the Béarn region.[33] The danger was that they could join Marie de' Medici and her rebels. Other factors favored a French appeasement in Germany. Frederick V, the Palatine prince elected by the Bohemians as their king, was a Francophile, and his native domain acted as a strategic buffer between France, the Spanish Netherlands, and the lands of the Austrian Habsburg. Should Frederick be endangered and the conflict spill out into his German possessions, enemies could dangerously encircle France.

In the Loire Valley where Marie de' Medici held court, rebellion continued to brew. The Duc de Mayenne, a prominent figure, left Paris at the end of March 1620 to join the queen mother's camp. Other high nobles immediately followed. Richelieu still tried to moderate the queen's actions. But how could the king and the favorite not view him again as the troublemaker? Danger materialized when Luynes sent an envoy to Angers to diffuse the queen's anxieties and renew his invitation that she join the court in Paris. These instructions carried the message that, actually, the king had a good disposition toward his mother: "A glance [from her to Louis] will alleviate any difficulty."[34] In addition, a personal missive from Luynes addressed Richelieu. The tone of this letter was remarkably different from the first. Promise of reward came along with a stern admonition that, after the extraordinary favor done to him in Avignon, the chief counselor of Marie de' Medici would be held responsible for any subsequent trouble.

Richelieu was again in a very tight spot. While he enjoyed great prestige and had the queen's trust, his efforts at calming her proved useless. In effect, Richelieu could still try to pacify her, but he risked losing influence should Marie declare an open conflict, no matter what the outcome. Certainly, the envious courtiers in Angers would not let him get away with such a faux pas. Richelieu finally opted to assist Marie de' Medici and her war projects. Years later, he described this choice as inevitable considering the kingdom's interests: "The torrent [of the belligerent party] took me away with such force that to keep pressing my point would have only brought me down. Detriment would have come to the queen and the public good, which were the same thing."[35]

When the Seigneur de Blainville, an envoy sent by Louis, arrived in Angers, Richelieu fooled him into thinking he was still an agent of peace, and gained enough time to rearm the queen's troops. Fontenay-Mareuil put it this way: "The queen and Monsieur de Luçon received Monsieur de Blainville when he arrived in Angers. He found all appearances promising, even though the talks often stumbled upon fallacious problems and well-wrought pretexts. Monsieur de Luçon wanting to gain time, he executed this whole strategy with such craft that Monsieur de Blainville convinced himself of the agreement's imminence."[36] Days later, once he was back in Paris, Blainville reported successful bargaining. When the Duc and Duchesse de Nemours joined the party of the malcontents, however, he was proven wrong and Richelieu's comedy was revealed.[37] For good measure, Richelieu published a manifesto to the queen, calling for peace.[38]

When the last of the queen's allies, the Comtesse de Soissons, escaped from Paris with her son to join the insurrection in Angers, at the end of June, it took little time for Louis to decide that from now on he would take on the rebels in person. The king pointed out his mother's contradictions and accused her of joining the ranks of wretched queens in history. During the breakup in Angoulême, the clergy had reminded him that divine commandments prescribed him to honor his mother. But this line of argument did not work anymore.[39] Against Louis, battalions were spreading across the entire territory and were readying to fight on behalf of his estranged mother and her friends, from Bordeaux and Angoulême, to Brittany and Normandy. Giving strongholds such as Angers to Marie de' Medici had been a mistake. On July 7, the king joined his army and threatened the beautiful garden valley of the Loire with armed conflict.

Meanwhile, Richelieu was trying to organize the queen's forces, amid the crowd of posturing grandees, women, teenagers, and priests that filled Marie de' Medici's lodgings in Angers. Louis and his army made quick inroads against the rebels in Normandy, capturing Rouen and Caen in no time. When the king took the direction of Angers, the pace of his conquest slowed noticeably. No matter how determined he was, he still wanted to avoid a clash of armies and an irreparable scandal for the family. After a time, the queen moved to the city of La Flèche, at the end of July. She traveled those thirty miles northeast of Angers in the hope of coming before the king to stop him, and allow the Duc de Mayenne, one of her most powerful allies, to fortify Angers with more men.

Richelieu intervened with a different plan. Given the rapid and triumphant advance of Louis, he persuaded the queen to hold back, return to Angers, and negotiate. This left the king with time to reconnoiter the region and to impress his enemies with a display of his army on August 4. He had twelve thousand soldiers and more than a thousand horsemen, even after many of his own troops deserted to join the rebels' stronger forces. The queen had about six or seven thousand troops of her own. Interestingly, Louis's relationship with his wife, Anne, deepened in this time of conflict with his mother, even though the royal spouses were separated and could only write to each other. A contemporary gazette said that on the day he conducted the grand review of his troops, "the king appeared at the head of all his armies with a face that stole the heart of everyone."[40] The king's letters to his wife, at the same time, reveal that on the occasion he wore a scarf that Anne had sent him for good luck, and that he took great comfort in this token of affection.[41] The day of the review he also made a pilgrimage to La Flèche, where the Jesuits kept the heart of his father, Henri, as a relic in the chapel of their college.

Negotiations led by a team of churchmen and court officers progressed, to Richelieu's relief. The Archbishop of Sens, Father Pierre de Bérulle, and the queen's equerry, Monsieur de Bellegarde, saw the king, on August 6, and made proposals that seemed acceptable. Luynes might have jumped at the offer, but Condé, ever impulsive, balked. Marie de' Medici wanted pardon for the soldiers who had defected from the king's army. Still, the king accepted this peace offer. The envoys reached Angers the day after, on the morning of August 7. Only the queen's final approval was needed for peace. Unfortunately, she was asleep, and waking her up, even at noon, would have unleashed a fit of very bad temper. Not even Richelieu found the courage to attempt it. Finally, long after they had arrived, Marie stepped out of bed and gave the envoys her signature. They went back to meet the king. Alas, it was too late, and the envoys found themselves in the midst of battle.

While awaiting Marie de' Medici's response, the royal troops, led by Louis, Luynes, and Condé, had moved southwest. Angers sits next to the Loire, and in those days it held the key to passing this river by owning a smaller fortified place called Les Ponts-de-Cé. Les Ponts consisted of two drawbridges leading to an island in the middle of the river, with a village and a castle on it. The royal army decided to keep that passage in check by standing close on a rise, facing about four thousand of the queen's men, some inside Les Ponts, some hiding behind a hastily dug trench that stretched from the bridge toward

Angers. No negotiators were in sight. Condé chafed at the bit with an urge to fight against Marie de' Medici. The king arrived at ten o'clock, mounting L'Armenille, his Spanish horse, at which point the prince persuaded him to proceed farther. The move would ensure a good place should the negotiators come back without the queen's signature, or otherwise make it look as if they had extracted peace sword in hand. That argument appealed to Luynes, who saw it as an opportunity to create a reputation as a good man of war, and he agreed. As soon as the troops moved on that scorching August day, the situation got out of control. One of the queen's chief leaders deserted the trenches. Spearheaded by the infantry, the royalists charged twice and routed what remained of their opponents down to the Ponts-de-Cé. A few exchanges of gunfire took place in the streets of the village. Some soldiers fell off the bridges and drowned in the Loire. Another of Marie de' Medici's leaders, the Duc de Vendôme, ran from the battlefield to the queen. "Your Majesty, I wish I were dead," he said. One of the queen's ladies tartly responded that he had only to stay on the field for that. The fort on the isle surrendered later that evening. Once the dust settled on what became known as *la drôlerie des Ponts-de-Cé*, the farce at the Ponts-de-Cé, the queen had lost about seven or eight hundred men, and the rest either were taken as prisoners or had fled toward Angers.[42] Not all was lost, however. Mayenne could still join the troops in Angers and put up a decent fight.

Richelieu, all this time, stayed with Marie de' Medici in Angers. This was again a critical juncture for him, both as the servant of the queen and as a man who wanted to contain the damage to his reputation. Should the queen miraculously get away, the king's ire would be terrifying, and he would surely find an opportunity for revenge. Richelieu's memoirs display stark realism at this event: "Those who fight against a legitimate power have already lost half of the battle, because imagination, which represents the king's executioner while they fight, makes the game uneven."[43] Notwithstanding the possible intervention of Mayenne, he pushed Marie to accept her son's peace offer. The parties signed the Peace of Angers on August 10. Louis was once again magnanimous toward his mother. He sent her the flags captured by his army, whereas those belonging to the princes' armies went to Anne in Paris.[44] Mother and son's formal reconciliation took place four days later, in a small town near Angers, in the presence of Condé, Luynes, and Richelieu.

*   *   *

Three weeks after the battle at the Pont-de-Cé, and after a stint in the south of France where his presence had an authoritative effect on the rebellious Protestants of the Béarn region, the young king Louis galloped into Paris with a troop of fifty noblemen, all horns blaring. It was noon. This unexpected arrival caught the guards at the Louvre by surprise, so much so that they did not recognize the king at first. Soon enough, though, Louis was flying up the staircases of his palace to surprise his wife and mother. Anne was particularly happy. In Paris, the boutiques closed for the occasion. Many banquets and fireworks celebrated the day when Louis came back to Paris his very own man.

Richelieu could hardly put all the turmoil behind him. How could the queen mother's party, which counted more than thirty thousand men, be ridiculed by the king's much smaller contingents? The Duc Henri de Rohan pointedly suspected Richelieu of having played down the significance of Mayenne's rescue effort, to throw Marie de' Medici into suing for peace. Still worse, claimed Rohan, Richelieu was secretly corresponding with Luynes to fix the results of the game just before the battle.[45] This part of Richelieu's life, when he handled the queen mother's affairs at Les Ponts-de-Cé, does indeed raise some curious questions, and they were pressing enough for Richelieu to prepare a lengthy statement in his own defense.[46] Making overtures to the opposition when he sensed imminent danger was nothing new to him. In any case, the one essential truth of this second war of mother and son, a fact that Richelieu acknowledges in his memoirs, is that he sided with the queen and deceived the king and Luynes.

The peace deal at Angers included a provision for Richelieu's promotion to cardinal, a necessary milestone for his career prospects. Marie de' Medici had a great interest in seeing her protégé obtain the red biretta. It would have been a boost to her credibility. For Richelieu, being a cardinal offered protection against any reversal of fortune. If he had been a cardinal, it would have been much harder to confine him to Avignon. But in the royal council, enthusiasm for his advancement was lukewarm, to say the least. The king wanted to satisfy his mother, and his prerogative included a right to present candidates to the pope for these promotions. On the other hand, he could not forget that her adviser had duped him while negotiating with the Seigneur de Blainville.[47] Luynes could only consider Richelieu's rising influence with suspicion, even if a familial alliance had united them. After the battle at the Ponts-de-Cé, Richelieu's niece, Mademoiselle Marie-Madeleine Vignerot de Pontcourlay, had been promised to Luynes's nephew, Monsieur de Combalet. This daughter of the cardinal's late sister Françoise was very dear to her uncle, and she remained his confidante all his life.

So, perhaps as early as the negotiations for the Treaty of Angers, the king, Luynes, and the ministers figured out a way to hamper Richelieu's progress while keeping the appearance of harmony between the king and his mother. On August 22, 1620, just two weeks after the peace, Louis XIII sent the promised letter to the pope asking him to consider the bishop for the next promotion of cardinals. The emissary arrived in Rome on September 6, gave the letter to the officials, and added that the missive meant the contrary, that the king's real wish was to adjourn the promotion.[48] In January 1621, Richelieu received a disappointing announcement: the Holy See had passed him over. Both queen and adviser got the news in Paris, where they had settled.

Richelieu's task was now to reinstate the queen smoothly in the position of power that she could rightly claim as the king's mother. The king and Luynes would then forget about their doubts concerning his character. The comeback necessitated an exercise in self-restraint. While he sat at his desk before the piles of mundane papers, invoices, inventories, and notes he had to compile, file, and send on as the superintendent of the queen's household and chargé d'affaires, Richelieu could only dream of red silk, just as one of Europe's ugliest conflicts was declared and more domestic turmoil threatened France.

CHAPTER 3

Jupiter's Favor (1621–1624)

FOLLOWING THE VISIT BY THE IMPERIAL ENVOY, and after first contemplating direct military intervention, the French ministers advised Louis to send a delegation of ambassadors to mediate the rapidly evolving central European conflict. This delegation, led by the Duc d'Angoulême, set its sights first on Germany, where two political and religious factions were in dispute. The Protestant Union included Calvinist princes such as Frederick V, the Elector Palatine who had accepted the crown of Bohemia in the place of Ferdinand, the new Holy Roman Emperor. The Catholic League centered on Maximilian I of Bavaria, who was a vassal of Ferdinand. Unlike Frederick V, this Bavarian duke did not have the privilege of being a German elector and voting in the imperial proceedings, and the emperor had promised him Frederick's voting rights—without consulting the diet. The Bohemian conflict risked becoming a proxy war between Protestants and Catholics, which could then spread over Germany. On July 3, 1620, in Ulm, the French diplomats persuaded the German princes to sign a treaty. No matter what their alliances represented with regard to the conflict in Bohemia, the princes agreed not to fight against each other on German soil.

Proud of their success, the French ambassadors headed to Vienna later in July 1620 with intentions to secure the same good results there. But nobody cared to hear them. As Victor-L. Tapié tells it in his standard account of the early phase of the Thirty Years' War, the diplomats then realized their critical misstep. Neutralizing the various German factions had allowed the emperor and his ally the Duke of Bavaria to direct efforts against the rebels in Prague, without fear of distraction on German soil. Indeed, the fate of Bohemia was sealed later in the fall of 1620, at the Battle of the White Mountain, near Prague, on a misty November 8. Imperial troops consisting mostly of Bavarian soldiers and led by General Jean Tserclaes de Tilly crushed Frederick V's army and left him no choice but to flee Bohemia with his English wife, Elizabeth.[1] Later Ferdinand banned him from the empire. Oppression befell Prague. Eight months later, after a summary trial and the final approval of Ferdinand, the heads of the most prominent Bohemian revolutionaries adorned the Charles Bridge over the Vltava River.

With the Habsburgs, problems were never simple. In the fall of 1620, just when French diplomacy contributed to tragedy in Bohemia, and when Louis put an end to his mother's rebellion with a campaign through the Loire Valley, the Spanish had made some strategic moves of their own to help their Austrian relatives. The Habsburgs' territories were spread out, making it difficult to move troops between their possessions in northern Italy, Austria, and the Spanish Netherlands. Adding to this difficulty were the English and their maritime resources, which made navigation in the English Channel risky. Hence the Spanish had a keen interest in a region called the Valtellina. A part of Italy nowadays, this mountain-encased valley begins at the north end of Lake Como and stretches to the northeast for about twenty-five miles. Control of the Valtellina enabled armies to travel from Milan to Vienna in ten days, and then onward to Bohemia.[2] It also allowed easy reach to the Spanish Netherlands, a feature all the more precious since the Spanish occupied the Palatinate of Frederick V, and when a truce between them and the Dutch Republic was to expire in 1621. The Spanish king Philip III, father of Louis's wife, had no right to use the Valtellina ever since Henri IV had negotiated an arrangement with the Swiss Gray Leagues (Grisons).

But soon an opportunity presented itself. In July 1620, the Catholic population of the Valtellina rose up and massacred their Swiss lords, who were Protestants. The Duke of Feria, representing the Spanish authority in Milan, took this occasion to invade the territory. France saw one of its most strategic assets seized and, for lack of sufficient resources in a time of domestic disturbances, could not put up a fight for it.

All Louis and his council could do was to send a military gentleman, François de Bassompierre, to Madrid to negotiate an agreement. In the end, negotiation was possible because the Spanish feared that this matter would draw upon too many of their resources just when their conflict with the Dutch was about to resume. They agreed to a treaty, signed on April 25, 1621, pledging to withdraw their army from the valley. This happened under the new rule of Gregory XV, who had been elected pope in February of 1621, and that of the new Spanish king Philip IV, who had acceded to the throne at his father's death on March 31, 1621.

Louis, despite the magnitude of these crucial events abroad, was rather drawn to domestic affairs, namely, to subdue Protestant agitation in the south and to the west of his kingdom. Besides, how could he stand up to the Habsburgs without a strong monarchy? At the end of December 1620, representatives from all regions of France had gathered in the coastal city of La Rochelle, even though the royal council had forbidden any meeting of this kind after the troubles in the Béarn. In February, Protestant rebels took control of the city of Privas. Cities in the south declared themselves under threat and promised they would fight for their religious freedom. In response, Louis made Luynes Connétable de France on April 2—even though the title of constable was the highest in the army and Luynes favored domestic quiet—and asked his treasury to raise taxes. Soon it was announced that the King of France would bring his army to the south. Louis XIII's stated goal was to tame a political insurrection, and not to fight over religious matters.

Marie de' Medici was taking her bearings in Angers. Hostility between her court and her son's had ceased, but she still had not regained a position of influence. It is hard to determine what Richelieu's exact positions were on the war with Protestants. Marie promoted peace within the kingdom, and given that Richelieu was her indispensable adviser, it is quite likely he influenced her position, or at least that they agreed.[3] More certain is that he thought the queen should stay near her son during these times of turmoil. War was unpredictable; it was a time when opportunities abounded. The queen and her bishop prepared to follow Louis and his court during the campaign, in mid-April 1621.

The first encounter with the Huguenots, in the long-established Protestant stronghold of Saumur, gave the impression that Louis and Luynes's war would be easy. The town surrendered without a fight. One hundred miles to the south, in Saint-Jean-d'Angély, however, they hit their first real obstacle. The king and Luynes were challenging the Protestant high nobility, including Duc

Henri de Rohan, a bigger-than-life character, and his brother Benjamin, Seigneur de Soubise, who ruled over the citadel of Saint-Jean. The royal presence
did not impress Soubise, and he declared that he would not open the citadel's
doors to his king.

The royal army launched a siege. Sieges were the substance of war in early
modern France, drawing on the resource of soldiers, but also on that of engineers and professional firemen. First, one had to reach the defensive fortifications by digging trenches, and then breach the wall either by cannon or with
mines. At that point soldiers might rush in, or, depending on the circumstances,
direct assaults with cannon fire might be preferred. The besieged put up resistance by various means. Fortifications and moats were the most elaborate
defenses, built at varying angles and preceded by bastions and half-moon
structures to hamper an enemy's advances; they allowed the firing of bullets,
cannonballs, and incendiary devices over a wide range while offering an an-
gled surface to deflect enemy fire. Should the assailants come too close, the
besieged could opt for a sortie, sending out soldiers in a flash attack. When the
siege of Saint-Jean began, it became clear that none of these sophisticated tech-
niques would be used. The royal army lacked recruits and was disorganized.
Also, the military did not take the new Connétable de Luynes seriously.[4]
Finally, after much more effort than such a place warranted, the army took
Saint-Jean on June 24. Louis ordered the fortifications razed and sent
d'Épernon with five thousand men to tackle La Rochelle, which was also rebel-
ling. The king continued his journey toward the south, where some of the
staunchest Protestants held towns.

As the long convoy of the French army made its way south, Richelieu and
Marie de' Medici realized that their presence was useless. In all likelihood, they
had hoped that the difficult circumstances would give them opportunities to
intervene at least on a few occasions. But all Louis and Luynes gave the queen
was a ceremonial role and no access to the council where decisions were made.
The bishop took time off in Coussay and in Richelieu, and he hosted the queen
in both places, a sure sign of great favor. Eventually, both Richelieu and Marie
de' Medici appropriately decided to leave. On July 1, near Blaye, Louis parted
with his mother, still on good terms, assuring her that she reigned in his kingdom. The official reason for her departure was that she could not keep up with
the advancing army and wanted to retire to the Loire region.

The royal army took a turn toward the east and the Languedoc. Frightened by the defeat in Saint-Jean, many smaller Protestant cities opted to submit before the king. If they resisted, it made no difference: the army took them with ease. All along, Louis rode on horseback with his troops, regardless of the weather, cooked meals for his companions, drew maps from memory, and stood impassive as bullets zipped past him. Then a formidable enemy rose: Montauban. Having resisted fierce sieges during the Wars of Religion, this town was deemed as independent as La Rochelle or Nîmes, with citizens "who think highly of themselves and do not suffer domination easily."[5] A location on a rocky plateau, the unruly Tarn River, and fine man-made fortifications protected it. The leadership was excellent, too. The Duc de Rohan, after he had left his brother Soubise to the defense of Saint-Jean-d'Angély, had quickly reached the city in June, to join a group of courageous and devoted civic councillors. Still, some effort to fortify was needed. Working tirelessly, citizens and soldiers strengthened their weaker defenses and installed forty pieces of artillery. With preparations well under way, Rohan gathered the citizens of Montauban in the main church and roused them with a fiery speech.

Louis and Luynes arrived to set up the army's camp on August 17, one month and a half after parting ways with Marie de' Medici and Richelieu. Given the late season, the fatigue of the soldiers, and the many smaller but still dangerous Protestant towns that surrounded Montauban, experienced strategists recommended postponement of the siege. But Luynes, now that war was well under way, wanted to make it his crowning achievement as a military leader. He relied on his brothers, including the Duc de Chaulnes who had been named marshal earlier, despite his own lack of experience. After sending Anne of Austria, his younger brother Gaston, and Luynes's wife, Marie, to reside in the vicinity, Louis took his own quarters in a small castle at Piquecos, a hilly village about four miles from Montauban. From there, the king could watch with a telescope as his soldiers built boat bridges and dug trenches. The royal army counted thirty thousand men and had about the same amount of artillery as Montauban.

Fierce fire signaled the onset of the siege, and, in no time, the operation turned into a nightmare for the royal army. Relentless cannon fire, explosive mines planted under the fortifications, and furious man-to-man combat never dented the Montalbanais' determination. Luynes's lack of military talent contributed to the floundering attacks and sometimes turned them into a senseless butchery. His political enemies seized the occasion to worsen an already tarnished reputation. They described him as an armchair general who was getting fat from eating the delicious local game.[6] The joke was that his personal surgeon boasted to his wife of being the safest man in the army: "Fear not for my life, my dear, the constable likes my company, and keeps me close to him at all times."[7] When Rohan brought reinforcements into Montauban with a daring rescue mission, the siege operation unraveled completely and a crisis befell the miserable royal camps. Torrential rains filled the trenches and turned the encampments into mud pits. Scarlet fever blossomed and spread across the entire army. The sick and the dying lay everywhere. One regiment that had come from Toulouse with one thousand men lost more than six hundred to the virulent fevers alone. In total it is estimated that the army lost more than fifteen thousand in combat or to disease during the siege of Montauban. The news from La Rochelle was depressing, too. D'Épernon could not tame the Protestants there either.

At long last, and after the citizens of Montauban rejected a negotiated settlement that would have required them to formally apologize to the king for their defiance, Louis gave orders to lift the siege on November 2.[8] The warrior king was crying bitter tears of rage. The army moved its cannons, ammunition, the sick. What had to be left behind they set on fire. Finally, the hardy warriors of Montauban watched the last royal battalions leave through a thick haze of smoke. "Adieu, Messieurs! Adieu!" shouted a soldier from the royal army.

All eyes at court turned to Luynes, who, with his two brothers and a few confidants, still wanted to keep his hold upon the young Louis.[9] François de Bassompierre narrated that Luynes confided that he felt for Louis, "like a man who fears being a cuckold, and dislikes seeing other men flirt with his wife."[10] But at Montauban, and in Richelieu's own words, Luynes had made decisions detrimental to his political safety, "like a man who stands atop a high tower, gets dizzy, and loses his judgment."[11] First, Louis finally realized the enormity of the rewards that Luynes kept asking for himself and his relatives. There was always a cohort of Provençal nobles, all dressed up in silk, near Luynes, and those courtiers cost him much. By contrast the king made a point of always dressing soberly and modestly.[12] Over time, Louis seems to have become aware of his friend's pretensions. He saw Luynes enter his lodging and said, "Look, it's the king coming in." Marie de' Medici and Richelieu, still stationed in the Loire Valley and the Poitou, undoubtedly asked whether the king's confidant and man of power had toppled from his pedestal at last. In retrospect, it must have seemed like a mistake to have let Louis pursue his military campaign alone after the stopover near Blaye. The court left Montauban on November 6 and traveled to Toulouse, where Louis decided to chastise Monheur, a small city nearby that had just rebelled. Luynes thought he could take advantage of this minor event to shore up his fallen fortune.[13]

Shortly after arriving near Monheur, the king's companion began to feel ill. A coup de théâtre stunned everyone. On the sixth day the dreaded red eruption appeared on his skin, signaling the scarlet fever that had decimated the army at Montauban and now traveled with the king's entourage. Doctors advised the king not to approach his sick friend, who was soon overtaken by terrible convulsions.[14] Four years and eight months after the coup d'état, on December 15, 1621, Charles d'Albert, Duc de Luynes and Connétable de France, was dead. The king's physician, Héroard, describes Louis as quite afflicted by the illness of his favorite, writing that the day before Luynes's passing, he played in his room, "to dupe the displeasure of Monsieur le Connétable's malady." Most observers saw indifference, however, and even a sense of relief. The Venetian ambassador reported Louis's only known comment: "I loved him because he loved me; however something lacked in this man."[15] In short order, the king was on his way to Paris, passing the scores of starving, wounded, and diseased soldiers who had served the military ambitions of his longtime companion.

Marie de' Medici sent the captain of her guards, Louis de Marillac, to express her good wishes. Shunning the court no longer made sense. Louis declared that he had had it with favorites and that he wanted to govern on his own. His mother applauded the decision. It seemed Louis still lacked in self-confidence, however, and that he would end up resorting to some kind of confidant again. No doubt, Marie de' Medici and Richelieu, the chief of her council, stood ready to seize such a unique opportunity and advance their interests. The first signs of recognition that Louis gave his mother after the unexpected death of his companion were reassuring. He declared that "never a son would so much cherish and love his mother." More tangible proof of his goodwill came when he admitted her to the royal council and, crucially, agreed to resubmit a petition for Richelieu's cardinalate. But courtiers thought that the king still feared his mother, even though he responded well to her wishes.[16] Apparently, he was still wary of Richelieu, a man whom the papal nuncio described as having a brain "made in such a way that he is capable of tyranny towards the mother and the son."[17]

In the end, Condé and the other ministers succeeded in drawing all the king's attention for themselves. Condé had joined the court as soon as he heard the news of Luynes's death. Since he had no interest in seeing the queen in the royal council, he incited Louis's taste for war and his need to avenge the insult of Montauban. This manipulation turned out to be easy as the Protestants were still provoking the monarchy in the south. Also, the powerful ministers that had remained in Louis's service since the coup believed that Richelieu scripted everything of substance said by the queen, and they, too, feared her possible influence over her son. They put their political weight behind Condé and his call for more military engagement with Protestant France.

Quickly, then, Richelieu understood that even though the king admitted his mother the queen to the council, business took place without her. "They showed her the displays in the boutique, but she did not get to see the back of the store," he commented.[18] Still, it was important that the queen keep affirming herself as a voice of reason, and this time we know that he prompted her to object to more open conflict with the Protestants. Marie urged her son, instead, to tackle Spain in the strategic Valtellina. Louis and his council ignored her opinion. While the court of France spent two winter months in hunting parties, comedies, and brilliant fêtes, traveling from one château in the Île-de-France to another, impetus for a second campaign against the Protestants grew stronger and stronger.

Louis departed for his second war as soon as springtime came, on March 20, 1622, and Richelieu urged Marie de' Medici to join the army again. The beginning of this trip was inauspicious. Anne had to stay at the Louvre after suffering a miscarriage. A few days after the court's departure, Louis learned what had caused the loss of a possible heir to his throne. Anne and Marie de Rohan—Luynes's widow, who had become the young queen's best friend—were coming back from a reception and were crossing the Great Hall in the Louvre. Still merry, both women started to run and glide on the wooden floor, but in the darkness, the queen tripped over the throne's platform and lost the child she was bearing. The king wrote harsh words to his wife and ordered Luynes's widow to stay away from the queen. Not only had Anne lost a baby and the respect of her husband; now she found herself lonely and increasingly depressed.

When the court and the army reached the Atlantic regions, another event dampened the king's morale. Marie de' Medici was not feeling very well. She and Richelieu decided to stay in Nantes. There was another motive for this change. Both queen and councillor had realized that because of Condé's influence, power was still far from within their reach. After pressing yet again for Richelieu's promotion, and ordering the captain of her guards to stay with the army, so that he could keep her abreast of any developments, Marie de' Medici left for the spa town of Pougues, where she spent the summer. Richelieu needed rest, too, actually. Over the previous months his migraines had tortured him with little respite. "My head is killing me!" he wrote one day. Years earlier, the general of the Carthusian order had sent him a bezoar stone, which had a reputation as a universal antidote and as a cure-all. The magic proved useless. Richelieu resorted to more conventional means. He vowed to Saint John the Evangelist that he would establish a weekly mass if he could be relieved of the atrocious pain.

Louis's second campaign began in earnest on the Atlantic coast, on the island of Riez, a piece of sandy terrain separated from the mainland by a shallow sound about six and half miles in width.[19] Monsieur de Soubise, brother of Rohan and defender of Saint-Jean-d'Angély the year before, had taken refuge there with five thousand men, five hundred horsemen, and some artillery.[20] The place gave him an excellent hold on the entire seaboard. Louis decided to dislodge Soubise. On April 16, he and his soldiers crossed the sound on horseback, in the middle of the night, and routed the enemy. With the rising tide it was impossible to retreat. One had to win or die. Following this brave action, the king took his army to the south. By June they stood again before Montauban. They set up camp to show they were not intimidated, but avoided conflict with the city. Instead, they took on the smaller towns that should have been tackled the year before in advance of laying the siege. Things turned ugly. In the town of Nègrepelisse, the entire royal garrison had been massacred during the previous campaign. This army wanted retribution. After an already murderous attack, the commanders lost control of their troops and terrible destruction took place. The rape of Nègrepelisse left behind a pile of bloodied and smoldering rubble. "The streets were so jammed with bodies and blood that one could barely walk," reported the royal gazette.[21] The citizens of Saint-Antonin, the next target, barely escaped the same extreme violence after they put up a desperate fight to save their town.

Louis and Condé followed up by setting Montpellier as their target, a much

more valuable and difficult stronghold. The Duc de Rohan had been fortifying it since the second campaign had begun that spring.[22] The king arrived at
the siege on the last day of August, to join a force of twenty thousand. Bassompierre, whom Louis had named marshal, proposed a sensible plan, but Condé
ignored this wise advice when he took over the operations. The prince did not
fare well in Montpellier. Attacks and siege operations were botched. Monsieur
de Combalet, Luynes's nephew who had married Richelieu's niece, was killed
in a bloody fight. Heavy rains filled up the trenches and created favorable conditions for another epidemic. Eventually, scarlet fever broke out again, taking
the lives of many combatants. Rohan, who remained outside the town, menaced the royal troops with reinforcements.

Louis did not let the faltering effort drag on unnecessarily this time. In spite
of the uncompromising attitude of Montpellier's citizenry, peace was agreed
upon on October 10 and signed on the nineteenth. To Condé, who argued
against it, Louis said, "There is no need to talk about it, this is what I have
resolved."[23] The king could enter the city to affirm his sovereignty, but the
Edict of Nantes remained and the Protestants retained the strongholds of Montauban and La Rochelle. In La Rochelle, where the general assembly of Reformed churches had gathered and where the uncompromising Huguenots had
fomented and encouraged the rebellion, it appeared that no army was invinci-
ble. Because the premature conclusion had not allowed Condé to finish the
siege and redeem his reputation as a warrior, he left in fury for Italy the very
day Louis announced he was ending the siege, pretending that he had to fulfill
a long-standing vow to visit the holy site of Loreto. Louis took the opposite
direction and slowly made his way up the Rhône Valley, spending his time
hunting and visiting holy sights.

The summer of 1622 had been a period of calm for Richelieu. On September 5,
he was taking some rest at a modest inn located in the village of La Pacau-
dière, on his way to meet the queen and the king, when a messenger arrived
with extraordinary news: after two years of disappointments and patience, he
had been made a cardinal. Legend has it that Richelieu's valet started dancing
and shouting: "We are a cardinal! We are a cardinal!"

Judging by the letters he sent the king to thank him, the new cardinal must
have found some fervent words to express his gratitude when he subsequently
met Louis in person, in Avignon. He was also in a much stronger position to

back up Marie de' Medici when she spoke against the forces that threatened French interests in the Valtellina. The situation had worsened since Bassompierre had signed the Treaty of Madrid in April of the previous year. With troops stationed all along the Rhine, the Spanish had even fewer incentives to give up the prized valley. Eventually, the cousin of the emperor Archduke Leopold attacked the Valtellina and forced the Swiss Gray Leagues to give up their claims on the valley altogether. The French, at last, showed some determination. The Duke of Savoy, Charles Emmanuel, arrived in Avignon to join another foreign player, the Venetian ambassador, and begin talks with the French king and his government to form an offensive league against the Spanish.

In Lyon, where the whole court of France moved in December, the mood was festive. After days of comedies and balls, two celebrations brought a magnificent end to the court's stay. On the morning of Saturday the tenth, 1622, in the arch-episcopal palace of Lyon and in the presence of the entire court, the king gave Richelieu the red biretta that represented his standing as a prince of the Catholic Church. The new cardinal affirmed his loyalty to his benefactor, Marie de' Medici, with these words: "Madame, this scarlet that I owe to the good will of Your Majesty will always remind me of the vow I took to shed my blood for your service."[24]

Later that evening, the cardinal held a magnificent banquet, and the next day, in a fitting conclusion to a remarkable week spent in the presence of their king, the citizens of Lyon offered Louis XIII a lavish ceremonial parade.

"When will you take the helm?"

Father Arnoux, whom Luynes had fired as the king's confessor shortly after the siege of Montauban, was not alone in wondering when the newly promoted Cardinal Richelieu would assume a greater role in the government. From all corners of the kingdom, the Good Frenchmen looked up to the cardinal as the man who could reaffirm France's stance against the Habsburgs' claims. Was he not the one who, during the regency, had showed leadership in foreign affairs, and who had stayed away from extreme Catholic Devout positions? A steady flow of stinging pamphlets, many of them written in a tart and satirical style, nourished this call for decisive international action in public opinion. Their author was an ecclesiastic of the church of Saint-Germain-l'Auxerrois, a man named François Dorval-Langlois, Sieur de Fancan. Suspiciously, he was also one of Richelieu's acquaintances.

But even with a cardinal's hat, the good wishes of many Frenchmen, and Fancan's verve, Marie de' Medici did not gain more clout at court, and Richelieu's own political career was not going anywhere. The ambitions of the ministers who now held most of the government's responsibilities—Chancellier Brûlart de Sillery, his son the Vicomte de Puisieux, who guided foreign affairs, and the Marquis Charles de La Vieuville, who supervised finances—were tenacious. The king's mother had a right to speak in the council but still had no vote or real influence. Richelieu watched the ministers' display of intrigue and mediocrity with disdain: "They recognized in me some force of judgment, they feared my mind, and thought with dread that if the king were to know me better, he would delegate the care of his affairs to me."[25]

Brûlart, in his advanced age, wanted to avoid the hassles of traveling. Ever since the coup d'état of 1617, he had followed Louis in his tribulations across France, and the last thing he wanted was to stir up things abroad and create another war that would require his presence in the field. Once the signing of a treaty in Paris on February 7, 1623, formalized the league to free the Valtellina from the Spanish, he and his son negotiated with the new Spanish king and his political mentor and counselor the Count Olivares.[26] They negotiated a compromise: Pope Gregory XV would receive the forts that the Duke of Feria had built in the Valtellina until a solution to the conflict could be found. It proved a ridiculous move considering how often Rome kept its policies in line with the Spanish. The Duke of Savoy and the Venetian senate immediately denounced these policies of Sillery and Puisieux as marks of French hypocrisy. "One is so crazy he should carry a jester's bauble, the other is malicious like an old monkey!" protested Fancan in his pamphlets.[27]

Louis, unfortunately, could not heed the calls of protest. Since his return to Paris, the king's exclusive occupation was hunting, which he pursued with such frenzy that it left everyone dismayed. The court often resided in the royal châteaux in the Parisian region, in Fontainebleau, Saint-Germain, or Compiègne. The king was also fond of the forests that surrounded the hamlet of Versailles, so much so that he ordered the building of a small manor there, for the days when dusk caught him on the hunt. Rain or shine, he rode through his domains as if trying to numb himself into oblivion. He thought his ministers did a fine job when they did not convene the council, asserted the Venetian ambassador Pesaro.[28] Marie de' Medici still pushed for the advancement of Richelieu, but she did so gently, so as not to upset her son. Louis and Anne barely spoke, and their estrangement caused so much distress to the young queen that she suffered what appears to be some kind of a nervous crisis in the month of April. The same kind of episode also happened in July. In this marital context, Louis turned to his mother when he needed comfort. Once in a while, Richelieu could get the king's attention.

Since September 1622, Richelieu had been *proviseur* at his alma mater, the Sorbonne. The post of protector of the institution gave him an opportunity to spend time in conversation with his peers and to participate in oratorical jousts. His closest friend was Father Joseph, who had developed a keen interest in German affairs and who gave him precious advice. Most of the time Richelieu followed Marie around Paris, sometimes at a nearby château with the court, or, during the summer, at the queen's estate in Monceaux. He still managed her household, which allowed him to place his relatives and acquaintances in comfortable employment. His niece, Madame de Combalet, was in charge of the queen's finery. The sons of Denis Bouthillier, the law clerk who is said to have taken care of Richelieu while he lived as a student in Paris, had all received various offices. Another staffer was Michel Le Masle, the cardinal's personal secretary. Richelieu demanded utmost loyalty from his trusted servants, and he rewarded their service with equal fidelity. Remarkably, Le Masle had worked for Richelieu ever since the early 1600s, when he was his academic tutor.

Richelieu's occupations also concerned house building and decorating projects. Construction frenzy had taken over Paris. On the Right Bank, in the area known as the Marais, aristocrats and financiers erected gorgeous mansions for their stays in the capital. The Île Saint-Louis was being built and developed as another residential neighborhood. In response to a rise in spiritual fervor, religious orders established new convents and churches throughout the city. All this paled when compared with the beauty and scale of Marie de' Medici's own projects, however. On the Left Bank, in the elegant and breezy new neighborhood of Le Luxembourg, the architect Salomon de Brosse built a palace fit for the aspirations of a Medici.[29] The queen mother wanted it as a residence for her old age. Richelieu, as superintendent of her house, supervised much of the project. By June of 1623, the gardens already looked very impressive with their mature trees, lively fountains, and grotto. In his ateliers, the painter Peter Paul Rubens produced a series of elaborate allegorical paintings to decorate the reception hall and tell the story of Marie de'

Medici—that is, the story as she understood it. Richelieu had projects of his own, too. He ordered ornaments from Italy for a property he purchased with the queen's financial help, right outside Paris, in Limours. Earlier, in 1621, he had bought the land and manor at Richelieu. Sorting out his brother Henri's financial affairs after his tragic death had been quite difficult. Much like their father, François, the elder brother had left his affairs in a "furious jumble." Eventually, the testament was annulled on the puzzling grounds that its author was psychologically unstable. With the acquisition of the manor and the settlement of his brother's estate, truly, Armand-Jean du Plessis was now *Cardinal de Richelieu.*

Chancellier Brûlart de Sillery and his son Puisieux fell from power in early 1624. Their mediocrity had become too obvious, and the king strongly suspected them of having embezzled money from the treasury. Marie de' Medici again pushed for the advancement of her trusted man, to no avail. The Marquis de La Vieuville took over the council, as Louis was still not convinced that he could rely on Richelieu. Upon seeing Richelieu enter one day, Fontenay-Mareuil reported, he leaned over to Maréchal de Praslin and said, "This is a man who wants to be in my council, but I cannot find the resolve to do it, after what he has done against me."[30] La Vieuville's foreign policy moves showed some nerve, as when, for example, he demanded that Spain observe the terms of the Treaty of Madrid that had settled the Valtellina affair. He then organized the marriage of Henriette Marie, Louis's third sister, to the protestant Prince of Wales (soon to be Charles I of England), in order to secure an alliance against Spain. Finally, he began talks with the Dutch, who strained under Spanish attacks. Since 1621, and after years of truce, the long-standing war between Spain and the Dutch Republic had resumed with the siege of Breda by General Ambrose Spinola. The Treaty of Compiègne subsidized the Dutch war effort with hefty loans.

In spite of these actions, however, La Vieuville became as unpopular as his predecessors. Besides his presumptuousness, he managed the public finances with a disregard for ethical principles that shocked even at a time when conflict of interest was a vague notion, and it looked worse considering that Louis had appointed him with a mandate to put some order in the royal finances. "His ruses are the Devil's work!" proclaimed the pamphleteer Fancan.

At long last, Richelieu got his break. La Vieuville found no other solution to the mounting political pressure than to call on him and secure the goodwill of the queen mother. The king, once consulted, agreed. Richelieu played it cool. Because La Vieuville feared that the talents of the cardinal might stand out and cast an unflattering light on his own aptitudes, he wanted him to remain a technical adviser to the Crown instead of being admitted to the council in a straightforward way. Richelieu politely declined the invitation, pretending that he would rather live quietly and take care of himself. On April 28, 1624, Louis XIII asked Cardinal Richelieu to meet him on the terrace of his bedroom at the Château de Compiègne, where the two men held a conversation. Then, on the next day, Louis went to see his mother, Marie de' Medici, as she awoke at eleven o'clock, and told her of his decision to admit the cardinal to his council. He welcomed Richelieu into the council that very afternoon, to every attendant's surprise.

Official letters announced the event all over France and Europe, and notes of congratulations and pledges of service came back from a remarkable range of Frenchmen: grandees such as the Duc Henri II de Montmorency, clergymen in the highest ranks, and magistrates. All in all, general approval and relief greeted Louis's choice. The Good Frenchmen rejoiced, and so did the Devouts, because he was a man of the Church. "Courtiers say that he is fine like twenty-two carat gold," assured Fancan. The foreign envoys, for their part, emphasized his ambition as much as they lauded his talents. Richelieu claimed that he accepted the job on the condition that he would not have to meet ambassadors and petitioners, and have more time for his affairs. The Florentine envoy tells another story, that the king and La Vieuville had set these terms so that the cardinal would not take too much advantage of his new position.[31] In any case, Richelieu put out another special request to the king. He argued that taking a post that he had neither sought nor wanted, but out of sheer obedience, required some special guarantee. "His Majesty must know that [the cardinal] has no other designs than the prosperity of his person and state, and must stand firmly in this belief so that the cardinal may be assured that the tricks of the malicious ones will have no power against him."[32]

Richelieu's subsequent actions surprised those who expected this eminent member of the clergy to be narrow-minded when it came to matters of religion and diplomacy. La Vieuville, in the hopes of securing the alliance with the English and the Dutch, paid little regard to the plight of Catholics in those countries. Richelieu demanded more security for the Catholics, but at the same time he never denounced the dealings with Protestants as zealous Catholics did.

Following Richelieu's nomination, La Vieuville continued to sink as the extent of his shady financial dealings became apparent. He ignored the royal council decisions concerning the Catholics abroad, thinking that they would derail his diplomacy. Fancan kept skewering him with his tracts. In *Le Mot à l'oreille*, the "word in the ear" of the king whispered that admitting Richelieu to the council had been a smart move.[33] Fancan also tackled Louis's enduring distrust of the newly admitted cardinal by proclaiming loudly that the latter would never seek any other support in his political career than that of the authority of the king.[34] On August 12, after his luncheon, Louis announced to his mother and her adviser that he had had enough of La Vieuville. The court left to visit a new estate Richelieu had just occupied in the village of Rueil to the west of Paris. La Vieuville, knowing that his political fortunes had rapidly dwindled, went to the king and offered his resignation, which, curiously, the king rejected. Louis told him that he should not worry about anything and that he expected him to follow the court to Saint-Germain that night. He promised his minister that he would let him know of his dismissal in person. Not quieted at all by this reassurance, La Vieuville spent a sleepless and anxious night at the château.[35] He was right to fear for his future. The following day, Louis summoned him to the council and told him that, as promised, he was announcing in person his removal from office. La Vieuville left. Upon crossing the courtyard of the château, guards arrested him for disrespecting the authority of the king.

At this early stage in his second political career, Richelieu still had to collaborate with other ministers, particularly those he met in the "restricted" meetings of the royal council, where vital and secret affairs were discussed. Nevertheless, many foreign envoys deemed him to be a man on the rise. The Connétable de France traditionally spoke first in the council, but Richelieu, as soon as he entered the council, claimed to have precedence, not because he was the council's chief, but because he was a dignitary of the Church. His *cappa magna*, the ceremonial dress of a cardinal, was a fitting costume not only for his growing power but also for the dignified décor he now set up for himself. His father's old debts were settled, and the memory of Luçon's meager days was gone. Benefits and lucrative charges accumulated.[36] He bought a Parisian lodging worthy of his standing, in the Faubourg Saint-Honoré, a stone's throw from the Louvre and the street where he was born.

Underneath all the prestige, however, the hardships of a turbulent rise to power were taking their toll. Richelieu was reaching the age of forty, a respectable age for the time. His migraines could paralyze him. Facing him was a strange character, an equally thin, dark-haired king whose youth had faded prematurely, worn out by inner torments, military battles, and furious hunting.[37] Richelieu knew that Louis's deep-seated distrust of others and of himself, combined with his royal conscience, could take away all nuances from his judgment. Louis, with his talent for dissimulation, was a disquieting master. Hence Richelieu asked Louis for a guarantee that he would not listen to his enemies, and took great care to profess his submission. To borrow the words of Saavedra Fajardo, the great Spanish diplomat, the minister Richelieu was, at the end of a difficult political climb, "closer to Jupiter, but also to its thunder."[38]

In the days that followed the demise of minister La Vieuville, surely Cardinal Richelieu thought more about the view he enjoyed from the Olympus he had finally reached than about the danger of lightning strikes. There were formidable challenges: to tame a violence-prone aristocracy that clung to its feudal ways, and to settle the enduring political agitation of the Protestants, all necessary steps to counter the Habsburgs. In practical terms, this meant the Spanish king, because this Habsburg was the most prominent and threatening to French interests.

Cardinal Richelieu's counterpart in Madrid could not have been more dissimilar at first glance. Philip IV's minister, the Count-Duke of Olivares, was a squat and bubbly Spaniard with a thick mustache curling upward, quite the opposite of the bony, aquiline, and poised Frenchman. But the two men had a good deal in common. Both were authoritarian, and hyperactive, yet also lovers of the arts, eloquent, and even hypersensitive. In his private study in the royal palace of Madrid, Olivares wielded immense power. His influence on the young Philip IV, whom he strived to fashion into a perfect monarch, was assured.

The splendor of Spain in the sixteenth century was gone, though, and the kingdom had become a fragile colossus. Early attempts at fiscal, administrative, and social reform had been unsuccessful. The Spanish population, long used to living on investment revenues, could hardly work to create enough wealth; worsening this situation was an alarming demographic decline that large numbers of priests and soldiers could not defy. Maritime contenders such as England had become formidable competitors to the legendary fleet, the Armada, and they made the gold and silver of America a less reliable source of wealth, leaving the kingdom gasping for revenues. The endless war with the Dutch was proving to be a drain on the precious energy and resources of Philip's kingdom. Emperor Ferdinand had his own military priorities in northern Europe and did not consider himself beholden to his Spanish cousin. The Habsburgs were far from being a unified block. Finally, who knew how the new pope, Urban VIII, who had succeeded Gregory XV on August 6, 1623, and who was known as a Francophile, would judge these French alliances with heretic powers as they were promoted by a cardinal.

The turbulent years following the assassination of Concini had taught Richelieu some good lessons on how to restrain his own opportunism, and on how to conceal it deftly. It remained to be seen how he would put these new skills to good use now that he was the minister of Louis XIII, and that the stakes were even higher for France, and for his own name. The veteran court poet François Malherbe declared that with Richelieu, France finally had a real chance to leave the troubles of the regency and of Louis's early reign for good: "I swear, there is something in this man that exceeds humanity; if our vessel ever goes through the storm, this glorious hand will hold the tiller."[39]

PART II

The Testing

CHAPTER 4

Angel or Demon? (1624–1626)

ONE YEAR AFTER RICHELIEU WAS ADMITTED to Louis XIII's council, the affairs of the French kingdom were on a steadier course. In the cardinal's words, all things conspired "to bring down the pride of Spain."[1] The marriage of Louis's sister Henriette Marie with the new English king Charles I, which was celebrated by proxy on May 11, 1625, isolated Philip IV and Olivares at a time when General Ambrose Spinola was preparing to besiege the Dutch city of Breda—the city fell on June 10. Spinola's offensive threatened the Dutch Republic with a dangerous blow, but also mobilized large contingents of forces and left the Spanish territories and possessions vulnerable to an attack. Richelieu took the opportunity to subsidize the Dutch war effort and to order French armies to enter the strategic Valtellina, to seize the forts held by papal troops, Spanish all but in name.[2] Finally, Richelieu reached out to Germans of all faiths, including the Catholic Maximilian of Bavaria, to challenge, albeit indirectly and by means of diplomacy, the other reigning branch of the powerful Habsburgs. Flurries of foreign Catholic pamphlets vehemently taunted this cardinal in "boots" and "spurs" who scandalously worked with Protestant powers and stood up to the House of Austria.[3]

On May 27, 1625, with an English delegation in Paris to fetch the new English queen, Cardinal Richelieu celebrated his political success by hosting a reception at the Palais du Luxembourg. Entertaining in the queen's new house was an outstanding honor for the cardinal. The royal family, the English envoy George Villiers, Duke of Buckingham, and throngs of courtiers converged toward the Luxembourg. Inside the palace, they gasped in awe. Flowers cascaded from all directions.[4] Fountains of perfumed waters leaped to the azure and gilt ceilings to the sound of music. Pyramids of candied fruits and dishes of preserves covered the buffets. Views of the magnificent gardens, with rows of ornamental trees and waterworks, ravished the eye. Finally, connoisseurs marveled at the long hall where the painter Peter Paul Rubens had placed his twenty-four scenes of the queen mother's life. The cardinal-minister, draped in his best red silk, could no doubt survey the scene with satisfaction.[5]

Except that at Richelieu's party, appearances were deceiving. Underneath the riches of the French court there was brewing what the cardinal would call "the most abominable conspiracy ever devised," a story so rich in outlandish events, romance, and politics that it gave Alexandre Dumas a canvas on which to compose the swashbuckling novel *The Three Musketeers*. That the details of this plot were good enough to become a bestselling tale should not lead one to dismiss them outright; there are actually reliable sources to document the incidents, and, with due precautions, they should be retained as integral to Richelieu's biography.

The first English ambassador who had come to Paris to discuss the marriage of Charles and Henriette was the Earl of Holland. In the French capital, Holland was a guest of the Duc and Duchesse de Chevreuse—the duchess being none other than Luynes's widow, Marie de Rohan, who had remarried into a prestigious family and returned to court as the queen's confidante. Holland and the duchess began an affair. If we believe the memoirs of François de La Rochefoucauld, their pillow talk led to quite a project: to arouse a love interest between Queen Anne of Austria and the Duke of Buckingham, the English king's dashing favorite, who would undoubtedly come to Paris if the marriage negotiations were successful. Now, La Rochefoucauld was an eleven-year-old child at the time, and because he wrote later, he is considered a less certifiable testimony in this whole affair. But other testimonies show, nonetheless, that some kind of a project to create bonds of friendship between the queen and the duke did exist.

Circumstances made such a project conceivable.[6] After the brief honeymoon that had followed the onset of the French royal couple's sexual relations, and the subsequent disaster of Anne's miscarriage, Louis had retreated into an indifferent, cold, if not downright mean, attitude toward his wife.

A new handsome page named François de Barradas rose in the king's esteem. Such indignity did not stifle joie de vivre in Anne, who kept a lively company in which the Duchesse de Chevreuse was ever present. Madame de Motteville, who became the queen's chambermaid and confidante, explained that for Anne there was an honest form of gallantry whereby women could acknowledge the platonic love of men and their homage without any harm. After decades of civil conflict, the French aristocracy was rediscovering the pleasures of polite society and, especially, all things literary and gallant.[7] From the salon at the Hôtel de Rambouillet where the chic set gathered, to the apartment of Anne of Austria in the Louvre, the romance sung by poets such as François Malherbe and Vincent Voiture defined the times. Little by little and with much art, the Duchesse de Chevreuse "incited the queen to think of Buckingham."[8]

Another twist gave this already bizarre plot added zest concerning Cardinal Richelieu. Richelieu's august title did not make him less of a man, and he liked the company of beautiful women who happened to belong to the highest aristocracy. It appears that Madame de Chevreuse, who summed up all these qualities and then some, had caught his attention, and it is true that many years later, even after she caused him unimaginable trouble and vexations, Richelieu still had a soft spot for the duchess.[9] One rumor has him paying her visits dressed up as a gentleman, bearing a sword and with red feathers in his hat. The story says that Chevreuse found the pursuit ridiculous and rebuked him. The French ambassador to England, the Comte Tanneguy Leveneur de Tillières, a man closely involved with the events of the time, does write that Richelieu then took a fancy to the queen herself.[10] The Comte de Brienne also tells a funny anecdote, but that one definitely seems far-fetched. In his words, the cardinal was so infatuated with Anne that he dressed up in a beautiful green velvet costume to dance a saraband just for the queen. People considered the saraband the most lascivious and devilish dance at the time. In any case, no frenzied dance to the sound of jingle bells could entice the queen to acknowledge the cardinal. Not only was he the "creature" of her mother-in-law, Marie de' Medici, with whom she had strained relations, but she suspected that he spoke ill of her to the king for fear that he could lose influence should Louis find interest in his wife again. According to Madame de Motteville, the Duchesse de Chevreuse alleviated the queen's scruples "by bringing forth the vexation that this thought of Buckingham represented for Richelieu."[11]

Buckingham arrived in Paris with Holland to fetch Henriette. He was tall, athletic, and blond, and, as Anne's personal valet La Porte reported, "with so much charm and magnificence that he gave admiration to the people, joy and something else to the ladies, jealousy to the gallants, and even more to husbands."[12] The queen still, as when she married, had quite ravishing features. It was love at first sight, according to Leveneur de Tillières. Madame de Motteville described the two feeling as if they were kindred spirits who had known each other for a long time. Both Holland and Buckingham were guests at the Hôtel de Chevreuse. Parisians saw the four friends—Buckingham, Anne, Holland, and Marie—around town for an entire week, while the royal marriage fired up the capital, the same week that Richelieu hosted his lavish reception at the Palais du Luxembourg.

During the day, the cardinal and the duke held discussions on the political situation and a possible military alliance. The English hoped to form in northern Europe a defensive and offensive league to restore Prince Frederick V of the Palatinate, the short-reigning monarch of Bohemia and King James's son-in-law. In spite of these favorable circumstances, Richelieu prudently abstained from directly engaging the Habsburgs. Siding too much with the English in this project would have been detrimental to his effort at winning the favor of Maximilian of Bavaria, who had moved a major step forward in gaining the coveted right of elector in the empire, a right his Palatine cousin had lost. Instead, Richelieu proposed to pay subsidies to the English-led league. Leveneur de Tillières described the two men's encounters as rather testy, and not only on account of the two men's political disagreement.[13]

Court protocol gave Buckingham and Anne a little more time together. A daughter of France always departed with an impressive cortege, and so, on June 2, a week after the Luxembourg party, Henriette Marie left Paris on a red velvet litter, followed by her mother, Marie de' Medici, and her sister-in-law, Anne. Naturally, the two English ambassadors followed, as did the Duc and Duchesse de Chevreuse, who traveled to England as representatives of the French government. Louis was recovering from illness. He remained in Paris with his minister. Shortly after leaving the capital, all arrived in Amiens, where they had to stay because Marie de' Medici had a cold. Amiens's governor organized a series of receptions to keep the court entertained, festivities where Anne was at her best. "The queen," wrote memoirist Louis-Henri de Loménie de Brienne, "shined over the entire court. Nature, who had given her so white a complexion that it could blind someone, eclipsed all the other beauties, and surprised everyone when she appeared like a new celestial body."[14]

One night, Buckingham decided to push his luck further. Anne lodged at an estate bordering the Somme River, where the court had taken a habit of enjoying a promenade late in the evening. Followed by his friend Holland, the Duchesse de Chevreuse, and the usual multitude of courtiers, officers, and valets, he led Anne though the garden. Holland and Chevreuse slowed their step to allow Buckingham to distance himself from the crowd. The duke discreetly took Anne into a dark alley. After a short while Anne let out a pressing call; her equerry, Monsieur de Putange, ran toward her.[15] The queen appeared disconcerted, Buckingham embarrassed. While speculations run wild on what exactly happened in those bushes, no one really knows. The duke disappeared into the night, without a word, and under the furious gaze of the queen's officers.

The day after this scene, at Henriette's departure from Amiens, Buckingham's behavior definitely confirmed that he was infatuated. He approached Anne's carriage and sobbed while hiding his face in the curtains. In Boulogne, rough seas prevented the English fleet from sailing right away. Under the pretext that he had received a letter from England, the duke rode back to Amiens with Holland, delivered some news to the queen mother, and went straight to Anne's room. Before her dumbfounded ladies, wrote Madame de Motteville, he then collapsed on her bed, sobbing and giving passionate kisses to the bed cover.[16]

Richelieu, who knew of all the details of the trip from the reports of his informants, thought that the English envoy gravely offended Louis XIII with his extravagant actions. The king fired a number of Anne's officers who were in Amiens. In the following months, the cardinal provoked widespread shock when he reversed French policy concerning England.

Richelieu's first move to counter the duke came in the summer of 1625 when he denied him a passport to reenter France. The purpose of the visit was suspicious. Officially, the discord that existed between Henriette's entourage and the English in general, and, as a consequence, between the English royal couple, motivated the duke's return to France. The huge crowd of courtiers that Henriette had brought from France included many Catholic clerics who thought that their mission was to spread their brand of Christianity in a country that was profoundly anti-Catholic in both public opinion and political institutions.[17] The French clerics came across as fanatical, intransigent, and tactless.[18] Henriette, as it turned out, missed few opportunities to quarrel with her husband. In the months that followed the French-born queen's arrival, and while the English court traveled from castle to castle to avoid the plague that ravaged London, it soon became obvious that anti-French sentiment was on the rise in Henriette's new kingdom. Not only did the English despise the Catholics, but they despised their king's trusted man, too. The Parliament had never warmed up to both the French alliance and Buckingham's war plans to save the Palatine prince. When Charles I dissolved the Parliament in August because it steadfastly refused to finance a German war, Buckingham agreed to anti-Catholic measures, and to the indignation of the French he sought to replace the women of Henriette Marie's entourage with other women he trusted. He then offered himself as a mediator in the situation and asked permission to travel to Paris. Perhaps the duke was sincere and was an honest broker in the royal household; to the French, it seemed he worsened the situation to take personal and political advantage of it. Richelieu needed little convincing to persuade the king to deny Buckingham's request.

From the English court where she spent the summer of 1625, Madame de Chevreuse wrote letters to her friend the queen to remind her of her suitor, while simultaneously provoking Buckingham's ill will against the cardinal. The duchess also continued her liaison with Count Holland, and, if we are to believe one of the reports Richelieu received, she started one with Buckingham at the same time.[19] Richelieu heard all the details from his trusted man within Henriette's circle, the Bishop of Mende, and he commented on them with a mix of indignation and titillation, not witholding at times a pun on the subject. The cardinal loved giving nicknames, and Madame de Chevreuse, in his parlance, was *la chevrette*, the little goat. With quite a train of thought, Richelieu wrote to one of his correspondents that Buckingham's moniker had to be *le bouquin* (evoking the duke's name and the male goat in French) because he had "bouquiné la chevrette."[20]

Richelieu denied Buckingham a second request to come to France later in 1625, when a new peril raised its head in Germany. Ferdinand had declared the Czech noble, rich landowner, and military entrepreneur Albert of Wallenstein the chief of his armies and had devised a new strategy in consultation with his

Spanish cousins, following what had turned out to be their inconclusive war against the Dutch. The goal was now to open a front toward the north, to threaten the lucrative and vital commerce that linked the cities of the Baltic Sea with those of the North Sea, including the Dutch ones. King Christian IV of Denmark declared war in response, and Buckingham traveled to The Hague to devise a general counterstrategy with the Dutch and the Danes. Then the duke solicited French military help and asked permission to come to Paris for talks. The request was rejected, and, out of spite, the duke called Richelieu a "fresh water admiral" who would never venture out in the seas given the maritime superiority of the English. In return, Richelieu enraged the duke when in one of his letters, he finished with the formula "your very humble servant," made a point of crossing it out with a stroke of his pen, and inserted a less respectful formula instead.

By the beginning of the year 1626, the personal enmity between these two men was an inopportune burden in the midst of other gathering political misfortunes, recounted Ambassador Leveneur de Tillières.[21] Richelieu's new troubles first concerned his foreign enterprises abroad. French troops were still stationed in the Valtellina, and they seemed likely to stay there after a papal legate failed to convince the French that they should renegotiate the terms of the treaty signed in Madrid in the year 1623. But then Germans soldiers used the passage in spite of the French presence. The provocation highlighted how soft the defense of the prized Alpine valley was in spite of French determination to keep it under their control.[22] In Madrid, despite Olivares's commitment to remain prudent in his relation with France, hawkish voices were heard more loudly. There were even rumors of a possible alliance between Spain and England. Another source of concern was the restless Huguenots. Since January of 1625, Benjamin de Rohan, Seigneur de Soubise, the defender of Saint-Jean-d'Angély and Riez, conducted sporadic raids along the Atlantic coast. On September 18, 1625, in front of La Rochelle, the Duc de Montmorency chased these rogue Protestant rebels, who then sought refuge in England. Who knew what trouble Soubise could stir up from there?

Cardinal Richelieu paused to reevaluate the situation. With the English alliance dithering, and some clear setbacks in the oblique confrontation with Spain, political pressure from the Devout party within France became much more insistent. In an earlier 1625 memo he had written to Louis—the paper where he declared that all things "conspired to bring down the pride of Spain"—the minister had also expressed some caution about France's prospective foreign strategy. Ever mindful of how internal dissent put France at great risk, he had stated that taming or quieting Protestant rebellion should always have priority over foreign enterprises. Backing up this opinion was that Spanish minister Olivares was providing secret help to the Huguenots, a guarantee that whenever France engaged with its southern enemy, it would have to face internal disturbance.[23] "Affairs of state," Richelieu wrote, "are similar to human bodies, which have their period of growth, perfection, and decline. Political prudence consists in nothing but to seize the most advantageous occasion to achieve what one wants."

On February 5, 1626, the French Crown signed a peace deal with the French Protestants, and, on May 5, with the Spanish.[24] So much for Richelieu's grand master plan to counter the Habsburgs, if there was any. The reposition showed that the minister's demonstrated opportunism could also be channeled into political flexibility. The second treaty, signed in Monzón with Olivares, allowed the French to retain their control over the Valtellina, although the two parties agreed that the forts that held the valley should be razed. The Devout party of France vehemently decried the agreement with the French Protestants, whom it considered heretics. Soon, however, the arrangement with Spain gave them reason to be content. The Duke of Savoy and the Venetians, who had sustained Richelieu's war effort against Spain by joining the league to defend the Valtellina and who had been left in the dark while Richelieu negotiated with Olivares, felt betrayed. The Dutch, who received subsidies in their own war against Spain, were equally incensed. Finally, the English saw the cardinal's move as a point of no return in their degrading relations with France. To make matters worse, news of the French treaty with Spain came just after Buckingham learned that Wallenstein had crushed his German coalition army at Dessau, on April 25. Tilly eventually defeated Danish king Christian IV on August 26, at Lutter.

Richelieu declared to his vociferous critics that the deal with Spain surprised him, too, and that Louis's ambassador in Madrid had overstepped his mandate. But tellingly, and as Maréchal de Bassompierre commented, the government spent more time blaming the "worker than demolishing the work."[25] Contemporaries and modern historians alike do not accept the excuse that a rogue ambassador had come up with the treaty with Spain.[26] Richelieu's opportunism had been elevated to a capacity to adapt; as for the lessons on how to slyly cover up or excuse shifts in strategy, they still were very much pertinent, as such. The cardinal feigned sickness, stayed in bed, and refused to meet with the ambassadors who wanted to complain in person about the betrayal.

Richelieu shelved his plans to counter the Habsburg House of Austria because, among many reasons, he could not do so as long as the Protestants posed a domestic threat. It is hard to discern whether he thought the fight abroad would soon resume. The challenge Richelieu ended up facing that summer, instead, was the one that had plagued the regency of Marie de' Medici, the unruliness of the high nobility. The trouble was an episode in Madame de Chevreuse's "most abominable conspiracy" known as the Conspiracy of the Dames.

This time, the duchess's plotting revolved around the person of Gaston, or, as the eighteen-year-old brother of the king and heir to the throne of France was called, Monsieur. Louis and his brother were contrasting siblings. The elder had quite a dark complexion, whereas the younger had pale skin and blue eyes, and was the more attractive. Differences of personality were even sharper. Louis's temperament was somber and melancholic. He often sought solitude. Gaston had a cheerful, witty, even farcical disposition that found an outlet in the lively company he always kept. Louis had little penchant for the arts, save for drawing, music, and dance. Gaston was learned, curious, even erudite, having a particular taste for literature, numismatics, and botany. As for character, a parallel could not be drawn, yet. For all his introverted ways, Louis had displayed good judgment and a determination to reign with justice. Gaston, at his young age, was still an enigma.

Marie de' Medici harbored some firm opinions on an important matter to Gaston's future: his marriage. Following her husband's wish, she wanted her younger son, the first in line to the throne, to wed Marie de Bourbon, Duchesse de Montpensier, a rich heiress related to the powerful ultra-Catholic dynasty of Guise. The king expressed ambivalent feelings about the union. The royal couple still had not produced a Dauphin. Louis XIII was often sick, and many astrologers predicted that he would die young. Should Gaston have a son, power would immediately shift toward him. Also, the question of Gaston's marriage reached a deeper emotional level. Louis thought that Marie's commitment to the match proved not only that she had the interest of the state and of the Bourbon dynasty in mind, but also that she preferred her younger child. One day the king even broke down in the arms of his confessor Father Suffren. Gaston's biographer stated that once the king told his confessor, out of the blue, that his mother would never forgive him for Concini's death, and that this was why she cared so much about Gaston's future.[27]

As he always did in such difficult situations, Richelieu analyzed the problem methodically. In his day-to-day workings with Louis XIII, the minister regularly sent memoirs in which he laid out all the possible ways of interpreting a situation, signaling to Louis XIII that his minister did not presume to decide for him. A piece Richelieu wrote on Gaston's marriage is a good example of this modus operandi. It shows how Richelieu needed to sympathize with Louis's fears without offending Marie de' Medici. Avoiding the semblance of Gaston's enemy was crucial, too, given that the prince could end up on the throne. Louis conceded, albeit reluctantly, that for the good of the state, Gaston had to marry. Father Joseph, Richelieu's trusted adviser, would try to convince Gaston without pressing the point too much, so as not to provoke an adverse reaction.[28]

The Duchesse de Chevreuse, who had come back from London in July of 1625, became an all-out adversary of the marriage. If Gaston produced an heir, he would gain influence and represent a strong opposition to Richelieu. But now that the decision to get him married had been made, countering the project would cause Richelieu's reputation to suffer, especially with Marie de' Medici. Chevreuse first explained to Anne of Austria that Gaston's marriage and possible progeny represented a grave threat to her own influence. Then she put forth an unsavory thought that floated for a quite a while at court: the queen had to oppose the marriage as well because in case Louis passed away, she could be the one to marry Gaston.[29] The siblings-in-law were quite fond of each other. In short order, then, and thanks to her skills and influence, the duchess spun a conspiracy from within Anne of Austria's inner circle, and its lethal threads first caught Gaston's tutor, Colonel Jean-Baptiste d'Ornano, in the spring of 1626.

This rather old and curt military officer was not, at first glance, the kind of man women could lure into court follies. Still, he was the perfect target for the plot because Gaston trusted d'Ornano completely since he had replaced the appointed tutors of Luynes and raised him with a mix of tough love and sincere devotion.[30] What gave Madame de Chevreuse and Anne hope that d'Ornano could be persuaded to join the plot against the marriage was his ambition and pride. All of a sudden, the unsightly colonel found himself the darling of the court's most beautiful dames. He contemplated what immense power he would hold should Gaston ascend to the throne. But that, of course, would all be moot if Gaston married a relative of the mighty Guises. To the surprise of many observers at the court, Gaston started showing strong reluctance toward the Montpensier marriage project.

Richelieu, deep in the midst of his English, Spanish, and Protestant worries, took little time to realize that a plot brewed and that it involved the colonel. The cardinal had one motto, according to the contemporary historian Vittorio Siri: "those not with him were against him."[31] He offered Colonel d'Ornano a promotion to the rank of marshal, with the hope of making him one of his allies. D'Ornano accepted. But the Duchesse de Chevreuse drew the marshal back again into the conspiracy. By springtime, d'Ornano asked that Gaston join the royal council, which would have granted him access to the inner workings of the government.[32] Taking the ensuing refusal as a personal slight, d'Ornano became an even more dangerous agent of dissent. By then, what had begun as a court intrigue had gathered those high aristocrats who felt threatened by the ever-growing power of the cardinal and his lack of interest in governing in consultation with them. It was a full-fledged effort to destabilize the throne. The king's two half brothers, César and Alexandre de Vendôme, were among the many who had come on board by offering safe havens and financial assistance should Gaston decide to start a rebellion.

On Saturday May 4, 1626, the royal family sojourned at Fontainebleau, one of the French king's most magnificent residences. Louis spent the day hunting and came back to watch military exercises in a courtyard of the château. As one of Gaston's courtiers recalled it in his memoirs, the whole court gathered for the spectacle, including d'Ornano. The king spoke amicably with him, although, strangely, in the midst of the conversation, he pointed to a window of the castle and casually asked, "Monsieur le Maréchal, did you know that this is the room where Maréchal de Biron was taken?"[33] The man to whom the king referred had fomented a conspiracy against Henri IV and had had his head cut off for his crime. The rest of the day went by without anything significant happening.

Louis retired. Once all his gentlemen went away, he stepped out of bed and asked a valet to fetch d'Ornano, saying that he needed company. The marshal arrived to find Louis alone playing his guitar. Both casually talked for a while about hunting. Then, according to the Venetian ambassador, Louis stood up, and, still playing his guitar, he went to his study.[34] Knocks sounded on the door of the bedroom. The captain of the guards came in and told the marshal that he was under arrest. He took d'Ornano to the very same room that Louis had brought to his attention earlier in the day, the one where ill-fated Biron had long ago preceded him. Should his allies have tried to free the colonel, they would have found all roads to Fontainebleau under a heavy guard. The military exercises were just a pretext to call troops in without attracting attention.

Richelieu's enemies, instead of being intimidated by the capture of d'Ornano, were fired up. Gaston said that he would find those responsible and feed their hearts to his dogs. The Duchesse de Chevreuse chose action in place of words of rage. She seduced a young noble in Louis's entourage, the Comte Henri de Chalais, who hailed from one of France's most ancient noble families, the Talleyrands-Périgord. After he was raised as a page in the royal household, his mother had sacrificed nearly all of her resources to buy him the charge of "master of the king's wardrobe," a place in the king's inner circle. Soon courtiers noted his good looks and success with women, and, after Chalais fought with valor in the Montauban and Montpellier campaigns, his athletic talents and courage. Unfortunately for the young man, he also happened to be madly in love with the duchess, whom he followed everywhere, at church or during her promenade. The duchess told him how Richelieu had tried to seduce her in the past, and that was enough to turn Chalais into a mortal enemy of the cardinal.

The conspirators realized that if anything was going to tip the balance of power toward Gaston, Cardinal Richelieu would have to be dealt with first in drastic fashion. Some proposed that he should be kidnapped and freed in exchange for the marshal's release. Others, including the newly recruited Chalais and the nobles in Gaston's entourage, wanted him simply eliminated. Gaston did not protest upon hearing these schemes, and so Chalais and his group decided to surprise the cardinal at a residence he occupied near Fontainebleau, ask for hospitality in advance of a courtesy visit by Gaston, and then provoke a brawl after dinner. In what would appear as a tragic accident, they wanted the cardinal to die from stabbing.[35]

Fortunately for Richelieu, Chalais confided the details of the plot to a relative, who then brought him before the cardinal to confess everything and ask for mercy. Meanwhile, the conspirators stood ready for action, even in Chalais's

absence. A group of nine men from Gaston's entourage traveled to the cardinal's house. There, Richelieu left them without an explanation, and, in the
middle of the night, protected by a heavy guard, he rushed to Fontainebleau,
where Gaston stayed. On the following morning of May 11, 1626, Gaston had
quite a surprise at his ritual awakening. When the servants pulled the curtains
of his bed, he did not see a courtier ready to announce the death of his enemy,
but Richelieu himself standing over him. The cardinal was the most prominent
person in attendance, and as such he stood ready to present the prince with his
shirt. Before proceeding, he very politely dropped that he would be very grateful if in the future the prince could give him advanced notice before coming to
his house, so that he might provide him with the best reception possible. Then
he handed Gaston his shirt and promptly left.

Richelieu retired to his country house in Limours. After showing a fine sense
of irony at Monsieur's bedside, he fell into a state of sadness and helplessness.
His were determined enemies. Many were women who could incite crimes
without risking too much because of their sex.[36] Later on, someone even tried
to kill him by placing a bomb under the seat of his carriage.[37] Mulling over
these somber thoughts led the cardinal to want to quit the game altogether.
What was the point of exhausting himself on behalf of France if death would be
his reward? he confided to Nuncio Spada.[38] From his country retreat, Richelieu wrote to Marie de' Medici and told her that he could not continue to help
the French king govern under these conditions.

Louis realized that if did not take quick action, he would lose the man with
whom he thought he had a chance to finally succeed as a monarch. On June 2,
the entire court left Paris and went to Blois. The king wrote a letter to his minister, after he received yet another request to resign: "Be assured that I will protect you against anyone, and that I will never abandon you. My mother the
queen says as much. I told you a while ago that my council should be fortified,
but you resisted, arguing that small steps led towards that goal. Time has come
to ignore those precautions. Suffice to say that this is what I want."[39] Thunder
struck on June 13 when Louis ordered his guards to arrest his two half brothers,
the Vendômes.[40] That same day, the king wrote again to his minister and pleaded
for his return, vowing that he would always stand by him, under any circum-
stance. For the rest of their turbulent collaboration, until the very end of their
lives, Louis would repeatedly remind his minister of this solemn commitment.
Richelieu agreed to rejoin the court.

Chalais still took his role in the conspiracy very seriously, even though Richelieu had set him free on the condition that he would keep him informed of ongoing affairs. At the royal Château de Blois where all the protagonists had gathered, in secret meetings held either in the gardens of the château or on one of the terraces, Chalais met with Madame de Chevreuse or Gaston to keep the plot going. He thought it was the only way he could win back his paramour's esteem. At the same time, the duchess kept prodding Gaston: "Have you forgotten what happened to d'Ornano?"

All these details of this dark affair, it should be pointed out, are known through the files of Chalais's subsequent interrogations and trial.

The plotters reached to include foreign powers. Because Richelieu had duped them when he signed the peace treaty with Spain, the Duke of Savoy and the Dutch were eager to communicate with Gaston. Also, the Duchesse de Chevreuse could easily convince Buckingham that the English should play a part, especially at a time when relations with France had taken a turn for the worse.[41] From London, Buckingham signaled to the town council of Protestant La Rochelle that they should support Monsieur's rebellion. All over France and Europe, a powerful network of conspirators expected Gaston to escape from Blois and depose his brother. Remarkably, the Duchesse de Chevreuse, Gaston, and Anne, all the primary players, remained very discreet in this web of betrayal. While courtly life kept on with its rituals, hunting parties, and festivities, Chalais ran from one end of the château to another, carrying messages, writing compromising letters on the behalf of others. The young man still sought to ingratiate himself with the cardinal, too, telling him that things were smoothing out while he actually plotted behind his back.

Richelieu offered the young man higher offices. At the same time, he kept asking, "What is Chalais in this story?" and he promised Gaston's acolytes riches if they persuaded the prince to stay quiet and to marry the Princesse de Montpensier.

As it turns out, Richelieu's question was unnecessary, since he paid spies everywhere, including near Anne of Austria, and he already had all the answers he needed.[42] On June 27, the court left Blois and headed toward Nantes, where the Estates of Brittany were about to meet. It so happened that Nantes was also a convenient place to hold a trial and resist attacks from rogue princes. Shortly after the court arrived in Nantes, Louis ordered Chalais's arrest, on July 8.

*   *   *

The attention of the commission formed for judging Chalais focused on his relationships with Gaston, the princes, and foreign powers. Chalais pretended he had acted as a go-between and an agent just to penetrate the conspiracy and to provide better information for the cardinal. In an attempt to prove his good faith, he even asked his judges if Richelieu could interrogate him. Richelieu was a sagacious priest who, after years of hearing confessions, knew his way into the darkest recesses of a soul. He came to Chalais's cell and barely had to ask a question. The inquiry papers that have survived show well how the hapless prisoner lost himself in his own contradictions. Sensing that he had slipped, the young man then suggested that he should rejoin the conspiracy, assuring that this time he would actually provide useful information. Richelieu dryly replied that there was little reason to trust him, and that at this point his only salvation would come from a full confession. The young man revealed that Anne and Gaston had plans to marry should Louis disappear.

Following these revelations, Chalais sank into dark despair. He stopped shaving and became disheveled, reported his guards to Richelieu. He spent nights uttering blasphemies and threatened to batter his brain out by running headfirst against the stone wall of his cell.[43] He wrote to his paramour, Madame de Chevreuse. A visitor passed her letters to him by hiding them in his ruff. Chalais responded: "I discerned what is divine in your beauty a long time ago. Now, however, I realize that I must really serve you as a true goddess, since declaring my love also puts my life at risk."[44] Richelieu did not miss a word of those exchanges. His secret agents were getting ahold of all the letters, which, beside precious compliments, yielded valuable information for the inquiry. When the Duchesse de Chevreuse prudently asked the young man to stop writing, Richelieu rewrote her letter, sealed it back, and gave it to the prisoner. Chalais continued the correspondence. Eventually, most likely because she suspected interference, the duchess stopped sending letters altogether. Richelieu now needed another stratagem to manipulate his prisoner. He visited Chalais again and insinuated that the duchess's silence meant that she mocked him in public for having been caught. Furious, the young man called her a "real Lucrezia Borgia" and revealed her role as the mastermind of the conspiracy. That day, the cardinal learned that after the failed attempt to stab him at his residence near Fontainebleau, Anne and the duchess had spent an entire dinner party laughing at the thought of his big scare.

Gaston was answering some tough questions, too. In a series of meetings

Richelieu held in the presence of his mother and brother, he had to confess everything he knew, which was not so difficult after all, because contrary to his unfortunate accomplice, the prince did not have much to fear: he was the heir to the throne. Gaston considered escape for a while. His acolytes, some of whom had cut deals of their own with Richelieu, suggested that he should seek an agreement with the cardinal before resorting to such an extreme solution. The prince went to see the cardinal. One of his courtiers wrote that in no time, "with three spoonfuls of preserves and two prunes from Genoa, he made [Gaston] forget all of what he had been planning for such a long time."[45] Louis, who until then still harbored some lingering doubts about the marriage, pressed ahead, and Gaston finally agreed to wed Mademoiselle de Montpensier. Gaston received a colossal sum of money for his cooperation, an appanage consisting of the Duchés d'Orléans, de Chartres, and the Comté de Blois in addition to his other landholdings.

The news of Gaston's looming marriage triggered a panic in the conspirators' circle. Those princes who had offered troops and strongholds for refuge wrote desperate letters asking the prince not to betray his loyal friends. The Duchesse de Chevreuse and Anne of Austria were in Nantes all this time. They cornered Gaston and begged him on their knees not to change his mind. But on August 5, 1626, in the king's room at Nantes's château, Cardinal Richelieu celebrated the prince's engagement with Mademoiselle de Montpensier. The day after, the two were wed in a nearby chapel, before the royal family and the courtiers, including many of the conspirators. The ceremony was a somber one, without music or any of the frills that should have enlivened such an occasion. Mademoiselle de Montpensier stood quietly. The groom did not even have time to have a new frock made.

Chalais, still secluded at the château, and, in an unfortunate coincidence, just below the room where the engagement happened, wondered about the cannon shots that marked the ceremonies. When the guard told him what they meant, he realized that his fate was sealed. The commission was tackling a most delicate part of its inquiry, whether the conspirators had contemplated assassinating Louis. Only vague testimonies and hearsay suggested that Chalais had entertained such a project. However, the mere existence of these rumors was alarming when it concerned a man who had been living in close proximity to the king and following his every move, day after day.

Once the judges of the commission finished collecting all the testimonies, the investigation continued with the sinister rituals of seventeenth-century justice. Guards took Chalais twice to the law courts and put him on the prover-bial hot seat, to pressure him to confess. He denied the judges' accusations that he had plans to assassinate his king. Following the second hearing, he went to the city's prison, where he had to look into a room filled with racks of torture instruments. The vision did nothing to move him. Again, the young man de-nied having anything to do with a murder plot against the king. He even re-tracted his accusations against the Duchesse de Chevreuse.

On August 18, 1626, the commission found the Comte de Chalais guilty of lèse-majesté. For his punishment, the judges decreed, he was to be decapi-tated, and after that, cut into four pieces. Then they ordered the quartered body to be displayed either at the city gates or on Nantes's major thorough-fares. The infamy went even farther. All of Chalais's family houses and forests were ordered razed. Finally, his posterity was declared ignoble and forever of common birth. Chalais's mother wrote a heart-wrenching letter to Louis and begged him to save the life of her son in remembrance of his valor in combat. All Louis could grant her was the remission of the infamous terms of the sen-tence. Chalais would die, but he would at least have the dignified death of an aristocrat belonging to one of France's finest families—that is, he would only be beheaded.

In spite of this royal intervention, there was no dignity in Chalais's death. Rather, the young man's execution turned out to be a butchery. His remaining friends kidnapped the executioner in a last attempt to save him. This bravado angered the judges. They found a prisoner who was also condemned to death and offered to commute the sentence if he would take on the role of the execu-tioner. The man, a shoemaker, agreed. Testimonies narrated that on the fate-ful day following his condemnation, at the end of the afternoon, Chalais came out of Nantes's courthouse on the Place du Bouffay to meet his fate. The con-demned man walked to the scaffold between two rows of guards, aided by a priest, and kissing the cross of a rosary he held in his tied hands. Once on the platform, the would-be executioner cut his hair and offered a blindfold, which Chalais refused. He asked for swiftness. The man had forgotten to sharpen his sword. At the first blow Chalais fell on his side, and the man kept striking. All he could do was to inflict horrible wounds. The crowd howled. The priest, one Father Desrosiers, shouted to the henchman to put him back on the wood block. Someone in the crowd gave the executioner a small hatchet, of the kind used by barrel makers. After nineteen more blows, with Chalais still crying "Jesus Maria," the improvised henchman finally severed the head from the body.[46] Chalais's mother prayed in a nearby church. She claimed the body of her son and, afterward, buried him with little ceremony.

Richelieu's enemies, and even his admirers, wondered what kind of angel he was—or demon. The Conspiracy of the Dames did not conclude with a general reconciliation with the high nobility, as in the days of Marie de' Medici's regency. Since November 1624, the cardinal minister had had a dispensation from the pope allowing him to participate in council deliberations—to form a judiciary commission, for example—that could cause death or loss of a limb. From then on, in a privilege normally reserved for the king, Richelieu moved around with a cohort of armed guards, and, even in his own house, the captain of those guards was a constant presence behind him. This was the time when he urged the king to enforce a long-existing ban against dueling. A year later, two young nobles from a most prominent family were sent to the scaffold for having held a duel right in the middle of the Marais. A purge of the king's staff followed Chalais's death. Richelieu dismissed all those who had been hired during the Luynes "reign," and who had weighed in against the marriage. He replaced them with men he trusted. The handsome Barradas, whom Louis could not do without, also chose the wrong camp. Eventually, the cardinal found a way to secure his disgrace. New staff came in. Michel de Marillac, a stern and staunch Catholic, became justice minister. On September 2, 1626, four months after his arrest, Maréchal d'Ornano died in prison. The cause was urinary retention, and, mindful of how this death would cause rumors of poisoning, the cardinal immediately published the report of the autopsy. Nevertheless, rumors thrived, much like those that accused him of having tricked Chalais into confessing with false offers of clemency.

Madame de Chevreuse vowed that she would rather give herself to a soldier than pardon a ruthlessness she squarely attributed to Richelieu. She found refuge at the court of Lorraine, an imperial territory at the time, after she was banned from France. This left her friend Anne of Austria to suffer the consequences for her involvement in the plot. On September 10, as the court journeyed back to Paris, Louis summoned the Queen of France to appear before him, Marie de' Medici, and Cardinal Richelieu. The king presented all the pieces of evidence, including the confessions of Gaston and Chalais. Adding to the humiliation, the queen had to sit on a small stool while the cardinal read all the pieces aloud, as if she was a common prisoner. When confronted with the accusation that she had contemplated the demise of her husband in order to marry Gaston, she claimed with defiance, "That would have been a mediocre bargain."

Gaston had left Nantes for good on the day of Chalais's execution. He was playing cards when he heard the details of the wretched man's final moments. One of his men observed that he kept on playing, "as if, instead of Chalais' death, he had heard of the man's deliverance."[47]

CHAPTER 5

Wonder by the Sea (1627–1628)

WITH A TREATY SIGNED IN 1626, peace was supposed to reign between the French king and his Protestant subjects. Yet near La Rochelle, the prosperous city of sea merchants and last standing citadel of French Protestantism, royal garrisons kept watch, stationed either in proximity to the walls of the city or offshore on the island of Ré. This continuing military presence left many thinking that the peace treaty was just a measure to gain time and shore up forces, and even more so after Gaston's interrogations during the Conspiracy of the Dames revealed that the citizens of La Rochelle had offered him asylum.[1]

Determining the intent of Richelieu's projects at that moment is difficult, however, because France's drastically deteriorating relations with England easily gave him another reason to prepare for war. Misunderstandings were still rife between the newly married English royal couple. When Queen Henriette Marie visited gallows where Catholics had been executed for political crimes, in the company of her clergy, as if she were leading a pilgrimage and paying her respects to martyrs, the provocation caused irreparable damage to her reputation. On July 1, Charles abruptly dismissed the members of his queen's French entourage, save for a few.[2] The French again saw all this as the work of Buckingham. The duke was, indeed, under much political pressure since the French had signed their Spanish treaty and refused to help him reinstate the Palatine prince Frederick V. Lastly, he harbored a grudge against the cardinal ever since he had denied him access to France because of

the divergence of political views and, quite possibly, on account of his infatuation with Anne of Austria. After Charles dissolved Parliament for a second
time, so unpopular were his confidant's policies, rumors that England was
arming vessels to attack France came to Richelieu's attention in Paris.

At the Lorraine court of twenty-one-year-old Duc Charles IV, hunting parties, tournaments, and lavish balls did not take the Duchesse de Chevreuse's
mind off her enemy the cardinal. Early in 1627, the English envoy Lord Montague arrived in Lorraine with a mission for de Chevreuse: she had to intercede
with Charles de Lorraine and get him to create a diversion during an English
attack on the French coast. As soon as the English arrived near the coasts of
France, armies from Lorraine would invade from the east. Between the se-
ductions of the duchess and some of his own territorial contentions with
France, Charles de Lorraine readily subscribed to Buckingham's plan and
began preparing for an attack on France of his own. Montague continued to
travel through Europe over the winter of 1626–1627, seeking more allies to
create diversions on behalf of Buckingham. In the Languedoc, he struck a deal
with the Duc de Rohan. In Turin, he asked the Duke of Savoy to join this
grand conspiracy as well.

Richelieu wasted no time in facing the gathering English threat. With another treaty agreed on March 20, he secured some help from Spain should the
English actually attack. France's naval forces were weak and useless. He ordered all ports and strategic posts on the Atlantic to be on alert and to fortify
their defenses. Those commanders in the vicinity of La Rochelle, such as the
Comte de Toiras on the nearby island of Ré, received detailed instructions. Car-
tographers and surveyors had to draw or update maps and plans. Quartermas-
ters began amassing supplies and munitions. Firm orders went out to purchase
and build ships. Finally, beginning in December, a general assembly of France's
most eminent personalities gathered to examine the kingdom's unhealthy budget and find cost-cutting measures in the hopes of bringing enough revenue to
sustain a war.[3] The nobles once again proposed to suppress the selling of administrative posts. But who knew when such a change could happen, when one
of the few means to bring in revenues was to create these offices?

On October 20, 1626, Richelieu received the brand-new title of Grand
Maître, Chef et Surintendant Général de la Navigation et Commerce de France
(Grand Master and General Superintendent of Sailing and Commerce). Then
he became Lieutenant Général in Le Havre and Gouverneur de Brouage et de

Honfleur, ports on the Atlantic. Later on, he eliminated the higher position of Connétable de France, and the competing one of Grand Amiral, thus saving money for the Crown and making himself the only master on board. There was an added personal benefit of this power grab. Richelieu had a keen interest in developing maritime trade and commerce, because he believed that the economic wealth of a country depended exclusively on a positive trade balance with other partners. With all those grand titles, he was in a prime position to reap hefty profits if his projects for France's naval development also bolstered commercial ventures. In the spring of 1627, he authorized an association of merchants to set up the fur trade in Canada, a milestone in the history of French colonial enterprises and the history of Québec.[4]

By March of 1627, all signs pointed toward conflict with England, and La Rochelle was in a state of high anxiety.[5] The English argued that they prepared for war on behalf of the Huguenots' threatened liberties. The cardinal, sensing La Rochelle's nervousness, continued to assure its citizens that they had nothing to fear if they remained obedient to the king. The Rochelois still felt that he was slowly and inexorably laying a trap for them. Some activist elements argued that getting involved in a war alongside the English was unavoidable and a necessary evil.[6]

On July 20, 1627, an imposing English navy led by the Duke of Buckingham showed up off the coast of Ré, and war between France and England began. The duke had set Ré as his first target because the island provided a good base from which one could control the French Atlantic seaboard and launch operations on the French mainland. The island also allowed easy access to La Rochelle, which lay a few miles away, across narrow straits. The English landed a few days later, and, after a short battle on the beach, the French commander Toiras retreated with the rest of his forces to the citadel of Saint-Martin, in the middle of the island's north coast. Immediately after this auspicious beginning, Buckingham sent a delegation led by Benjamin de Rohan—the Seigneur de Soubise who had fled France in 1625—to La Rochelle. The aldermen of La Rochelle feared that Richelieu would misinterpret Soubise and the English's presence as a sign of defiance from the city. As a result, the mayor did not invite them into the city, but rather ventured outside the walls to speak with them. Soubise kept his cool and pretended he had come to visit his mother, the Duchesse de Rohan. This woman brought the tense situation to an end when she marched to the gate and, pointing to her son, proudly declared to the gathering crowd that the house of Rohan had always defended La Rochelle and its liberties. Soubise and the others entered the city to the sound of loud cheers, forcing La Rochelle's council to hear his proposals. All that the men in the council agreed to, however, was to name some deputies and send them to talk with Buckingham. No matter what, they said, they would take no action before consulting with the other Reformed churches of France. The Duke of Buckingham, in the meantime, waited for his armaments to be unloaded. By July 27, he and his troops camped in sight of the citadel of Saint-Martin and prepared to lay siege.

Louis and Cardinal Richelieu were on their way to the Atlantic, not aware yet that the English had arrived. Suddenly, the king fell gravely ill with an intestinal infection, similar to the one that preceded the coup d'état of 1617. Marie de' Medici and Anne of Austria quickly joined them and watched Louis waste away as news of Buckingham's landing arrived. Richelieu, the king's mother, and his wife, realizing that the king's warrior instincts would push him to take the road again if he learned of the attack, decided to keep the news of the invasion a secret. Louis went to Versailles to recuperate without knowing that his brother-in-law Charles I had declared war on his kingdom.

The responsibility of countering Buckingham's attack was squarely on Richelieu's shoulders. It was a daunting task indeed for him to stay at Louis's bedside, pretending that nothing happened, and excusing himself under false pretexts whenever he needed to hear reports or give orders. Despite the earlier treaty, Spanish aid had not materialized. The war fleet he arduously had worked on was still at the docks, with weeks of additional efforts needed before it could operate. A rescue effort on Ré was impossible, and the only hope of saving the island rested on Toiras's capacity to resist the siege until those forces were ready. Richelieu began a frantic search for available ships of any kind and promised a fortune to anyone who succeeded in delivering provisions to Toiras. He even advanced his own money when the royal treasury could not send funds quickly enough to builders and suppliers.

Louis XIII's daring minister had to be realistic: Ré could be lost. He ordered the Duc d'Angoulême to take his position on the strategic site of Coreille, on La Rochelle's bay, on August 13. From this vantage point, one could keep the English off the mainland, and control access to the port city, should it choose to join the enemy, or should the cardinal need it as a hostage during negotiations with the invaders: "Taking Coreille without a major Huguenot uprising had always proven impossible" in the past, wrote Richelieu, "so we should not waste the opportunity to take it at a time when La Rochelle shows so much ill-will, and is only waiting for the fall of Ré to take arms."[7]

The citizens of La Rochelle contemplated an increasingly impossible situation. The royal army had slowly surrounded them, and they perfectly understood that the most tenuous sign of hostility could be a pretext for attack. Work began to strengthen the city's defenses. A detachment of several hundred English soldiers came from Ré to assist, and in return the Rochelois sent food and provisions to Buckingham. On September 10, 1627, soldiers in La Rochelle fired cannon shots at workers of the royal army who were building bastions around the walls of the city. The citadel of French Protestantism had decisively chosen the English camp over its sovereign, King Louis XIII. The siege began for good on September 12.

Louis was now fully recovered. By the end of the September, he and his minister were again on their way to the camp at La Rochelle. The cardinal made a stop at Richelieu, the ancestral home where he had not set foot in six years. There, he met with the Prince de Condé and asked him to tackle the Duc de Rohan. Condé, always a fierce enemy of the Protestants, gladly obliged. A brutal scorched-earth campaign began around the southern mountains of the Cévennes, the area from which Rohan launched small but persistent military attacks against royalist towns in the south. When Louis XIII and Richelieu arrived at La Rochelle, respectively by October 12 and November 6, they joined Gaston, whom they had sent to La Rochelle just in time for the open declaration of hostilities.

The reasons for Gaston's presence at the siege went beyond the need for yet another chief. Mademoiselle de Montpensier had died less than a year after their marriage, and a few days after giving birth to a baby girl.[8] Ever since, the heir to the French throne gambled, slept with prostitutes, and hosted rowdy banquets with a gang of free thinkers he called his "Council of Good-for-Nothings." His family hoped that by sending him to the army and giving him responsibilities he would reform his ways. And, indeed, Gaston got his act together. First, he helped in taking supplies to Toiras and in evacuating the women and some wounded. A big breakthrough came on October 7. Using boats that the prince had ordered from the southern Atlantic regions, two daring captains named Beaulieu-Persac and Razilly forced their way through

Buckingham's blockade at Saint-Martin and delivered a large quantity of food, medicine, and equipment.[9] In their joy, the French stuck capons and hams on pikes and paraded them above the walls of the citadel, in full view of the English army whose shortage of food was becoming a problem, too. Unfortunately for Gaston, the presence of Louis and Richelieu at the camp of La Rochelle also marked the end of his redeeming exploits. The king, ever jealous of his own prerogatives, could not let his brother take too much credit in the operations, and Richelieu was not the kind to cede control either. Gaston eventually left the camp, feeling useless and resentful.

Louis reviewed his army and personally selected the best soldiers to conduct a commando attack on Buckingham. He also gathered tactical information about the terrain, the coast, the winds, and the tides. Meanwhile, Richelieu traveled to the island of Oléron, where the major operation would be launched, to review equipment. These maneuvers did not augur very well for Buckingham. Now that new provisions had reached the besieged citadel, any hope of a surrender faded. His own fresh supplies were rapidly dwindling, and no reinforcements were coming.

The first French contingent landed at Ré on October 30, a few miles away from Saint-Martin. Buckingham, at the other end of the island, ordered a general assault on the fort, showering cannonballs and sending his men crashing through the fortifications, hoping that their sheer number would overwhelm Toiras's worn-out forces. The ladders the assailants used to climb the walls of the fortress were too short, and that left them at the mercy of enemy fire. For two hours, all Buckingham could see were the bodies of his men piling up in the moats of the fort. The only option remaining after this bloody fight was to cut losses by sailing back to England. Grave tactical mistakes made the retreat another massacre. On November 12, Buckingham wrote to the city councillors of La Rochelle and assured them that King Charles would not abandon them. The task the duke contemplated was even harder since Richelieu's police had arrested Montague and found him carrying a bag full of documents that left little doubt about the role played by the Duchesse de Chevreuse on behalf of Buckingham and the intentions of the Dukes of Lorraine and Savoy. Only Rohan remained to continue the fight.[10]

How does one take hold of one of Europe's most well-protected cities, a coastal fortress so impregnable that it had sustained fierce sieges during the Wars of

Religion without incurring a dent? La Rochelle was renowned for having the
tallest and strongest fortifications in the kingdom, and, because the city lay in
the midst of a complicated mosaic of salt marshes and inlets traversed by narrow, heavily guarded causeways, nature offered additional protection. Navi-
gating the long bay that separated the city from the Atlantic was the easiest
way to reach it. But the walls of the city enclosed the port itself, leaving only
a well-guarded entry, overlooked by an outlying fort called Tadon. This fort
was built above the bay on the only elevation of the region and offered a vantage point from which to shoot at vessels approaching the city. Boats could re-
supply La Rochelle safely. In the words of a contemporary gazette, not even an
army of fifty thousand and a fleet of 250 vessels could take this mighty town by
force, numbers that far exceeded French resources.[11]

For Richelieu's quick wit, it had been obvious from the start that a full military blockade rather than a classical siege was the only way to bring La Rochelle
down. A most daring project came about. A Parisian architect, Clément Mé-
tezeau, proposed to close off La Rochelle's bay and separate it from the Atlantic
Ocean. This is how Alexander the Great had subdued the antique city of
Tyre.[12] Richelieu consulted with an engineer, Jean Thiriot, and the plan took
off. The cardinal and these two men conceived of twin structures, one on each
side of the bay, built with piles of rocks and reinforced with vertical beams
sunk into the sea floor. The bay was about a half mile wide, but its waters were
not very deep. Only at the center did depth prevent any construction, and this
was not necessarily an obstacle, since an opening into the bulwark was needed
in order to allow tidal movements.

Richelieu launched the project at the end of November 1627. The works
quickly got under way. From La Rochelle, one could see hordes of soldiers
tirelessly carrying rocks and throwing them into the ocean. The dam was built
to be out of reach of the city's cannons, a precaution that had the drawback of
exposing it to the ocean's rough waters. By the beginning of February, the two
branches of the bulwark jutted out in the harbor, tens of yards out into the sea,
and they kept getting longer as the thousands of soldiers continued with their
relentless task. Winter brought a fierce storm, the waves of which toppled the
stones that made up the bulwark. Once the storm had passed, Richelieu's engineers observed that the stones now formed a sloped embankment on which
the waves crashed and lost their violence. Evidently, building a dam wide at
the top was useless. Workers immediately put to use a new design. Not only

did it allow the bulwark to withstand the force of the ocean, but the structure now retained mounds of silt that further solidified it.

In January, a distinguished visitor inspected this grandiose work. It was Ambrose Spinola, the famed victor of Breda who had stopped at La Rochelle while on his way to Madrid, where Olivares had recalled him to strategize. Spinola's prediction on Richelieu's grand design? "Es tomada la ciudad." (The city is already taken.) Of Spinola, Richelieu commented in a letter, "One must confess that he is one of the better men in this world, and that his kindness is as good as his talent."[13]

On the mainland there was much effort as well. Construction continued to encircle the city with a three-mile-long line of defense, dotted at regular intervals by strong bastions and redoubts. The villages of the surrounding countryside became headquarters for the commanding officers. Louis took his lodging at Aytré, south of the besieged city, while Richelieu stayed nearby in a hamlet called Pont-de-Pierre. More and more troops arrived from all corners of the kingdom. Eventually, the total number of soldiers exceeded thirty thousand. The cardinal lodged these men in decent encampment, supplied them with clothes, and paid them regularly. At nine o'clock every evening, a cannon shot signaled the onset of curfew, requiring everyone to leave the shops and the taverns that had sprung up around the camps.[14] Hangings for breaches of discipline were common. Father Joseph, when not consulting with the cardinal on foreign affairs, joined the cohorts of Capuchin friars who patrolled the camps and ministered to the soldiers.

Since the very beginning of the siege, no one was allowed out of the city. The Duchesse de Rohan asked for special permission to leave and take with her a large group of women, but Richelieu denied a passport. In retrospect, having sent supplies to Buckingham appeared to have been a grave miscalculation to La Rochelle's councilmen. Food prices began to rise in the city. Everyone looked for any sign of a coming English rescue, but Charles's kingdom suffered from enduring political turmoil and budgetary crisis. As the weeks passed, a sinking feeling pervaded La Rochelle. A few envoys managed to sneak out. They went straight to England and begged Charles and Buckingham not to abandon them.

Surprisingly, Louis found this bustling activity of the siege a disappointment. Besides construction and logistical tasks, there was little to satisfy a king who liked some fighting action. He missed his royal domains of the Île-de-France where he spent restless days on horseback tracking a stag, smoking out foxes and badgers, or sending out his hawks. Making matters worse, it had rained continually since the beginning of the siege. The young nobles of the king's close entourage, including the new favorite, Claude de Rouvroy de Saint-Simon, who had replaced Barradas, voiced their impatience. Was there really such a pressing need for the king's presence when the cardinal took such good care of everything? This was Carnival season. The court should have been in Paris planning for masked balls and romantic rendezvous, not cavorting in a mud pit.

Richelieu naturally needed Louis by his side to motivate the troops and back up his role as an organizer and a disciplinarian. If Louis left for Paris, an exodus of officers would follow, morale and order in the troops would suffer greatly, and the success of the siege would be put at risk. Also, with Louis far away, keeping a watch over potential loss of favor would be much harder. Perhaps this was the very reason why the king's entourage wanted so much to leave for Paris. Richelieu asked the king to stay. The Venetian ambassador reported some "brisk and resentful" words between the two.[15] On February 10, 1628, Louis left the camp at La Rochelle, supposedly to inspect his other army stationed in Champagne. He arrived in Paris two weeks later and immediately went hunting at Versailles. Shortly after his departure, and making Richelieu the lieutenant general of the army, he had written an affectionate letter to his minister, assuring him of his complete trust and that he was grateful for all his efforts. Richelieu wrote back to say that "his heart was pierced altogether" by the king's kindness. Nevertheless, he was still quite wounded. In a letter to his good friend Cardinal Louis de La Valette, a son of d'Épernon, the cardinal wrote, "I used to be a zero, which in mathematics means something when real numbers follow; now that the king is gone and that I am the leader, the same zero that I remain means nothing."[16] He even told the papal nuncio that if God gave him the satisfaction of taking La Rochelle, he would retire soon after.

Count-Duke Olivares and Duke Charles Emmanuel of Savoy must have heard of all this agitation at the siege of La Rochelle. When a controversial matter of succession arose in the Duchy of Mantua, in Italy, they did not fail to take advantage of the situation when all of France's resources were committed on the Atlantic coast. The Duke of Mantua, Vincent II, had died on

December 26, 1627, without leaving a direct male heir. He had, however, taken precautions by designating as his successor Charles de Nevers. This French duke—who had raised trouble during the regency of Marie de' Medici, right after Condé's arrest—was actually a Gonzague: he belonged to Mantua's reigning dynasty and was a legitimate candidate for the succession. Nevertheless, his loyalties remained in France. Having already left for Mantua when news came of his relative's passing, the Duc de Nevers arrived to take up his new possessions in a climate of deep political tension. The Duchy of Mantua, which lay to the west of northern Italy, also included the territory of the Monferrato, a source of dispute since the years of Richelieu's first ministry. Its capital city, Casale, was on the strategic road that leads from Genoa to Milan. Olivares faced great political difficulties at home after failing to enact his reforms and to bring the conflict with the Dutch to an end, even after the success at Breda. A coup against French interests in Italy not only was essential, but could shore up his standing as well. On December 25, 1627, while Charles de Nevers was on his way to Italy, Olivares and Savoy struck a deal. Should Nevers persist in his desire to stay in Italy, they would drive him out by force.

Incredibly, Gaston complicated the story. In the months following the death of his wife, while he assiduously patronized those dubious Parisian hangouts "where one very much fears the police chief," Gaston did not neglect the salons of the aristocracy.[17] Perhaps at the Hôtel de Rambouillet, a woman caught his eye: Marie Louise de Gonzague, who was none other than the daughter of Charles de Nevers. After an intense courtship, Gaston figured he was destined to wed Marie. Her father, of course, viewed this as a positive development at a time when he needed help to secure his hold on Mantua. But given the burden of sustaining La Rochelle's siege, a prospect made notably longer by the king's absence, Richelieu could only express sympathy to the duke while skirting any promise of a military intervention in Italy. As far as Gaston's marriage project was concerned, both Louis and Richelieu would have none of it. The 1626 Conspiracy of the Dames had amply proven the highly sensitive nature of matrimonial alliances. The heir to the French throne was kindly asked not to think of getting married for the moment.

With the king out of sight, and with mounting problems in Italy, Richelieu realized that he had to speed up the siege. On February 19, he formally demanded that La Rochelle surrender and open its doors. The aldermen denied the request. A royal officer who had lived in La Rochelle remembered an opening where the canal to transport salt into the city passed under the walls. Not only was the passage poorly guarded, but it was sealed by a weak wooden gate. It seemed like the perfect place to penetrate the fortifications and allow troops to enter and take the nearest entrance to the city from the inside. Richelieu decided to take the city by force. On the night of March 12, a group of fifty men from the cardinal's personal guard, followed by a contingent of five hundred of his best soldiers, set out to blow up the wooden gate that blocked the canal. Richelieu, meanwhile, on horseback and wearing his finest armor, waited near another city gate with a cavalry of one thousand and a contingent of four thousand pike men. He and his men waited for hours, until dawn. Apparently, those who had to bring the explosives and the rest of the material to the first group had gotten lost in the countryside, and by the time they found their way, it was too late. A day later, Richelieu made an attempt at taking the fort at Tadon. The effort went nowhere, this time resulting in many casualties on the royal side. Eventually, the Rochelois learned of Richelieu's embarrassing snafu, and many took the mysterious failings as miraculous signs of God's protection. One Joseph Guillaudeau wrote in his diary: "God, with his might, providence, and clemency, God who never fails to keep watch, cast over [the attackers] such a dizzying spell, weakness, and powerlessness in their limbs, that they could barely move and go forward; they could not even hold their weapons."[18]

Another miracle—the kind more readily ascertained—came to raise morale inside La Rochelle. On March 21, a ship from England passed between the two bulwarks and managed to reach the port unscathed after a hot pursuit. It carried the deputy Jean David, barrels of wheat, and some heartening news from London. The English Parliament was in session, and its members, having been moved by the thought of their brethren in religion trapped in La Rochelle, would most likely vote for subsidies. Buckingham prepared for a rescue operation and planned on coming to supply the city in April. Unfortunately for the Rochelois, the chase in the harbor had frightened David so much that he had thrown the official letters that announced the help overboard. These letters ended up in the hands of the cardinal, who also learned of the forthcoming supply operation.

Richelieu sent the English letters to the king in Paris. The upcoming menace convinced Louis that he had to return to the siege. He responded to his minister with a gracious note, saying that he returned as much to satisfy the wishes of his minister as because of the sheer menace of the English. He added, "Please believe that I love you, and that I will always love you as I promised I would."[19] But the nuncio reported in his own diary that three days after writing his conciliatory letter, Louis complained about the actions of his minister and said that he only kept him out of deference to his mother.[20] Marie de' Medici, as it turns out, was now less keen to support the minister. She felt that he did not consult properly when he made his decisions. The reports that Richelieu heard from Paris were so serious that he wrote to the queen to claim his allegiance: "You told M. that I used you like a child's bauble: please do consider how that stabbing blow is mortal to a person like me, who has never thought of anything but your grandeur and glory."[21]

In late March of 1628, as Louis was returning to prepare for the arrival of an English fleet, the Mantua affair became a full-blown international crisis. By another quirk of history, the Mantuan duchy was a fief of the Habsburg empire, and Ferdinand II had the prerogative to legitimize Charles de Nevers with the new title. Naturally, the emperor declared on March 20 that until Nevers's claim to the Duchy of Mantua was adjudicated, he could not take hold of his possessions. When Charles de Nevers refused to obey, the Duke of Savoy invaded the Monferrato in the areas that bordered his own estates, while Olivares ordered the Spanish governor in Milan to lay siege to Casale. It was quite a gamble—the armies were already stretched thin—but Olivares figured that opportunities such as that rarely came along.

The king was on his way, but Cardinal Richelieu counted on his own resources. He still viewed his success as depending on the bulwark. One crucial problem that needed a resolution, though, was how to prevent boats from passing in the middle canal. Already some special ships loaded with stones lay sunk in the middle of the bay. But as the exploit on March 21 had demonstrated, this blockage did not deter smaller ships. On April 8, Richelieu boarded his carriage and went to see Maréchal de Bassompierre at his quarters in Laleu. Gale-force winds blew and sheets of rain fell, but the meeting was crucial. After lunch, the cardinal heard the marshal talk about an officer named Bernard du Plessis-Besançon. This man had an idea of how to close off the bay of La Rochelle, even to the mightiest of fleets, but it would take at least two months to put his plan to work. Cardinal Richelieu had heard of many fanciful solutions already. The sorry remnants of a floating fort built by the Italian engineer Pompeo Targone still lay toppled in the middle of the bay after the passage of a storm. The cardinal ordered Bassompierre to follow up on the plan.

On May 11, an English fleet led by Buckingham's brother-in-law the Earl of Denbigh showed up and failed to rescue La Rochelle. Then, a few weeks later, the sentinels of La Rochelle noticed unusual activity on the coast of the bay, near one of the bulwarks. Nine strange structures lay on the ground. From afar, they looked like an elaborate assembly of wooden beams, with metal parts jutting out, and measuring several yards. In the following days, anyone in La Rochelle with a looking glass kept it pointed at the bulwarks. Whatever it was, the spectacle drew large crowds of observers from the royal army. Workers first sunk long thick poles into the sea floor, each pointing outward and sustained by rafters. These poles ran in two staggered rows parallel to the bulwark and right before the opening of the canal. On the sixteenth, King Louis, Cardinal Richelieu, and other high-ranking officers gathered on the sides of the bay to watch the workers fit the nine "machines," as they were called, on top of the poles, which made them look like candelabras emerging from the sea.[22] Finally, the soldiers tightly bound these machines with sets of wooden beams. When the entire installation was completed, a frightening sight greeted any ship approaching the bulwark at La Rochelle: fierce spikes emerging at an angle from the sea and pointing menacingly to any would-be intruder.[23]

Morale inside La Rochelle fell to a new low. The unsuccessful mission of Lord Denbigh had left the city to its own devices. With fear and hunger, tensions began to mount between the citizens themselves. A few advocated for peace with Louis XIII, arguing that further resistance was useless and would only get the city less favorable terms of surrender. At opposite ends were the radicals, both religious and political. These included the preachers, the Duchesse de Rohan, and Jean Guiton, the newly elected mayor.[24] Guiton was a stern and uncompromising character, coming from a generations-old family of La Rochelle leaders. Lore has it that when the citizens pushed him to take the mayor's office, he stuck his dagger in the city council's table and declared: "I shall be mayor if you really want me to, but behold this knife: I swear I will stick it in the heart of the first one who talks of surrendering, and I ask to be stabbed likewise if I should ever propose to capitulate."

With phrases like that, one can perceive how stark Guiton's views on the conflict between the Huguenots and the French monarchy were. To him and to his followers, surrender put the city at risk of a second Saint-Barthélemy, the worse massacre of the sixteenth-century Wars of Religion. Richelieu maintained regular contacts with some city elders. Unfortunately, no resolution could be reached because Richelieu demanded an unconditional surrender, while those in power insisted on having the King of England as a mediator. In England, Charles and Buckingham set up yet another rescue. A nasty dispute with Parliament about what defined sovereign power paralyzed the political culture. Nevertheless, religious kinship and political loyalty prevailed, and Parliament voted for new subsidies to liberate La Rochelle after Denbigh's failed attempt. This time, Buckingham would come in person with a fleet so mighty that nothing would stop it.

La Rochelle's terrible summer of 1628 began. Food reserves inside the city would last for two months at most, and so the municipal authorities instituted rationing. Prices shot up even higher than they had before. Horses had to be butchered, even those belonging to the Duchesse de Rohan. Yet meat could only make up for part of one's normal diet. As a consequence, scurvy began its ravages among the neediest, leaving them with rotting gums and black, swollen limbs.

In the royal camp, an altogether different mood prevailed, and it was more than just a sense that this unlikely siege could succeed. The entire operation now took place in a crusading atmosphere. All around France, masses were sung to speed up the demise of the Protestant citadel. The French clergy, albeit after many prevarications, voted to give the Crown three million pounds to help with the war. Religious fervor absorbed Louis. On Whit Sunday, he touched several sick people. In what seemed like a miracle, a twelve-year-old mute girl began to speak. That same week, the king celebrated a jubilee in a church, praying for hours while he beat his chest, raised his hands, and bowed repeatedly before the altar. He was offering his heart to God, explained an official gazette.[25] A month later, in July, a prominent noble converted to Catholicism. To many in the royal army and across the kingdom, these were the many signs that God's wrath would necessarily descend upon La Rochelle.

And God struck, or, at least, this is what many surmised when in early September, shocking news reached France: the Duke of Buckingham had died on August 23, stabbed to death in Portsmouth by a man named John Felton. This soldier was a veteran of the botched campaign at Ré, and the perceived tyranny of Buckingham over King Charles had led him to his desperate act.[26] The news of Buckingham's assassination made less difference to the staunchest holdouts in La Rochelle. Tension rose further between the extremists and those who wanted to surrender. One man who ventured a few words of criticism went to jail. Suspected traitors were hanged. The day when the messenger came to announce Buckingham's death, Guiton harangued the citizens at church and exhorted them to be patient. A brawl erupted at the end of his speech. The same day, those who believed that the city could still survive took heart when a strange phenomenon lit up in the sky above the city and showed what they thought were visions of an army of fire attacking the bulwark.[27]

The population resorted to feeding on anything it could find. Dogs, cats, even rats—all comestible animals disappeared. The royal army systematically uprooted crops outside the walls.[28] The men and women still went out to collect weeds, or any living creature they could find in the moats, but gunshots chased them back inside. People then ate leather, from shoes, belts, or harnesses, and exchanged recipes to make this miserable substance edible. One Rochelois who lived through the siege, Pierre Mervault, reports in his journal that people would find any type of leather, "cut it in small pieces, just like beef tripe, and would cook it fricassee-style in a pan with a bit of tallow and water, while some made jams out of it with a bit of sugar."[29] Hunger led people to desperate acts. The royal army was under strict orders not to let anyone out. Soldiers killed a woman who ignored the warning to stay away, right in front of her two children, and after that they slaughtered the children, too. This cruelty appeared so horrific that the cardinal ordered that sticks should be used to push back the starving Rocheloises.[30] Men suffered a harsher treatment. The soldiers systematically hanged those who reached the lines. If they were in a group, these wretched drew lots to designate one victim, and the rest went back into La Rochelle. In the end, some people decided that they would rather risk dying by execution than suffer a long, drawn-out martyrdom, and they continued to show up at the lines.[31] Cemeteries overflowed in the city. Because gravediggers were either dead or too weak to do their job, people simply dragged themselves there or died in their houses. In September of 1628, up to three hundred people died every day from starvation inside the walls of La Rochelle.

The Rochelois did not have to be such zealots and die in throngs. But those who desperately wanted to continue their fight to the bitter end not only feared the king, who demanded unconditional surrender with no strings attached and would only then consider if the city was "worthy of his mercy," but also believed in their freedoms and were willing to take a stand. They kept their faith and lay in wait for any sign that would certify their divine intuition. Louis XIII and his minister could have taken the city as soon as its defenders became too weakened by their starvation. Nonetheless, Richelieu believed, as he wrote in his memoirs, that letting the siege run its course affirmed royal power. This might seem rather counterintuitive. What better stand on his power could Louis have taken than by ordering the attack on the city with force, at a time when the guard could not offer a meaningful resistance? But as the cardinal put it, "it is unfortunate when one has to take with authority what reason should concede."[32] Cardinal Richelieu did not have the hypocrisy to hope that La Rochelle would actually recognize Louis XIII's sovereign authority as good. He wanted to force La Rochelle to reach a consensus on the king's power. Granted, religion justified La Rochelle's suffering for Richelieu, too. In his view, letting the Rochelois decide on their fate, even at the cost of thousands of lives, allowed divine will's accomplishment: "The vengeful wrath of God gave them a new extraordinary [force] by means of the Devil, so that their woes would be prolonged, and that their punishment would be more proportionate to their excessive crimes."[33]

Louis often went to see the bulwark, sometimes in the middle of night. He wandered alone on the mighty structure, breathing the salty air of the Atlantic before the terrifying machines, the waves crashing at his feet. One of those gazetteers whom his minister paid for propaganda wrote that the bulwark had something that exceeded human genius, the proof of a supernatural force at work that not only announced the coming victory at La Rochelle but justified it as well: "Was there a more visible miracle, than because those who built the bulwark did not design it properly, it was the sea itself that rearranged the shape of it, giving it a slope, and achieving in one instant what months of human work could not have done?"[34]

At daybreak on October 3, 1628, cannon shots were heard, sending tremors throughout La Rochelle's harbor, echoing as far as the coast of Ré. A mighty English fleet had come to save the bastion of French Protestantism. The attack took place in a fearsome war theater. The Earl of Lindsey, who had replaced Buckingham as commander of the navy, laid out his 120 vessels in a crescent formation before the harbor. Six thousand men were on board. Facing them stood an armada of smaller French boats that was still no match for them. Cardinal Richelieu stood on his flagship, directly behind the mighty defense, ready to forbid access to the enemy city in the background. The very morning of the attack, he still pressed his engineer to install more of his "machines": "His Majesty would get angry if it did not happen, because they are vital." La Rochelle was exhausted yet still defiant, all bells ringing and standards flying. Thousands of armed French soldiers crowded the coastline as far as the eye could see. Louis himself manned one of the batteries that added further protection to the blockade. Hordes of civilians, either volunteers who wanted to help or just onlookers, had converged on La Rochelle as soon as they heard of the arrival of the English. An unbelievable traffic jam of fancy coaches, ox-drawn carts, and horses clogged the roads leading to this long-awaited showdown.

When action began in the morning, a good east-southeasterly wind favored the English. The ships of Charles's fleet deployed their sails, and one after the other, they approached the harbor. Every time a boat reached its position, all hell broke loose. Rounds of cannon fire targeted the fleet of French boats, the bulwark, and the batteries on the coast. The French responded with equally furious fire. This periodic hail of cannonballs lasted for about two hours. A military officer present on the scene recalled that, since the English had lighted fire ships to cover their moves, a cloud of black smoke hung over the entire scene, so thickly at times that it only let out the thunder and lightning strikes of cannon fire. But in all this terrifying pandemonium, there was no breach. The English commanders kept their warships at a safe distance from the coast. Their ships' drafts were too high, or they did not want to take too many risks. Most of the shots were wasted, and when the tide began to recede, the fleet sailed back toward Ré.[35] The following day, the same roaring and useless exchanges took place. Eventually, the sea became very rough, putting an end to the fighting. The English lost one boat, and casualties on both sides were minimal.

During this battle, Lindsey took time to study the French defenses. Landing seemed out of the question. A message of encouragement went to La Rochelle, but at the same time, on the fourteenth, an envoy left to meet with Cardinal Richelieu. This envoy was Lord Montague, who had been freed from the Bastille a few months earlier and served Charles I again. Richelieu welcomed his former prisoner with civility. Both men discussed the terms of a surrender. Montague proposed that Charles act as a mediator and a guarantor of the peace; Richelieu maintained that foreign powers had nothing to do in this contention between the French sovereign and the Rochelois. A few days later the two men met again and went out for a tour of the bulwark. Montague left the cardinal, took one boat, and set sail to England to consult with his king.

The Rochelois deputies who represented their city at the English court of Charles had traveled back to La Rochelle. Knowing that their starving city could not wait any longer, they asked Cardinal Richelieu for a pardon, which the cardinal granted with a promise to leave the Protestants their liberty of conscience, provided that those in the city would agree to the condition, too. At the same time, the aldermen of La Rochelle were coming to their own conclusions, and they also asked for an audience with the cardinal.

On October 28, two of the Rochelois deputies from the English fleet were at Cardinal Richelieu's house: Pastor Philippe Vincent and a financier named Jean Gobert. The cardinal heard that six delegates from La Rochelle were on their way. He asked the two men to move to another room, and then he met with the city's deputies. They asked to keep La Rochelle's municipal privileges and fortifications, to obtain pardons for the Duchesse de Rohan and Soubise, and finally, to get the English king to act as a mediator. Richelieu told the deputies that they were not in a position to negotiate, but only to ask for the king's mercy, which had already been shown to the other delegates. He added that if they did not believe his claim that the deputies from England had settled, he could prove it on the spot by fetching them in the other room. The cardinal asked that everyone remain silent.[36] He went to other room and told Vincent and Gobert that they would meet with their fellow citizens, but likewise, it was on the condition that they would not utter one single word during the encounter. Cardinal Richelieu then opened the doors. When the men from La Rochelle saw each other in silence, with joy, but also with months of pain and suffering etched on their faces and bodies, they all broke down in a torrent of tears.

La Rochelle surrendered without conditions the same day. Louis XIII followed Cardinal Richelieu's recommendations. Most important, the Edict of Nantes, which granted the French Protestants their liberty of conscience, was upheld. But La Rochelle lost all of its municipal privileges and franchises, the king ordered the fortifications razed, and he refused to grant a remission to the Rohan family, of which one prominent member was still at war with Condé in the south. Two days later, a delegation of eight prominent citizens arrived from the city and formally asked for grace, kneeling before Louis XIII. As a sign of their humble remorse, they should have walked to Louis's camp at Aytré. Instead, given their weakness, Maréchal de Bassompierre took them to meet with the king in a carriage, leaving them to walk on foot just the last one hundred yards. Louis granted their request. Negotiations for peace began with England soon after.

On All Saints' Day, Cardinal Richelieu celebrated mass in La Rochelle. He entered the city first, and as with all of his contemporaries, the sight of La Rochelle after the year-long siege left him dumbfounded.[37] Out of a population of twenty-eight thousand, a staggering twelve thousand had starved to death during the siege. Louis XIII held a victorious parade through the city, from the main gate to the Catholic church, where a Te Deum was sung in the king's presence. This celebration was simple, with none of the pageantry that usually marked these occasions. Companies of musketeers marched first, followed by the generals. Cardinal Richelieu came right after. Only Louis rode on horseback. Emaciated survivors lined the streets, chanting with sepulchral voices, "Long live the king who showed us mercy!"

CHAPTER 6

Great Storm (1629–1630)

Non, non, ce n'est point aux humains,	No! No! The privilege of writing
A venir mettre ici les mains,	And singing your praise
Ni à vous chanter vos louanges;	Does not belong to humans.
Grand Cardinal vos faits guerriers	Great Cardinal, your warring feats,
De la bouche et des mains des Anges	Demand chants and laurels,
Veulent des chants et des lauriers.	From the mouths and the hands of
	Angels.[1]

FRANCE, IT SEEMS, COULD NOT FIND words strong enough to celebrate Richelieu's victory at La Rochelle. From all corners of the kingdom, praise rose in honor of the "New Alexander," who slowly made his way back to Paris after a stop at his family estate in the Poitou. The pope wrote to congratulate him. Meanwhile, on December 15, the king entered his capital city and marched from Notre-Dame Cathedral to the Louvre through the cheers of an ecstatic crowd.

Richelieu contemplated the tasks that awaited him. He could settle the Crown's feud with the Protestant party by moving troops in the Languedoc, where Condé had so far been unable the vanquish the last Protestant holdout, the Duc de Rohan. Otherwise, he could take the army to Italy, where the Duc de Nevers urgently called for French help. There were many reasons to take the latter option. Under attack from Spanish troops, the city of Casale in the Monferrato could not resist for much longer, and should the territories of the duke fall, the rest of northern Italy's independent powers—namely, the Duchy of Savoy and the Republic of Venice—could end up decisively within the Spanish sphere of influence and further tighten the Habsburg grip around France. Acting in Italy would disturb the Spanish offensive against the Dutch, who were allies of the French. Also favoring action in Italy: the emperor was showing no interest in lending resources to help his Spanish cousin's fight. In 1626, his general Wallenstein had defeated the Danish king Christian IV, and for a while he had extended his control over the entire northern seaboard, thereby cutting the lucrative merchant routes that ensured the wealth of the Dutch Republic. But a new player had appeared with much panache: Sweden's king and Lutheran stalwart, Gustavus Adolphus, a man firmly intent on establishing dominance around the Baltic Sea at the expense of the Habsburgs. That fact had not been lost on Richelieu, who had initiated contacts with Gustavus Adolphus during the siege at La Rochelle.

Perturbing Richelieu's projects, however, were his souring relations with Marie de' Medici. The cardinal still held the offices of the queen's chancellor and superintendent, and his relatives and friends occupied almost all of the key posts in her household. For example, his favorite niece, Madame de Combalet, had been in charge of the queen's finery for many years. Now that Richelieu led unchallenged in the king's council, Marie de' Medici felt entitled to consider him as her agent, but to her great dismay the man had a mind of his own. The queen opposed the rescue of the Duc de Nevers in Mantua. For one thing, Nevers had taken over Condé's role as chief rebel during the regency, in 1616. Furthermore, he had gravely offended the queen mother by comparing unfavorably the Medici dynasty to his own, the Gonzague.[2] In another complication, Gaston still entertained the dream of marrying Marie de Gonzague, which the queen understood as a ploy imagined by Nevers.

These seemingly superficial motivations went along with deeper political ones.[3] Since the regency, the queen mother had showed a balanced political judgment, but lately she was paying more attention to the voices of militant Catholics. This, as the rest of the story will show, was a change of crucial consequences. There was Pierre de Bérulle, newly elevated to the dignity of cardinal, who had a mystical view of politics. Minister of Justice Michel de Marillac also stood out as a leader of the Devouts. Marillac was a man with enough outstanding capacities to excuse a certain dryness of character and marked authoritarian disposition. For some time he had been trying to enact a broad program of legal, fiscal, and commercial reforms to help France thwart endemic poverty—some of these reforms originated from the assembly of notables held in 1626–1627. Marillac's loyalty to the sacred office of the king sprung from a deeply held Catholic credence, and this belief made him consider the struggle against the Habsburgs and the cooperation with Protestant potentates as inherently evil.[4]

On December 26, the king, his principal minister, Marie de' Medici, the minister Marillac, and other members of the government gathered at the Palais du Luxembourg for a crucial meeting on what course to take after La Rochelle. Marie voiced her concerns about such a risky enterprise. Richelieu explained that Olivares had made a crucial mistake by venturing into Italy. Reports from Casale suggested that the besieging Spanish army was demoralized. For sure, one had to consider the exhaustion of Louis's troops, too, and the increasing unrest of a French population hard-pressed by the taxman. In conclusion, he simply remarked that the French king's glory was at stake when a prominent member of his nobility suffered abroad. Marie de' Medici lashed out against Richelieu for contradicting her in full view of the council. She called him ungrateful. This kind of excess made the shy Louis recoil, and his mother realized that this round of the game belonged to her former protégé. The subject of Gaston came up. Marie de' Medici got something to relieve her wounded pride when all agreed to have Gaston lead the army across the Alps, on the condition that he would uphold his promise not to marry without his family's consent.[5]

A few days after the meeting at the Luxembourg, the king went out hunting at Saint-Germain and failed to bring down a beautiful stag, which Gaston ended up killing the following day. That mere incident reawoke the powerful jealousy of the older sibling. Louis retreated to Versailles, and, after two sleepless nights spent mulling dark thoughts, he decided to pay a visit to Richelieu, who stayed at a villa in Chaillot. Louis opened up to the cardinal as if he were his own confessor and told him how much he feared for his own reputation if Gaston pulled off a victory on behalf of the Duc de Nevers. Richelieu was keenly aware of the depth of the king's inner conflicts: "Jealousy is a malady that only time can cure much better than remedies, which can even worsen the condition if they are not applied with great care."[6] His answer was straightforward: "Your Majesty has no other choice but to go by himself."

A few days passed. On the evening of January 13, after hearing that Louis's decision to lead his army in Italy stood, Cardinal Richelieu asked to see the king and Marie de' Medici in a private audience. The only other person he wanted present was the king's own confessor, Father Suffren. Richelieu set the record straight on many counts. After exposing again the strategic options that lay before the king if he wanted to affirm France's standing in Europe, he scolded Louis for being suspicious, jealous, quick to take offense, and lacking in dedication and steadiness. He reminded him how Luynes had remarked that he took much more interest in meting out punishment than rewarding good service. The queen mother was next. How could she expect the cardinal to work efficiently if her thin-skinned and unpredictable nature caused him endless worries? "Sometimes I am well with the queen, sometimes not; sometimes the king is delighted with my service, sometimes he shows disgust," Richelieu cried out to both. In conclusion, he declared that he could hardly serve the French monarchy in the midst of such uncertainty. Perhaps he could put up with the "extraordinary hatred" that Gaston showed ever since d'Ornano and Chalais had been arrested, he said, but only with the king and his mother's support. Otherwise, he would rather resign than keep eroding his already worn-out body for ungrateful masters. Richelieu's memoirs describe the king's reaction to this scolding as patient and benevolent, and perhaps it was. It all depended on whom they were hearing, the priest, or the servant.

Two months after this confrontation, and four months after leaving the shores of the Atlantic, Louis XIII and Cardinal Richelieu were in the middle of the Alps, standing at the border with Savoy and ready to descend toward the plain of the Po River. Count-Duke Olivares had not seen it coming. Spanish kings almost never left Madrid, let alone ventured into such treacherous conditions as the harsh Alpine winter.[7] Terrible storms had battered the French army. On steep icy roads, and under the constant threat of avalanches, the troops had to pull the cannons with ropes or carry baskets of ammunition and cannonballs. Frostbite tormented the soldiers when deadly hypothermia did not kill them. The local populations often used sleighs to descend the most treacherous slopes. Amid all the sights of this alpine campaign, the image of Louis XIII and Cardinal Richelieu going along for a hair-rising ride, all bundled up and sporting beaver hats, was not the least curious.

Before Louis and Richelieu, the deep and snow-covered valley of the Dora Riparia River offered a gateway to reach the Monferrato and Casale. But that valley crossed Savoy, and so the French army needed permission from Duke Charles Emmanuel to take it. For a few days now, Cardinal Richelieu had been negotiating with the son of the duke, Victor Amadeus, who happened to be Louis's brother-in-law. But even though Savoy had supported the French in their earlier claims on the Valtellina, Charles Emmanuel was now allied with the Spanish with the hopes of obtaining parts of the Monferrato for himself. Just a few miles down from where the French army stood was the city of Susa and its well-armed citadel, perched on a rocky peak. To hold on to to his valley even more tightly, the duke had frantically built three barricades at a particularly narrow point, the Susa Pass. On March 5, yet another Savoy emissary came to see Richelieu in the village of Chiomonte and offered nothing more than a delaying tactic. Richelieu sent a message to Louis, who was stationed in another village, about ten miles behind, that the army would attack early the next day. Louis left his camp right away, at ten o'clock at night. After a four-hour walk spent knee-deep in snow and in total darkness, the king and a few trusted men arrived at the cardinal's camp, just in time to participate in a meeting of the principal army chiefs.

It was March 6, 1629. In the early hours, three army corps took their positions at the forefront of the French camp: one in the middle of the valley, the other two high up on each side. The Sault regiment of hardy mountaineers also left camp. Guided by local shepherds, they trekked up the mountain and showed up from the rear of the barricades. At eight o'clock, Maréchal de Bassompierre reported to the king that everyone waited for his command: "Sire, the spectators have gathered, the violins are in, and the masks stand ready. The ballet can begin whenever it pleases Your Majesty!"[8]

The three corps of the avant-garde quickly reached the pass and the twelve-foot barricades. At the same time, the regiment of Sault erupted from the mountains in the back. Panic took over in the enemy camp, throwing the Savoy soldiers into disarray, and allowing a hefty contingent of French nobility to force the passage through the barricades. King Louis and Richelieu followed at a good gallop. As was often the case with the French, their attack was more courageous than disciplined. In the rumble of the cavalcade, of gunfire, and warring shouts, a noise made all the more deafening by its echo in the encased valley, the French troops reached Susa in just half an hour, barely allowing Charles Emmanuel and his son a narrow escape.

On March 11, Duke Charles Emmanuel once again shifted his allegiance

toward the French king by signing the Treaty of Susa. Against some landholdings in the Monferrato and a yearly stipend from the Duc de Nevers,
Charles Emmanuel agreed to leave the citadel of Susa in the hands of the
French king and to supply his armies should they cross his territories. This left
the Spanish in a very vulnerable position, and the commander had no other
choice but to let go of Casale and retreat back to Milan. Ten days after the attack at the Susa Pass, carts carrying bags of wheat and barrels of wine began
entering Casale. All this significantly boosted the Duc de Nevers's claim on the
Mantuan succession.[9] The "New Alexander" Richelieu was now hailed as the
"New Hannibal," after the legendary Carthaginian military commander who
had taken the same mountain route to travel from Spain to Italy in the third
century B.C. From a strategic point of view, the victory at the Susa Pass was
crucial, for it allowed the French easy access to northern Italy, preventing the
Spanish from making aggressive moves and sending troops to northern Europe.
Cardinal Richelieu even had the option to take the fight against the Spanish
directly to Milan and inflict further damage to Olivares's reputation.

Days later, a courier arrived at the court with startling news. Gaston, who
fumed after being unceremoniously removed as commander of the army, still
wanted to marry Marie de Gonzague against his family's wishes. This thought
had frightened Marie de' Medici so much that she had locked up the princess
in the château at Vincennes, leaving Gaston to make threats of leaving the
kingdom to seek refuge abroad. Even though Richelieu had kept writing
Marie de' Medici during the campaign, to inform her of the unfolding events,
she blamed him for not supporting her action against the princess, while Gaston somehow found ways to blame the cardinal for the entire situation. It
seemed that both mother and son could end up rallying in their hatred of the
cardinal while the king was in foreign lands.[10]

Louis XIII and Cardinal Richelieu set their sights on bringing the army into
Languedoc and stomping out the last embers of Huguenot political dissent.
Louis left the camp at Susa on April 28, 1629. Two weeks later, he besieged the
city of Privas, which lies seventy-two miles south of Lyon. The king also sent
small detachments to tackle all the surrounding minor towns, thus preventing
the kind of rescue that had made Montauban such a tenacious foe. Cardinal
Richelieu, who had stayed behind to lay out the organization of a permanent
French force in Susa, arrived in the middle of the siege. A lasting peace with

the English king Charles I was announced. It signified to the Protestants that their chances of getting help from abroad were nonexistent.

Richelieu must have hoped that the news would please Marie de' Medici, too, given that King Charles was her son-in-law. The news from the Palais du Luxembourg was not good, however. The queen publicly voiced her animosity against the minister, provoking a stream of rumors about the cardinal's imminent downfall. The cardinal wrote to the queen on May 25. In humble words, he told her that she undermined the strength of the government with her public displays, and that he would resign if asked to: "All I care to know is what you want me to do."[11] Whether the queen would even want to engage with her former protégé remained impossible to predict. Characteristically, Richelieu had also written with a note of frankness and independence that could easily pass as pretension and further irritate the queen.

On May 27, a catastrophe ended the siege at Privas. Privas offered to surrender, and for reasons that remain difficult to elucidate, an explosion occurred while the soldiers of the royal army occupied the town. It triggered a two-night orgy of looting and killing.[12] The king and the cardinal then laid siege to Alais, about fifty miles to the southwest. In an effort to save Alais, Rohan kidnapped the governor of the town, whom he viewed as too soft. Richelieu in person defended the city from the duke's rescue. He spent the night of June 15 on horseback, surrounded by a cohort of two hundred men, and handily prevented Rohan from reaching his goal. Alais surrendered on the seventeenth. The Duc de Rohan was the only leader left in the Huguenot resistance after the disaster at Privas and the surrender at Alais dampened the little will to resist left in the French Protestant communities. Even though he had accepted subsidies from Olivares to keep on fighting, the duke had to face a settlement with the Crown.[13] Richelieu was also eager to come to an agreement and put an end to the conflict. From Italy came reports that imperial troops were crossing Switzerland, on their way to Mantua. Then, of course, there was Gaston, who gave ominous signs of unrest, even though Marie de Gonzague had been freed from her prison at Vincennes.

After representatives of the Reformed Churches of France gathered to deliberate on a peace deal, Louis XIII signed the Grace of Alais, on June 28, 1629. This landmark text declared peace with the king's Protestant subjects and agreed to uphold their liberty of conscience and some of their rights. The

Grace of Alais was also remarkable given that a prelate whom Pope Gregory XV had once called "the rampart of Catholic religion and the scourge
of heretics" promulgated it. There were limits to the king and the cardinal's
tolerance, however. The Grace of Alais was only a promise neither to punish
the Protestants for their faith nor to force their conversions. The king ordered
that all fortifications in the cities that counted a majority Protestant population
be razed. The Duc de Rohan, who had fought on behalf of his religious brethren since 1621, went to live in Venice. Richelieu still hoped that one day the
French subjects of the king would unite in the same faith, so much so that
many initiatives designed to promote Catholicism were mandated in the regions with a predominantly Protestant population. Father Joseph, who had
followed Richelieu during the entire campaign, was a fanatical auxiliary in that
effort.[14]

Richelieu and the king continued on a journey toward Montpellier and
Montauban, where the rebellion still pulsed, albeit weakly. Louis, who longed
for his northern hunting grounds, chose to go back to Paris at this point, but
it was not without a stern reminder from Richelieu that instead he should be
carrying his duties to the end and not abandon his minister. Much as in La
Rochelle, Louis first felt angry and resentful, then he hurried to assure the cardinal of his deep gratitude and affection as soon as he left: "I will love you until
death!" In Protestant Nîmes, Richelieu ditched his usual entourage of body-
guards and circulated in the streets all by himself, mingling casually with the
citizens who suddenly realized that he was not a monster, at least in appearance. The same charm operation took place in Montauban. The citizens offered
Richelieu a grand entry into the city, but the cardinal, ever mindful of looking
subservient to the king's power, declined the offer. Instead he entered the city
by foot, on August 21, followed by his guards in their red tabards, taking time
to entertain the city's officers with fine conversation. The hardy Montalbanais
wondered how this man, so simple and yet so elegant in his manners, could be
the ruthless engineer of La Rochelle.

"Vive le Roi! Vive le Grand Cardinal!" was their response.

And so it was under cheers and celebrations that Richelieu began the long
journey that would lead him back to the court in Paris. Unfortunately, he fell
ill on his return. Marie de' Medici sent her well wishes, but who could predict
what kind of treatment the irascible Italian matron would give him upon his

return? In a last complication, Gaston had finally heeded the most irresponsible advice of his favorites and left the Kingdom of France to stay at the court of Lorraine. The heir to the French throne taking his family feud into Habsburg territory—that would be enough to give Richelieu one of his mighty migraines.

On September 14, Cardinal Richelieu's carriage, escorted by an impressive cavalry of the most prominent nobles, pulled into the courtyard at the royal Château de Fontainebleau. It was the middle of the afternoon. Louis was out hunting. Marie de' Medici entertained in her apartments, and so court protocol required the cardinal to go and salute her immediately. After entering the queen's salon and bowing before her, Cardinal Richelieu rose to discover an unfriendly face. A long and awkward silence left everyone embarrassed. Accounts of this first public breakdown between Richelieu and Marie de' Medici differ. One source favorable to the cardinal recalled that he then excused himself and left the room. Mathieu de Morgues, a courtier of Marie who later became her pamphleteer and an enemy of the cardinal, also narrated this incident. While this source, naturally, must be treated with caution, the account it provides is quite precise. According to de Morgues, the queen finally asked how the cardinal was.

"My health is better than what many people here would like it to be," Richelieu is said to have responded, "with a frown, thinned out nose, and trembling lips."

Marie de' Medici, continued de Morgues, saw Cardinal Bérulle, the prelate who had replaced Richelieu in her good graces, enter the room. Bérulle, unlike Richelieu, lacked worldly manners. That day he wore white boots, which gave him a comical appearance. The queen used this entry as a pretext to change the conversation, and made a playful remark. But at that point the cardinal had lost his temper.

"I wish I was in as much favor as is the man that you are now mocking," he said before leaving the room.[15]

In any event, it took two days for the situation to calm down. Louis, who had been delighted at the thought of seeing Richelieu again, teared up when he heard of the incident and how his mother refused to reconcile with her erstwhile confidant. He begged her to change her attitude. Meanwhile, Richelieu offered his resignation to the queen mother and advised his relatives in her household to prepare for sudden dismissal. Marie de' Medici grudgingly agreed to a public reconciliation. The court was genuinely relieved and happy, and to help the cardinal forget about the incident, the king gave him the new title of Principal Minister of State.

Respite was short for Richelieu. Reports from Switzerland confirmed the presence of more than ten thousand imperial troops, and, worst of all, that these troops were now headed for northern Italy. If the Duke of Savoy had been a reliable ally for Nevers, the situation would not have been urgent. Casale was well guarded and had good supplies. The duke, however, was still reeling from his stinging and humiliating rout at Susa, and if the past was any indication, he could easily betray the French and switch his loyalty to the Habsburgs again, leaving Mantua and the Monferrato vulnerable. Charles Emmanuel also knew well how much the personal trouble in the French royal family could hamper another effort at rescuing Nevers. After weeks spent in the Duchy of Lorraine, Gaston had finally come back to France and given up on his dream of marrying Marie de Gonzague, against offers of more riches.[16] But even so, with Gaston, one never knew what to expect.

Italy, inevitably, was yet again the theater of the French and Habsburg contention. Because the situation remained unstable in the royal family, Louis XIII gave Richelieu the command of the army that would once again protect Nevers. On December 28, 1629, at his mansion on the Rue Saint-Honoré, the cardinal regaled the royal family and throngs of courtiers with a lavish banquet, comedies, music, and ballets. The following day, he bid farewell to Louis XIII and the two queens at the Louvre, held a luncheon with his niece Madame de Combalet, and boarded his grand carriage with the principal officers of the French army. Richelieu, with his suite of hundreds of horsemen in their finest uniforms, then joined the regiments that were stationed outside of the capital, to lead the French army to Italy for a second time. One had to know the name of this proud cavalier to realize he was a man of the Church. Richelieu had no use for the robes of the cardinal when he conducted a military campaign, explained an officer of the army who followed him in this new campaign. He wore fine armor, under a coat of rust-brown cloth embroidered in gold, and a feather on his hat. Four pages always rode beside him, two carrying his gloves and his helmet, the others holding two of the finest horses one could find. To give further proof that he was a knight at heart, Richelieu gladly gave displays of his horsemanship and performed elaborate figures and pirouettes.[17]

*   *   *

By mid-January 1630, the cardinal-cavalier was in Lyon, where he began all
the necessary preparations to cross the Alps in punishing weather, reach
Casale, and settle once and for all the dispute over the Mantuan succession.
The Duke of Savoy sent his son to extract more advantageous conditions
from the French. In exchange for his cooperation, the duke now wanted the
French to join him in an attack against Milan and Genoa. Adding to the
confusion were the efforts of Pope Urban VIII, who tried to avoid an open
conflict. A twenty-seven-year-old papal secretary, Giulio Mazarini, began
shuttling between various camps, traveling hundreds of miles in the winter,
but he could not avoid the situation's unraveling. Charles Emmanuel thought
he had nothing to lose with his hard bargain. Either he obtained enormous
gifts, or else he would sell himself to the Spanish. He let the talks drag on, to
allow the imperial army to reach Italy and buttress his own position. Richelieu called Charles Emmanuel's bluff by advancing through the Alps along the
valley of the Dora Riparia, beyond Susa and toward the plain of the Po River.
The foulest weather imaginable made this a miserable journey for everyone.[18]
When Charles Emmanuel saw the first of the French army and the artillery
getting close to Turin, he quickly retreated to his capital and even called back
all the troops he had in the region, including those that guarded the fortress of
Pinerolo, south of Rivoli. Pinerolo was the strategic key to another valley that
allowed communication between the Kingdom of France and northern Italy. In
a brilliant move, Richelieu ordered the rear of his army to clamp down on the
citadel, and he took it on March 29, 1630.

Olivares and his Spanish generals signaled that they could settle on Mantua's succession in exchange for letting the Duke of Savoy keep Pinerolo, and
Giulio Mazarini doubled his efforts at negotiating a peace deal. But Richelieu
sought to maximize his gains. He wanted to neutralize Charles Emmanuel completely by taking the last passageways that remained unsecured between France
and Italy, in Savoy, even though imperial troops had reached Italy, and General Spinola was on his way from Madrid with reinforcements. The letter he
wrote the king on April 13 detailed the situation with clarity. Should Louis
XIII choose the path of war, "one will need to attack Savoy at the earliest, and
the soonest one will do will always be too late." Then, "all thoughts of resting,
of balancing the kingdom's budget, and of settling domestic unrest would have
to be cast aside." In this stark assessment, Richelieu did not conceal how a
prolonged conflict would necessarily bring about new taxes and would stir up

domestic revolts. By the time his letter arrived in the king's hands, the court had
moved to Dijon, to tackle some violent protests against the heavy fiscal burden
brought about by the war. Keeping Gaston quiet was also essential to the success of the operation. Though the prince had returned to Paris from Lorraine
and bid adieu to Marie de Gonzague, he still had not formally met with his
brother to reconcile. Richelieu took pains to highlight this necessity in the conclusion to his missive to the king: "I dare say freely that one must obtain a true
and solid reconciliation between Monsieur, the king and the queen mother, and
also with Monsieur's courtiers; otherwise, one might as well settle and give
back Pinerolo, because it will be impossible to achieve anything of lasting importance."[19] A touchy subject was left out, however: Marie de' Medici's continuing anger at the minister and his anti-Habsburg policies.

Louis departed from Dijon with the two queens, heading southeast. Most
likely he had set his mind on continuing the fight against the Habsburgs in
Italy, as his martial temperament inclined him. But Louis could also be timo-
rous, especially with respect to his mother, and he waited to be with his chief
minister to make his decision public. Courtiers noted that the king's melancholy manifested itself more prominently in those days. Signs of ill health further added to his funk. In the meantime, Richelieu was returning from Italy,
leaving behind a well-equipped fortress in Pinerolo. On May 10, king and
minister reunited in Grenoble and finalized their projects to invade Savoy. Unexpectedly, Marie de' Medici also opted to support the war, even though she
feared for her son's life at a time when news of sporadic outbreaks of disease
came from the Alps. Did she realize that nothing could change her son's determination, and that she risked alienating him if she kept on with her steadfast
refusals? Her motivations at this point remain obscure.

Louis XIII, Cardinal Richelieu, and the army made their way deep into the
Savoy Alps, leaving Marie de' Medici, Marillac, and much of the court in
Lyon. The armies of Duke Charles Emmanuel had no other choice but to retreat. By June, king and minister had set their camp in the Maurienne, a region
encased between majestic mountain ranges, forming a natural conduit toward
Italy. The correspondence between the army camp and the court, kept in
thickly bound manuscripts in the archives of the Bibliothèque Nationale in
Paris, reveals a climate of rising political tension. Richelieu made sure to
keep the queen mother abreast of all the military developments and informed

of her son's well-being. Unfortunately, the king's health was still bad, and he suffered from a recurrent fever. The cardinal took pains to describe to Marie how Louis took good care of himself, even if he hated doctors and their paraphernalia: "We could not get him to take a certain medicine until yesterday, then we told him how much that would cause you chagrin; upon hearing that, he opined out of respect for your person. This, in return, brought great satisfaction to the true servants of Your Majesty, as much for the sheer utility of the gesture as for how it showed the power your name holds on him."[20]

Epistolary niceties aside, Richelieu still faced some difficult choices that could irritate the queen again. The first question was whether Louis himself would take the fight to Italy from Savoy. As soon as Louis and Richelieu had arrived in the Maurienne, an advanced corps headed by the Duc de Montmorency had gone to Pinerolo, to show that the French would not abandon Toiras, secluded in Casale to sustain a siege begun by Spinola on May 30. In any event, Richelieu needed the king to stay by his side. Leading the Italian rescue demanded a prodigious effort in terms of logistics. Richelieu had to know that the monarch would fully support his course of action. As days passed, Louis's health remained stubbornly weak, so much so that he started to worry, saying that he would surely end up dead if he stayed at the mountain camp any longer.[21] At the same time, Marie de' Medici refused to move to Grenoble with Marillac, to get closer to the army headquarters. Richelieu did not insist further on keeping the king with him. On July 25, Louis traveled back to Lyon, via Grenoble, through typhus-ridden regions, on roads where the air was thick with the smoke of bonfires lit up to fight the miasma of disease. A full-fledged epidemic had taken over the Alps, devastating its villages.

A month of bitter worries began for Cardinal Richelieu. With the king gone, he had to work twice as hard to keep his war effort going and everyone's morale up. In Mantua, the die was cast when, on July 18, German troops sacked the glorious capital of the Gonzague, inflicting suffering and devastation, and furiously destroying the priceless art collections of the ducal palace. Casale still resisted, but without greater French support its future was anything but certain. Sensitive diplomatic action in Germany caused added difficulties. Ferdinand's confessor, the politically influential Jesuit William Lamormaini, pressed his master for radical actions. On March 6, 1629, in a text named the Edict of Restitution, the emperor had demanded the return of all the territories and possessions that the Catholics had lost to the Protestants during the

Reformation. Then, just as war raged in northern Italy, he had summoned imperial electors to the city of Regensburg for a formal meeting of the diet. Ferdinand's objective was to make his imperial throne hereditary, and he entered Regensburg at the end of June 1630 in a style that befit the grandeur of his claim. Accounts describe a fifty-five-year-old man, not tall, sporting a short beard and graying red hair, traveling in a red car drawn by eight horses and followed by two thousand horsemen and three thousand soldiers. In the swarm of diplomats that descended on Regensburg were the French envoy extraordinaire Noël Brûlart de Sillery and, naturally, Father Joseph, the cardinal's point man for German affairs.[22] Their mission was to prevent a Habsburg consolidation of power. If that effort wasn't successful, they had to vouch for France's interests in the talks over this ascent of the Habsburgs to the hereditary imperial dignity.

Michel de Marillac, backed by Marie de' Medici, pressured Louis to accept a peace that Urban VIII's envoy, Giulio Mazarini, had proposed. The dreadful state of France's population at the time, when disease and famine compounded with the miseries of war to make the tax burden seem like tyranny, was truly disheartening. News of agitation in the parlement flowed from Paris. Throughout the kingdom, people were now decrying Richelieu's politics of grandeur, and throngs of hardened and cynical courtiers were betting on how many days were left before the cardinal's demise. Forgotten were the images of "New Alexander" and "New Hannibal."

In the middle of the plague-ridden Alps, struggling to direct several armies in Italy, trying to keep the Habsburgs' ambitions in check, and, to top it off, tortured by a variety of ailments, the harried Richelieu made a dramatic decision.[23] He left the Maurienne on August 17 for Lyon, to explain himself again to the king and avoid the unraveling of his plans. In Grenoble, he and his men changed all their clothes and discarded any objects and supplies brought from the mountains to keep the contagion from spreading down the valley.

A political showdown was not to happen. Fate conspired against Richelieu. After the cardinal's arrival in Lyon, Louis fell gravely ill from an intestinal infection. On September 22, 1630, he told his confessor Suffren, "Father, I am sicker than what is thought."[24] Astrologers' predictions were grim. Members of the clergy brought a most sacred relic, the heart of Saint François de Sales, for him to pray over. A week after the beginning of the crisis, on a Sunday at around eleven in the evening, the royal patient's condition became critical.

Louis let out large quantities of blood and pus, his abdomen was painfully swollen, and a tenacious fever drenched him in sweat. Suffren, who left us a moving narrative of Louis's illness, let him understand gently that he had to prepare for a good Christian death. The king received the news with calm and courage. He took communion from Alphonse du Plessis, Richelieu's brother whom the cardinal had plucked from his monastery and made the archbishop of Lyon. Then he asked that the doors of his bedchamber be flung open. The king's room at the residence of the archbishop's palace, even at a nightly hour, was full. His wife and Cardinal Richelieu stood before him. Louis gathered his meager strength and spoke to all quietly. "I ask forgiveness for anything that may have caused offense, and will not pass away happily without knowing that you have forgiven me. Please let that be known to all of my subjects."[25]

Anne of Austria had spent hours at her husband's bedside with little rest. Louis bid her farewell with genuine signs of affection. Richelieu's turn came after that. The cardinal broke down when the king thanked him for all his good service to the Crown. Marie de' Medici arrived. She offered heartfelt sentiments of motherly attention. He told her that he felt sorry for all of their past feuds. Many shed tears again at this spectacle.

But in the heavy atmosphere of the dying king's bedroom, everyone had more on their mind than just the mere thought of losing a loved one. Based on multiple testimonies from courtiers and officers present on the scene, there has been little doubt that these dramatic hours were also a time of intense plotting and maneuvering. Every day since Louis's condition had worsened, Marie de' Medici held meetings in her apartments to decide on Richelieu's fate. The governor in Lyon, whom the queen counted as a man in her party, stood ready to arrest the cardinal.[26] Needless to say, little help to Richelieu would come from the new sovereign, Gaston, who treated him with the barest civility. Could the well-informed Richelieu not have known of what was happening in Marie de' Medici's apartments? Louis, well aware of the danger that lurked for his minister, told him that the Duc de Montmorency, who had come back from Italy earlier, stood by to help him in the aftermath of his passing. The duke was even ready to whisk him to the port of Brouage if needed. As dawn broke over Lyon, on September 30, no one knew who would be King of France by sunset. All one could hear were sobs and prayers. What Richelieu could hear, too, was the sharpening of knives.

Then, what seemed like a miracle occurred. The intestinal abscess that threatened Louis burst, and, by the end of the day, an astonished court saw the king arise and walk around his bedroom. Cardinal Richelieu rushed to his desk. He needed to inform all of his officers that war operations should proceed according to the plan. His closest collaborators heard frank description of the fear that had been gripping him over the last days. To the Maréchal de Schomberg in Italy: "I do not know if I am dead or alive." Another missive has the tone of a man who had been on the edge of a precipice: "By the Grace of God the king is out of danger, and, to tell you the truth, I really do not know in what state I am myself."[27]

By mid-October, Louis spoke of hunting at Versailles and of how much he missed the fresh air of the Île-de-France. All understood that in this case, good morale was essential for the king's full recovery, and the doctors allowed him to go as soon as his strength made the trip possible. But before parting ways in Roanne, the king confided to Richelieu that Marie de' Medici was dissatisfied with his service.

The cardinal decided to confront the danger by traveling back to Paris with the queen mother. She was still in Lyon, and scheduled to arrive in Roanne in just a few days, to take a barge and navigate down the Loire River. During this waiting time, the cardinal received some stunning news from Regensburg. Ambassador Brûlart and Father Joseph had signed on October 13 a treaty that guaranteed peace in Italy by allowing the Duc de Nevers to keep his territories. The price to pay was high, however: France pledged not to enter in any alliance detrimental to Ferdinand. In other words, all the patient efforts that Ambassador Hercule de Charnacé pursued at the court of the Swedish king Gustavus Adolphus since the siege of La Rochelle, and the possibility of countering Habsburg power throughout Europe by forging strategic ties with this Lutheran king, were rendered moot just to ensure the safety of Nevers. Granted, Catholic German princes who feared Wallenstein's ambitions had persuaded Ferdinand to dismiss the general, bringing some relief to French allies the Dutch and German Protestants. But that could not make up for the weak position France was in now because of that treaty. Making matters even worse, the French diplomats had sent news of the treaty directly from Germany to the army in Italy. If the French army decided to stop its operations while waiting to hear confirmation from the government, Richelieu's painstaking efforts would suffer irreparable damage. General Spinola had died from illness at the siege, and even if disease decimated the French army, there was a real chance of gaining the upper hand if the army kept marching toward Casale.

The cardinal immediately sent messengers to both Germany and Italy to disown the treaty. In his personal letters, he described himself as "desperate" and "extremely afflicted."[28] Meanwhile, envoys sent to Lyon informed Marie de' Medici that the cardinal minister was reneging on the treaty. The news plunged her into a state that contemporaries described as symptoms of hysteria: uncontrollable tears, blinding flashes, and whistling sounds.[29] The queen had a secret. Testimonies differ on its exact nature, but at the very least she had extracted from Louis the promise that he would reconsider his trust in the cardinal at the end of the war in Italy.[30] One wonders if Louis's near-death experience and the amazement of discovering that his mother could care for him had not brought painful remorse for waging war against her during Luynes's "reign," prompting him to make this astounding commitment. To the queen's dismay, however, the cardinal now disowned the treaty with the Habsburgs that would have meant his ouster.[31]

Unexpectedly, once Marie de' Medici recovered and was able to reach Richelieu in Roanne, she appeared most gracious. For the memoirist Brienne, "the queen, who was born a Florentine, showed Richelieu that even after nearly thirty years spent in France, she still had not forgotten the art of masking her sentiment, an art that can be learned anywhere in the world, but is a natural talent in Italy."[32] Was the cardinal able to see through this appearance?[33] Certainly, he took the cue from Marie and lavished her with attention and compliments during that trip. Years later, Marie de' Medici confided to Gaston's courtier Goulas that on the boat that took them back to Paris, the cardinal "did not forget anything of what a refined, astute, and shrewd courtier can invent and practice in such circumstances."[34]

Louis was already in Versailles, all giddy at the thought of prowling again in his beloved forests: "As far as my health is concerned, it's getting better and better. I can walk half a mile without any trouble. Chairs and stretchers have been dismissed and God willing tomorrow I will be on horseback on Tuesday in Versailles."[35] His doctor, Charles Bouvard, described him as "singing, laughing, sleeping, and eating."[36]

Unbeknownst to all, yet another coup de théâtre had taken place. Maréchal de Schomberg, upon receiving news directly from Regensburg, had dismissed the treaty as irreconcilable with what he thought were Richelieu's real interests.

He kept the French army marching, to finally gather on a plain near Casale. Facing the French were the imperial contingents led by Octave Piccolomini. On October 26, the battle for the strategic Monferrato was imminent. Both armies were on the verge of collapsing, yet all were ready to settle the dispute. Then, suddenly, a galloping horseman was seen breaking through the ranks of the imperials. It was Giulio Mazarini, waving his hat, shouting frantically: *Pace! Pace!* At the last minute, and thanks to this papal envoy's tireless effort, the two army commanders had reached an advantageous agreement for France. Casale was rescued. After two years of incredible efforts, France now kept Habsburg power in check in northern Italy.

Marie de' Medici, upon hearing news of the peace accord back in Paris, immediately asked Louis to dismiss the minister she had come to hate with a passion. The way the queen saw it, it was not a choice between two policies; it was a choice between a mere valet and a mother. Louis came back from Versailles in a rush and took lodging near the Palais du Luxembourg, in Concini's former Rive Gauche mansion. He tried everything he could to change his mother's mind. Cardinal Richelieu proposed to resign. The king rejected the offer and assured his minister that he would keep his promise of standing up for him, even against his mother. All the king would grant his minister were a few days of respite in the countryside. But before Richelieu could do that, he had to formally excuse himself from the queen mother's own service.

On November 11, 1630, at around ten in the morning, Richelieu walked to the Palais du Luxembourg from the Petit Luxembourg, an annex given to him by Marie de' Medici. Those short steps that separated the two houses were more a bitter walk down times past than a convenience for the cardinal's exhausted body. How incredible that, five and half years earlier, the man had marked his grand entrance on the European political stage with an awe-inspiring reception in that very palace. Now, Cardinal Richelieu was coming to the Luxembourg with one last hope of saving everything he had done on behalf of France, and on behalf of the Richelieu name.

Danger lurked. In spite of all assurances, Louis had yet again criticized his minister's imperious manners, and now the king was paying an unannounced visit to his mother.[37] Who could tell what the ever-impenetrable Louis really had in mind? Much more than during the period leading to his appointment to the king's council in 1624, Richelieu's second ministerial career was the time when he learned the survival arts, or, rather, when his political talent proved to be a primordial drive to act. Would this force serve him as well this time?

What followed made that day one of the most famous in French history, the so-called Day of the Dupes. Richelieu himself would one day call it "the strangest revolution that ever was."[38] There are many versions of these events. For a long time the dubious testimony of Louis's close companion Saint-Simon skewed historians' reconstitution of the events. But in 1974, Pierre Chevallier, based on a careful confrontation of the various diplomatic testimonies and memoirs, was able to present a timeline and description that have been widely accepted ever since.

On the Day of the Dupes, Richelieu entered the Luxembourg by the great gallery where all the paintings by Rubens were displayed. No one stood before the queen's study. He tried to open the door, but it was locked. Then, according to one version of the events, the house personnel—perhaps a maid of the queen, La Zuccoli—signaled another way. Few but Richelieu, who had signed off on all the building's invoices, knew that a narrow corridor linked the queen's private place of worship to her study. After another dash through the palace's rooms, the cardinal found himself before a small door leading to Marie de' Medici's most private retreat. He opened the door, which had remained unlocked. Marie and Louis stood in the middle of the room, cut short in what appeared to have been an intense conversation.

"Were Your Majesties speaking of me?" asked Richelieu.

"Yes," responded the queen.

Marie then burst into recriminations. She called Richelieu an ingrate, a traitor, a false-hearted con man. Louis stuttered a few words to calm his mother, but they drowned in a swelling rant. The cardinal, so those who heard the story say, then fell to his knees, asking if he had ever done anything but wear himself out for the greater glory of the kingdom. Marie de' Medici responded by yelling more insults. Still on his knees, his body shaken by violent sobs, Cardinal Richelieu ended up begging for mercy and kissing the hem of her dress. His former protector turned her back on him with disdain. She thought he could cry at will, like "a crocodile," she even said once.

All Richelieu could do was to leave the room. Louis also quit the scene. As he left the palace, he saw his minister waiting for him at the bottom of the stairs, but he ignored him.

Cardinal Richelieu went back home. He ordered that his carriage be ready for immediate departure, right after luncheon. He scribbled a note to the king begging for his mercy and then threw it away.[39] The spectacle of Marie de' Medici constrained Louis to fire him; otherwise he would bring great shame upon his mother and, to a certain extent, on himself, the king. Richelieu planned to flee to Le Havre, the fortified port-city he controlled. There, at least, he could withstand an attack. With Marie de' Medici in power, anything was possible, including an ignominious death. Already, the capital buzzed with astonishment. Ambassadors, breathless over their desks, scrambled to dispatch the news all over Europe: Louis had just disgraced Cardinal Richelieu!

A messenger came in, carrying an order from Louis XIII: he summoned his minister to Versailles. Was it a trap? Cardinal La Valette arrived in the middle of this panic, one of the few who dared to come and offer some support. When Richelieu told him of the king's orders, and of his intent to ignore them, La Valette responded categorically: no one knew what the king really wanted, and the one who quits the game is the loser. Richelieu had to obey the order, or else face the direst of consequences.

It is hard to fathom how Richelieu found enough fortitude to board his carriage and present himself before Louis XIII that evening. His decision, arguably, changed the course of France's history.

At Versailles, King Louis gave his minister a guest room, right above his own apartment. This hunting manor was a simple house, a retreat for an introverted king who shunned fuss and artifice and who reserved it for his few intimates. Later on, before a crackling fire, the two spent four hours together. Louis confided the deep sorrow he felt for having to hurt his mother. Such was the price of royal fame, he admitted. Long into the November night, Richelieu and Louis XIII defined the details of their next moves to make France the most prominent kingdom of Europe. Just a few hours after separating, Richelieu wrote to Louis a vivid testimony of his gratitude: "I feel so extraordinarily obliged that it is hard for me to describe the feeling. I urge your Majesty, by the name of God, not to trouble himself with useless melancholy."[40]

That same night, in the salons of the Luxembourg, courtiers celebrated with Marie de' Medici what they thought was her triumph over the hated minister. The crowd was so thick that people could barely turn around. The Duc d'Épernon made a rare appearance. Anne of Austria sent a message of congratulations. Reports had the cardinal at Versailles, and some prudent minds advised the queen to join her son, too, and make sure that he would not betray her. But instead Marie de' Medici spent the night breathing in the intoxicating perfume of success and flattery.

When Marie woke up the next day, she learned, to her horror, that Louis had ordered both Michel de Marillac and his brother Louis, the marshal, arrested. The Palais du Luxembourg remained empty throughout the day, leaving the duped queen with dark thoughts. The woman, who knew the cardinal better than anyone else, once said, "He is utterly depressed when fortune is contrary to him; but when wind is in his sails, he is worse than a dragon."

PART III

The Passion

CHAPTER 7

Restless Dragon (1631–1634)

SIX YEARS AFTER ENGAGING IN A show of strength with Spain and minister Olivares, and in the aftermath of the Day of the Dupes, Cardinal Richelieu boldly widened his challenge to the Habsburgs and confronted the Austrian branch of France's enemy dynasty. For a subsidy of one million pounds, King Gustavus Adolphus of Sweden agreed to wage war against the emperor with thirty thousand of his soldiers and six thousand horsemen, and he promised that he would always respect the religious rights of Catholics. France and Sweden formalized this alliance in Berwäld, on January 23, 1631. Then, on May 8, France struck another alliance with Duke Maximilian of Bavaria, to lead an opposing Catholic party in the empire.

Had not King Solomon and King David themselves resorted to the help of miscreants in their fights against enemies? Richelieu asked the king in order to justify these alliances.[1] Pope Urban VIII, it seemed, was worried enough about Habsburg power in Italy and the safety of his own states not to protest Richelieu's dubious alliance with Sweden. Besides, after having spent many years in France as a diplomat, this pope had an affectionate attitude toward the kingdom of Louis XIII.

One who did not accept the arguments, even from a cardinal theologian, was Marie de' Medici, as well as the intensely pro-Catholic party she had come to represent. Louis had assured his mother that she remained a most prominent figure at court. He even invited her to attend the royal council sessions, provided that she would not ask to vote. The gesture gave the queen hopes of eventually reclaiming her influence, and, in the meantime, it encouraged her to display overt political hostility to the cardinal. Richelieu protested his good-will: "I can hardly represent how much I want an accommodation," he wrote.[2] Eventually, the queen showed up for a session of the royal council. Her icy cold attitude during the meeting left little hopes of an arrangement with the minister. She then stopped attending altogether, for fear of dampening the angry resentment that animated her followers. It was Gaston, in the end, who caused the situation to unravel.

On the morning of January 30, 1631, as Richelieu was tending to his ordinary business at the Palais-Cardinal, the prince stormed in with his gang of hotheaded young courtiers and stunned him with an open declaration of war.

"I am here for a strange reason" were Gaston's first words, as reported by Antoine Aubery, the cardinal's first biographer. "As long as I thought you could serve me well I was content with loving you. Now that you are reneging on everything you promised, I've come to tell you that I am taking back my word that I would care for you."[3]

With the cardinal's guards out of the room due to protocol, Gaston's men looked ready to pounce. But after a few tense moments, Gaston cursed, turned around, and walked back to his carriage, uttering more threats on the way. Richelieu followed on his steps, speechless. Louis was hunting that day. As he heard of his brother's tantrum, he rushed to the cardinal's house and tried to reassure the minister as best as he could. Richelieu once again offered to resign. Gaston, after his outburst, had secured the precious stones he had inherited from his late wife and left for his fiefdom in the Loire Valley.

About three weeks passed after Gaston's scene. The court made preparations to move to the Château de Compiègne for the winter. For Carnival, Richelieu planned some entertaining of his own with comedies and ballets. Stage sets and machineries were sent on their way to the château. The question for Marie de' Medici was whether she should join the court or not. Some of her courtiers recommended she stay safely in Paris, but she decided to accompany her son the king to Compiègne. No doubt, the crucial mistake of not having followed him to Versailles, when perhaps she still had a chance of obtaining the minister's dismissal, was present in the queen's mind. At the château, the true motives of the king and his minister were revealed.

In the early hours of February 23, Louis left with a few of his men, pretending to go out hunting. Once at a good distance, he dispatched a messenger to

Anne, telling her that for the good of the state Marie de' Medici would have to stay under house arrest at the château, and that Anne should leave immediately, too, and meet him at a nearby convent. Lately, their common loathing of Richelieu had brought the two queens closer. Anne, wearing only a night robe, and while her servants scrambled to prepare for the hurried departure, ran through the cold corridors of the château. She found her mother-in-law sitting on her bed, her arms wrapped around her knees, recalled Anne's chambermaid Madame de Motteville.

"Oh, my daughter, I am either dead or a prisoner. Is the king leaving me here? What does he want from me?"[4]

Soon after this episode, Richelieu urged the king to dismiss many of Anne's ladies, because the spies the cardinal paid in her entourage were reporting that her apartments were a hotbed of ill will against him.[5] Maréchal de Bassompierre, that diplomat and hero of many wars, was the lover of one of the ladies chased from Anne's court, and he dared to speak a bit too freely on Richelieu's actions. A captain of the guards took him to the Bastille. No charges were ever brought up during the more than a decade the marshal stayed at the dreaded fortress. For Richelieu, exceptional circumstances justified this kind of action: "While justice requires authentic proof, things are not the same when the state is concerned, because in that case, what is the result of pressing conjectures must be deemed sufficiently proven."[6]

Gaston stayed at large in Orléans. After seeing the backlash triggered by his outburst at the Palais-Cardinal, the prince was now writing to disgruntled nobles and foreign powers. Louis left Paris with an army corps, and soon he found himself in hot pursuit after his brother, not toward the west of the kingdom and Orléans, but rather toward the Holy Roman Empire, where Gaston had again decided to seek refuge. Gaston declared that he acted for the good of France. The parlement in Paris gave him the benefit of the doubt when it refused to register a declaration of lèse-majesté published by Louis against those who enabled his brother.[7] "Vive Monsieur and the freedom of the people!" shouted Gaston's heralds while he charged toward Franche-Comté, a region which lies to the south of Lorraine. Before and after crossing the border of the empire and leaving an enraged Louis behind, Gaston wrote scathing public letters to his brother, in which he denounced what he viewed as the tyranny of the cardinal and the ills and miseries that his quest for international grandeur and personal profit inflicted on France: "There is barely one third of your peasants who eat ordinary bread, the next eats oats, and finally the rest are not only reduced to begging, but languish in such sorry necessity that some end up dying of hunger, while the others live on acorns, weeds, and similar things, just like beasts. As far as the least miserable of those are concerned, they eat bran and the blood that they can find in the gutters of butchers. I have seen this with my own eyes in many places, since I've left Paris."[8] Richelieu duly responded by publishing the letters himself, but with point-by-point responses to every accusation. Gaston eventually moved to Lorraine and settled at the court of Duc Charles IV, in Nancy, on April 28, 1631.

An acrimonious and tiresome exchange began between the government and Marie de' Medici. Her confidant, the physician François Vautier, had also been sent to the Bastille. The queen asked to stay in the town of Nevers, yet once she obtained that satisfaction, she delayed. She feared being exiled to Florence, and her astrologers had predicted that Louis would soon die.[9] Other factors provoked the queen's anger. Both Marillac brothers were detained. On the one hand, there was not much to warrant a trial against Michel, the minister of justice; on the other, there were strong suspicions that Marillac's brother, Maréchal Louis, whom Richelieu himself had pointlessly promoted to placate the queen early on, had mishandled military funds. In May, a royal decree summoned Louis de Marillac to justice before an ad hoc judicial commission in Verdun, where the marshal had been a governor and the commander of the army of Champagne.[10] Marillac's supporters denounced the trial as sheer retribution for the conspiracy in Lyon.

Special envoys shuttled between Paris and Compiègne. Now the queen delayed her departure on the pretext of bad weather or illness. She locked herself in her room, spent hours hearing read-aloud the anti-Richelieu pamphlets that her supporters were spreading through Paris. Finally, Louis himself intervened and offered to remove the armed guards that patrolled the surrounding country, to show his mother that he did not mean any direct threat against her. In response, she petitioned the Paris Parlement to have the cardinal publicly censured, a request the parlement politely declined, given its already strained relations with the Crown after its refusal to act against Gaston.

On July 18, just after nightfall, a veiled woman showed up at a service gate at Compiègne. She was in the company of a man who said that this lady-in-waiting to the queen mother was getting secretly married. The porter warned the two that the door would be shut for the night. They replied that they were not coming back and walked away. The woman was Marie de' Medici, who thought she would relive the 1619–1620 epic years of the war with her son with another stunt.[11] This time, however, there was no d'Épernon to help her, and her faithful Bishop of Luçon was not a precious adviser anymore. After walking a few hundred yards from the château, said the police report that Richelieu eventually received, she boarded a carriage and took the northern road. The day after, once in sight of La Capelle, a stronghold held by a man loyal to her, the queen heard distressing news: the cardinal had already discovered the plot.

The absence of guards at Compiègne, or around La Capelle—it was all a bit suspicious considering the cardinal's information and extensive resources. Had the queen pondered this mystery, perhaps she would have realized that it was to Richelieu's advantage to see her out of the kingdom. But Marie de' Medici ordered her carriage to proceed toward the border of the Spanish Netherlands, where Infanta Isabella reigned. Soon after, she wrote to her son and implored him to disgrace the cardinal. Louis responded: "Thank God I know quite well what I am doing, and please allow me to tell you that your own decisions, or the advice that others have given you, have put you in a position whence reason dictates that I should not receive any counsel from you, and that you should not try to give me any."[12]

A month after the queen mother's flight, and after a formal request by Louis, the parlement officially made Richelieu a Duc and a Pair of the French kingdom, the highest honor a Frenchman could attain. To affirm the legitimacy of his newly acquired distinction, the cardinal published a genealogy of his family that proved its antique roots in the French nobility. It went as far as affirming that he had some royal blood in his veins—a rather suspicious claim. Then the newly promoted duke spent part of the summer planning and supervising a grandiose project that would consolidate his newly found prestige: the building of a new château and an innovative urban project at Richelieu. First, Richelieu set up an aggressive program to purchase the lands surrounding the ancestral domain of his family. The architect Jacques Lemercier drew plans for the most lavish château ever built by a subject of the French king. A dream in creamy white stone, a model of regular, well-ordered architecture rose as the perfect setting for the art collections that the cardinal was amassing. In letter after letter, Richelieu gave instructions on the minutest aspects of the project. The adjacent new town was a gridlike and rectangular development set at a perfect angle from the château. A church, a religious mission, a town hall, a covered marketplace, and a main street lined with townhouses, the brand-new town had everything to become a prosperous provincial center. Except that Richelieu's land still lay out of Poitou's main thoroughfares. The cardinal remedied this difficulty by transferring the fiscal institutions of nearby localities.

Paris, naturally, remained a place to show off. In his palace on the Rue Saint-Honoré or at Rueil, Cardinal Richelieu lived surrounded by cohorts of personnel, including the clergy of his ecclesiastical house, and the nobles who served as equerries or pages. It was quite a spectacle when he hosted, and his guests took their place at immense tables where the finest candles from Venice brightened the white linens, crystal, the goldware, all to the sound of fine music.[13] He went around Paris in a grand carriage trimmed with red velvet and gold, pulled by six horses sporting red feather tufts, surrounded by handsome, proud, and devoted mounted guards who wore red uniforms.[14] This opulence showcased a worthy noble actor. The principal minister of Louis XIII was always well groomed and elegant. People found him alluring. They deemed his conversation refined and urbane, his sense of humor biting. The very title Eminence, which all cardinals received by papal decree in June of 1630, could have been coined to describe Richelieu alone.

All of this resplendence cost colossal amounts of money, but Richelieu now possessed a growing fortune. There were the revenues from the admiralty, offices, lands, domains, monasteries he supervised such as Cluny, and other various investments.[15] Never again would the name Richelieu seem antithetical to the modest country manor where it had originated.

With the French heir to the throne once again in Lorraine, Cardinal Richelieu cast a dark gaze upon Duc Charles IV's possessions, a fiefdom of the emperor. Louis and Duc Charles were embroiled in long-standing sovereignty disputes over certain parts of Lorraine. At a time when the cardinal affirmed a strong political line against Habsburg power, solving these problems was ever more urgent. The region was a passage for Habsburg troops traveling from northern Italy and Germany to Flanders.[16] The other concerns to the east, ironically, related to France's ally the King of Sweden. Less than a year after signing the Treaty of Berwäld, and thanks to innovative methods of warfare, Gustavus Adolphus had made inroads in Germany that warranted his nickname "Lion of the North." The imperial troops Gustavus Adolphus had found on his path were led by General Tilly, who after defeat went on to attack the city of Magdeburg on the Elbe River, provoking one of the most infamous carnages of the Thirty Years' War and rallying Protestant princes such as the military entrepreneur Bernard of Saxe-Weimar and the Saxony elector John George around the Swedish king.[17] On September 17, Gustavus Adolphus won another crushing battle against Tilly at Breitenfeld. Then he reached the rich lands of the Rhine that the Spanish had occupied since the ban of Frederick V, the Elector Palatine, taking Mainz in December and settling there for the winter. Meanwhile, the Duke of Saxony, John George, entered Prague. These Swedish advances were increasingly worrisome for Richelieu.[18] The Catholic League, that gathering of princely interests that he had envisioned as a political counterweight to the emperor's power and who had pledged neutrality, was growing increasingly nervous, too. Lorraine needed to become a firewall against the Swedish king's growing force.

At the end of the year 1631, Louis and Richelieu left the Île-de-France to wage war against Charles de Lorraine. The campaign was a quick one. Charles, already exhausted from having participated in the battle at Breitenfeld, could offer no resistance. Louis's army took his fortified city of Moyenvic, and on January 6, 1632, by the Treaty of Vic, Charles IV pledged himself to Louis XIII.

Just three days before the signing, however, a very secret ceremony had taken place in Nancy: the marriage of Gaston and the duke's sister, Marguerite de Lorraine. Gaston had met this princess during his previous stay at the court of Lorraine, and, although he was still infatuated with Marie de Gonzague at the time, the blond Marguerite had left a lasting impression on him. Once a fugitive at the court of Lorraine, he decided to marry her without consulting his brother. Among the few witnesses to the ceremony were the duke himself and Gaston's new confidant, Antoine de L'Age, soon to become Duc de Puylaurens.

On January 28, with his brother nearby and his host the duke pledged to him, Gaston left his new wife and headed for Brussels to join his mother, who welcomed him with open arms. A real community of French expatriates was now settled amid the gothic splendors of Brussels, and festivities and gallantries of all kinds marked those winter months of 1632. It was all at the expense of Infanta Isabella, who paid Marie and Gaston generous allowances. Marie used this Spanish money to keep a sizable entourage of ladies-in-waiting, maids of honor, servants, and favorites, including the inevitable plotters and the pamphlet writers she used to defame her enemy Richelieu. Gaston went around with his court of rowdy nobles and amusers. Both mother and son, mindful to project the image of a legitimate government in exile, dined in public ceremonies, during which they also fed dozens of people at the lower tables. Everyone spent the days in brilliant hunting parties, the nights in balls and comedies. As one of Gaston's courtiers put it realistically, "The Spanish were not paying us for gallantry, but to cause trouble on their behalf."[19] With Gaston, Marie thought she would be able to teach a lesson to the cardinal. She borrowed against her precious stones, and, with the help of the Spanish, she encouraged her son to raise troops. In Madrid, the minister Olivares found the enterprise quite "fragile," but with the French heir present, he thought it was worth a try.[20]

Richelieu monitored this new hotbed of sedition with concern. In March of 1632, a royal decree created a new extraordinary commission to judge Maréchal Louis de Marillac on charges of embezzlement. In spite of the earlier commission's zeal, not enough evidence had been found to guarantee a guilty verdict. The judges were ordered to deliberate at Richelieu's favorite château of Rueil, to the west of Paris, the place where he went to escape the hustle and bustle of Paris and enjoy walks in beautiful gardens. The judges even slept there during the trial, lodging two per room—this way they could keep watch on each other, observed Marillac's partisans. The man in charge of the judicial inquiry doubled as one of the judges. Another judge, Paul Hay du Chastelet, had written pieces against the accused during the first trial. He had to be removed. Marillac put up a strong defense and fought the charges and the irregular procedures as hard as he could. But after the king repeatedly admonished parlement not to mingle with affairs of the state, the accused lost his legal right to make appeals to a third party.[21] By the end of March, Richelieu wrote to the king, "One must speed up the trial of Marillac . . . because it is certain that length and negligence in such business show [the state's] weakness and give great hopes [to its enemies]."[22] Two month later, the jury found Louis de Marillac guilty by thirteen votes out of twenty-four.[23] His judges scoured old legal texts and found language ambiguous enough to be interpreted as calling for the death penalty in cases of theft from the Crown.[24]

Marillac's relatives rushed to see Richelieu as soon as they heard of the seemingly inevitable death sentence. Their version of the encounter, which they published soon after, is intriguing. They claim that they found the cardinal in his garden at Rueil, strolling in the midst of his blooming flowerbeds. Once at his feet, they begged for mercy.

Richelieu looked surprised. "You are announcing to me, Messieurs, something I was unaware of. I am sorry that Maréchal de Marillac put himself in such a situation by his own actions. See the king, he is good."

"Monseigneur, would you not grant us the favor of speaking to the king and interceding in his favor?"

"I told you the king was good," insisted Richelieu.

Coming from a tract published by one of Marillac's partisans, these details should be read with prudence. Yet one should also consider seriously how they represent Richelieu as unaware of the trial's recent outcome, and declaring that Louis held the man's fate. Contemporaries and historians have often considered that the minister was the mastermind behind Marillac's demise. But isn't it possible that Louis actually played the determining role? For sure, Richelieu did contribute to Marillac's fate, and he might well have been the one to excite the king's anger at the beginning. If Louis had decided on the man's fate, however, there was actually not much Richelieu could do to alter the course of events. The day after the encounter, Marillac's relatives somehow managed to reach the cardinal again, even though he gave orders not to let them in. He sent them away with angry and sour words this time.[25] Louis, whom they finally petitioned, was equally implacable.

The execution of Louis de Marillac took place two days after the judgment, in Paris's Place de Grève, on May 10. Marillac, contrary to his stern brother Michel, was a rather showy man, not exactly announcing constancy and stoicism. He died a brave Christian death nonetheless. His brother Michel followed him in death soon after, when he passed away in prison on August 7. The cause was deemed natural.

Paris grumbled. One morning, verses "infamous to the honor of the king" were found on a piece of paper fixed to the Louvre's gate. Later on, a picture showing the king and his minister in a shocking sexual position appeared on the walls of city hall.[26] The weight of political surveillance became increasingly heavy, to the point where people became wary of speaking out even in the safest confines of private gatherings. Authors of political tracts who criticized the government were sent to the galleys. Richelieu countered the bad publicity by hiring the dismissed judge, Hay du Chastelet, to write an apology of the government's swift justice.[27] He could also use a novel and efficient means for his propaganda. Since May 30, 1631, the *Gazette de France* published what is considered one of the very first newspapers. The redactor, a man named Théophraste Renaudot, gave news from the kingdom and abroad, described court spectacles, and published everything Louis and Richelieu saw fit to print.

In May of 1632, Gaston left the Spanish Netherlands to join his newly gathered troops near Trier. The news of Marillac's death added to his determination, but the soldiers the Spanish had given him were a motley crew of tired recruits and thugs. The only thing that looked bright in Gaston's prospects was the arrival of an unlikely ally, the handsome Duc Henri de Montmorency, whose name the French nobility revered. The man had chased the Huguenots from the Atlantic coast in 1625 and made decisive inroads during the Italian campaign of 1630. He rode masterfully, danced well, and protected men of letters. Finally, Montmorency had political credit: Louis had called him to his deathbed in Lyon when he needed a protector for the minister. But small grudges had built up to motivate the duke's rebellion. In 1626, he had let go of his admiralty so that Richelieu could become superintendent of the navy. Nothing had come in return. More recently, he was at odds with the minister over taxation in the province he governed, the Languedoc. His wife, a relative of Marie de' Medici, hated the minister with a passion.

"Well, Madam, you want it," admitted the duke when for one more time his wife urged him to join the rebellion. "I'll do it to content your ambition, but remember that it will only cost me my life."[28]

Montmorency might have chosen his camp with inauspicious words but had no intent of failing at this enterprise. He specifically told Gaston that he could not fight before the end of August. By then, an assembly in the Languedoc would have deliberated on the fiscal demands set by Richelieu and, in all probability, rejected them. The time would then be ripe to call for an uprising across the province.

Gaston left Trier in June thinking that he would join Montmorency in the south and conquer the kingdom to chase Richelieu away. The first stop was the capital of Lorraine, Nancy, where he reunited with his wife and waited for Montmorency to be ready. News came that Louis and Richelieu were headed for Lorraine. Aside from Gaston, Charles de Lorraine's suspicious activities motivated them. Contrary to the terms of the treaty he had signed, the duke was rearming, allegedly because Gustavus Adolphus was threatening his duchy. The Swedish king's advances were indeed cause for alarm, especially after he had invaded Catholic Bavaria and conquered its capital, Munich, on May 17, causing great damage to the French and German Catholic alliance and prompting Pope Urban VIII to send a team of diplomats to mediate. On June 12, 1632, two months earlier than it had been agreed, Gaston and his courtiers began a picaresque summer cavalcade. The citizens of Dijon fired cannon shots at the heir to the French throne and his troops to scare them away. Gaston kept on and was able to rest for a while in backwater Vichy. Auvergne did not prove a more hospitable region. His tart-tongued court poet, Vincent Voiture, wondered if this moment did not call for declaring *veni, vidi, Vichy*.[29] The bad troops, unable to find sustenance, were disbanding or causing so much trouble that the would-be liberator became an object of scorn. Meanwhile, Gaston's courtiers found any opportunities to revel and frolick at every halt. Montmorency realized he had made a mistake aligning himself with Gaston. Nevertheless, he declared himself by arresting officers Richelieu had sent to his province. When Gaston arrived in sun-parched Languedoc in August, his forces were reduced to a paltry contingent of eighteen hundred soldiers. Louis and Richelieu, after forcing Charles to sign an even more constraining treaty, were on their way to Lyon.[30] The much-anticipated rise of the Languedoc's nobility failed to materialize.

On September 1, in the morning, the fateful meeting of the rebels and an advancing corps of the royal army—it was Maréchal de Schomberg's—took place on a plain near the small town of Castelnaudary. Gaston and Montmorency were at some distance from each other, the former with his closest men on the hill, the latter with some troops on the plain. Out of the blue, Montmorency spurred on his horse and threw himself in the midst of the royal battalions. The contemporary chronicles describe him as fighting like those knights of old chivalric tales, mowing down soldiers seven rows deep. Even after ten wounds, he was still fighting. Only when his horse fell on him was he caught. A flabbergasted Gaston watched this scene from the nearby hill. Did Montmorency mistakenly think that the fight had begun without him, and that he might leave the laurels of victory to someone else? Was this the suicide of a man who had come to realize the foolishness of his enterprise? Witnesses say that Gaston chafed at the bit and wanted to join his ally as soon he saw the engagement, but that his men advised him to stay put, given how narrow the chances were of winning after such a poorly planned start. The rebels' army, as soon as the news of Montmorency's capture spread, quickly disbanded. The prince had no choice but to flee southeast to the city of Béziers.

Louis and Richelieu joined the royal army in the Languedoc three weeks after this battle. As always, the heir to the throne was untouchable. Once Gaston signed an agreement on September 29 that granted him a pardon, Richelieu turned his attention to the duke. The state owed much to Montmorency, and the aristocracy and his own people admired him. The cardinal, however, professed a sharp distinction between the realm of human feelings and that of the state. Charity wants to pardon. Reason, on the other hand, demands the rebel's punishment. This is why the cardinal famously wrote that "in matters of state crimes, doors must shut pity out," and why the man of letters Jean-Louis Guez de Balzac, in a panegyric of Louis XIII that Richelieu commissioned, defined the perfect prince as a sheer intellectual substance, a man endowed with unwavering reason.[31] Still, Richelieu sent Louis a memoir that blackened the reputation of the duke, to press for his condemnation should the king prove less than dispassionate.[32]

On October 22, 1632, Louis XIII and Anne of Austria performed their solemn entry into the capital of the Languedoc, Toulouse. Cardinal Richelieu followed. Then it was Montmorency's turn to enter his city. Hundreds of musketeers and soldiers guarded the badly wounded duke, and the streets were lined with men in arms. Since he did not contest the charges, the trial was a quick affair. The execution took place in the courtyard of the town hall a week later, on October 30.

"Strike boldly!" Montmorency urged the headsman.

One blow severed the duke's neck. The people of Toulouse, who had been kept outside for fear they might try to prevent the beheading, poured into the courtyard. They ran to the scaffold, crying and wailing. Some dipped their handkerchief in the blood and brought it to their lips, noted a contemporary account.[33] Not only had they lost a beloved governor, but with Henri's death, the illustrious lineage of the Montmorency was terminated. The childless duke was thirty-seven years old.

Gaston, from Blois where he had retreated after his pardon, professed shock at the execution. He was now completely discredited, not only after his miserable loss but also because it seemed he had sold out his ally Montmorency to return to the good graces of his brother and the principal minister he hated. The treaty he signed had not brought harmony between the two brothers. During the trial, the secret of his marriage with Marguerite of Lorraine had been revealed. News that Gaston had once again fled the kingdom for the Spanish Netherlands reached the court later in November.

Louis headed straight to Paris. Cardinal Richelieu, who had planned a ceremonial parade for Anne in La Rochelle, accompanied the queen. The trip also allowed him to visit Brouage, a center for salt trade on the Atlantic that he had been fortifying for many years. Both the queen and the minister boarded a convoy of ships on the Garonne River. Because Anne wished to visit the fiefdom and château of the d'Épernons, a stopover in Cadillac was added.

There, an incident marred the trip. This queen took with her such an imposing retinue that the Duc d'Épernon misjudged the number of carriages he needed to take her to his majestic château over the Garonne. By the time the duke finished showing Anne her apartments and rushed back to the water to fetch Richelieu, he found the cardinal walking the steady climb that leads to the house. As the duke's secretary, Guillaume Girard, narrated it, no apology or prayer could persuade the cardinal to accept this belated offer of proper transport. Richelieu looked both angry and in great discomfort—and indeed he was, because he was feeling the first symptoms of a severe case of a prostate condition and related urinary retention. He finished the climb and went straight to his room.

Some panic ensued. The cardinal thought d'Épernon's oversight was an intentional mistake. That haughty feudal lord, the former friend of Henri III and Henri IV, did not like what he saw: a man who chased the heir to the throne and the queen mother away, who was bringing down the high nobility, and who tried to take a hold on all of the key strategic posts in the kingdom.[34] Most of Richelieu's guards had been sent away to faraway lodgings, and so he was practically alone in the duke's house. The cardinal ordered his most trusted men to stay with him. They slept on the floor of his room.

At the earliest hour the following day, without touching the food that d'Épernon offered, Richelieu fled Cadillac and sought refuge in Bordeaux, where his health deteriorated rapidly.[35] Day after day, he suffered increasing pain, to the point where Father Joseph feared for his life. All this time, d'Épernon paid him daily visits, always showing up with a contingent of two hundred of his own guards.

"I'm not coming to bother you, but to hear about your well-being," insisted the duke.

The cardinal's condition took a turn for the worse, raising his pain to atrocious levels. Doctors lost hope, and news of the cardinal's death spread through the kingdom. Then, out of the blue, a physician from the town asked to meet the desperately sick man. A few days later, Richelieu wrote this curious letter that explains how that doctor had saved his life in Bordeaux with an ingenious type of catheter: "A surgeon with an admirable secret lives in Bordeaux: with a thin, grooved candle of wax, he released all the urine kept in that bladder that was killing me, and so gave me indescribable relief."[36] Father Joseph was still concerned, finding him very weak, having spent many sleepless nights, and having been bled many times. At last, Richelieu's condition stabilized. By the time he reached Brouage, his fortified port on the Atlantic, he felt much better. He had missed Anne's solemn entry into La Rochelle, but now, at least, he could work to his full capacity and enjoy security.[37]

News of some startling developments in international politics came in. Gustavus Adolphus had died at Lützen, on November 16, in a battle with the imperial forces of Wallenstein, whom Ferdinand had recalled in extremis.[38] "There is no place for two cocks on the same pile of manure," said Wallenstein in a prosaic eulogy for the man who had been terrorizing Catholic Germany for the last two years. Father Joseph, it is said, had described the alliance with the Swedish Protestant stalwart as a venom, which, used in tiny quantities, is an antidote. Richelieu's dosage in creating a balance of powers, however, could well have killed the patient, had fate not taken the life of Gustavus Adolphus at Lützen.

Finally, on January 3, 1633, Richelieu made it to the château at Rochefort-en-Yvelines, near Paris. Louis came in from Versailles. The *Gazette de France* reported: "As soon as he saw the king, the Cardinal threw himself at the feet of his His Majesty, who, while he lifted him up with one hand, embraced him with the other one, doubling his gestures of tenderness so much that tears starting flowing in all those attending. All confessed to having never seen such testimony of a master's more cordial kindness, or the testimony of a more respectful affection from any subject."[39]

France chose to renew its alliance with Sweden.[40] Since the new queen, Christine, was a nine-year-old child, Chancellor Axel Oxenstierna now conducted the destiny of her kingdom, and he had made the crucial decision that Sweden should keep its armed forces in Germany after the death of Gustavus. The new pact, signed in April, still left Richelieu with cause for concern. The emperor's influence in Germany, after the lull of the Diet of Regensburg, was on the upswing. The German Protestant princes were increasingly alarmed by Wallenstein's return and military successes. Even the Dutch Republic strained in its fight against Spain. What would happen then if the Dutch, or the German Protestant princes, opted for peace with the Habsburgs on their terms, leaving France dangerously isolated and exposed?

Richelieu sent the Marquis de Feuquières to Germany with a mission to shore up Protestant Germany's resolve to counter the ambitions of Ferdinand. Good news first came when, under the leadership of Oxenstierna, the League of Heilbronn, on April 13, 1633, created a Protestant party in Germany. John George of Saxony, who was more interested in negotiating with Wallenstein, did not join the league. During his travels, the French envoy Feuquières also began some most secret talks with a member of Wallenstein's closest guard. Wallenstein had not forgotten the sour taste of his unceremonious ouster by Ferdinand in 1630. Feuquières reported to the cardinal that Wallenstein, provided the French would support his accession to Bohemia's throne, could easily become Ferdinand's implacable enemy.[41]

Next to require Cardinal Richelieu's attention in 1633 was Lorraine. Fickle Duc Charles IV was still a most unreliable neighbor. Notably, he helped the Spanish gather troops and fought the Swedish in Germany. After the Parlement of Paris declared that the duke's actions allowed France to annex the territories that had been at the center of the ongoing litigation, Louis and Cardinal Richelieu left Paris in the middle of the summer and once again moved toward Lorraine with their army. They nurtured wider ambitions than just the territories they disputed. When Marguerite, the wife of Gaston and sister of Charles, managed to flee Nancy disguised as a man and reach Brussels, Louis resolved to take Lorraine's capital. France's gradual takeover of Charles's estates and its building of a territorial and strategic barrier to the east had begun in earnest.[42]

The year 1634 saw even more French military conquests there.[43] By then, many Alsatian princes had placed themselves under French protection, widening and deepening this eastern front. Diplomatic efforts with Sweden continued to foster France's good relations in Protestant Germany and against the emperor. Chancellor Oxenstierna gathered a general assembly of Protestant powers in Frankfurt. The meeting ended up extending the terms of the League of Heilbronn to include, this time, John George of Saxony. It also formalized France's own participation in the deal, on May 9.

All these weighty concerns took a personal toll on the already feeble Richelieu. The cardinal was described by his first biographer, Aubery, as sleeping just for a few hours a night during his ministerial career, and often waking up in the middle of the night to dictate memoirs and letters to a secretary whose unique mission was to stand by at all hours. Reality was a little more prosaic. That nightly secretary's first role was that of a nurse tending to an aging man's miseries.[44] In October of 1633, and then in May of 1634, the anguishing symptoms of another bout of prostate problems came. The English ambassadors observed that the minister looked not only tired and fearful, but also very sad.[45]

For quite a while, Louis XIII had been the kind of concerned and attentive king that Richelieu needed to govern efficiently. Three years after the Day of the Dupes, however, the king fell again into one of those moods where he appeared withdrawn and disinterested. He spent most of those winter days hunting with even more ardor than usual. Back at his châteaus, at Anne's salon, his only concern was for a blond beauty in his wife's retinue, Marie de Hautefort.[46] The king had, unexpectedly, fallen in love with a woman. He spent most of his time with de Hautefort talking about the only matters he was versed in, hunting and making war. Sometimes he played his guitar, singing romantic songs he composed for her. The queen did not have much to fear from this liaison, all the more so since Mademoiselle de Hautefort seized any opportunity to decry the poor standing of Anne at court before the king. It led to an improbable situation where Louis was jealous of his wife: "The king expressed his passion to [Mlle de Hautefort] much more by lengthy and painful assiduousness and marks of his jealousy, than by the graces he bestowed on her," thought the memoirist La Rochefoucauld.[47] Once de Hautefort took the full measure of her influence on Louis, she boldly criticized the immense power of his principal minister and the consequences this had for so many at court, including her friend the queen.

If, in spite of the warm notes Louis often sent to Richelieu, a malaise existed between the king and the minister, it was surely confirmed once Wallenstein was assassinated, on February 25 of 1634.[48] Many signs indicated that the *generalissimo* had been ready to defect from the Habsburgs. When Swedish troops under the lead of Bernard of Saxe-Weimar began to ravage Bavaria in November of 1633, Wallenstein did not bother to move the enormous army Ferdinand sustained financially. Meanwhile he had been negotiating for peace with the Duke of Saxony. Vienna was losing patience, and hopes were rising in Paris. Wallenstein was an awkward man who surrounded himself with astrologers and lived in a world of dark ghosts. Emperor Ferdinand came to the conclusion that his general was a direct threat, and he issued a secret declaration of lèse-majesté, which encouraged his officers to kill him.[49] It was not so much the imperial "act of majesty" that shook Richelieu to his core as what Louis said when he heard the news. The king declared publicly that Ferdinand's victim had met the just fate of those servants who betray their master. The king, it seems, had forgotten the role his own minister played in this affair. "His Majesty must refrain from expressing such views candidly," Richelieu commented in extraordinarily rare public criticism. For him, the story was a vivid proof of how hard it is "for the good servant to completely trust his master." "This is all the more true when the servant has thousands who envy his glory, that so many enemies created by his service accuse him with thousands of unflattering words. It is all the more true when the mind of a prince is jealous, defiant, and credulous, and when he has the power to exert his ill will indiscriminately against him."[50]

The Venetian ambassador Giovanni Soranzo noticed that Cardinal Richelieu's attention to his own well-being verged on paranoia. But the cardinal's worries were not unfounded: he did have to fear assassins sent from Brussels. On September 22, 1633, a man named Alpheston had been broken on the wheel after confessing under torture that his mission was to eliminate the minister.[51] In October, the cardinal's secret police discovered yet another plot. Under the guise of conducting a negotiation with Richelieu, an impostor was to give him a letter drenched in poison.[52] To his already mighty corps of mounted guards, Richelieu added a company of one hundred musketeers. They wore the red tabard with a white cross and a trim of gold and silver. The palaces of the cardinal had been under high security for a long time. Now, wherever he was, in Rueil or on the road campaigning, the cardinal's men had to beat the countryside a mile around.

On September 5 and 6, 1634, a terrible and decisive battle took place near the Bavarian town of Nördlingen. In the Habsburg camp, two armies had just joined their forces. The King of Hungary, Ferdinand's oldest son, led the first one, which consisted of Wallenstein's former contingents. Don Juan of Austria, who was the younger brother of the Spanish king and Anne of Austria herself—he also went by the name Cardinal-Infant—had just taken the other one from Italy to Germany, across the Valtellina and right under the nose of the meager French battalions that guarded the valley. The move was in flagrant violation of a treaty signed in Cherasco between France and Spain, in the aftermath of the wars of northern Italy. Facing these imperial and Spanish corps were the Swedish army that General Gustav Karlsson Horn commanded, as well as the German army constituted by the League of Heilbronn, under the command of Bernard of Saxe-Weimar.

The King of Hungary besieged Nördlingen. The Protestant contingents of Horn and Saxe-Weimar tried to rescue it when the Cardinal-Infant arrived with reinforcements. Not only were the Protestant armies outnumbered at that point, but they also suffered from a lack of coordination between the chiefs and an unfavorable position on the field. General Horn, who left a good description of the battle, estimated that the final engagement lasted more than seven hours. At the end, twelve thousand men of the Protestant coalition lay dead on the ground. More than six thousand were taken prisoners, including Horn. It was an unmitigated catastrophe for Protestant Germany and a terrible setback for Richelieu. Imperial troops could now retake control of southern Germany. "It is the greatest military victory of our times," declared Olivares emphatically.[53]

A cry of desperation rose in Protestant Germany. It called for a direct French intervention now that the Leagues of Heilbronn and Frankfurt appeared useless and that many of its subscribers negotiated for peace. There was still a risk that the Dutch, in the face of such uncertainty, would decide to settle with Spain, thereby freeing Olivares to attack France from the Flemish front. The cardinal immediately called for a negotiation with the Swedes to define the terms of a more vigorous French commitment to their cause.[54] But these efforts went nowhere. Richelieu was still wary of directly engaging the Habsburgs, and the price he put was too high for Oxenstierna to accept it.

Over in Brussels, Gaston had grown disappointed with his mother, Marie de' Medici. She resented the deal he had signed after his last rebellion because it included nothing concerning her return to France. And to think that she had bankrolled the expedition with her dear jewels. There was more upset for the queen when she realized that Gaston's favorite, Puylaurens, had held talks with Richelieu. She made some overtures to come back, too. The king reacted favorably, but when he asked if she would agree to receive the cardinal's well wishes, she responded that she would rather still endure his persecutions. Mostly, she wanted to show her younger son that she could act alone as well. Eventually, Marie de' Medici took the full measure of her adversary's power and resources, and she decided to negotiate in earnest in February of 1634. It was too late. The trial of her collaborators such as the polemicist Mathieu de Morgues or the dangerous priest Jacques Chanteloube—a man behind the assassination attempts of 1633—was now the price of her return.[55] Richelieu wrote the queen a well-crafted letter to affirm his desire to see her again. On the same day, however, he also wrote to Marie's confessor, Father Suffren, to stand firm on the conditions for the queen mother's return to France. Mindful that his enemies always questioned his motives, he added, "If someone falsely tells you that [these conditions] are a pretext to make this arrangement impossible, I do affirm before God that what I am telling is sincere."[56]

The defeat of the Protestant coalition at Nördlingen precipitated everything in this family situation. Since the death of Infanta Isabella in December of 1633, the new Spanish representative in the Spanish Netherlands was Francisco de Moncada, Marquis d'Aytona, who viewed the French expatriates with suspicion. The people of Brussels found the French expatriates' frolicking no more amusing. After the battle at Nördlingen, they demanded displays of pro-Habsburg fervor. Gaston could not show support, for, as his contemporary biographer Jean Lasséré explained, he had seemingly rediscovered his patriotic fiber.

On October 8, 1634, the heir to the French throne left his Brussels residence pretending he would be spending the day fox hunting. An eighteen-hour horseback ride took him and a few of his men to the nearest French stronghold, La Capelle.[57] It was the middle of night. "C'est Monsieur frère du Roi!" responded Gaston's men to the startled sentinels who asked for the visitor's identity. The governor, in high alert, ascended the walls of the fort and asked again who was there before he let Gaston in. No one had said good-bye to Marie de' Medici and Marguerite de Lorraine before leaving Brussels, not even Gaston.

The French treasury paid off all of Gaston's debts, including those in the Spanish Netherlands.[58] Some provisions concerned his marriage, because at the king's request, the Paris Parlement had declared the union invalid from a royal constitutional point of view.[59] The French clergy still had to pronounce its opinion on the matter. To facilitate Gaston's return, all parties agreed that the parlement's verdict would stand but that the Crown would never try to force him into another marriage. Finally, Richelieu promised Puylaurens, who had made the deal possible, the hand of one of his relatives, a duchy, and a hefty sum of money.

On October 21, 1634, around two o'clock, Gaston's carriage pulled into the courtyard at Saint-Germain-en-Laye. Crowds of courtiers stood riveted. Many had doubted that a return of the prodigal brother could ever occur after four years of exile. Louis received Gaston and his entourage in his private apartment, surrounded by the most prominent nobility of the kingdom. According to the official description of the event, the prince bowed as low as he could before his brother the king and said, "Monsieur, I do not know if I am left speechless because of fear or joy, so all I am left to do is to ask forgiveness for what happened."

The two brothers embraced three times, said the account.

"My brother, I have forgiven you, let us not talk about the past any longer, but let us talk, instead, of the great joy I have to see you here," responded Louis while he led Gaston toward his study.

Richelieu arrived from Rueil shortly after. He told the prince that his biggest regret lately had been the impossibility of serving him as he wished. The rest of the conversation was cordial, although the cardinal did tell the prince half jokingly that he hoped he would not patronize places of ill repute anymore and stop his cursing and blasphemy.

Following that, the king said, "Monsieur, I pray for you to love Monsieur le Cardinal."

"Monsieur, I shall love him like myself, and I declare my resolve to follow his advice," responded Gaston.[60]

Gaston held his luncheon in public, before a huge crowd. Then he went to salute Anne of Austria. The day after, the cardinal paid his own respects by hosting Gaston at Rueil with a splendid meal and a concert. The ever-present guards of the cardinal, for once, lay down their arms instead of hiding them under their coats.[61]

The cardinal showed again his entertaining talents when, on November 11, the newly titled Duc de Puylaurens married his niece Mademoiselle de Pontchâteau during a day of festivities. Cardinal Richelieu counted on Puylaurens's

Armand-Jean du Plessis, Cardinal Richelieu by Philippe de Champaigne.

Louis XIII as a Boy by Frans Pourbus the Younger.

Louis XIII by Philippe de Champaigne.

Marie de' Medici by Peter Paul Rubens.

Gaston d'Orléans by Anthony van Dyck.

Anne of Austria by Peter Paul Rubens.

Louis XIII, Anne of Austria, and Cardinal Richelieu at the Theater of the Palais-Cardinal in 1641 (Ballet de la Prospérité des armes de France) by Juste d'Egmont.

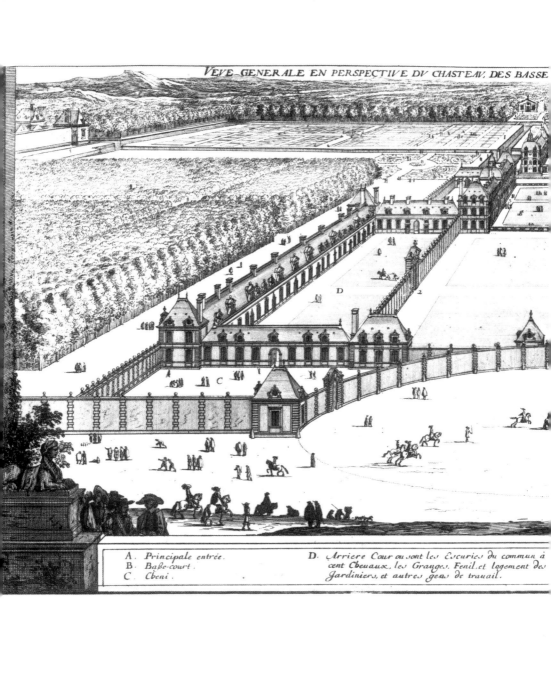

VEVE GENERALE EN PERSPECTIVE DV CHASTEAV DES BASSE

A. Principale entrée.
B. Basse-court.
C. Cheni.

D. Arriere Cour ou sont les Escuries du commun à
cent Cheuaux, les Granges, Fenil, et logement des
Jardiniers, et autres gens de trauail.

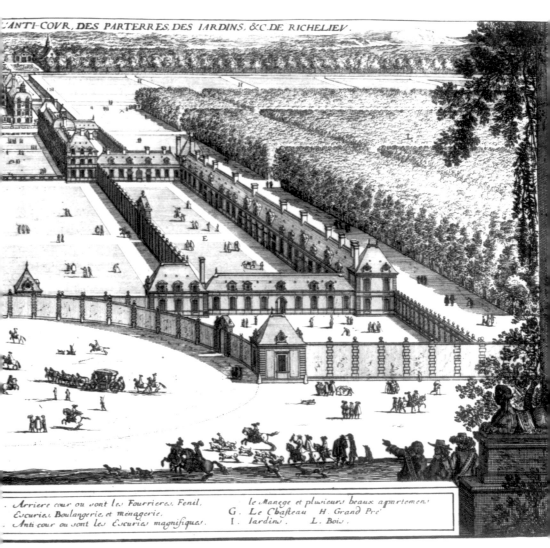

ANTI-COVR, DES PARTERRES, DES IARDINS, &C. DE RICHELIEV.

Arriere cour ou sont les Fourrieres, Fenil.   le Manege et plusieurs beaux apartemens.
Escuries, Boulangerie, et ménagerie.   G. Le Chasteau   H. Grand Pré
Anti-cour ou sont les Escuries magnifiques.   I. Iardins.   L. Bois.

View of the Château and Gardens of Richelieu by Jean Marot.

The Marquis de Cinq-Mars by an unknown artist.

cooperation to dissolve Gaston's marriage with Marguerite de Lorraine, a vivid testimonial of disregard for the king's authority. Court gossip also said that he had long been nurturing the idea of giving the prince the hand of his niece Madame de Combalet. But soon it appeared that Gaston's friend had lost interest in the cause. Worse still, Richelieu suspected him of keeping contacts with Brussels. When Richelieu learned that before leaving the Spanish Netherlands, Gaston had secretly written to Pope Urban VIII to inform him that any petition he should write on dissolving his marriage would have been written under duress, Richelieu considered this as the last straw in Puylaurens's insolence.[62]

The arrest of Puylaurens took place in early February 1635, during Carnival. Louis invited his brother to the Louvre to participate in the rehearsal of a ballet: "I placed you, as you can imagine, as the leading man in a group of the best dancers, and have not forgotten the Duc de Puylaurens. Should you want to come and claim your rightful place in this ballet, the man who loves and will always love you will greet you like the child of the house that you are."[63] The ballet in question, titled *De la vieille cour* (Of the old court), was in the style Louis favored, with a burlesque and fantastic atmosphere. It featured the ghosts of deceased courtiers. The king was seen dancing dressed up as an old woman, and the printed program described the whole show as a "representation of human vicissitudes, which continual-movement dance symbolizes best."[64] Puylaurens was caught just as he arrived at the Louvre for the rehearsal.[65] The guards took him to the dungeon at Vincennes. They blocked the window of the cell to make it even darker. The duke had brought some novels. The guards promptly replaced them with books of devotion, which he could barely read anyway because he only had one candle. When it dawned on him that he was in the very same place where first d'Ornano and then one of Louis's Vendôme half brothers had died after a few months of incarceration, the usually calm Puylaurens broke down. He lasted seven and half months before he too died of illness. Madame de Rambouillet, the famous *salonnière*, commented that this infamous cell "was worth its weight in arsenic."[66]

A few days after the arrest, and after a meeting when their relations seemed to be at their most cordial, Richelieu wrote a short note to his master: "These three lines to tell Your Majesty that the honor of his conversation yesterday made me sleep without interruption until seven in the morning, which indeed lets one know that the mind's content is the best medicine there is for delicate bodies."[67] Indeed, Richelieu had some energy and initiative. He took over the management of Gaston's household and sent more of his courtiers to jail, to be replaced with loyal men.[68] The prince did not protest. The night of his favorite's arrest, he had danced until the wee hours at the Louvre with the whole court.

Should Louis have spared his marks of trust and affection, Richelieu still had another type of distraction to rely on, the theater, an art form which naturally took its place in his general interest for the art of eloquence.[69] The cardinal was a fine speaker and writer himself, and his own French was simple, measured, and elegant—in contrast to Louis's rather plain elocution. The minister always kept near him a witty and eloquent companion named François Le Métel de Boisrobert, whose agile conversation and bons mots were an antidote to the bouts of melancholia that clouded his mind. In January of 1635, at the behest of his minister, Louis XIII authorized the Académie Française.[70] The mission of this body was to cultivate the purity and elegance of the French language so as to make it the modern equivalent of Latin. This way, language could become a cement of national unity, and furthermore, a way to showcase the je ne sais quoi of exquisite urbanity that charmed visitors to Paris, and to Cardinal Richelieu's own palaces. Theater, though, showcased the art of eloquence as a total spectacle, with visuals and music, and that color exerted an even greater appeal on the cardinal.

Sixteen thirty-five was truly the year when the stage became his passion. For centuries, the Church had condemned playwrights and actors as evildoers. These times were long gone. Louis XIII offered his patronage to three groups of comedians, and Richelieu organized more and more sophisticated spectacles. In early March of 1635, at the Arsenal where he stayed in Paris because of renovations needed to expand the buildings and gardens of the Palais-Cardinal, Richelieu invited Anne to a show titled *La Comédie des Tuileries*. A team of five writers, including the famed author Pierre Corneille, wrote the play. What few knew at the time was that Richelieu himself had provided the subject and canvas for the story, with a strict order not to reveal his contribution. The play was a romantic comedy where young love faces the social imperatives that their parents represent. The ending managed to satisfy everyone—it was meant, after all, as lighthearted entertainment.

On February 8, 1635, the French renewed their treaty with the Dutch Republic.[71] At the same time, their enemies made some bold moves of their own.

On March 26, Habsburg troops attacked an essential French ally on the Rhine front, the Elector of Trier, and took him prisoner. Following this, the emperor engaged in a process of reconciliation with the German Protestant princes, notably John George of Saxony, by which he agreed to suspend the Edict of Restitution.[72] There was action on the northern front, too, when Christine of Savoy's brother-in-law, Thomas, joined a gathering Spanish army in March.[73] This army could have been a response to the Dutch renewed commitment toward France, but it could also have been a direct threat to the kingdom. Richelieu ordered the Duc de Rohan, in exile in Venice ever since the Peace of Alais, back into service. The duke's mission was to intervene in the Valtellina and restore French authority over the passage, which he did brilliantly at the end of March.

Once again, Cardinal Richelieu and Louis XIII were at a crossroads for France's fate on the continent. The king, always the warrior at heart, wanted to wage war against the Habsburgs ever since the defeat at Nördlingen.[74] For Richelieu, war first had to be envisaged in a moral and religious perspective. His writings show that he was deeply aware of the misery it brought, and of the canonical teachings on the subject, such as those of Thomas Aquinas, who wrote that wars had to be justified. War was a decision that even the cardinal could not base on sheer political motives. The kidnapping of the Elector of Trier, however, did justify armed conflict as a means to extract the most favorable conditions in a general settlement of European affairs.

Concretely, launching France in an armed conflict was not a decision Richelieu could take lightly either. The seventeenth century is often cited as a time of rationalization in the art of warfare. But in Richelieu's time, these changes merely concerned the armies of a few countries such as the Dutch Republic or Sweden. For the French, warfare was still very much thought of as the art of laying siege rather than open combat. Even after waging successful campaigns at La Rochelle and in Italy, the concept of an efficient nationwide army did not exist. A considerable number of soldiers the cardinal could use were mercenaries who, except for a few elite regiments of veterans, had little sense of loyalty. The cavalry was disorganized and lacked discipline. There were few French commanders, in fact, who knew the art of war, how to place their troops for combat and prepare them by drills. The cardinal often divided the responsibilities of a post between chiefs so as to encourage mutual surveillance. The strategy led the prickly nobles in the military to waste time and opportunities in frivolous disputes of honor.[75] Arms and ammunitions were old-fashioned, expensive, and rare, especially cannons, because the French produced few of them. Barracks or military hospitals were nonexistent. Money to pay all these troops was often lacking, prompting the officers who raised them and were in charge of their livelihood to let the recruits live off the lands where they were stationed, even if that was at the expense of the peasantry and tax revenues. Armies, then, invariably came with a cortege of "peasant girls dragged from plundered farms, children kidnapped for ransom and forgotten, hawkers, tricksters, quacks and vagabonds."[76] Last but not least in the cardinal's sober assessment of what handicapped his chances of success was what he called "the natural whimsy" of the French nation.[77]

Yet Richelieu kept on securing his alliances. Chancellor Oxenstierna arrived at Compiègne in April to finally bring the Franco-Swedish talks to fruition with a treaty signed on April 28, 1635. France could now count on a reliable army should it need to defend itself in Germany. Bernard of Saxe-Weimar, the capable man of war who had been one of Gustavus Adolphus's generals and now turned into a military entrepreneur of his own, led these troops.

In this time of rising tension, and whenever he was not in Paris for an official event or a play, Richelieu spent most of his time at Rueil. He loved to wander in the estate's beautiful gardens, with his friend Father Joseph and just a few guards, far from all his worries, along the majestic central allée and the porticos, by the reflecting pools, the waterworks, and the great cascade.[78] Springtime brought back his favorite kind of tulips, a special breed in violet and white. Courtiers clamored for his presence in Paris, the grandees waited in his antechambers, but Richelieu insisted on keeping his time for leisure. Secrecy, after all, adds mystique to power.[79]

CHAPTER 8

War (1635–1637)

I N   T H E   B U S Y   M O R N I N G   H O U R S   O F   May 19, 1635, the guards at Brussels's Hau gate witnessed a curious spectacle. A proud-looking man arrived on horseback, wearing a maroon coat decorated with a gold motif of French lilies, and a wide black velvet cap. He held a blue baton, also decorated with a motif of lilies. Next to him was a drummer, on horseback as well, who beat his instrument before the gate. Once the drumbeat stopped, the first horseman shouted solemnly that he was Louis XIII's herald and that he carried a message for the Cardinal-Infant, the brother of the Spanish king. The puzzled guards sent out for instructions. After a while, the two Frenchmen were let inside the city and taken to a house, where they waited for several hours. But the Spanish mistook them for impostors, and the envoy, Jean Gratiolet, charged back to France with his drummer once he understood that nobody wanted to see him. Before crossing back over the border, however, he nailed a formal declaration of war on a pole as his companion beat the drum again.[1]

And so, in the wake of what was in essence a German religious and civil conflict, the long awaited, great pan-European war between France and the Habsburgs began with an old-fashioned ritual that Richelieu had resuscitated as a publicity stunt.[2] The cardinal insisted that war had to be justified by an overt attack from the enemy. Yet war was not an ordeal in the medieval sense of the term, for once war was deemed appropriate it did serve political ends. The point was to push the Habsburgs into a negotiated settlement that would resolve the conflict to France's best advantage. It would, indeed, thus laying the foundations of modern Europe. But, in truth, Gratiolet's emphatic declaration of war against Spain fell a bit flat.

In Richelieu's strategy, the French and Dutch were to combine forces and shock the Spanish Netherlands. Short on military resources and preparations, he thought a blitz was the soultion. War against the Dutch had exhausted the Spanish territory. Ever since the death of Infanta Isabella on December 1, 1633, and the end of the semiautonomous rule that her reign guaranteed, the local population felt increasingly dissatisfied with its Spanish rulers. It was for this reason that the cardinal opened hostilities only with Spain. He thought he could compartmentalize the conflict, strike audaciously, and overwhelm the Habsburgs.

Led by Gaspard III de Coligny, Maréchal de Châtillon, and Urbain, Maréchal de Maillé-Brézé—the latter was the husband of Richelieu's sister Nicole—French battalions of twenty-two thousand soldiers and four thousand horsemen entered the Spanish Netherlands to face the smaller armies of Prince Thomas of Savoy. The clash happened in Avein, on May 22, just a few days after the herald left Brussels. A resounding French success, this battle left five thousand enemy soldiers dead on the field and spread tales of French fury all around Europe. Te Deum hymns rose everywhere.

What followed this hopeful opening, however, turned out to be a catastrophe. After their success in Avein, the French joined in with the army led by Frederick of Nassau and headed for Brussels. The two French chiefs had begun to bicker, which in turn led to difficulties with the Dutch. When the coalition army took Tirlemont, the situation got out of control. Soldiers pillaged the city and committed atrocious acts of violence, burning hospitals down while the sick were still inside, desecrating convents, and raping nuns. The population of the Spanish Netherlands, on whom Cardinal Richelieu counted so much in his war effort, turned against the coalition instead of supporting it. With Brussels now too much of a difficult target, the coalition's chiefs set their sight on Louvain and laid siege on June 25, which proved impossible. This failed attempt revealed the deep flaws in the French army and, ultimately, lack of real stamina in the lower ranks of the fighting nobility. Sickness broke out. The early advantage of the French was completely reversed.

Richelieu, who had advised Louis against joining the fight in person, had to suffer the king's irritation.[3] The symptoms of prostate ailments returned to further undermine his morale. Louis wrote to wish him well. His minister, in reply, told him that his condition prevented him from traveling, and that this cast doubt on his capacity to serve. "If so far I have been deemed a diamond, right now I see myself as one of those diamonds from Alençon, which are actually barely harder than common glass," he wrote from Rueil.[4] Characteristically, this was both a sincere recognition of the difficulty of his task and a way to shore up Louis's support by evoking the possibility of a retirement.

By the end of the summer, other military upsets worsened the cardinal's dissatisfaction. While some contingents fought in the Spanish Netherlands, the French armies in Lorraine and Alsace waged war against imperial troops led, notably, by Duc Charles. The situation in occupied Lorraine was particularly worrisome, because the duke kept conducting raids in his native lands, where the population received him well. Louis himself decided to tackle this menace and announced his intention to join the campaign. The cardinal, now immobilized by illness, was even less inclined to let the king go than he had been at the beginning of the war. He opposed the project. Quarrels ensued. This time, however, Louis ignored his minister. He called for a general raising of the lower orders of the French nobility and left for Lorraine on August 23, in the company of two of Richelieu's most trusted men, Surintendant Claude Bouthillier and his son Léon, Comte de Chavigny, who was secretary of state.

The two minders had little good to write about in the following weeks. In Châlons, where he was supposed to meet his gathering troops, Louis found just a few men, no money, and no supplies. Richelieu's administration was not enough to carry out his carefully laid plans. Louis thought his minister had purposely created this sorry state of affairs to discourage him from joining his army, and he wrote a mean-spirited letter to voice his displeasure. Richelieu kept his cool: "Your Majesty is too kind not to accept that an old, faithful, and privy servant should take the liberty to say, with all due respect, that if he keeps thinking that the intentions of his most assured creatures do not correspond to what they profess, they should so much fear his suspicions, that it would become difficult to serve him as they wish in the future."[5] The king apologized and even begged him to burn the letter. The army's disorganization persisted, and the mutual defiance continued, leading the Bouthilliers to write about the king's digestive problems, twitchy agitation, somber face, and high body temperature.[6] At last, Louis gathered a decent contingent, some supplies, and reached Saint-Mihiel, one of Duc Charles's possessions. After a short siege he entered the town on October 3. The confidential news from the camp still described the king as devoured by "such a cutting melancholia that it gives His Majesty bloating of the belly and attacks of gout; any positive news one could give him would only serve to make him more sick."[7] Making matters worse, Charles of Lorraine remained undaunted. Most of the nobles Louis had brought with him had never been at war before, and they thought that conflicts between princes were settled like the brawls in their backwater provinces. They quickly disbanded, leaving behind the bountiful Lorraine in the ravaged state that the master-engraver Jacques Callot presented in gruesome images, the *Misères de la guerre*.

A dispirited Louis made his way back to Saint-Germain-en-Laye to meet a minister he could hardly trust wholeheartedly anymore. Other news added to the cardinal's vexation. The King of France had signed on July 11 the Treaty of Rivoli with the Dukes of Savoy, of Parma, and of Mantua, to strike at the heart of Spanish possessions in the Milan area, but this ambitious project yielded nothing significant. In mid-September, the Spanish fleet took a key strategic post on the Mediterranean, the islands of Lérins in the Bay of Cannes. In northern Europe, Swedish troops under General Johan Baner were ravaging Saxony in a protracted fight with John George's army. The only sources of hope in this underwhelming military tableau were Rohan's strong position in the Valtellina and the signing of another treaty with Bernard of Saxe-Weimar, which guaranteed that the duke would fight for the French on German soil.[8]

The overall sorry state of affairs called for the finance minister Claude de Bullion to take bold, if not risky and desperate, measures. The finances of the kingdom, ever catastrophic in spite of a manyfold increase in the main tax on peasants, necessitated the creation and selling of offices, and inventing all sorts of fiscal acrobatics, including a devaluing of the main currency, the *livre tournois*. Mindful that disorganization had weighed heavily in the year's setbacks, the cardinal-minister restructured the cavalry into regiments to improve its discipline and efficiency. He dispatched royal officers—called intendants—with great powers to control provincial fiscal administrations, and also to manage the logistics of the army and maintain the rule of law among soldiers, even if that put the monarchy at risk of a clash with those local powers and the aristocratic military leaders. These intendants were able to communicate more rapidly thanks to a new network of postal relays.

Last but not least, Richelieu confronted Marie de' Medici again. The queen, in a letter she placed in the care of Nuncio Mazarini—he was in France in a new capacity as nuncio extraordinaire, after he became a priest to pursue a career for the pope—urged Louis with much motherly pathos to save his soul by stopping a war that brought suffering to his people. Richelieu read the letter himself in spite of the queen's precaution in sending it to the nuncio, since Mazarini was entirely loyal to him. He advised the king not to respond in person.[9]

Sometimes Louis came from Saint-Germain or Versailles to hold his council at Reuil because Richelieu was ailing. Courtiers, however, noted that although Richelieu's health was certainly poor, he never missed his walks in his gardens. It seemed that the cardinal wanted to stay as close as he could to his companies of guards. Once in a while he did go to see the king in one of his châteaus, always unannounced.[10] Whatever Richelieu actually feared, it seemed to wear him out. The ambassadors found his complexion waxy and his face showing "great travails of the soul."

Fortunately for Richelieu, he was able to pursue his passion for building and the theater. In May of 1635, he laid the first stone for the chapel at the Sorbonne, which was designed by the architect of his country house and town, Jacques Lemercier. Work at his château in Richelieu was also now well under way. The central wing stood proudly. It featured, right above the entry door, two famous statues of slaves by Michelangelo. Formerly the property of Henri de Montmorency, the duke had given them to the cardinal to obtain mercy for his family after his execution. To further enlarge his duchy, Richelieu obtained from Gaston the nearby domain of the prestigious Montpensier family and managed to raze the château at the prince's own expense. Even the magnificent gothic church where the generations of Montpensiers rested would be destroyed. After the pope intervened, the cardinal only reluctantly agreed to keep the church. In the town, the cardinal had offered free lots to those who agreed to build rich townhouses on the main street. A blueprint provided by Lemercier ensured the perfect harmony and symmetry of the urban landscape. To Richelieu's great annoyance, the few who bought houses were his own courtiers, who had no intention to live in Poitou. The town began to look eerily empty.

On February 19, 1636, at the Palais-Cardinal, Richelieu entertained the Duke of Parma, who was visiting France to strategize how to fight the Spanish armies that occupied his territories. Italian aristocrats were fine connoisseurs of the dramatic arts, so the cardinal was eager to showcase what the

French could do. He treated his guest and the court to a comedy titled *Aspasie*, the work of Desmarets de Saint-Sorlin, an author who had become a favorite companion during leisure. (The cardinal found the hall he used as a theater quite small for his dramatic ambitions. He later ordered plans for a brand-new one in his Parisian palace.) Richelieu then took the duke to two buffets, one where everything, including the food, shined like silver, and another where all was gold.

For the campaign of 1636, Richelieu launched the full brunt of the French attack on the eastern war front. The cardinal-minister told the papal nuncio that war was still a necessary step toward lasting peace, even if it brought immense suffering for the population.[11] The overall goal was to secure those positions along the Rhine and in Alsace that were already under French control and then gain some more. Also part of this strategy was a takeover of the Franche-Comté. This region was a Habsburg territory that observed neutrality in the conflicts between the House of Austria and the French Bourbons. The cardinal, however, saw it as another key position to set a barrier between the Spanish Netherlands and northern Italy. Richelieu gave Condé the command of an army, and, by May 29, 1636, the prince laid siege to the town of Dole. The besieged put up a stubborn resistance. Even the new firebombs used by the French could not scare the small town. In the north, at the border with the Spanish Netherlands, Prince Thomas of Savoy gathered a mighty army by quickly adding to his troops some imperial contingents brought by Piccolomini, other ones from the Catholic League commanded by Jean de Werth, and even soldiers from the armies of Charles of Lorraine.

The terrible Spanish invasion of 1636 began. The French strongholds that defended Picardy to the north of Paris were structurally weak and ill equipped. François Sublet de Noyers's mission as secretary of state for war was to reinforce those positions, but the task was herculean. Richelieu's cousin, the grand master of the artillery Charles de La Meilleraye, had the equally impossible task of arming those forts. On July 9, the fort of La Capelle near the border with the Spanish Netherlands fell first. Cardinal Richelieu was left scrambling to organize a defense. He wrote frantically to Maréchal de Maillé-Brézé to fortify the last defense post before the capital at all costs: "It is most important to provide for Corbie, for this is the weakest place on the Somme river and the one most likely target after Le Catelet."[12] Indeed, the stakes at Corbie became crucial when Le Catelet fell two weeks after the invasion began. The soldiers of these almost defenseless places gave up their position without any resistance. The small army of Champagne led by the Comte Louis de Soissons—Condé's cousin and son of the rebel countess made famous during the wars between mother and son—could do little to rescue them. Making matters worse was the usual jealousy between commanders.[13] Pandemonium overtook Paris when bad news from Le Catelet and tales of destruction and savagery came in from Picardy's villages. The road from Paris to Orléans became one long line of carts wobbling under the weight of baggage.

Louis XIII's leadership at this time was exemplary. On the afternoon of August 4, he summoned to the Louvre his council, some high-ranking military officers, a delegation from the parlement, and the city's provost of merchants. By the end of the day, Paris heard a drumbeat. It called on able men to join an emergency corps and for all subjects to donate money, horses, and equipment. The day after, representatives from all trade guilds appeared before the sovereign in the Grande Galerie at the Louvre. They promised unwavering support in touching scenes of devotion. Distressing news of the enemy's advance and ravages kept coming in a steady stream, however. Thomas's armies had just crossed the river Somme, which was as much a strategic goal as it was a psychological threshold. The horsemen of Jean de Werth's much-feared Croatian cavalry came to scout near Pontoise. Some Parisians claimed they could see them from Montmartre.

If Louis needed to act, it was because his minister could not. Contemporary memoirs and diplomatic reports show that the invasion caused Richelieu to fall into the kind of deep despair he had known many times in the past, and this time, it was debilitating. Even in the midst of the parlement's sessions, people openly expressed anger. Was he not the one who wanted this risky and expensive war when a larger part of the population lived so poorly? Had he not spent millions to make his own strongholds on the Atlantic showcases for military defense while leaving the more important north defenseless? Had he not hastened the demolition of Paris's walls to lay out immense gardens at the Palais-Cardinal? Mostly, though, Richelieu must have feared the king's reprobation.

Father Joseph, the companion of so many adventures, saved him this time. Seeing how the cardinal was in imminent danger, he shook him out of his depressive torpor with pointed words: "Do you think your weakness is going to call divine mercy upon you? Is it not more a means to excite the wrath of God and inflame his vengeance?"[14]

Cardinal Richelieu recovered his courage and stood up. For good form he again offered Louis his resignation, which the king refused, and he announced that he would fight by his side. Then he left his palace and went to meet the frightened and infuriated Parisians. He took no menacing squads of muske-teers armed to the teeth, no armored carriage. He just went out in a simple ve-hicle and with only a couple of men. His closest confidants begged him to stay and not to endanger his life so recklessly. Richelieu ignored them and visited, of all places, the Pont-Neuf. The memoirist Fontenay-Mareuil described the scene: "The streets were so full of people that one could barely circulate, and all were so animated that they only spoke of killing [the cardinal]. As soon as they saw him approach, either they shut up, or they prayed to God to make his trip successful."[15]

The king and the minister's first moves to reclaim France's north were to secure the bridges on the river Oise. On August 15, 1636, the long-dreaded news of Corbie's fall arrived, followed by that of Roye's. Richelieu recalled Condé's troops that still labored to take Dole in Franche-Comté. More help came from the Loire. Gaston had been quiet in Blois, dedicating himself to the good life, even though an assembly of the French clergy had declared his mar-riage to Marguerite de Lorraine null at Richelieu's request.[16] With diligence, the prince mustered all the men of his nobility. The volunteer army ended up counting about twelve thousand recruits. Louis and Cardinal Richelieu left Paris in the first days of September after giving the command of the army to Gaston, ordering the capital to reinforce its defenses, and forbidding the sale of bread at a higher price. Perhaps there were a few too many feathers and fancy ribbons on the uniforms of the improvised army for anyone to be utterly con-vinced that it could halt the progress of the rapidly advancing Spanish troops, yet Gaston quickly went to reclaim the town of Roye.

What Richelieu needed was another stroke of luck. It came. After hearing the news of an imminent Dutch attack in the northern Spanish Netherlands, the Spanish army suddenly retreated toward Belgium, leaving garrisons in all the posts they had seized, including about three thousand men in Corbie. Gaston, who had been chasing more enemies from the south of Picardy, set his sight on the town. Corbie lay in the midst of a network of small rivers and canals. The best option to retake it, it seemed, was a blockade. Another consideration was the king's reputation, which had already suffered so much that failing to take the city by force had to be avoided at all costs. Corbie's siege began on

September 9. Eventually, Louis took command away from Gaston, leaving his brother, once again, denied the full reward of glory in victory. Over the next few weeks, and even though he had relapsed into a state of melancholia and irritability, Louis rode tirelessly to supervise the siege. Work on a circular line of defense began. Dams were built so that entire fields could flood at will. These works prevented both an excursion from the besieged city and a rescue operation from the north, from which the Cardinal-Infant, Prince Thomas, Piccolomini, and de Werth could attack again. Conditions were dreadful. The enemies had burned down most of the surrounding villages and ruined the wells by throwing dead horses in them. Illness quickly mounted.

Richelieu stayed in Amiens, where he established a general command center. He ordered the making of bread for the troops and the delivery of oats and fodder by sea. With winter fast approaching, he enrolled carpenters and bought tools so that the best troops would have cover when the weather turned inclement. Sometimes he went to visit the defense works. Back at his desk, he tried to shore up his reputation as much as he could. "His Majesty's design can only be realized if extraordinary care is used, and also with much money, of which there is little in abundance. Care there is plenty of, however, or at least according to me. There shall be no sparing of work as far as Your Majesty's closest servants are concerned."[17] Last but not least, Richelieu made sure to punish the governor of Corbie, Soyécourt, for dereliction of duty. The cardinal, even when a stronghold was ill equipped, expected its officers to fight until death.[18] Jurists applied the Roman sentence of death for cowardice, and Soyécourt had to escape to England.

On the eastern front, after Condé left the Franche-Comté to rescue Picardy, General Matthias Gallas and Charles de Lorraine joined forces to form a fifty-thousand man army and prey on Burgundy. They laid siege to the small town of Saint-Jean-de-Losne, toward the end of October, hoping to establish a base for future incursions into France. Saint-Jean put up a strong defense. This respite for Richelieu was short-lived. Soon the Spanish fleet would act in the south. Not content with holding the key Mediterranean post on the islands of Lérins, the Spanish sought another advantage on the seas by making an incursion on the southern Atlantic coast, seizing the port of Saint-Jean-de-Luz and going so far as to menace Bayonne.

By the end of October, in spite of his best efforts, Richelieu began to doubt that Corbie would surrender anytime soon. Reports came that the Spanish governor of the place had died and that food was becoming dramatically scarce inside. In spite of many false alarms, an enemy rescue failed to materialize after Gallas's unsuccessful campaign in Burgundy. But one could never be sure that the French volunteer army would not disband with the cold weather's onset, and so, even though the Comte de Soissons would have rather kept up the blockade, Richelieu advised the king to change the method and to take Corbie by force. Louis agreed to the change in strategy. On November 5, soldiers began to dig trenches to reach Corbie's walls and place mines under them. Cannon fire battered the city. In the end, full force was unnecessary. The garrison at Corbie capitulated on November 10. The *Gazette de France* duly published the news and highlighted how the bold decisions by the cardinal, "whose solid judgment cannot be underestimated," had brought an end to the 1636 Spanish invasion of France.[19]

Strange news kept Louis and Cardinal Richelieu from fully rejoicing. Gaston and the Comte de Soissons had ridden out of Paris in a storm, so quickly in fact that they had left their baggage behind. Gaston went to Blois, while Soissons went to the fortress of Sedan, just outside France, in the Ardennes. Eventually, the two justified their quick exit by insisting that they had been subject to a harassing climate of suspicion.

Back at Rueil, the autumn delights in his gardens could hardly distract Richelieu from the stark reality of the situation of France. Devastated were Picardy and Burgundy. The attack on Franche-Comté had pushed the emperor to declare war openly. With a faltering war machine, pamphlets railed against him. The superintendent of finances was, as ever, desperate.[20] During the siege of Corbie, Father Joseph had spoken of an alchemist called Dubois who claimed that he could turn lead into gold. The cardinal gave the man a chance, providing for a comfortable place to work and all the resources necessary. Predictably, Dubois failed to produce the precious metal, and Richelieu had him executed for sorcery on short order. In light of this, some historians make much of the cardinal's earlier interest in the infamous sorcery trial of Urbain Grandier, in Loudun.[21] Surely Richelieu believed in the devil, but does that mean that he thought humans could channel occult forces? Based on his writings and actions, the cardinal did not come across as a believer in the presence of supernatural forces. He did not seem to have had an intense religiosity, let alone mystical tendencies. He celebrated mass on religious holidays or on special occasions, but his days were so busy that the pope had to give him special permission to recite a shorter version of the breviary.

What one can say about the infamous year of Corbie is that it gave Cardinal Richelieu a stronger sense of his faith: "Having in all things a general trust in God is a much better cure than all of the occult remedies of the world," wrote Richelieu just a few days before Dubois's death, in a letter to Chavigny where he described the difficulties of the siege.[22] In July, as he understood that the Spanish were on the verge of invading Picardy, he gave the religious order of the Calvairiennes a large sum of money, with a request that they keep a votive lamp at all times before the altar of their church, and celebrate a special mass every Saturday for his sake. In the midst of his despair, while Paris clamored for his head, he promised Father Joseph that he would confess and take communion more often. This is also when the cardinal began to compose another work of devotion, the *Treatise on a Christian's Perfection*. This work simply and accessibly explained why and how the ends of the human being are in God. Here was the Richelieu of good practical sense, the man with strong willpower and faith in reason, who thought that God bestows his grace on those who act in the world. "Every Christian," he wrote, "must adapt his devotional practices to his own condition, and not its condition to certain spiritual rules. Otherwise these rules, because they are not proportionate to the life of the one who wishes to practice such rules, will be like grafts of one excellent plant put on another plant of an entirely different nature: they shall die instead of bearing fruit."[23]

Despite all his weighty concerns after the Spanish invasion of 1636, Cardinal Richelieu's newfound passion for the theater was still very much alive, and the splendid show he mounted for the Carnival of 1637, *La Grande Pastorale*, saw him involved at every step.[24] First, he composed five hundred verses for the play. Then he opted for a grand production with all kinds of special effects. Before a dazzled audience that included the king, Anne of Austria, and the papal nuncio, one beautiful set succeeded another. At one point in the story, a storm breaks out, simulated on stage by a rain of sugar-coated anise seeds and bonbons, and fountains of perfumed water.[25] News of these festivities as sycophantically narrated by the *Gazette de France* left Parisians angry. A famous anti-Richelieu pamphlet of the time, *La Miliade*, evokes bitingly how Richelieu entertained his passion for the theater while he asked so many sacrifices from Louis's subjects.

Il trace une pièce nouvelle	He writes a new play
Quand on emporte La Capelle	When La Capelle is taken down
Et consulte encore Boisrobert	And also looks to Boisrobert
Quand une province se perd.	When a province is lost.[26]

Pursuing leisure was all the more imperative in the spring of 1637, because, in addition to preparing for a new war campaign, the cardinal faced the return of poisonous palace intrigues and a string of scandals. The king had a new favorite, a sixteen-year-old brunette named Louise-Angélique Motier de La Fayette. She, too, was one of Anne's ladies. Having tired of how Mademoiselle de Hautefort undermined his authority, Richelieu had instructed all his devotees at court to bring the king's attention to La Fayette's sweetness and moral purity. Louis was smitten, and La Fayette accepted his homage. But then, just like her predecessor, the new favorite began to undermine the authority of the minister. It was common knowledge at court that La Fayette's religious devotion prompted her to openly question the alliances that Louis made with Protestant princes and the rigid determination with which he kept his mother in exile. Through the reports of his spies, Richelieu became aware that the equally devout Louis listened to the pleas of La Fayette with ever increasing apprehension for his own soul. In a reversal of his plan, Richelieu secretly asked a Dominican priest who frequented the woman's society, Father Carré, to encourage her long-held desire to enter the religious orders.

Then a new character stepped onto the court's stage. In March, after the king's confessor, Father Gordon, fell ill, Cardinal Richelieu found for him a new one, a Jesuit named Nicolas Caussin. Caussin's superiors at the Society of Jesus flinched. The man was simple and good, but his knowledge of the court remained speculative—he was, after all, the author of a popular book of devotion titled *The Holy Court*. Indeed, when the Jesuit realized what kind of intrigues surrounded the predisposition of La Fayette for a convent's life, he urged her to wait.[27] She did not seem ready for it, and he appreciated the beneficial effects of her platonic love on the monarch. He also appreciated how the staunch credence of the young woman led Louis to question his minister's policies. Louis was torn between his desire for La Fayette and his respect for her presumed vocation. On May 5, for example, the king wrote to his minister: "If tomorrow she persists in her resolution . . . I shall leave on Monday for Versailles or Chantilly to try to forget my affliction, which from time to time takes a hold of me with extreme force, especially when I am alone. It's not worth your coming here. I hope God will give me consolation."[28] Richelieu, who was well aware of the king's anguish through the reports of a valet in his pay, responded: "It is hard to represent to Your Majesty the displeasure that His sorrow provokes in me, but I bear at least half of it with my good wishes, and cannot doubt that God, in whose name Your Majesty supports these travails, will soon console Him. Kings who submit to His will and prefer His glory to their satisfaction receive rewards not only in that other world, but also in this one."[29]

Louis's passion was not so spiritual after all. If we trust the memoirs of Madame de Motteville, the king eventually asked La Fayette if she would agree to live at Versailles and become his mistress.[30] Perhaps this would explain why, on May 19, in Anne's apartment at the Louvre, La Fayette saw the king and asked his permission to leave the court and this worldly life. She entered the Convent of the Visitation, on the Rue Saint-Antoine that leads from city hall to the Bastille, to begin her novitiate. Her sudden departure left Louis profoundly distraught; he went to visit her soon after her entry and then many times after that.

As Louis's love story unfolded in the intimacy of a convent's parlor, the campaign of 1637 began. Emperor Ferdinand II had died on February 15, 1637. His son Ferdinand III took over and ensured a seamless transition of power. Lack of resources and sufficient attention from Paris had caused the collapse of the Duc de Rohan's war effort in the Valtellina. It left the prized passage in the Alps in the hands of the Habsburgs and further demoralized the French allies. The Spanish took Alba in the Piedmont. When the Duke of Mantua, Charles de Nevers, died on September 20, his wife decided to leave the league formed in 1635. Then the Duke of Parma abandoned the French cause, too. Finally, on October 8, the Duke of Savoy, Victor Amadeus, died, making his wife, Christine, the sister of Louis, the regent. It did not augur well for French influence in Savoy, considering how unpopular she was in her own duchy.

At the opposite end of the Italian war theater, in Picardy, the army under the command of Cardinal de La Valette besieged Landrecies in June and took it on July 26, 1637. Richelieu then set his sights on La Capelle, the first place the Spanish had conquered the year before, and took it as well. The simultaneous—and eventually successful—Dutch effort to take back the often contested town of Breda greatly facilitated this victory. In the Franche-Comté, the goals were more realistic than the previous year, and the army gained many smaller places. When Bernard of Saxe-Weimar's army arrived to second the corps led by the Duc de Longueville, an energetic push back against the forces of Charles de Lorraine further strengthened the French hold on the province. Unfortunately, Bernard's absence from Alsace allowed the imperial forces to retake key posts they had lost earlier on the Rhine. The duke became more and more impatient with the French for their increasing inability to provide supplies to his campaign.

These modest successes were far from heralding a French breakthrough. A peasant revolt arose in the southwest to protest the heavy tax burden brought on by the war. At the worst moment of the revolt, six to seven thousand of the rebels—called "Les Croquants"—took the city of Bergerac, and an entire royal army was needed to reestablish order in the region. Better news came from the Mediterranean.[31] In late March, after stunning the enemy with a heavy bombing, the French soldiers of Louis's fleet, led by the Comte d'Harcourt, had landed on the islands of Lérins in the bay of Cannes. The Spanish, who had considerably improved the fortifications, successfully resisted the attack. The Parlement of Provence sent in four thousand more troops in reinforcements. More than six weeks of ferocious fighting were necessary to reclaim the islands from the twelve hundred soldiers who kept the fort. Once this was achieved, the French fleet traveled toward the Spanish border, where Olivares was gathering a substantial army. At the end of August, these enemy troops lay siege to the fort of Leucate. This post on the road between Perpignan and Narbonne lay on a rocky mountain, right on the sea, and it guarded a strategic sea inlet. With backing from the fleet, the French troops chased away the invaders on September 28. This loss caused the Spanish to also abandon the positions they held on the Atlantic coast, including Saint-Jean-de-Luz.

Louis still divided his time between the war cabinet and the convent's parlor on the Rue Saint-Antoine during these months of contrasting outcomes. He brought La Fayette music that he had written for her. Sometimes the two simply stood in melancholic silence; at other times they were absorbed in deep, hushed discussions. Perhaps they were still concerned about Marie de' Medici. The queen's reputation had sunk to dangerous lows in her adoptive country of the Spanish Netherlands, so much so that when La Valette began his attack in the north, the people of Brussels mounted anti-French demonstrations and demanded that the queen give them lists of all her household staff, some of whom they suspected of spying and plotting on behalf of Cardinal Richelieu. To quiet the emotion, Marie de' Medici opened the door of her residence and let the mob search every corner of it, from attic to cellar. It was a humiliation not only for the immensely proud queen mother but also for her son, the king. She signaled her intent to come home.

Meanwhile, another scandal hatched. Anne of Austria had been living a tranquil life in the royal palaces, with a standing at court far below what she could have aspired to. War with her native country had done nothing to improve her misfortunes after the Day of the Dupes. The queen's loneliness, however, was less innocent than it appeared. Her longtime friend Madame de Chevreuse lived in exile at one of her châteaus in Touraine, and the two wrote to each other in secret. Sometimes, the duchess put on a disguise and rode to Paris to meet the queen at the convent of the Val-de-Grâce in the southern suburbs of the capital.[32] From this safe place where the superior of the convent put an apartment at her disposal, Anne was writing letters. Through Madame de Chevreuse and an English diplomat, she wrote to the Marquis of Mirabel, former Spanish ambassador to France, who himself reported to Olivares. She corresponded with Marie de' Medici and her courtiers, as well as Charles de Lorraine. Much of Anne's writing was complaints about Marie de' Medici and her own miserable conditions. One day, however, she informed France's enemies that Richelieu intended to win back the Duc de Lorraine.[33]

As always, spies surrounded Anne, and Richelieu had been informed of the queen's shady transactions for quite a while.[34] The cardinal's secret police kept a particularly close eye on the comings and goings of her servant Pierre de La Porte. This thirty-four-year-old was one of the men that Louis had summarily dismissed after Buckingham's seduction in Amiens, and whom the minister had eventually allowed to return to her service. Proof of the queen's treason came when a letter to Mirabel was intercepted. The cardinal decided he needed to inform the king. Anne's recent biographer, Ruth Kleinman, suggests that maybe the cardinal was just waiting for a propitious time, for example, when he would need to distract the king's attention from the faltering war effort or from a dangerous confidant.[35] The queen's incriminating letter can still be found at the archives of the Bibliothèque Nationale, in a file that contains all the pieces of this Affaire du Val-de-Grâce.[36] Louis, outraged, gave full authority to Richelieu on this matter.

On August 11, 1637, after visiting an acquaintance, the queen's valet, La Porte, stepped out onto the Rue des Vieux-Augustins without paying attention to a two-horse carriage that waited farther down the street. As soon as La Porte walked by this coach, men dressed in plain gray clothes jumped out of it and shoved him inside. All doors were locked behind him. After a short ride, Anne's trusted man arrived at the Bastille, where the guards threw him in a dark cell. An extensive investigation began. The cardinal's agents found a letter for Madame de Chevreuse on La Porte, but they were looking for more. They searched his lodging at the Hôtel de Chevreuse. There, La Porte kept some very compromising papers, including pamphlets against the cardinal and the secret codes used by the queen to correspond with her friends, but the search yielded nothing because the papers were well concealed in a space carved in a window frame, behind what looked like a tightly sealed stone block. Searching the Val-de-Grâce demanded the intervention of no less than Chancellier Pierre Séguier and the Archbishop of Paris. There was nothing there either.

Richelieu's hope of finding the whole truth thus ended up resting on a confession from Anne, and so he suggested that the queen be summoned to Chantilly. Chancellier Séguier interrogated her at first. The queen knew that her actions could prompt Louis to repudiate her and send her back to Spain. She denied any wrongdoing. Nevertheless, the ordeal left her in a such a state that she could not eat for two days, until she swore on the Holy Sacrament that she did not correspond with foreign agents. Courtiers were afraid even of looking toward the windows of her room. On August 17, she asked to see Cardinal Richelieu.

A detailed description of this encounter with Anne can be found in Richelieu's memoirs. She first confessed that she had written to the Cardinal-Infant in the Spanish Netherlands, but pretended that it was only to exchange good wishes. The cardinal was ignorant of the exact nature of the exchanges but knew there was more to them than that. He objected with a bluff: "But there is more, Madame . . ."

He assured her that he would gladly serve her interests before the king, provided that she tell the whole truth. Anne asked if the other persons present in the room would excuse her and the cardinal. Once the two were left alone, she told Richelieu everything he wanted to hear.

"How good you must be, Monsieur le Cardinal!" Anne exclaimed while she confessed the details of her betrayal to France.

Then, according to Richelieu, came this surprising and desperate move from a queen who, by protocol, almost never touched anyone: "Give me your hand," she said while extending her own.

Richelieu, in his own words, "refused out of respect, and for that very reason moved away from her instead."[37]

All this time, Pierre de La Porte was still at the Bastille, where an officer of justice interrogated him repeatedly. Anne's valet was entirely devoted to the queen's cause, and he deftly evaded all questions and ploys laid before him. Clearly, a more impressive interrogator needed to intervene. One evening, around eight, as La Porte readied for the night, the doors of his cell burst open. Guards dragged him to a carriage. As it kept passing the places where the executioner carried out his duty, the prisoner realized that he was going somewhere else. Finally, the carriage stopped in the service courtyard of a large house that La Porte recognized as the Palais-Cardinal. The captain of the guards appeared to escort him, and, after a long walk through many rooms and hallways, La Porte found himself standing before no less than Cardinal Richelieu.

The cardinal was polite at first. He urged Anne's servant to give details about the queen's correspondence and even went as far as promising great riches in exchange for his testimony. La Porte responded that he knew nothing of the queen's contacts with the enemy. This silence threw Richelieu off. "He became a bit angry, and told me that since I was not telling him the truths he already knew, I could rest assured that he had the power to put me to trial, and that such things went very fast when the interest of the state and the king's service were concerned," La Porte recounted sometime later.[38] After five hours, and in spite of the cardinal's best effort and menaces, he still had revealed nothing of the queen's commerce.

La Porte's troubles were far from over. Anne had spoken in Chantilly, but Richelieu still wanted her valet to reveal everything he knew so as to corroborate his version with the queen's own. This caused the queen great anguish. La Porte had to speak if he was to avoid more forceful interrogative methods, but he would never do so if he thought he was betraying the queen. Mademoiselle de Hautefort, who had remained the queen's friend, saved the situation. She put on a disguise, went to the Bastille, and succeeded in conveying the queen's message that he was free to divulge her secrets.[39] It was high time for La Porte to speak. One of Richelieu's most feared intendants, Isaac de Laffemas, a justice officer whom critics refered to as the cardinal's favorite headsman, had arrived to interrogate him. After dangling both promises of rewards and menaces, the cardinal's headsman took his prisoner to the torture chamber of the Bastille. There, he showed him all the instruments and elaborated cheerfully on the intolerable pain they could inflict.

Cardinal Richelieu advised Louis to reconcile with his wife for the sake of his kingdom. Anne of Austria ended up more isolated than before. A minder now read all her correspondence before it went out. Another victim in this story was Madame de Chevreuse, who had been implicated in the plot since the beginning. Understandably, she feared arrest and had stayed on high alert in her retreat in Touraine. The duchess had an agreement with Anne. In case of an imminent danger, a common friend and intermediary would send the duchess a prayer book bound in a certain color of leather; if flight was unnecessary, a different color would be sent. Once peril subsided, the friend sent the book to tell Chevreuse that she should not worry. But the woman mistook the code and sent a book with the wrong color. Believing her life to be at stake, Madame de Chevreuse would not wait to be caught by her archenemy Richelieu. On September 6, 1637, she put on some men's clothing, a wig, dyed the white hair of her favorite horse, and began a flight on horseback toward Spain. When she reached the border, after many adventures, she found the kind of rich cortege that Count-Duke Olivares deemed worthy of such an illustrious adventurer. This unnecessary escape further contributed to suspicions the queen was still up to no good, and it was all the more useless since Cardinal Richelieu had actually wanted to pardon Madame de Chevreuse, too. He wrote in an effort to get her to come back: "I lament more than I can tell you the hardship of your trip, and confess that I could not help laughing at certain of your exploits. You have reacted disproportionately to this alarm. I can assure you no one wants to harm you, but I also understand that everything seems shadowy when one lives in fear."[40]

While the Val-de-Grâce affair shook the court at the end of the summer of 1637, Louis was still paying frequent visits to the Convent of the Visitation to meet with his lost love, and the Jesuit Nicolas Caussin still tended to the king's spiritual well-being with dedication. Caussin was touched by Anne's plight, and by that of La Fayette, too. He put even more zeal in his attempt to convert Louis to a more Christian attitude toward his suffering people and his mother. For Father Caussin, the affairs of state and those of the soul were indistinguishable. Louis responded with ambivalence to the minister's criticism. He recognized that Richelieu's influence on his entire life appeared to many as incomprehensible, and that much of what reached him had been either filtered or intended by the cardinal and his "creatures." This modest king also understood that, after years of war, it was scandalous to see gold and silver shoveled to the cardinal's palaces to purchase works of art and put on extravagant spectacles. At the same time, though, he wrote to Richelieu such kind words as "I am feeling well today and can assure you that I have never been so happy with your services."[41] King and confessor Caussin spent long hours in the study to discuss these grave matters under the pretext that they were composing the text of masses. Discretion and precaution were certainly required, because whenever these conversations lasted for too long, Cardinal Richelieu would arrive in an unannounced visit.

Occasionally, Caussin thought that he had finally succeeded in persuading the king to assert his will more forcefully. But every time, to his great dismay, the confessor observed that as soon as the king went back to Rueil to see the cardinal, "it seemed as if [the cardinal] had emitted towards him some kind of active and penetrating venom, some enchanted fumes that altered his judgment, and made him suddenly like all he previously hated, approve all he condemned, and embrace with trouble of the mind and unnatural passion, everything that the cardinal wanted."[42] The Jesuit came to the conclusion that only a great showdown between him and the cardinal, in the presence of Louis, could dispel the sulphurous enchantment that clouded the king's judgment. The king consented, provided that the encounter with his minister would appear to happen by chance, so as not to provoke him too much.

On December 9, 1637, Father Caussin went to Rueil and found a man well aware that something significant was happening. The day before, Chavigny and the Duc d'Angoulême had noticed the unusual length of the king's conversation with Caussin, and how unusually troubled Louis appeared. Richelieu welcomed the Jesuit to his study with chilly politeness and casually entertained him with a conversation on the vanity of the world. Suddenly, noise announcing the king's arrival interrupted their conversation. Without missing a beat,

Richelieu asked Caussin to take a secret passage and to wait in another room until the king would leave, because, he said, the king had such a suspicious nature that he might take umbrage to see the two together. Caussin was in an awkward situation: he could not tell the cardinal the reason for Louis's visit, and so he agreed to retreat in the other room. Louis inquired about the confessor. His minister simply responded that he had not seen him. He then took the opportunity to explain once again why Marie de' Medici should remain in exile and why the Protestant alliances were justified, drawing examples from the foremost theologians. He also challenged Caussin's credibility: the man's arguments were so weak, he said, that he had not dared to show up.

The hapless Father Caussin waited for hours, alone in the backroom. He described in his report to the Jesuits' general that only at nightfall did he realize he had been duped, and then went back home. Lightning struck immediately. Caussin received a letter informing him that he was no longer the king's confessor. Guards came to search his lodging and found a copy of a heart-wrenching letter Marie de' Medici had written to her son and sent in care of Caussin.[43] Eventually, the guards took him away to a convent in Brittany, where, Richelieu commented, the Jesuit "could spend as much time as he wanted in the conversation with the wisest men of his order, and write a sequel to his book *The Holy Court*, with examples of what he had seen and practiced in Paris."[44] For a while, Richelieu even contemplated the idea of sending Caussin as a missionary to Québec. From the place of his exile, Caussin taunted the cardinal in a brutal harangue: "It is said that you were born under the sign of the most bellicose scorpio, but you should rather consider God's lamb to whom you have consecrated your life."[45]

The last scandal to break out in the winter season 1637–1638 concerned the Abbot of Saint-Cyran, Jean Duvergier de Hauranne, and it also pertained to the privilege of hearing royal confession. Richelieu and Saint-Cyran knew each other well, having been in contact since the Luçon years. In a time of worldly turmoil, Saint-Cyran preached a personal and lived relationship to God and a return to the essential truths taught by fathers of the Church such as Augustine. His ever-growing circle of followers gathered in a place near the abbey of Port-Royal. They lived modestly, hence their nickname, Les Solitaires. This inward spirituality did not cut them away from the world. The Solitaires were primarily Parisian bourgeois, specifically from the milieu of magistrates.

The Solitaires had much admiration for the religious writings of Cornelius Jansen, a bishop of the Spanish Netherlands who had written in 1635 a fierce pamphlet against Richelieu's foreign policies, the *Mars Gallicus*. After Saint-Cyran voiced open criticism of the state's attempt at dissolving Gaston's union with Marguerite with little respect for the institution of marriage, Richelieu rapidly perceived the Solitaires to be threats to the state and to his own power. Also, their brand of inward spirituality disturbed him. The cardinal believed a Christian's duty is to act in this world. "To act, to suffer, and to love are the real foundations of human merit in this world," he wrote in the religious treatise he had been composing since the Spanish invasion of 1636.

Then there was the subtler and more personal question of how one lives in God's presence and whether there are people who have the authority to mediate in that relationship. The sacrament of confession was the controversy's flashpoint. For Saint-Cyran, the sinner can only be redeemed if he feels contrition, that is, a profound regret that is experienced as newfound love of God. For Richelieu the theologian, a confessor can deem attrition to be sufficient to grant the sinner pardon, that is, if the sinner merely wants to improve because he fears eternal damnation. Richelieu defended the concept of attrition because, while giving much freedom to the human creature, it necessarily invested figures of authority with an essential mediating role in religious life.[46] It is the priest who decides whether a penitent can receive pardon, even if this penitent wants absolution for fear of eternal damnation. In other words, attrition gave Richelieu the latitude to absolve the king, who feared that keeping his mother away and striking alliances with Protestants would send him to hell. The notion of attrition, incidentally, also fitted the way Richelieu the man lived his own relationship to God. Aubery, the early biographer who benefited from firsthand accounts of the cardinal's life, wrote, "He often mentioned that he felt sorrow for not experiencing as deeply as he wanted remorse over his mistakes, and the love of God."

In March of 1638, a man named Claude Séguenot published a treatise that spelled out in unambiguous terms the creed of contritionists like Saint-Cyran. It triggered a controversy that resonated in the hallways of Paris's theological schools, but also at court. The party of the Devouts felt emboldened. How could the king think that Richelieu's political advice and theological justifications were less than grave sins before God when it tormented his own soul? For Richelieu, this controversy was definite proof of Saint-Cyran's threat. Perhaps there were even deeper motives to the cardinal's ruthlessness. Saint-Cyran's biographer says that the abbot knew some very secret details "that would not have enhanced" the life of the Bishop of Luçon, and that God sometimes gave him "terrible thoughts" when he reflected upon these secrets.[47] In short order, Richelieu had Saint-Cyran arrested on May 14, 1638, and taken to Vincennes, in one of those infamous cells where the Ducs de Vendômes and de Puylaurens had died. Even Madame de Combalet expressed dismay at so much rigor.[48] Richelieu answered that if someone had stopped Luther early in his life, many catastrophes would have been avoided. He put another one of his feared headsmen, Jean Martin de Laubardemont, in charge of the prosecution. A tribunal convicted Saint-Cyran of having rejected the teachings of the Council of Trent, and of other crimes against the state. He remained in jail, between life and death, until the cardinal passed away.

CHAPTER 9

Turning Points (1638–1640)

O N DECEMBER 10, 1637, Louis XIII placed France under the protection of the Virgin Mary with a special vow, seeking intercession for his
military effort.[1] But the Virgin Mother interceded in a different matter. To
everyone's astonishment, Anne announced her pregnancy in the early months
of 1638. The Queen of France was thirty-six years old. The royal couple had
tried in vain to conceive for almost twenty years, and, after the Val-de-Grâce
affair, Louis's icy demeanor toward his wife left the court thinking that a direct heir to his throne would never appear. Still, while the circumstances of
that heir's conception were as surprising as the pregnancy itself, no one at the
time ever doubted that the king was really the prospective father.[2]

The *Gazette de France* announced the happy news of the queen's pregnancy
on January 30. Throughout the Kingdom of France, special masses and prayers
asked for the birth of a healthy heir. Richelieu's prayers, undoubtedly, were
not the least fervent in this choir. After the poor showings of 1637, and under
what seemed better auspices, he assigned more troops and resources to the
war with the Habsburgs and urged his commanders to be bolder.[3] Meanwhile, a general peace conference opened in Hamburg. For some months already, French envoys tested the mood in the private study in Madrid, to see if
Olivares would consider a settlement. Similar talks with Spain in Hamburg
ended up yielding nothing. It prompted Richelieu to guarantee the Swedish
more financial support. This was a considerable move because Chancellor
Oxenstierna, who for the last months had led his armies against the Elector of

Saxony, John George, in northern Germany, was thinking of leaving the war altogether.

Maréchal de Châtillon undertook the siege of Saint-Omer in the Spanish Netherlands, at the end of May. Prince Thomas and Piccolomini managed to bring more troops into the city. France's own attempt at reinforcements proved useless, and so Châtillon had to abandon his siege in mid-July. All conspired to deny Richelieu the military leverage he needed to negotiate a favorable peace settlement. For lack of a better target, troops under the command of François du Hallier went to besiege Le Catelet, one of the last French places that remained in Spanish hands after the 1636 invasion. On the eastern front, Bernard of Saxe-Weimar had won an early victory against imperial troops at Rheinfelden, on March 3. This battle gave the duke a bridge point over the Rhine and resulted in the capture of Jean de Werth, one of the generals who had threatened Paris two years earlier. De Werth was brought back to Paris in a triumphant parade and jailed at Vincennes.[4] At the end of April, Saxe-Weimar laid siege on Brisach, an Alsatian fortress built on a rocky mountain overlooking the Rhine and facing the spruce-covered mountains of the Black Forest. With both natural and man-made fortifications, Brisach's defenses were formidable. Bernard, however, knew that only two months' worth of food remained inside the place. Work on a circular line of defense began under the command of Jean-Baptiste Budes, Comte de Guébriant, a talented French officer. More than two thousand peasants and two hundred specialized construction workers labored in this colossal operation.[5] "This siege was so considerable that the eyes of Europe were set on it, as the key to overall success in the affairs of Germany," explained the memoirist Charles de Montglat.[6]

After trying to observe a safe neutrality in the conflict that pitted the French Bourbons against the Habsburgs, Christine of Savoy finally recognized that she had no choice but to place herself under her brother's protection. The regent signed a treaty that renewed the terms of the 1635 Treaty of Rivoli. Given how anti-French her people were, and how her own brothers-in-law Thomas and Maurice leaned toward an alliance with the Spanish, Louis's sister risked much. In addition, the scale of the French involvement in the north surely prohibited committing many troops to the Duchy of Savoy. The Spanish seized the opportunity and occupied the Monferrato town of Vercelli on July 5.

In the south of France, the past campaign's success at Leucate emboldened Richelieu to try some aggressive moves directly into Spanish territory. This was also a preventive action, since for the two previous years Olivares had given signs that this was where he might strike at France. The cardinal set his sights on the fort of Fuenterrabía, which commanded a lake formed at the opening of the Bidassoa River at the western border between the two kingdoms, and placed all his hopes on the success of this siege after it appeared that no significant inroads could be made to the north. The French had to take Fuenterrabía to seize more towns on the Atlantic coast. Always mindful to place men of certain loyalty in key positions, Richelieu designated the Prince de Condé as his commander. Also, he ordered the Atlantic fleet, commanded by the Archbishop of Bordeaux, Henri d'Escoubleau de Sourdis, to gather near the island of Ré and sail toward the border with Spain. As the month of July began, Condé ordered the opening of trenches in front of Fuenterrabía. Twelve thousand men participated in the operation.

In an all-too-familiar pattern, the chiefs of this southern army began to squabble over questions of honor, precedence, and strategy. Particularly, Lieutenant Général the Duc Bernard de La Valette showed much ill will because Condé's intervention shifted power away from his father, the Duc d'Épernon, who was governor of the nearest French province and no friend of the cardinal. The French troops were, as usual, malnourished and ill equipped. Adding to the misery of the wretched soldiers, rain continually filled the trenches. Meanwhile, under the personal supervision of Olivares, the Spanish began to organize a counteroffensive. Richelieu still thought that soon enough Fuenterrabía would fall into French hands. In a letter written to Condé from Amiens, where he watched over the siege of Le Catelet with Louis, he already gave advice on how to proceed after the surrender: "It is quite possible that the King of Spain might imitate what the king did after Corbie, by attacking right after the taking of the place; this is why nothing must be forgotten to thwart that design should he take it."[7]

A few days later, news that the naval forces of Archbishop de Sourdis had won a superb victory on August 22 gave Richelieu further reasons to hope for resounding success. Having heard that a large Spanish fleet had come to the rescue and waited in front of Guetaria, near San Sebastian, Sourdis went straight to the enemy. He made good use of incendiary boats and started a blaze over the water, sinking thirteen Spanish galleons and killing more than three thousand enemy troops. Richelieu assured the king of his own victory. "Fuenterrabía remains close to my heart although I do not expect any inconvenience to happen there." Then: "If Fuenterrabía is taken, as it will undoubtedly happen, and provided that this campaign [in Picardy] is successful, we will be in a position to enjoy an ever lasting quiet."[8]

Louis left the siege of Le Catelet to join Anne in Saint-Germain-en-Laye, where he had been born in 1601 and where he expected to see his first child. The cloying atmosphere at the château irritated him. He wrote to Richelieu: "I have found the feminine sex with as little sense and as full with impertinent questions as is customary. I am bothered that the queen's delivery has not yet allowed me to go back to Picardy, should you deem that appropriate, and even elsewhere for that matter, as long as I am away from all these women."[9] Much of the king's ill temper was caused by Mademoiselle de Hautefort. The exile of Father Caussin had marked the end of the king's visits to the Convent of the Visitation, and de Hautefort, now twenty-three years old, had reclaimed her hold on the monarch. Clearly Madame de Motteville voiced some truth when she wrote in her memoirs that the king "felt tenderness only to feel even more the grief and the pain of that feeling."[10] Louis spent time arguing and bickering with the brash lady-in-waiting to his wife. De Hautefort still voiced open criticism of Richelieu, and in turn her lover threatened her with his minister. Thus Richelieu had to mediate between king and favorite even though the king presented him as a fierce castigator. When, at the end of August, Louis and Mademoiselle de Hautefort reconciled after another nasty fight, the cardinal complimented Louis: "I am delighted to hear of his Majesty's appeasement with his inclination [for de Hautefort], a person who will always be, in my judgment, as innocent and devoid of malice, as it sometimes happens during these kind of excusable rows."[11]

In spite of these reassurances, Richelieu had tired of de Hautefort, and he wanted to replace her with an alternative favorite. Eighteen-year-old Henri Coëffier de Ruzé, Marquis de Cinq-Mars, whose father, the Maréchal d'Effiat, had campaigned valiantly before dying in Italy in 1632, seemed like the perfect candidate. Cinq-Mars was very well put together, with chestnut brown locks, a thin mustache, and pouty lips. He had an elegant demeanor, much charm, and spirited conversation. After the death of the marshal, the cardinal had taken d'Effiat's second son under his protection, giving the young Cinq-Mars a company of the king's guards, and then making him grand master of the king's wardrobe in March of 1638. Those courtiers the cardinal paid to spy on the king were told to discreetly bring Louis's attention to his new wardrobe keeper.

At last, on September 4, 1638, the day of Anne's confinement arrived. Tradition demanded that the queen give birth in public, and so the midwife Dame Peronne helped the queen take her place on a delivery bed in full view of the court. Gaston was back at court and with much at stake. An assembly of the French clergy had recommended that his marriage be declared null, but having reconciled with his brother and the cardinal after his inexplicable flight from Paris, he had obtained assurances that he could remain married to Marguerite de Lorraine. With this reprieve, Gaston was in a legitimate position to produce another heir to the throne. Should Anne have a male baby, all this would become moot.

On September 5, at eleven thirty in the morning, and after a difficult labor, Anne of Austria gave France a big and healthy boy with dark hair. The future Sun King, Louis XIV, was born. Church bells rang. Envoys darted throughout the kingdom and abroad to spread the news of the healthy birth. The new father shed many tears. Two letters of congratulations, one for the king, another for the queen, arrived from Richelieu in Picardy. Witnesses describe Gaston as looking quite stunned when the midwife showed him, "by means of physical reason," that he was now much less likely to claim the throne.[12] After a few days of feigning happiness, Gaston went to his château in Limours, where, according to his courtier Goulas, he finally broke down with "tears that flowed along his two cheeks like rivers."[13] Anne asked to hear mass as soon as she was able to stand. While the Bishop of Lisieux officiated in her room, she came to the altar with her newborn child in her arms and offered him to God. Then she took communion "with a great profusion of tears, from her and all of those assembled."[14]

Even though his queen had given him a Dauphin, Louis made her no offer of new affections. Cardinal Richelieu did not intend to cede much to the queen, either. During the pregnancy he had liberated her erstwhile valet, Pierre de La Porte, a gesture Anne received with great contentment. The *Gazette de France* began to make frequent mention of her great qualities, but the cardinal still ruled over the queen's household—and now the Dauphin—with as much authority as ever.[15]

Marie de' Medici sent wishes to her son after the birth of the Dauphin. Louis answered politely but without effusion. Early on, in anticipation of the birth, he had inquired of his minister, "I beg you to tell me what to do if the queen my mother sends someone concerning the coming delivery of the queen."[16] In fact,

Marie had other more pressing matters at hand. Frightened by the hostility she had encountered in the Spanish Netherlands, she had decided to seek out a more hospitable land, even if that meant leaving behind a mountain of debts and many servants who refused to follow. After first setting her sights on the Dutch Republic, she sought protection from the English king Charles I. Her son-in-law was not happy at the prospect of her visit, at a time when religious trouble stirred up Scotland, trouble which he could ill afford. Marie de' Medici ignored the discouraging signs that came from London, and, after a trying navigation, she landed on English soil, in November, an exhausted and dispirited woman. The English king and her daughter Henriette Marie put her at Saint James's Palace, hoping for a temporary stay. "I found her a little changed," tactfully wrote Henriette to her sister Christine.[17]

Soon, and to England's relief, it became apparent that Marie had left Spanish territory to better bargain for her return to France. Richelieu, ever distrustful of the queen mother's temper, could not agree to this return. The French ambassador in London made sure that he only saw her in public settings, where no serious discussion could take place. Her options dwindling, and resources so tight that she had to pawn all her jewels, Marie de' Medici cornered the ambassador to place her official request. In a final act of desperation, she wrote to her archenemy the cardinal to ask if she could return. She was sixty-five years old.

Richelieu ignored her assurances that she had forgotten the past and that she would strictly submit to the will of her son. Mindful not to look as if he was pursuing a personal vendetta, he abstained from the royal council deliberations on what course to take. Of course, he didn't need to: the secretaries of state, the chancellor, and the superintendents—all loyal to Richelieu—recommended that Marie de' Medici move to Florence and be given money to do so.

While jubilant masses were sung, fountains of wine flowed, and fireworks lit up the sky to celebrate the birth of the Dauphin, still the war went on. Cardinal Richelieu tended to the siege of Le Catelet in Picardy and anxiously waited for news from the southwest border and Fuenterrabía. His letters to the army chiefs became ever more pressing. After much effort, Le Catelet fell on September 14. But Richelieu had learned that just one week earlier, on the seventh, Fuenterrabía spawned a new disaster. Just as French explosives had opened in the Spanish walls a breach so wide that twelve horses could have entered at the same time, and with only three or four hundred men remaining inside, the sudden appearance of a Spanish army of about seven thousand men had forced away the French. Two thousand French soldiers were killed, some of them drowned in the Bidassoa River while fleeing the scene. Others fled in the boats that had been used to bring reinforcements from the navy. The enemies captured cannons and ensigns. For many days Madrid was lit up with bonfires.[18]

"The pain of Fuenterrabía kills me" were the opening words of the letter the minister wrote Louis upon learning of the news.[19] There were many excuses given for this defeat: the faulty layout of the camp's defenses, the missed opportunity of taking the fort as soon as its walls were breached, and, finally, the suspicious lethargy of La Valette's contingents. Richelieu still needed Condé's alliance, and the loyalty of Archbishop de Sourdis. Knowing this, perhaps, the Duc de La Valette prudently fled the kingdom before the cardinal could punish him, and joined a growing cohort of French expatriates in London. Among them was the Duchesse de Chevreuse, who had arrived from Spain with a firm intent of brokering a rapprochement between Charles I and Philip IV. For lack of direct culprits to punish for the defeat, Richelieu ordered the old Duc d'Épernon to leave Cadillac, and to move to a modest country house.

Other news from abroad was mixed. In Italy, more dynastic confusion disrupted the cardinal's plans to control the House of Savoy. The heir to the duchy, Francis Hyacinth, died in October at the age of five. Christine had another male child, four-year-old Victor Emmanuel, but he was weak. That left the regent's two brothers-in-law ever more determined to play to take the reins. Meanwhile, Bernard of Saxe-Weimar still besieged the Alsatian citadel of Brisach. In early October, all the troops that Emperor Ferdinand III could rally converged on the siege, including a four-thousand-man corps led by Charles de Lorraine. Saxe-Weimar went on to defeat him, on October 15, near Thann. Back at Brisach, and even though he suffered from persistent high fever, Saxe-Weimar pushed back another terrible attack at the end of October, during which Comte de Guébriant and Henri de La Tour-d'Auvergne, Vicomte de Turenne, displayed great valor.

Plagued by disease, lack of food, and money to pay the soldiers, the imperial forces eventually had to give up on their rescue plans. Alsace, at this point in the war, was a barren land that could not feed its population, let alone an army. On December 18, after an almost eight-month siege, the governor of Brisach capitulated. Bernard's army found inside the citadel the usual catalog of horrors: their food having long ago ran out, between eighteen and twenty-four thousand citizens of the town and soldiers had died after eating the most inconceivable things, including human flesh.

The *Gazette* could not find enough hyperbole to praise the Duke of Saxe-Weimar: holding Brisach gave the French the precious advantage of controlling the passage that Habsburg armies took to travel from Germany to Alsace, Lorraine, and Franche-Comté. It was also a good outpost to intercept armies moving between Italy and Flanders, an all the more essential advantage after the loss of the Valtellina. But the duke's ambitions dampened Richelieu and Louis's enthusiasm. Success made him quite independent, and many thought that he contemplated becoming the sovereign of Alsace. His death in the summer of the following year came as a relief to Richelieu, much as that of Gustavus Adolphus had five years earlier.[20]

While Richelieu received the news of Brisach's fall, he mourned the loss of his dear friend, companion, and precious adviser Father Joseph. An apoplectic attack had greatly diminished the Capuchin friar weeks earlier. He passed away at Rueil, on December 18, 1638. Richelieu put his casket on his own grand six-horse carriage and sent him back to his monastery on the Rue Saint-Honoré with a cortege formed by all the men in the cardinal's household.[21]

For the campaign of 1639, Richelieu gave the command of the army to his cousin, La Meilleraye, who decided to besiege the Flemish city of Hesdin, a base from which the enemy launched excursions into Picardy. The retreat before Saint-Omer in 1638 called for firm action to avenge the honor of the king. Soon after La Meilleraye's army reached Hesdin, on May 20, the trenches were open. Meanwhile, Louis and Richelieu had left Saint-Germain-en-Laye. Their first goal was to secure a path for the convoys that transported food and supplies from France to the siege. Richelieu and Louis then set up their camp in Abbeville, closer to Hesdin.[22] The cardinal wrote down the most minute advice to his relative: "Don't lose time responding to the letters I write, and only do what needs to be accomplished; if you need anything from us, ask for it."[23] The city was protected by large moats that could be filled by an ingenious system of locks and gates. It took many working hands to fill them with dirt, and this diverted resources away from other theaters, allowing Piccolomini and his imperial troops to win a murderous battle against the French army in Lorraine, at Thionville. Following this victory, the imperial forces showed up at Hesdin. The besieged were putting up a strong defense, too. In the middle of the siege, they almost broke through French lines, forcing Louis to take command. Fortunately, all the French defense works made a rescue by Piccolomini impossible. The assault continued in the most awful weather. Two mines blew up a large hole in the town's wall. On June 29, the city finally surrendered. La Meilleraye became a marshal.

The ongoing crisis in the princely family of Savoy, and the adverse effects it had on French interests in Italy, prompted a voyage by the court to Grenoble. Prince Thomas, after waging war in Flanders, had gone back to his native country and struck an alliance with his brother Maurice and the Spanish. The rift between Louis's sister Christine and her two brothers-in-law was open, and the small French army that was present in the region could do little to protect her. In July, Thomas attacked Turin, forcing the regent to find shelter in the city's citadel and defend herself by bombing her own capital. Eventually, she fled Piedmont for Savoy.

As the king and his minister spent the fall traveling toward the Alps to meet with Christine, courtiers noted that the king was giving his wardrobe keeper, Cinq-Mars, more and more attention. At a dinner, Cinq-Mars and another noble of his age, the Duc de Nemours, began to tease each other. What was playful banter at first soon became bickering. Nemours spat a cherry pit at Cinq-Mars's nose, the latter replied in kind, and the two ended up with hands at the pommels of their swords. Louis took sides with Cinq-Mars. The court understood this as an official declaration of favor.[24]

Louis and his sister Christine had not seen each other since the Suza Pass episode, ten years earlier. She told her brother that after losing her husband, her son, and an important part of her estates, her only consolation in life was to see him. Louis replied that he had come all the way just for that. Richelieu was not in the mood for tender feelings. He treated the king's sister quite harshly after she refused to give him control over all of the strategic places in the Piedmont that he wanted. Christine had taken lovers while her husband was alive. This allowed her brother-in-law Thomas to spread rumors that her son was not the legitimate heir to the duchy. Richelieu did not miss this opportunity to castigate Christine: "Besides the fact that women's government usually represents the misfortune of states, this one had so many bad qualities to conduct her people, that it was impossible to lead her to accept what was necessary for her own good."[25] Notwithstanding the vexing issue of strategic locations, the regent of Savoy refused to let the cardinal take custody of her child, which he wanted as a guarantee of her goodwill. The regent knew that such a move would destroy the little legitimacy she enjoyed among her own people.

On November 3, the king, his favorite, Cinq-Mars, and his minister were back in the Île-de-France, in Fontainebleau, where Anne waited for her husband. Louis introduced his new young male friend to his wife and paid little attention to Mademoiselle de Hautefort. Eventually, de Hautefort received an written order telling her to leave the court. "We have a new favorite at court, Monsieur de Cinq-Mars, son of the late Maréchal d'Effiat," wrote Chavigny to his correspondent Mazarini in the fall of 1639. "This young man is entirely dependent on Monseigneur the Cardinal. Never has the king felt so violent a passion. His Majesty will pay off the office of Grand Écuyer de France [Grand Squire], which belongs to the Duc de Bellegarde, just so that [Cinq-Mars] can have it. It's not a bad start for a man who is nineteen years old."[26] From now on, Cinq-Mars would often be refered to as Monsieur le Grand.

Cardinal Richelieu had hastened to Rueil, spurred by the need to suppress a domestic revolt that had begun over the summer in Normandy. The region, like the rest of the kingdom, had to give more to the Crown, even if the war was already taxing its resources intolerably. When the government decreed new impositions, including a higher tax on salt, and then put in place extraordinary measures to punish those localities that could not contribute, crowds rioted to manifest their anger. On July 16, in Avranches, the rebels killed a tax collector and ransacked the offices of the fiscal administration. The unrest then spread from Rouen to Caen. The diverse social origins of these rebels made this a unique event. There were peasants and poor people, hence their name: the Nu-Pieds, or "barefooted." But the revolt also concerned nobles and officers, even priests. "I must confess that I do not understand how you can ignore the consequences of the resolutions you take in the council of finances," Richelieu wrote his minister of finance, before concluding that only the utmost severity could prevent further uprisings.[27] Late in November, royal troops quashed the rebels. The cardinal then dispatched Chancellier Séguier to the region. From December to March, 1640, Séguier exercised the harshest repression. When he arrived in Normandy, he suspended the local court, the Parlement of Rouen, because it had favored some subjects in the early contentions that had led to the revolt, and then he proceeded to judge in person those accused of sedition. Sentences that carried the death penalty were executed right away. He sent many to the fleet of galleys in the Mediterranean.

Richelieu dedicated himself fully to preparing for the next year's campaign and pursuing his winning strike. The presence of Cinq-Mars by the king's side, however, was turning out to have the opposite effect of what he had hoped for. No matter how infatuated Louis was with his new friend, the two were too different to get along easily.[28] The burden of life had prematurely aged Louis. He lived austerely, not to say thriftily. Richelieu chided him for not demanding that his servants clean his apartments properly.[29] Cinq-Mars, a young man catapulted to the highest reaches of the court, was fully determined to enjoy life. The elegance of his clothing and the richness of his décor delighted Paris and the court. He was rumored to have three hundred pairs of boots. "One has never seen at court a table better furnished than that of Monsieur le Grand," wrote one admirer. At first, Louis gave signs that he might enjoy injecting a bit of glamour into his quiet life. On November 13, he went to a dinner that Cinq-Mars gave in his honor at Saint-Germain-en-Laye. But soon he began to resent the flashy ways of his *cher ami*, as he called Cinq-Mars. A few days later he scolded the young man for having bought an extravagantly lavish carriage.

That was mere grumbling compared to Louis's reaction when he discovered Cinq-Mars's activities upon retiring for the night. Cinq-Mars had a lover in Paris named Marion de Lorme, whose townhouse on the Place Royale, in the Marais, had become the gathering point for the hip set of the time. Every night, after Louis went to bed, Cinq-Mars mounted his fastest horse and flew from Saint-Germain to Paris to spend the night in revelry and torrid lovemaking with the demoiselle. At dawn, he rode back to the château just in time for the king to rise. A day of yawning on the royal hunting grounds would follow. Sometimes the exhausted favorite went straight to bed, only to emerge for lunch.

Over time, Cinq-Mars's disputes with his elder royal companion became more frequent. One contemporary wrote that, one day, Cinq-Mars was found sobbing in his bedroom, sniffing that he could not live in his golden cage anymore.[30] On November 27, Louis mailed a statement to Richelieu that both he and the favorite had signed after a particularly acrimonious quarrel. That was their way to prove to each other that they truly wanted to live in harmony. He added the following note: "You will realize by reading the certificate here included how the reconciliation you arranged yesterday went. When you intervene nothing can go wrong. Have a nice day."[31] Just a few days later, however, the mood again turned stormy in Saint-Germain-en-Laye. Richelieu wrote from Rueil: "I cannot help but feel the pain when I sense that your Majesty is not happy . . . I urge you to believe and to hold as certain that, if you do not resolve to voice your discontent and your will to Monsieur le Grand, you will be in a state of sorrow that could be avoided otherwise, provided that you act as I recommend. Consider it may be impossible to be young and wise at the same time."[32]

On June 13, 1640, the man who kept watch on top of the belfry at Arras in the Spanish Netherlands, near the French border, sounded the alarm and placed his flag to signal the source of the danger. In that region of Artois, troop movement was frequent, and so the people did not pay much attention at first. When a second, more pressing call resounded through the city, the citizens looked again. To their great surprise, the flag now indicated danger from the opposite direction. The watchman shouted that soldiers were coming. Quickly the population gathered on the fortifications and discovered a mighty spectacle. Two powerful French armies slowly poured into the plains that surrounded them. The citizens of Arras thought their city's fortifications made it impregnable. A proverb even said, *Quand les Français prendront Arras, les souris mangeront les chats* (When the French will take Arras, the mice will eat the cats).[33]

Putting all his chips on Arras was quite a daring move for Richelieu, for the stakes were doubly high. Not only was it a key to keep the north secure, but taking this city would pressure the Spanish at a time when they had to face unrest within their own territory, especially in Catalonia. Although it benefited from a particular independent status within Spain, Catalonia had given much money and many men since the beginning of the war. Now its population was asked to lodge troops whose brutality against their own could not be controlled. On June 7, crowds of peasants who had descended on Barcelona for a fair rose and killed the viceroy. Richelieu's project, all things considered, was worth neglecting the other theater that mattered that year, the Piedmont, where the Comte d'Harcourt had begun an effort to take back Turin from Thomas of Savoy.

Settled at Arras, French soldiers immediately began to construct a line of fortification. Because they were operating deep within enemy territory, these commanders had to think as much of defending themselves as of preparing for the siege. Their target was large. Yet in a mere two weeks, the soldiers finished the line of defense and built a bridge over the river Scarpe to allow easy communication between the quarters. The defense featured deep, wide moats and well-placed redoubts and forts. Another difficulty of this colossal enterprise was the feeding of an army that counted around twenty-three thousand recruits and about nine thousand horsemen. Convoys had to leave from Picardy, cross the border, and then reach the siege in Spanish territory without being caught by the enemy. Richelieu, who joined the king in Amiens, keenly knew that this question of supply represented the key to the operation's success. On July 1, just as the diggers were about to open the trenches needed to reach underneath the walls of Arras, he reproached his generals for not sending enough troops to guard a large convoy that was on its way: "I must say that unless God has revealed to these gentlemen that the enemies will not get this convoy, I am unable to find the reason why they would put at risk the success of such an important matter with their lack of security."[34] Fortunately, the convoy arrived safely with food, munitions, and some cannons.

First attempts by the Spanish to throw some reinforcements into Arras failed. The besieged tried a few excursions on their own, but the French pushed back. This led the Cardinal-Infant to conclude that only a massive rescue operation could save the town. He gathered all the nobility of the country, called General Guillaume de Lamboy and Charles of Lorraine to help, and, with an army that counted almost thirty thousand men, took over a hill just a few miles from Arras. From there, the Cardinal-Infant could easily spot the arriving convoys and stop them. The strategy was to turn the siege onto the French, so to speak. By mid-July, the French works needed to blow up the walls of the city were well under way, but rationing of bread began. Equally dramatic was the shortage of wine on the officers' tables. Richelieu relentlessly urged, begged, and threatened. A new convoy had to reach the siege, and for that La Meilleraye needed to send contingents to protect them from the enemy: "The principal goal on the side of Messieurs the generals, and likewise on our side, is the passage of a convoy and the fall of Arras."[35]

On July 18, La Meilleraye and three thousand men of the cavalry tried to meet with a small incoming convoy that had used a less-traveled route. By sheer bad luck, he stumbled upon a contingent of Spanish cavalry passing by.

The French were able to chase away their enemy but ended up losing the convoy. Around the same time, an officer named Saint-Preuil succeeded in bringing enough food to last eight more days. This modest achievement allowed better preparations for the larger operation. Richelieu then moved an army he had first intended for a campaign in Lorraine toward the plains of Picardy, to provide additional protection for a last, crucial supply operation. François du Hallier led this force. From Amiens, the minister kept admonishing his cousin La Meilleraye and his subordinates not to let themselves fall into a false sense of security.

At the end of July, the dull plains of Picardy offered quite a spectacle. Hundreds and hundreds of carts filled to capacity with provisions and ammunition, herds of bellowing oxen to pull them, and entire regiments of the army waited in hot clouds of dust. All able men from the French army and the court were there, even the king's guard. Young Cinq-Mars, who wanted to distinguish himself as a military man, led a contingent of twelve hundred voluntary recruits from the finest nobility. It had taken a lot of begging to persuade Louis to let his *cher ami* put himself before enemy fire. Standing out in this corps of volunteers was the nineteen-year-old son of Condé, Louis, the Duc d'Enghien, who after brilliant studies with the Jesuits had made a much-remarked entry into the court. With so much at stake and the presence of young stars, Paris held its breath: "We are waiting with marvelous impatience some news from the great convoy," wrote a correspondent from the capital.[36]

Finally, on August 1, 1640, a message came in from La Meilleraye. It informed du Hallier that he would leave that night from Arras with three thousand soldiers and three thousand horsemen.[37] When the time came, La Meilleraye ordered his men to leave camp with as much discretion as possible, no drum beating, no trumpeting. No matter how great the risk of a surprise attack, not even the matches of muskets could be lit. At dawn, after hours of marching south, the marshal saw troops from afar and heard an exchange of fire. All thought the Spanish had showed up. Actually, it was du Hallier and his own convoy coming from France, and they were just as frightened. All hell broke loose: "Drums, kettledrums, and trumpets played in a cacophony, all the soldiers shouted in rejoicing now that the bread had arrived, and they threw their hats in the air to show their enthusiasm," related officer Montglat, who was on the scene.[38] The two armies of rescuers spread tablecloths on the grass, pierced the barrels of wine, and broke bread. In no time, a happy crowd mixing the tanned, dirty, and disheveled officers from the siege with the volunteers led by Cinq-Mars, who sported fancy war outfits covered in golden and silver embroidery with the inevitable feathered hats, was toasting their successful union. The party did not last long. An out-of-breath messenger appeared, announcing that the Spanish were attacking the siege at Arras. Everyone grabbed their arms and left the picnic behind.

La Meilleraye and Cinq-Mars arrived at Arras in the midst of a fiercely contested battle.[39] After two hours of fighting—it was around noon—the Cardinal-Infant and an army of forty thousand men had already taken one of the forts built by the French and broke through the defense lines. The town's gates, from which the soldiers of the garrison shot at the French, were within their easy reach. Amazingly, the French soldiers pushed the Spanish troops out of their lines with their naked swords and took back the fort. Du Hallier arrived with the convoy to add further reinforcement. The hail of cannon fire was so thick at this point that pieces of horse and mangled human bodies flew through the air. At last, the Cardinal-Infant called for retreat. It was quite a French victory against the best troops the Habsburgs could muster, not least, as Montglat says, when they were led by a young prince "still crowned with the laurels of Nördlingen." Over the following days the French attack on the city continued. The workers finished digging the trenches, and the pyrotechnicians placed explosives under the wall of the city. It opened a sizable breach. La Meilleraye ordered the final assault. The bourgeois of Arras, fearing the looting and rape that would naturally follow a hostile takeover, begged their governor to surrender. After the Cardinal-Infant failed at one last attempt to rescue the city, the articles of surrender were signed on August 9.

At last, a bold coup crowned with success for Richelieu. In Catalonia, the population clamored for French intervention. French talks with the revolutionary junta began. Surely the once superb Armada would have a hard time coming to the rescue should Louis mingle in the affairs of Catalonians. Dutch naval forces had battered it mightily at the Battle of the Downs, on October 21, 1639, and Richelieu's nephew Jean-Armand de Maillé-Brézé in front of Cadix had further diminished what was left in late July. That same month of July, at a new diet in Regensburg, Emperor Ferdinand III and the electors had gathered to consider a peace agreement. France, Sweden, and the Protestant princes of Germany were present to demand a comprehensive solution to the conflict. After the woes of Olivares in his own territory, the French victory at

Arras had thwarted Habsburg ambitions. There was even talk of revolutionary unrest in Portugal.

Alas, rejoicing after Arras was cut short by stunning revelations. The new
governor Richelieu had named at Arras thanked his benefactor by revealing
the secret reason for Gaston and Soissons's flight right after Corbie, in 1636.
The princes had not fled because of lack of rewards for chasing the Spanish
invaders, or, as they claimed, because of a vague climate of suspicion; stun-
ningly, they had fled in a panic after failing to assassinate the cardinal. The plot
had been the brainchild of Gaston and Soissons's two courtiers, Claude de
Bourdeille, Comte de Montrésor, and one Saint-Ysbal. The memoirs of the
first one of these conspirators, it must be said, is the only detailed source for
this story, and Gaston's secretary, Goulas, deemed it an invention in his own
memoirs. Yet other documents suggest that indeed a dramatic attempt at getting rid of Richelieu had taken place four years earlier, in the fall of 1636.

If Montrésor is to be trusted, he and Saint-Ysbal had convinced their masters that Richelieu had to be eliminated by drastic means. While the cardinal
was in Amiens, Louis often came to hold the sessions of his council in the
governor's house near where Richelieu lived. He returned to military camp
right after. Montrésor and Saint-Ysbal thought it was an ideal place for killing
the cardinal because there his guards had to stay away in the presence of the
king. The day of the attempt, after a council meeting, Louis boarded his carriage in the courtyard. Gaston, Soissons, and Richelieu were at the bottom of a
flight of steps, surrounded by a crowd of followers. Montrésor and Saint-Ysbal
stood by with knives concealed under their coats. All that the conspirators
needed to dispatch the cardinal was a sign from Gaston. But suddenly, as Montrésor tells it, Gaston bolted from the group and ran up the stairs to retreat into
the house. Killing a priest proved too criminal even for Gaston. He was scared.
Back in the courtyard, Saint-Ysbal waited for a signal from Soissons that never
came.[40]

Then Louis fell into a somber and irritable mood that further dampened
the cardinal's own good spirits after Arras. Was this the melancholy of a new
father? The Dauphin was now a vigorous two-year-old child. But the day the
king arrived at Saint-Germain-en-Laye from Arras and went to see him in
the company of Cinq-Mars, the child shrieked uncontrollably.[41] This angered
Louis, who immediately wrote to Richelieu to report the incident. "I shall not
accept this kind of bad humor," he said. Two days later, Richelieu heard the

same complaint, with real menace this time: "I am very dissatisfied with my son; as soon as he sees me he screams as if he were confronting the devil, and calls for his mother. One must dissipate this bad temper, and take him away from the queen as soon as possible."[42] Anne, who was pregnant with a second child, burst into tears upon hearing the king's ultimatum. The woman Richelieu had placed as governess to the Dauphin gave him secret reports on any significant event in the young life of the heir to the French throne. He instructed her to quiet the situation. Six days after the disastrous reunion with his son, Louis wrote to the cardinal: "My son asked me for forgiveness on his knees today, and then he played with me for over an hour. I gave him toys so that he might amuse himself. We are the best friends in the world."[43] Anne gave birth to a second son, Philippe, a week later, on September 21.

The king's bad temper nevertheless continued. Chavigny wrote to Mazarini: "His Majesty has been showing some ill will towards the cardinal-duke. I have to tell you that I fear what they announce, yet Monsieur de Noyers assures me that it's nothing. There are many strange details on this matter that I cannot write about." Was it Cinq-Mars, then, who was responsible for Louis's somber mood? After the siege at Arras, there were reasons to believe that Cinq-Mars waged a secret campaign against the cardinal. The twenty-year-old now dreamed of martial glory, and he had asked Louis if he could have the command of du Hallier's army. Louis had heard contrasting opinions regarding how Cinq-Mars had fought. Some found that he showed valor. Others reported to the king that he was quite stunned by gunfire, and that in spite of his allure and fashionable attire he "did not have that noble pride that suits so well a man of war."[44] In response to his friend's request, he explained patiently that he could not remove the hero of a siege this way, and that in any case Cinq-Mars still needed to get more experience in the art of war.[45] Richelieu declared in public that his unwieldy former protégé was cowardly. The slight threw Cinq-Mars into a fit of rage.[46] Adding insult to injury, the *Gazette de France* published a narrative of the siege that did not even mention Cinq-Mars's name, even though he had been the leader of the volunteers' corps.

Eventually, Cinq-Mars showed his hand. He openly harassed the cardinal by boasting about his influence over Louis and how the king felt deeply conflicted about his minister. He told him how angry the king was after Richelieu had published a commemorative book of the siege at Hesdin that gave all the glory of the enterprise to La Meilleraye. He let him know of the king's frustration when he saw the minister reject his master's advice and propose it a little later, just to make it look as if only he could find solutions to problems. There was little in Richelieu's ways that escaped the king's attention, apparently, by Cinq-Mars's telling. "Monsieur le Grand has told me on many occasions that the king confided he had to endure me because he needed me for the sake of his affairs; from that he inferred and warned me that I had to watch for my security, because the king was not the kind of person one could hold for reasons of necessity," noted Richelieu in a memorandum he wrote to remind himself of Cinq-Mars's provocations.[47]

Louis, indeed, bore a share of responsibility in this dubious affair. He did complain to the young man about his miserable relationship with Richelieu, and about how he wished to reign by himself. Cinq-Mars must have observed how Louis often questioned foreign ambassadors and other officials to find out whether the cardinal conducted business without his knowledge.[48] Even after the victory at Arras, Louis remained tired of a war that cost so much and made his people suffer so greatly. At other times, however, Louis would tell Cinq-Mars that while he loved him, and although he could not stand Richelieu, he would undoubtedly keep his minister if he had to choose between the two. Louis even went as far as stirring up the twenty-year-old's sentiments against him by revealing how his former mentor discreetly tried to tarnish his reputation and get him ousted.

The Comte de Soissons, still at the fortress of Sedan where he had fled in 1636, thought Richelieu had discovered the assassination project. He heard of the worsening relations between the cardinal and the king's favorite. Through one of the courtiers, a young man named François-Auguste de Thou, he offered Cinq-Mars the hand of his niece, provided that Monsieur le Grand would double his efforts at taking down the cardinal. Cinq-Mars declined, but he kept this overture to himself, not even sharing it with the king.[49]

CHAPTER 10

The Final Scene (1641–1642)

O N THE EVENING OF JANUARY 14, 1641, Cardinal Richelieu presented Desmarets de Saint-Sorlin's new play *Mirame* for the opening of his theater at the Palais-Cardinal. *Mirame* tells the story of a princess, who falls in love with a foreign king's favorite who had been sent to woo the princess on his master's behalf. At the cardinal's theater, the curtain rose to a lush garden, framed by porticos that looked onto a sea. Two fleets glided past in the distance, sails deployed under a bright sun, moving all together as in a ballet. Then night plunged the stage into darkness to reveal the moon slowly emerging from the back of the stage, bathing the scene in a silvery light.

Paris had been abuzz in anticipation of the premiere.[1] Grandees, prelates, financiers, artists, and the few fortunate laymen who waited patiently to get into the cardinal's theater were not disappointed. Richelieu's new theater was an enchanting place. It cost a fortune, and, considering the effort it took to bring to Paris the colossal beams for the vaulted ceilings of the theater, the skills and ingenuity the Italian engineers deployed to mount all the sophisticated machinery, how much gold went into the gilding of the Corinthian columns, the balustrades of the balconies, and the chandeliers, surely the extravagant numbers people whispered to each other were not far-fetched. On the other side of the palace, artists Simon Vouet and Philippe de Champaigne had just finished a gallery with a series of historical portraits. The rest of the Palais-Cardinal was filled with precious objets d'art and rare books. Richelieu was not alone in embellishing Paris. In spite of the war, aristocrats erected sumptuous mansions in the

Marais and near the Luxembourg. The Palais du Louvre underwent much-needed repairs and improvements, too. Notably, Richelieu's architect, Lemercier, added the Pavillon de l'Horloge in the Renaissance courtyard. Still, all this paled when compared with the cardinal's grand home.

From his box on the first balcony of his theater, Cardinal Richelieu was again at a moment when he could survey the scene with satisfaction. Not only was he responsible for the magnificient theater and remarkable entertainment that evening, but the cardinal celebrated an engagement, that of his niece Claire-Clémence de Maillé-Brézé with Condé's son, the Duc d'Enghien.[2] This alliance of Richelieu's niece with a prince of the blood was so out of proportion that, even considering the immense power and wealth of his future uncle, it embarrassed d'Enghien. Other things made this an odd match. The fiancée, a very petite twelve years old, still played with her dolls. Her late mother, Nicole, had suffered from a mental condition and for that reason had spent most of her life out of the public eye. D'Enghien's mother, Charlotte-Marguerite, who was the sister of the late Duc de Montmorency, lamented the marriage project.[3] But in the end, it was up to the elder Condé to decide, and he had put aside his pride a long time ago by pledging himself to the cardinal.[4]

After the victory at Arras, news of another brilliant success had come from Italy. Late in September 1640, the Comte d'Harcourt had taken back Turin, leading Christine's brother-in-law, Thomas of Savoy, to consider abandoning the Spanish and switching his allegiance to Louis XIII. In October, French troops reached Catalonia to buttress the local militia's defense. There were not enough French soldiers to prevent the Castilian army from taking Tarragona, just south of Barcelona, but the province still held tight. Portugal was also causing Olivares much trouble. On December 1, the new king John IV had declared his kingdom's independence and signed a treaty of cooperation with Louis XIII. Then, at a new meeting of the diet in Regensburg, the emperor had agreed to open discussions with France and its allies.

When the curtain was lowered after the premiere of *Mirame*, everyone in the audience turned their heads to acknowledge the cardinal. He was overtaken with emotion, related a spectator: "he was standing up, then sitting again, then leaning over from his box to show himself to the assembly."[5] Courtiers saw that he wore a long coat of taffeta the color of fire, over a bodice of black cloth trimmed at the collar and hem with ermine.[6] Thirty-two young pages dressed in his livery appeared, each carrying a large golden vessel filled with candied fruit. They offered these treats to Queen Anne and to the most prominent ladies. Next, two floats in the shape of peacocks pulled a footbridge from the stage. As soon as this bridge touched the platform at Anne's feet, the theater's curtain went up again to reveal a dance hall lit with sixteen crystal chandeliers and furnished with seats covered in gray and silver silk. Trompe-l'oeil panels made the impromptu hall look infinitely large. Because Louis had left immediately after the comedy, Gaston led Anne to this stage, where she opened the ball.[7]

Suddenly, as the music took the guests in a whirl of dance figures, the entire theater burst in laughter. Tiny Claire-Clémence had just fallen flat on her face while dancing, showing the extravagantly high platform shoes she wore to look taller. The courtiers noticed that the Duc d'Enghien, who had looked quite pale and tired until then, looked as amused as the rest of the court.

Cardinal Richelieu spent yet another winter at Rueil after his grand premiere, preparing for the upcoming 1641 campaign. There were occasional stints in Paris, including the marriage celebration of his niece. Another theatrical extravaganza marked the event. Mostly, though, with the help of the members of the king's council, he was focused on how to maintain his momentum. There was Surintendant Claude Bouthillier; his son Chavigny, the secretary of foreign affairs; Sublet de Noyers, the secretary of war; and Chancellier Séguier, in charge of justice. Close to him one could also find a man whose talents Richelieu had come to appreciate more and more over the years, especially now that Father Joseph had passed away. After his stint as nuncio extraordinaire to France in 1634 and 1635, Giulio Mazarini had been recalled by the pope to be vice-legate in Avignon, and then to Rome in the service of the pope's nephew Cardinal Barberini. But Mazarini missed France. In January of 1640, with a letter of naturalization, he had returned to Paris to begin a remarkable career and be called from then on Jules Mazarin.

France's treasury remained as empty as ever, leading it to more daring monetary operations, including an increase in the nominal value of the currency and the recoinage of Spanish currency into the French one. Still, the state pressed the people of France for more funds, at the risk of more revolts. Even more public offices in the magistrature and the administration were created and sold for money. This led to grave conflicts with the Parlement of Paris, which had the prerogative of approving this creation. Because the new posts took away power from existing officers and represented a progressive takeover of the justice system by the Crown, the parlement refused to register the government's decree and formally protested. On February 21, 1641, the king officially declared that he forbade the parlement to mingle in the affairs of the state once and for all.

Still needing more money, Louis asked the French clergy to contribute to the war effort. A general assembly of the clergy convened in February. The government demanded an extraordinary contribution of six million pounds; the assembly offered four. Richelieu, since he had come to power, had taken pains to oversee the Church of France. Notably, he fostered a reform of the Benedictine orders. He had also placed loyal men in the bishoprics. But there were still very vocal prelates who acted independently, and who thought that giving money for the siege of Protestant La Rochelle was one thing, but giving to a war against the Catholic Habsburgs quite another. The cardinal dismissed the bishops and ordered them to leave Mantes, where the clergy's assembly sat. This action soured already tense relations between Cardinal Richelieu and Pope Urban VIII. The French Church had always been independent; it even gave a name, Gallicanism, to a line of thinking that the affair of Gaston's marriage had further underscored. When Richelieu demanded the resources of the French Church to serve his own political purposes, the pope could only wonder where it would all end. One of the bishops the cardinal had chased from the assembly, Montchal, accused the cardinal of fomenting a schism such as the one that had torn England apart in the sixteenth century.[8]

On January 23, the Catalonians had reneged on their Spanish sovereign, Philip IV, and pledged themselves to Louis XIII by naming him Count of Barcelona. Three days later, they successfully pushed back the Castilian army at the Battle of Montjuïc. This meant that Spain still needed to be pressured in the Netherlands, but that the French also had to commit seriously in the south. For months already, Richelieu urged Condé, who commanded in the Languedoc, to raise and bring more troops to help Catalonia. The Spanish commanders, however, anticipated their nemesis's plan. In March, as preparations for the spring campaign were under way, the Cardinal-Infant wrote to his brother, King Philip IV, to suggest that it was time to foster rebellion within France and create a diversion.

Ever since the assassination plot at Amiens in 1636 and his subsequent flight from the court, the Comte de Soissons had lived in Sedan, at the northeast border of France within the territories of the Holy Roman Empire. This town was a sovereign entity that belonged to Frédéric Maurice de La Tour-d'Auvergne, the Duc de Bouillon, and it protected its independence with some of the best fortifications in Europe. Because he ignored at the time the reason for Soissons's flight, Richelieu had found it acceptable to allow the count to retire there for a period of four years. With this period coming to an end, Soissons worried that the cardinal harbored ill designs against him, in all likelihood because he had finally discovered the real reason for the count's retreat from Amiens. The Duc de Bouillon also lived in a state of alarm, knowing the kind of asset Sedan represented. The Cardinal-Infant reached out to Soissons and Bouillon and offered them troops if they would provoke a general rebellion to topple Richelieu's government. They struck a deal.

By the end of April, Richelieu realized that Soissons and Bouillon were preparing a revolt and that his patience had been a mistake.[9] He sent Maréchal de La Meilleraye and his troops to the town of Aire in the Spanish Netherlands, where siege was laid on May 19. Since marshes surrounded most of Aire, this undertaking represented quite a challenge. "It's a place of great value, much stronger that what we thought, with nine bastions, a good counterscarp with a moat, and many advanced fortifications," communicated Richelieu to Condé. Weeks into the siege, one could hardly determine which side held the advantage. Meanwhile, another corps of six thousand soldiers, led by the Maréchal de Châtillon, approached Sedan with a menacing intent. Near Soissons and Bouillon's lair, on June 25, a first skirmish took place. The Cardinal-Infant took this as a signal to intervene. He sent his general Lamboy with some strong contingents. All in all, the rebel forces formed an army of about twelve thousand men. Richelieu had been far from imagining that he would face such strong opposition. The clash between rebel, Spanish, and royal contingents happened on July 6 in a place called La Marfée. The princes and Lamboy's forces routed the royal army so badly that it fled, even leaving behind a cart that carried one hundred thousand crowns meant for the payment of the soldiers.[10] The rebels formed plans to overthrow the government of Richelieu.

But as they rode back to Sedan, Soissons and Bouillon spotted a skirmish between their own men and laggards of the royal army's retreat. Soissons approached the scene. Suddenly, the count fell off his horse, one foot still in a stirrup. He was dead, his head mangled and burned in such a way that he could only have been shot point-blank. The circumstances of this stunning death have never been explained. Some, including Bouillon himself, claimed that Soissons had shot himself when he tried to raise the visor of his helmet with his pistol, a habit against which people had warned him many times.[11] Others say that a double agent paid by the cardinal had killed him. It was either chance or dubious political prudence that saved the cardinal this time. Anyhow, the mysterious death cut short the rebels' cause. Lamboy left with his troops to try to rescue Aire, which, despite his intervention, fell to the French on July 26. In August, the Duc de Bouillon surrendered to the king.

In Catalonia, Philippe de La Mothe-Houdancourt tried to reclaim Tarragona from the Spanish with additional troops and help from the navy. After the commander of the French fleet failed to prevent the town's supply, the blockade of Tarragona had to be lifted on August 20. The army Olivares sent to tame this rebellion in Barcelona was quite strong. One additional difficulty for the Catalonians and the French was the many fortified places that the Spanish still held north of Barcelona, in a region called Roussillon. As autumn arrived, the cardinal ordered the fleet to retire for the winter in Barcelona and asked for more troops to prevent the Spanish from supplying Perpignan, the principal city they held in the Roussillon.

Grand theatrical productions and balls were out of the question at the outset of 1642. On February 3, Louis XIII and Cardinal Richelieu departed from Fontainebleau for a long voyage toward the south. Having heard that Olivares was arming forcefully to subdue Catalonia and secure the Roussillon, they headed for decisive confrontation. This early start took place under good auspices. On January 17, the Franco-Weimarian army, now led by Guébriant, had won a battle against the imperial army at Kempen, in Germany. It made it much harder for either Spanish or imperial troops to attack the eastern or the northern fronts while king and minister waged war in the Roussillon. Adding to this success in Kempen was the capture of that army's leader, Lamboy, the war chief who had threatened the French in Arras and in Sedan.

All the while, relations between Richelieu and his former protégé Cinq-Mars had continued to deteriorate. When the king's *cher ami* announced that he wanted to marry Marie de Gonzague—the same woman Gaston had courted during the siege at La Rochelle fourteen years earlier—Richelieu scoffed at the idea and told the young man his nobility was not good enough. To impress Marie de Gonzague, Cinq-Mars convinced Louis that he should attend the privy council's sessions. Richelieu bluntly warned the king that affairs of state were not the business of children. The day after the young man made this demand, wrote Montglat, the cardinal "berated him like a valet, told him he was an insolent child, and threatened that he would sink even lower than where he began."[12]

Cinq-Mars vowed to take revenge. The cardinal's spies did not notice that immediately after a meeting during which the Duc de Bouillon had formally apologized to Louis XIII for his uprising with Soissons, Cinq-Mars had had dinner with the duke. In the following weeks, a young man who had relayed Soissons's marriage proposition to Cinq-Mars in the fall, François-Auguste de Thou, shuttled between Bouillon and Cinq-Mars to help advance their relationship. A thirty-year-old redhead, de Thou held a low office in the government and was also a librarian to the king. Primarily, however, he belonged to Soissons and Bouillon's circle, and like many of his contemporaries he had a visceral hatred for Richelieu. Gaston, still deeply angered by the death of Soissons, also had a courtier who hated the cardinal, a hunchback named Louis d'Astarac, Marquis de Fontrailles, who facilitated contacts between the prince and Cinq-Mars. Louis showed frequent signs of illness, and many of his doctors predicted that he would not live for more than six months, adding urgency to the conspiracy. Cardinal Richelieu, it was presumed, aimed to be declared regent.

One evening in November of 1641, in the strictest secrecy, Cinq-Mars, Gaston, and the Duc de Bouillon met in a townhouse—the Hôtel de Venise, in the Marais, where Gaston's stables were and where his equerry lived—to finalize the details of a plot to finally get rid of Richelieu. Fontrailles could not attend. De Thou waited outside. The plotters agreed that the Spanish needed to provide support again. Fontrailles was to travel to Madrid and present Olivares with a signed request from Gaston. Although the others trusted de Thou, they chose to keep such an explosive secret to themselves.

Cinq-Mars still pressured Louis to dismiss his minister by putting forth that Richelieu waged war to keep himself in power, and that the permanent exile of his mother, Marie de' Medici, tarnished his reign. In the sole company of her longtime confessor, Father Suffren, and an Italian confidant who stole the little money she had, Marie de' Medici had departed from England in August of 1641, after it appeared that increasing political and religious unrest in the kingdom of Charles threatened her safety. A long journey, during which Father Suffren passed away, took her to Cologne. Astoundingly, Marie de' Medici was so poor and sick at this point that some say she could hardly pay the rent of the house where she sojourned.

The court of France headed south. Gaston went back to Blois, while Bouillon, to whom an unsuspecting Richelieu had given the command of the Italian army, made his preparations for the campaign in Sedan. Luck was on Cardinal Richelieu's side during this trip. Cinq-Mars realized that his best way to succeed was to assassinate Cardinal Richelieu. As the cardinal himself later recounted, Cinq-Mars first attempted to kill him in the town of Briare, but for some reason could not.[13] Once in Lyon, where the court took some rest for a week, Cinq-Mars summoned a band of young nobles from Auvergne, the ancestral region of his family, to support him. Cinq-Mars, however, backed down at the last minute because he thought it was preferable to obtain Gaston and de Bouillon's consent before acting.

The court traveled down the Rhône Valley. In Valence, Richelieu reunited with Mazarini, who at France's request had just been nominated a cardinal. Louis XIII solemnly conveyed the man his red biretta. Louis's minister coordinated operations for the army that awaited them in the Roussillon. Money was so short that he feared the soldiers would begin pillaging the land and alienate the local population. That had been a crucial mistake at the beginning of the war, in 1635, and it could not happen again. The minister sent a courier *exprès en diligence* with money to Surintendant Bouthillier.[15] Once Louis and the cardinal's convoys reached the Rhône Delta, they veered to the right to follow the coastline of the Mediterranean Sea. By mid-March, the entire court had settled in the city of Narbonne.

Louis and Cardinal Richelieu first ordered Maréchal de La Meilleraye to besiege Collioure. This small but strategically fortified port was encased at the foot of the mountains that plunge into the Mediterranean Sea between Barcelona and Perpignan, and holding it was essential for the larger goal of taking Perpignan, the capital of the Roussillon. Siege operations began in mid-March 1642 after a few days of unusually stormy weather with heavy snowfall. The regiment of Cinq-Mars showed courage in the many fierce attacks on the place. The port surrendered to the French on April 10. There were about twelve hundred Spanish troops in the château, and only sixteen horsemen out of the four hundred that guarded it initially.

Louis, who resided at the palace of the Archbishop of Narbonne, spent most of his time with Cinq-Mars, while his minister lived in another mansion just across the town square. Perhaps witnessing his favorite's courage made Louis realize the unjust nature of Richelieu's past mockeries. Perhaps Cinq-Mars's relentless campaign of persuasion had its effect. The king barely spoke to Richelieu, who fell ill. A strange inflammation took hold of his right arm. From the beginning of April, the minister could not even sign his name, so bad was his condition. Rumors of a conspiracy hovered over the court, and even in Paris. Richelieu knew of suspicious movements between France and Spain, too. Olivares, whose reputation was in a tailspin, had readily agreed to the treaty with Gaston on March 13.[15] When Fontrailles came back to France with the treaty in hand, he heard that a spy had followed him on his way to Madrid. The cardinal's insecurity worsened when, on April 21, Louis left Narbonne to lead the siege of Perpignan. The king went away without saluting his minister.

Perpignan lies on a plain, but a citadel perched on a rocky hill protected it. It was also amply supplied and had many wells. Clearly, then, only a blockade would enable the French to take the town, and everyone expected a long, drawn-out siege until at least mid-June. Louis took his lodging in a modest house built on an elevation, about one mile from the siege. The memoirs of an officer of the army, Aymar de Chouppes, provide useful details of the ongoing intrigue. Cinq-Mars confided to him that he had harbored a grudge ever since the cardinal had dishonored him following the siege at Arras, when he had tried to obtain the command of du Hallier's army. Chouppes, who was a *cardinaliste*, diplomatically explained that it might have been because he had not spoken to the cardinal about it before, and the minister was jealous of his power. Surely a reconciliation was possible, he added.

"You know Monsieur le Cardinal," responded Cinq-Mars after reflecting for a while. "There is no going back with him, he never forgives."

A day later, this officer came back to Cinq-Mars. Richelieu had urged him to convince the young man that good relations could be restored. Cinq-Mars lay in bed as he heard this. He turned over and sighed. "Ah! Monsieur de Chouppes, it's too late now."[16]

A week after the siege began, Secretary Sublet de Noyers took his turn as the king's minder. He began a correspondence with Chavigny, who had remained by the cardinal's side. Their letters are still preserved in the diplomatic archives of the French Foreign Ministry, on the famed Quai d'Orsay. Nothing reveals more the unfolding drama and the heavy atmosphere at court than these documents. Knowing that their exchanges could be intercepted at any time, Sublet de Noyers and Chavigny expressed themselves in oblique language, and that tone gives their account a fascinating intensity. The situation Sublet de Noyers found by Louis's side was discouraging: "The thick air of the Pyrenees has come down to obscure the court," he wrote upon arrival.[17]

Day after day during that month of May 1642, the strange disease that had attacked Richelieu's arm progressed. Painful ulcers formed and required the constant intervention of surgeons. "I can't be carried from one bed to another one without hurting extraordinarily," the cardinal wrote to Sublet de Noyers on May 3. Three days later, he spoke of a wound in the fold of his arm: "There is new inflammation in my arm, and the older opening that God and nature created has now reopened and pus oozes in great quantity. Only to console me the doctors speak of playing with their knives again; it will be hard for me to accept, because I have no courage or strength left. I pray for God to give me some so that I can submit to His will." On May 12 the news was hardly better: "I am always in the same state: one day I hope, the next I'm in doubt, and all nights are bad. God will give what is necessary, and what He has prescribed is what I want."[18]

Beyond perfunctory notes of good wishes, Louis remained strangely silent. De Noyers reported that Cinq-Mars held such power over the king's mind that he could destroy in an hour what the cardinal's envoy had convinced him of over an entire eight days. The king fell ill, too, with his characteristic signs of emotional turmoil.[19] From all over Europe, in letters from allies in the Dutch Republic, but also in newspapers from Brussels and Cologne, the wildest rumors spoke of the cardinal's dismissal. Richelieu's secret police reported that Marie de' Medici was packing her bags for her return. Intercepted letters from Madame de Chevreuse spoke of her archenemy Richelieu's imminent demise.

On May 23, 1642, Cardinal Richelieu dictated his last will and testament to his secretary and decided to leave Narbonne. There were many reasons why such a move was ill-timed. On the one hand, there was no wine left, and only two dogs were still alive, in Perpignan.[20] Victory for the French seemed imminent. On the other hand, news had come in that Olivares was sending relief by land and by sea. Together with his king, Philip IV, the Spanish minister had taken the unusual step of moving closer to the action, in the Aragonese city of Aranjuez, to supervise better the operations. Who knew what resistance the nineteen thousand French troops in Perpignan would offer as they were sweltering under the hot sun of the Roussillon?[21] So far Perpignan's attempts at forcing the defense lines had been a failure, but desperation sometimes works wonders. For these reasons, too, Richelieu should have remained close by.

Yet Richelieu suddenly departed on May 27, stating that his doctors had recommended a change of air, which was true. Not only did he not ask the king's permission, but he left him an ultimatum: if he wanted his minister back by his side, Louis would have to publicly declare his continuing trust in the cardinal and punish those who showed ill will toward him. In an extraordinary memorandum he penned to inform Chavigny and Sublet de Noyers of his hasty departure, Richelieu wrote with his past trials in mind: "God's design was for me to find an unlocked door, so that I could defend myself when one tried to hasten my ruin. To let a place that is not fortified be attacked, is to let it be taken. It is certain that they are attacking my innocence, and to say nothing is to allow the malefactors to succeed."[22] Of course, the unlocked door of which Richelieu wrote was the door that had allowed him to enter Marie de' Medici's study at the Palais du Luxembourg, on the Day of the Dupes, when he won Louis's allegiance from the queen mother and saved his career, if not his life. Time for dramatic action had come yet again.

The days after Richelieu left Narbonne were harrowing for him. He wandered aimlessly with his convoy, having no place to go in this southern region of France. "At night no one knew where they would be sleeping the following day," related Montglat.[23] Rain battered his convoy. Because he could not endure travel in a carriage, his men had to carry him in his litter, which slowed their progress. Madame de Combalet sent her uncle more warnings that Paris was abuzz with his demise. News of a French defeat suffered against the Spanish army of Flanders on May 26, at the Battle of Honnecourt, raised fear of another enemy descent upon Picardy.[24] After many detours, Richelieu finally heard from one of his faithful, the governor of Provence. The cardinal had found a destination in Tarascon, on the right bank of the Rhône, and not far from the papal enclave of Avignon.

Ironically, by the time Richelieu had departed from Narbonne, there were fewer reasons for him to leave. Over the preceding weeks, Louis had tired of his favorite, with his ambitions and arrogance. On one or two occasions, the king even let his impatience show in public. He repeated to Cinq-Mars how much he valued Cardinal Richelieu's service. Yet few could understand that Cinq-Mars was not really the king's confidant anymore. Richelieu's precipitate departure caused many to think that, indeed, Louis would soon replace him, or, at least, that this would give Cinq-Mars an opportunity to consolidate his hold over the monarch. Also, the young man deftly concealed his dwindling fortunes. One day he came to the king's apartment in the company of his courtiers. An usher stopped him at the door, but Cinq-Mars did not lose his composure. He told the usher that this was just because of one of their habitual fights, and promised that if he would let him wait in the hallway that led to king's room, he would receive great rewards later on. For the next two weeks, Cinq-Mars spent a few hours per day in the king's hallway, reading romance novels, unbeknownst to Louis. "This is the kind of news that spread through France to confirm the cardinal's disgrace, and double his defiance," concluded the memoirist Montglat.[25] On June 3, Louis penned a short note to assure his minister: "Whatever rumor he [Richelieu] can hear, I have never loved you so much. We've been together for too long to ever be separated."[26] But Richelieu ran away, until a copy of the treaty signed by Gaston and Olivares mysteriously surfaced. "God assists the king with marvelous discoveries," Richelieu wrote to Sublet de Noyers on June 11, 1642.

Historians have never figured out how Richelieu got his hands on the document that incriminated Gaston and Cinq-Mars. Some say a spy at the court of Spain obtained it. Other have speculated that Anne of Austria sent it after getting hold of a copy, to shore up her reputation with Richelieu.[27] Whoever it was, this proof of conspiracy surely afforded Richelieu the coup de théâtre of his life. His secretary, Charpentier, later recounted that once Richelieu read the document the messenger had brought to him, the cardinal almost fainted.

"Let someone bring me a cup of broth," he panted, "I am most troubled!" After a few of sips he was able to calm down. "O God! You must care deeply for this kingdom and for my person!"[28]

The cardinal ordered Chavigny to bring proof of Cinq-Mars's betrayal to the king right away. Louis had left the ongoing siege of Perpignan with Cinq-Mars and was back in Narbonne. He had fallen ill and showed yet again those symptoms that his contemporaries interpreted as marks of great stress: fever and intestinal inflammation. When Chavigny and Sublet de Noyers were introduced, they found the king conversing with Cinq-Mars. The two took him aside to explain what startling documents they had in hand. Louis was perhaps too stunned to realize the magnitude of this event and what it represented.

When Cinq-Mars returned to see him after spending the day playing croquet and watching the training of a horse he had just received, Louis behaved as if nothing had happened. Someone warned Cinq-Mars that the king had ordered his arrest. The young man took refuge in the attic of a house. Eventually, the town's militia tracked him down and took him to the nearest safe place, Montpellier. De Thou, in the meantime, had also been arrested.

The king took de Thou with him while he traveled farther north in search of a milder climate. As with Richelieu, doctors had advised Louis that he should leave the hot south and take waters in a town which, coincidentally, was close to where Richelieu had safely landed. Richelieu, in the haven of Tarascon, heard from Sublet de Noyers that Louis was deeply melancholic. "Strange thoughts haunted him," Sublet de Noyers wrote.[29] "Are you sure his [Cinq-Mars's] name was not mistaken for another?" the king asked at one point. News from the fronts even left this otherwise martial king indifferent. Richelieu ordered Chavigny and Sublet de Noyers to stir up the anger of the king against Cinq-Mars by all means possible, while he kept writing affectionate letters to reassure him. "Having just heard that Your Majesty's ailments have not relented, I am sending this messenger right away to hear more news, while I pray to God with all my heart that the news he will bring back shall be that which I seek."[30]

When Louis arrived at the springs of Montfrin, he stayed away from Tarascon for a while. Finally, on June 28, he reunited with Cardinal Richelieu in the minister's own house. Richelieu's staff placed a bed next to the cardinal's own, in order for the two to talk as much as they wanted, and even take some rest if needed. This conversation lasted for about four hours. Nothing of its terms has ever been revealed. The correspondence that the two men exchanged right after Louis began his return to Paris shows no sign of tension. Richelieu sent a warm letter the day following the interview, where he announced that seeing his king had been so beneficial that he could raise his arm for the first time in a long time.

Most important, Richelieu did not accuse Louis of any wrongdoing. The king's minders, however, repeatedly charged Cinq-Mars with having plotted to kill the cardinal, and denigrated the former favorite. Louis ordered that Cinq-Mars's imprisonment in Montpellier be made harsher. Richelieu, after a while, sent Louis this letter: "I recognize that it would have been easy for Monsieur le Grand to execute his design, which I would have never suspected, it being impossible to believe that he would be evil enough to sully himself with the blood of a cardinal, who, for the last twenty-five years, has with God's permission quite happily served his master. Reason wants kings to protect their servants; yet it is your own goodness, which has caused you to protect me on all the occasions that Cinq-Mars had wanted to end my life."[31] Perhaps Louis found relief in those words, thinking that his minister did not hold any grudge for his suspicious behavior, and had accepted his renewed expressions of heart-felt support, trust, and friendship.[32] But Richelieu's words could also have been ironic, because he could now afford it. Two days after leaving Tarascon, King Louis XIII had given him full executive power over the southern regions of France, with responsibilities for all judicial affairs, including the trial of the conspirators.

Soon after, surprising news arrived from the Roussillon. Richelieu's nephew Jean-Armand de Maillé-Brézé had sailed with the Atlantic fleet from the port of Brest early in the summer to join with the Mediterranean fleet and protect the blockade of Perpignan from any relief Olivares could send. Indeed, a powerful Spanish naval force had advanced in late June to oust the French from the Roussillon. From June 30 to July 3, in full view of Barcelona, Maillé-Brézé laid out his ships and maneuvered brilliantly to win a stunning victory against the Spanish, pushing as far as the Balearic in hot pursuit of what was left of the navy after he routed them. The siege of Perpignan could continue without any more threats coming from the sea.

Maillé-Brézé's victory was not the only news. Marie de' Medici had died of gangrene in Cologne, on July 3, alone and miserable, the prey of unscrupu-lous courtiers who had taken what little she had left. Before her death she made the point that "despite everything that happened before her exit from France, and after her entry into Flanders, she had always kept and would al-ways keep in her heart the affection and the sentiment of a queen for her king and of a mother for her son."[33] Actually, she spent the last years of her life hanging on to her astrologist's predictions, hoping that Louis's ill health would shorten his days and allow her return as regent. Even though her last will ig-nored Richelieu, after her death the queen's servants set aside for him a pet parrot he had given her in happier days.

From the small town of Bourbon where he had moved and awaited Cinq-Mars to realize his projects, Gaston now sent letter after letter of submission to the cardinal. He revealed the details of the Spanish plot. Richelieu was inclined to exile him to Venice, where he would offer him a pension equal to what the Spanish had agreed to give the prince for his betrayal. Bouillon came back to France as a prisoner. He saved his life by ceding the stronghold of Sedan to the French king. Fontrailles had fled to England even before the threat was discovered.

This left Richelieu with two subjects to bring to justice. He spent the summer month of July and most of August in Tarascon investigating the conspiracy and preparing the prosecution of Louis's former confidant and de Thou. First, he formed an extraordinary commission in Lyon.[34] Then he compiled all the elements of the dossiers. He certified witness testimonies and prepared questions that the guardians were to ask in the course of their everyday exchanges with the prisoners.[35] He set up in minute detail the material arrangements of Cinq-Mars's captivity in Montpellier. Richelieu stayed in a house that sat in front of Tarascon's château, where de Thou was kept. The cardinal had the man brought to his room and questioned him while lying in bed. Richelieu's infected arm still weakened him much. A well-informed Parisian described the cardinal's schedule in Tarascon: "He works and dictates from seven to eight. From eight to nine his doctors dress his wounds. From nine to ten he speaks with those who have some business with him. From ten to eleven he works, and then he hears mass and has lunch. Until two he discusses with Monsieur le Cardinal Mazarin and others. From two to four he works again, and then gives audience." The author of the letter added, "Never has the affair of Perpignan taken up so much of his time."[36] The everyday business of his ministry demanded the cardinal's attention, but the trial of Cinq-Mars and de Thou was also very much on his mind.

Cinq-Mars and de Thou denied all involvement in the conspiracy. All the young man and his friend would say, and with much double entendre, was that whatever they had done the king knew about. Gaston's confession caused their downfall. His testimony was vague about de Thou's involvement, however, and Bouillon's own declaration even said that the man had only heard of a project to retire in Sedan, without any knowledge of Spanish cooperation. Cinq-Mars's guilty verdict, by contrast, seemed a foregone conclusion. The cardinal declared that the trial could open in Lyon. Cinq-Mars was transferred from Montpellier to Tarascon. On August 20, after he attended a service to honor the memory of Marie de' Medici—a magnificent ceremony that did not feature a eulogy—Richelieu began his journey to Lyon.

To avoid the discomfort of traveling by carriage, the cardinal had ordered an entire fleet to travel by river. Tens of horses towed the boats from along the banks of the mighty Rhône. First came two frigates carrying musketeers armed to the teeth. The cardinal's own vessel, decorated with gold and crimson velvet, followed. A smaller boat attached to Richelieu's own carried de Thou and his guards. Cinq-Mars had been sent to Lyon by carriage. Four more boats completed the convoy, loaded with Richelieu's courtiers and his luggage. Along each side of the Rhône, two companies of cavalry provided added security. The sound of their trumpets echoed in the rugged, dry, rocky landscape of the valley. Landing in any town was quite a challenge. Any movement still caused much pain to the ailing cardinal. So when the boats arrived, the crowds saw six men carry out the cardinal in a huge litter bed built especially for the trip, which they could conveniently transport thanks to padded slings that hung from their shoulders. "What surprised people," says the eyewitness who described the scene, "was that [Cardinal Richelieu] entered houses through windows. Before he came, masons would come to remove the window frames, or make openings in the walls of the rooms where he was to stay. Then, they erected wooden bridges from the street to the window, or opening of the lodging. Thus, while he remained on this portable bed, he went on the streets and then up this bridge, after which he was put in another bed, in a room that his officers hung with crimson and purple damask and decorated with very rich pieces of furniture."[37] The cardinal's entourage and guards gave an impression of "civility, affability, and courtesy." His guards and his soldiers lived chastely, "like virgins," never blasphemed, and showed great piety when they went to church.

Cardinal Richelieu finally arrived in Lyon after two weeks. He took his lodging at his brother Alphonse's palace and waited while the magistrates examined the dossiers. Cinq-Mars and de Thou were jailed at the fortress of Pierre-Cîse and persisted in denying all charges. Gaston's and Bouillon's testimonies denied that de Thou had ever heard of a project to join forces with the Spanish. When Chancellier Séguier exposed this matter to the cardinal, Jean Martin de Laubardemont intervened. Laubardemont used one of the oldest tricks in the book. He interrogated Cinq-Mars and let him know that de Thou had confessed everything. Only a full confession could save Cinq-Mars from torture and death. Cinq-Mars fell into the trap. He explained that his companion knew of the Spanish treaty ever since he had met with Fontrailles on his return from Madrid, in Carcassonne.

In the early morning of Friday, September 12, 1642, guards took Cinq-Mars and de Thou to the courthouse for the last day of proceedings. While the two men waited, Laubardemont played the role of the prosecutor and read a report that, quite possibly, the cardinal had prepared. Then the accused appeared separately. Cinq-Mars reiterated his confession. When his turn came, de Thou had no choice but to recognize that, indeed, he knew of the treaty from his encounter with Fontrailles in Carcassonne.[38] The two met for a final confrontation, and Cinq-Mars, outmaneuvered, realized he had been duped and had precipitated the condemnation of his friend.[39]

Richelieu had left Lyon on his boat earlier that day. While on his way a messenger arrived at full gallop to bring some startling news: on August 29, Perpignan had opened its doors and surrendered. Louis XIII's possessions now extended to the border between Catalonia and Spain. Another messenger sent by the chancellor announced to him that the jury was sending his two enemies to the scaffold.[40]

Cinq-Mars and de Thou spent the afternoon with two Jesuits, Father Mambrun and Father Malavalette, who took their confessions and guided them in their prayers. Mambrun left us a detailed and vivid description of the two men's final hours. This priest might have embellished his narrative to make it instructional and exemplary, but the text reconciles with another detailed account of Cinq-Mars and de Thou's last day. According to these documents, Cinq-Mars remained calm throughout. He wrote a letter to his mother. De Thou told him that he forgave him and fell in trancelike devotion. Around five o'clock, an officer came in to announce that it was time to go. When they stepped out of the courthouse, the two friends saw an immense crowd. They waved. Cinq-Mars wore a frock cut in a maroon Dutch cloth and covered with wide bands of gold lace. His silk stockings were green, a good match for his fancy shoes. Over this outfit was an ample scarlet coat with silver buttons. His hat, in the latest fashion à la Catalane, had one side folded upward. De Thou wore a simple black frock with a short coat. The judges and a carriage waited at the bottom of the steps.

"Look, my friends!" said de Thou to two guards, "they are taking us to heaven in a carriage."

Cinq-Mars and de Thou looked joyful at this point. After saluting their judges, they boarded the carriage and sat in the back, with the Jesuits on each side, at the windows. One hundred archers escorted them, and yet so many people filled the streets that the cortege could move only very slowly. Cinq-Mars and de Thou continued to say their prayers. They exchanged a few words of consolation and saluted the crowd that lined the streets. A group of young ladies swooned when Cinq-Mars waved and shouted at them, "Pray for me!"

When both men volunteered to go first, Father Malavalette solved the matter by noting that de Thou was the elder one, and that he should show the most generosity by stepping aside.

"Well, Monsieur, you want to open the path to glory for me," said de Thou to Cinq-Mars.

"Oh!" responded Cinq-Mars, "I opened a precipice for you before; let us now hurry towards death, to then surge into immortal life."

On the Place des Terreaux where the scaffold stood, people from all over Lyon lined windows, balconies, and roofs. Four hundred guards struggled to form a perimeter around the place of execution. Cinq-Mars and de Thou embraced before the younger man stepped out of the carriage to meet his fate. Trumpets sounded three times. Once on the platform, Cinq-Mars took time to compose himself, Mambrun said. After that he walked around the block holding his hat, took more time to adjust his lace collar, put the hat back, and smiled to the public while he struck a pose, his foot forward and his hand on his hip. Then he realized that the block where his head was going to be cut off did not look like the ones used in Paris. A two-foot log stood upright, with another wood section in front of it. Father Malavalette and a companion explained that the executioner had requested this unusual setup. Lyon's headsman had broken his leg, and because Chancellier Séguier wanted the sentence executed right away, he had hired a handyman to carry it out. Just to be sure that everything would go well, Cinq-Mars took off his hat and kneeled in front of the block, placing his head in the proper position.

"Is that where I am supposed to put it, Father?"

Malavalette and the friar helped him to undress and cut his hair. The young man finally took his place in front of the block, which he surrounded with his two arms while he tried to place his head in the best position. He prayed. The executioner opened a bag and took out some sort of cleaver, of the kind used by butchers. He placed himself next to Cinq-Mars and raised his instrument in the air with his two hands. The crowd that filled the Place des Terreaux "broke the profound silence it observed until then with a terrible moan. The sobs, the sighs, and the laments made such a horrible noise that one could hardly tell where this was happening."[41]

"Here I am, I must die. Dear God, have mercy," said Cinq-Mars.

The blow fell slowly and heavily. Blood drowned Cinq-Mars's scream. For a moment, his body straightened completely while he still held to the block, then fell on its knees again. Because the blow had not detached the head completely, the headsman grabbed it by the hair and sawed it off. Eventually, the head fell off and rolled on the ground. Many people observed that it remained animated for quite a while with eyes open. After struggling a bit to detach the arms that still clenched the block, the henchman placed the body on the side on the platform, together with the severed head that the Jesuit had fetched, and covered both parts with a piece of cloth.

De Thou climbed the ladder to the scaffold so fast that it seemed he was flying, and then he hugged the headsman.

"O my brother, my dear friend, how much I love you! I must hold you in my arms, since today you will give me eternal happiness by sending me to heaven."

He went around a few times to salute the crowd, more modestly than Cinq-Mars. He recited Psalm 115: "The dead praise not the Lord, neither any that go into silence. But we will bless the Lord from this forth and for evermore."[42] After the customary preparations, he took his place on the block. The first blow missed the neck and struck the back of his skull. Reflexively, de Thou brought his hand to his neck and tried to rise. The henchman prepared to strike again. Malavalette, seeing that this would only end up cutting off his fingers, halted him. Another blow inflicted a wound under the ear, and this time it completely threw de Thou on the platform. His legs twitched. The screaming in the crowd of spectators put the ersatz headsman in a panic. He jumped on the body and hacked the head off by striking furiously at the throat.[43]

Cardinal Richelieu was making his way back to Paris from Lyon, on a road he had traveled so often and in so many states of mind. Not only had Cinq-Mars wanted to assassinate him, but, mirabile dictu, now the cardinal knew that Louis had had some knowledge of his favorite's intention all along. Cinq-Mars said many times to his guardian in Montpellier, "The king knows everything I've done."[44] But it was not only that; Louis incriminated himself. Shortly before the trial took place in Lyon, the king heard that Cinq-Mars was speaking of his ambiguous role in the conspiracy, and he felt the need to refute any suggestion that he had ordered Richelieu's assassination. The letter he sent to Chancellier Séguier, the man in charge of the proceedings in Lyon, is startling: "Monsieur le Chancellier . . . the Sire of Cinq-Mars employed all means to irritate me against my cousin [Richelieu], and I suffered that as long as those ill-designs remained within the bounds of moderation. However, when he went as far as proposing to get rid of my cousin and offered to do it himself, I loathed his evil thoughts and detested them. It is sufficient for me to say it for you to believe it." Cinq-Mars would have never felt the need to ally himself to the King of Spain, Louis added, "if I had given him enough support for his evil projects."[45] Worse even, then: Cinq-Mars's desire to assassinate Richelieu existed and was known even before he mounted the conspiracy with Gaston and Bouillon, with knowledge of the king.

In light of this evidence, what the memoirs of Montglat say about Louis's involvement must be considered with attention. Montglat wrote that one day, as Louis once again lamented his situation, Cinq-Mars openly suggested that killing the minister was the natural solution to his problems, and to those of France. The king's reaction, narrated Montglat, was cautious: "[The king] responded that he would be excommunicated, because [Richelieu] was a priest and a cardinal."[46] The captain of the king's musketeers and an ally of Cinq-Mars, Monsieur de Tréville, then said that he would do it and later seek absolution in Rome. No wonder, then, that for many of Louis and Richelieu's contemporaries, the king's silence had tacitly made him the chief of the conspiracy.[47] Louis, blinded by his passion, had taken some very dangerous liberties with his promise to protect his minister Richelieu.

King and minister reunited in Fontainebleau on October 13. Richelieu was exhausted by the trip and in even worse health than before, and so he asked if the king would care to visit him in the house where he stayed. Quite possibly he was also mindful of his own security. Louis acceded to this request. Because he could not ride, the king had spent the last weeks on a new hobby, cooking: he built a stove with stones and learned how to preserve apricots in sugar. People found him sad, but then he claimed he was rejoicing at the thought of seeing his minister, and vowed to live in good harmony with him. The encounter lasted three hours. Chavigny and Sublet de Noyers had to hold Richelieu up so he could stand. King and minister embraced without saying one word, choked with emotion. Richelieu protested his enduring respect for his sovereign the king and struck a conciliatory tone by praising him for getting back his senses after so strong an infatuation with the young man. A few days later, on October 17, 1642, Cardinal Richelieu entered Paris after an absence of eighteen months. Crowds descended in the streets in such numbers that the lord mayor ordered that chains be hung to hold them back. Everyone, of course, had followed the situation in the Roussillon and all the details of the conspiracy. Parisians watched in quiet fascination the mighty cardinal returning twice a victor. Perpignan had fallen, and Cinq-Mars and de Thou's heads, too. The cardinal saluted the crowds graciously.

Once he was settled, Richelieu wrote to Louis that he would resign unless the king "cleansed the court" of all malicious spirits and renounced having a favorite. The object of the first demand concerned, specifically, Monsieur de Tréville, the captain of the musketeers who had been a sympathizer of Cinq-Mars. Richelieu's tone was intransigent, unlike anything he had used before. Then he invited Anne of Austria to the château at Rueil and offered her a superb afternoon reception. The purpose of the invitation became clearer when Richelieu let it be known to Gaston that the king had agreed earlier to several punitive measures against him. Gaston lost his military companies, the government of Auvergne, and, most important, the right to exercise any administrative function in the kingdom. The courtiers assumed Richelieu was maneuvering to retain his power in the likely event of a regency.

Louis appreciated Monsieur de Tréville's loyalty very much, and so he did not respond to Richelieu's request. But the cardinal was undeterred. After waiting for a week, Richelieu sent Chavigny with the following instruction on how to speak to the monarch. No pretense of reconciliation softened his declaration. He reiterated his demands and added these words: "His Majesty should be aware that Monsieur le Grand has said many things he has not yet heard of. His Majesty should know, as well, that Cinq-Mars was spared torture to avoid a public confession of what he said in secret. His Majesty should know that Cinq-Mars's confessor could hardly prevent him from speaking on the scaffold, after he said that once pressed and hopeless, he would not spare anyone."[48] What were these mysterious revelations about which so few people knew? Did they only have to do with Louis's role in the conspiracy?

Louis rebuffed the cardinal's threats and persisted in denying his minister's wishes. Richelieu sent Chavigny to announce that from then on he would not see his king without his own armed guards present. This time, Louis could not ignore the extraordinary provocation. On the subject of dismissing Tréville, he angrily said that he did not intervene in the cardinal's affairs, and so should the cardinal behave with his own. Chavigny objected that the cardinal would never allow the presence of a man that the king did not like. The king, who had always resented his minders, responded mordantly, "Then he would never see you, because I cannot stand you." He then chased the cardinal's envoy away.

Superintendent Sublet de Noyers received the same treatment a few days later when he came to renew Richelieu's demands.

With each day, Richelieu's health deteriorated. Louis appeared to be as melancholic and sickly as ever. The question that courtiers and diplomats asked was not so much who would have the upper hand, but, rather, which of the two would go first. Eventually, Richelieu left Rueil and came to Paris. He felt an urgent need to indulge in his cherished pastime, the theater. For a long time now, the cardinal had wanted to celebrate his political accomplishments in grand style. After months of collaboration and effort with his favorite playwright and producer, Desmarets de Saint-Sorlin, he was ready to present a machine-play titled *Europe*. There could be no blazing gala at the Palais-Cardinal under such dramatic circumstances, however. On November 19, the cardinal asked his servants to lift him off his bed and to transport him to his theater, where the comedians staged a private dress rehearsal for him.

The play's title character, Europe, is ravished by a prince named Ibère—an allegory of Spain—after she refuses his advances. Enter Francion, the French hero who will save the damsel from Ibère's lurid designs.

> *Il sait parler de paix, et moi je la sais faire*
> *Il la fuit et la craint, je la cherche et l'espère.*
> *Il dit bien qu'il ne veut que le commun repos,*
> *Puis soudain ses effets démentent ses propos;*
> *Et moi sans affecter d'être un pacifique,*
> *J'établis en effet la liberté publique.*[49]

[Ibère] can speak of peace, but I know how to procure it.
He runs away from peace and even fears it;

I seek peace and put my hopes in it.
He insists that all he desires is common repose,
Then suddenly his actions his intentions expose.
It is I, with no pretense of being a lover of peace,
Who will actually define common liberty.

The cardinal and Desmarets worked on the play up to the very last days, hence the text's pointed references to the conspiracy of Cinq-Mars. The citadel of Sedan appeared as "the lair of the monsters," and there was mention of the "bloody scaffold of Lyon."[50] The play featured an extravagant display of ever-changing sets, flying machines, and special effects.

On November 20, 1642, one day after Cardinal Richelieu saw *Europe*, and after more than a month of tense exchanges, the king finally acceded to all of his minister's demands. No, Louis XIII would never take a favorite again, and the men he trusted in his guard would be sent away.[51] On the paper wherein he bowed to Richelieu's willpower, Louis wrote the following note: "I have nothing to say to my cousin Cardinal Richelieu, other than he knows too well what the malice, the imposture, and the artifice of Cinq-Mars were while he was by my side; to give credence to anything Cinq-Mars said would disprove the friendship I have for my said cousin and the esteem in which I hold his person."[52]

Cardinal Richelieu came back to Paris thinking that he could survive the king. This time, however, he would not have it his way. A week after the performance of *Europe*, on Friday, November 28, he complained of a sharp pain in his side. A high fever took hold of him. Doctors diagnosed a kind of pleurisy. Both the pain and the fever grew through that Sunday. Fearing the worst, his relatives the Maréchaux de Maillé-Brézé, de La Meilleraye, and Madame de Combalet decided to stay for the night at the Palais-Cardinal. On the following Monday the cardinal coughed blood and could hardly breathe. Doctors recognized that there was nothing they could do.

Since the beginning of this illness, courtiers advised Louis that a visit to his dying minister would be appropriate. On Tuesday, December 2, at around two o'clock in the afternoon, the king entered Richelieu's bedroom at the Palais-Cardinal in the company of several captains of his guard. With Louis by his bedside, Richelieu declared that he would die with the satisfaction of leaving France at a high point. He asked the king to protect his relatives and recommended to him those he esteemed capable of helping him rule his kingdom after his passing, men such as Mazarin. Louis appeared genuinely moved. He fed the cardinal two egg yolks. To exit the palace, as he returned to the Louvre, Louis crossed the grand gallery where the cardinal had hung his own portrait by Philippe de Champaigne, alongside that of the king, and of other illustrious men in French history. One of these figures was Suger, an abbot-statesman who had been a regent of the kingdom. Louis took time to stroll through the gallery and observe the paintings. For some reason he burst into laughter, a laugh that was heard as far back as the chambers of his dying servant.[53]

Cardinal Richelieu's fever and pain in the chest worsened later that evening. He asked for communion, which the priest of the Church of Saint-Eustache delivered. "Here is the judge who will soon decide my fate," said Richelieu before the Eucharist. "I pray with all my heart that He will convict me if I ever had any other intention than the good of religion and the state."

At three o'clock in the morning, the priest performed the last rites before a swell of onlookers, including an inconsolable Madame de Combalet, and many dignitaries of the Church and government. By all accounts, the cardinal showed courage, constancy, and genuine piety in his agony. He prayed constantly, worshipped, and kissed his crucifix.

On Wednesday, December 3, a doctor from Troyes who had a reputation as a wise man gave him a pill that improved his condition. The cardinal rallied, enough to raise hopes of his recovery. But it was merely a sedative, probably an opiate concoction. Louis came to pay a last visit at the end of the afternoon. He had just asked the parlement to ratify the declaration that forbade Gaston to have any future involvement in the government of France. His words to the cardinal were gentle. He assured Richelieu that he would continue his minister's work with diligence, and that he would obtain lasting peace with the Habsburgs in terms honorable for France. The king, many Parisians thought, seemed liberated, and much less chagrined than one would have expected.[54]

Cardinal Richelieu's condition improved once more the next morning, enough for rumors to spread that he was out of trouble. Most of those who watched over him went to have their luncheon. But around eleven, Richelieu felt great dizziness and his body became drenched with cold sweat. The doctors, the relatives, and the priests came back at once and filled the room with sobs and prayers. The cardinal offered more signs of religious devotion. To

Madame de Combalet, who was nearby, he said: "My niece, I am not well at all, I am going to die. Please excuse yourself. Your tenderness already touches me so much."

Shortly after she left the room, he sighed and passed away. It was Thursday, December 4, 1642. Armand-Jean du Plessis, Cardinal-Duc de Richelieu, was dead at the age of fifty-seven. He had been the principal minister of King Louis XIII for eighteen years.

Two days after this death, the Spanish king Philip IV and his minister Olivares retreated from Aranjuez following the failure of their army at Perpignan. Both king and minister returned to Madrid's royal palace in the middle of the night, as discreetly as possible.

Conclusion

ON A NIGHT IN DECEMBER OF 1642, parents, friends, members of the clergy, officers, and his entire household accompanied Cardinal Richelieu's casket to the church of the Sorbonne. The procession made its way from the Palais-Cardinal to the Left Bank, through crowded streets. A six-horse carriage, decorated in black velvet with a chevron motif of white satin, representing the Richelieu arms, carried the cardinal's casket. Every marcher held a large white candle. The streets of Paris, says the *Gazette de France*, appeared as bright as if it were still daylight.

At the same time, for a large part of France's population, Richelieu's death came with relief, because they had come to associate him with public executions and the heavy tolls of a seemingly endless war. One eighteenth-century historian of Louis XIII's reign, the Jesuit Henri Griffet, wrote of old men who remembered the joyous bonfires that lit up France when news of the cardinal's passing spread. Consider this epitaph, one of hundreds, that read:

Ci-gît en ce lieu	Here rests
Le Cardinal de Richelieu	Cardinal Richelieu
À qui il faudrait un tombeau	Who surely deserves a tomb
Plus magnifique et plus beau	More magnificient and beautiful
Puisque avec Son Éminence	Since with His Eminence
Repose toute la France.[1]	Rests all of France.

Those who revered him—and even many who loathed him—understood that Richelieu was an exceptional statesman. After the siege at La Rochelle, the Huguenots remained subdued. Visions of bloody scaffolds discouraged rebellion in the high nobility. Perpignan in the Roussillon, Pinerolo and Susa in Savoy, Lorraine and Franche-Comté, Brisach in the Rhineland, Arras and Hesdin in Flanders—all these contested territories and outposts constituted a defensive belt from which the French king threatened the possessions of Habsburg monarchs Philip IV and Ferdinand III. The French navy, which was nonexistent when Louis came to power, was rebuilt, and a new generation of capable men of war had emerged. In the context of a France made up of a mosaic of institutions and corporations, each with its own regional specificity and privileges, the minister had affirmed the king's power with his extraordinary judicial commissions, or by laying the foundations of a national administration, notably when he increased the number and responsibilities of his intendants. These were the crucial assets on which Mazarin could build to assert France's influence in 1648, six years after Cardinal Richelieu's passing, when the Treaties of Westphalia delineated a new European map based less on religious orthodoxy than political sentiment, and in 1659, when the Treaty of the Pyrenees put an end to the war with Spain, to France's advantage. Cardinal Richelieu's œuvre might have been a work in progress when he died, so much so that his successor had to live through one last jolt of princely and parliamentary independence, the Fronde, but still, he allowed his countrymen to think of a grand future for themselves, and that is no small legacy for a leader.

Yet recognizing the value of this legacy raises the question of how Richelieu made it through it all. The achievements listed above were surely the products of Richelieu's ingenuity, adaptability, and tenacity. The cardinal was not a religious fanatic. He understood that without domestic peace with the Protestants, France would never be able to stand up to the Habsburgs. Thus he signed the Treaty of Monzón with Spain, in 1626, gaining valuable time to restore the kingdom's forces. After La Rochelle, he left those he considered heretics their liberty of conscience, and he carefully avoided the kind of drastic action that Louis's son took by revoking the Edict of Nantes in 1685, with damaging consequences when the Protestants took their wealth and economic expertise abroad. That Richelieu was a pragmatic, rational politician seeking the political unity of the kingdom and a balance of power in Europe is true, provided that one also accepts that his long-term goal was to make France, and possibly Europe, an entirely Catholic land. Let us quote him again on this subject: "The kingdom of God is the principle of government, and, indeed, it is such a necessity that without this foundation, no prince can ever reign well and no state can be happy."[2] Following one of Richelieu's great scholars, Orest Ranum, the key to what may appear to be a seemingly intractable reconciliation of Church interests with the use of human reason is actually simple: Richelieu believed in the sacred nature of the monarchy, that the French king was the Lord's anointed. "Reason of state," then, was the king's God-given prerogative.[3] Louis was pious, even to the point of being prudish and overly scrupulous. He earnestly wanted to be known as *The Just*. Rulers, naturally, are rarely ever fully rational. Yet Richelieu also thought that God gave unquestionable authority to the King of France, and, indeed, he steadfastly affirmed that power throughout his entire career, bypassing regional law courts, or countering the high nobles who, in the feudal tradition, considered the king to be but a prince primus inter pares.[4]

Richelieu, to be sure, made some costly mistakes and took some very dangerous risks. After the Swedes failed to create a German Protestant party that could ward off Ferdinand II and Philip IV's forces, he launched France in an all-out war with Spain in 1635, without securing proper defenses. Had it not been for France's vast natural and human resources, and remarkable resilience, Richelieu might well have lost. Loyalty and familial ties were often valued more than talent when he chose his men, although this *clientèle*, as suggested by the historian David Parrott, provided vital support in difficult times, too. The cardinal was surely an organized man who sought the best to affirm Louis XIII's fiscal, judicial, and military authority. Nonetheless, many of Richelieu's administrative programs were circumstantial responses to problems raised by his constant wars. His command of finances and commerce was meager, and the actual reforms he tried to carry out could not be implemented. Sometimes, it was because of inertia and sheer resistance from local powers. Other times, it was because his men were prone to use too heavy a hand or were just incompetent. When he passed away, France actually teetered on the edge of bankruptcy. Finally, in the realm of court intrigues, the stories of the Jesuit Caussin and of Cinq-Mars provide additional evidence that Richelieu was not such a good judge of men after all.

Credit must be given to Louis XIII for taking over when his minister fell to discouragement and depression after he blundered, but, as the memoirist

Montrésor argued, luck was also with the king's minister many times. Between Gustavus Adolphus's convenient timing by death in battle and Soissons's possibly accidental shooting, it is hard to believe that the dice were not loaded in the cardinal's favor. Without the opportunity offered by the revolt in Catalonia, who knows if we would care so much about Richelieu today. One might argue that mysteries of state are truly impenetrable, and that Cardinal Richelieu's strokes of luck could well have been the effects of carefully laid out but unsavory strategies and transactions, or the work of paid stealth agents whose identities are lost forever.

So, to remain on more secure ground in this assessment of Richelieu's genius, it seems that, above all, sense of opportunity, amazing decisiveness, and courage were the cardinal's most extraordinary political qualities; these were the heroic traits that allowed him to succeed, often *in spite* of himself. What is striking in Cardinal Richelieu's life is how he displayed this talent in settings both large and small. He took advantage of Olivares's faux pas during the succession of Mantua, in spite of Marie de' Medici's opposition, to give France a first advantage at the Susa Pass. Confronting the angry crowds on the Pont-Neuf while the Spanish army threatened Paris in 1636 is another moment that defines Cardinal Richelieu as a man of wonders. The way he swiftly hastened the submission of La Rochelle's aldermen in his gallery at Aytré, or destroyed Louis's trust in his confessor, Father Caussin, at Rueil, was masterful political staging. The long held view that Richelieu acted from the beginning of his career with a master plan to fight the Habsburgs and make France a modern administrative state, as old schoolbooks taught the French, can stand, because he did raise the bar of expectations for France. More than as a calculating, prescient eagle of politics, though, Cardinal Richelieu did it by becoming one of history's most intrepid and fiery actors, a man who was moved by an uncommon force and who lived politics deeply, viscerally.

"A capable prince represents a great treasure in a state. A skillful counsel, as it should be, is no less a treasure, but the acting of both in concert is invaluable, because from it derives the true happiness of states."[5] The God-given absolute power and genuine intelligence of Louis XIII did not make Richelieu think less of his role as adviser. In his logic, and as early as his speech to the Estates General of 1614, clergymen had to play a crucial role in the royal council. The theological quarrel with the abbot Saint-Cyran and the "contritionists" in 1638, for this reason, is deeply illuminating. The "contritionists" emphasized the necessity of God's grace in human redemption, whereas the "attritionists" emphasized human volition and the intercession of priests in seeking salvation. No one understood Richelieu's stakes in this dispute better than Ambassador Angelo Correr, who wrote to the Venetian Senate: "He made himself his [Louis XIII's] director of conscience, because, as the most famous doctor of the Sorbonne, he wanted to be the only one to resolve the doubts and scruples that worried that [royal] conscience; and it was foolish of the last Jesuit confessor [Caussin] to think that he could approach that conscience from another angle, as it appeared when he was chased away from court."[6]

Naturally, then, many of Richelieu's contemporaries thought that he was a despot, driven by his own thirst for power and violent instincts, and hated him with a passion for that. One of his fiercest critics, Montchal, the Bishop of Toulouse, narrates in his memoirs that on the very day of Richelieu's death, in a small village of the Languedoc, a priest envisioned an arsenal of torture instruments hanging from the walls of his church. As he celebrated mass a few moments later, the priest concluded that those were the instruments that Divine Justice reserved for Cardinal Richelieu.[7] But one would be hard-pressed to find one single event where personal, private instinct appeared to have exclusively motivated Richelieu to commit crimes. He could always argue that it was Louis XIII who spoke in the French state's interest, and that he only used his brilliant eloquence on behalf of a king who could be shy and suffered from a stutter. By Richelieu's own system of thought, that his obeying these royal decisions was irreconcilable with the vows of a priest missed the point. It is hard not to shake off the feeling that quite often the cardinal's advice to the king and his own actions were also an outlet for a power-hungry, vindictive, and mean temperament, however. There is meanness in the way he hired Louis de Marillac's judge to defend the marshal's own political trial, or how he punished officers who surrendered to the enemy for lack of sufficient resources. There is hypocrisy in the way he spied on Louis's mistress La Fayette and conducted the trial of Cinq-Mars. All of this mattered because, while he asked Frenchmen to accept "reason of state" with blind faith in their sovereign, Louis, he used priestly privilege and the moral authority of the Church to achieve his own political aims and to manipulate the king.

Provided that the reader will allow a bit of speculation, let us venture that personal dynamics with Louis and those modern Atreides at the French court played a substantial role in shaping Richelieu's character as a statesman.

Richelieu often reached his goals by exciting the king's somewhat mean disposition, when he prompted his ill will against Montmorency, for example, or to prevent him from rescuing Cinq-Mars. At the same time, Louis often felt let down by his minister's political and military shortcomings. Richelieu had to fear his master, all the more so since, "in the king's disposition, one was either the object of hatred or one enjoyed his full confidence; falling from his grace never happened gradually, but rather as if one stepped into a precipice."[8] The specter of Concini hovered over Richelieu for all of his life, and he had no choice but to carry on.[9] Mathieu de Morgues, the secretary of Marie de' Medici in Brussels who knew the cardinal well and who churned out stinging pamphlets against him, said that his mind was always on the move because he lived "suspended between hope and fear."[10] That is a sure truth about Richelieu. Critics often accused Richelieu of keeping war alive so as to remain indispensable to the king. But giving up would have meant more than losing power; it would have called for the king's judgment. As long as he labored in the name of France and King Louis XIII, the jury was still out as to whether all this human suffering was warranted or not. Perhaps it is the very perception of his minister's fear that led Louis to be less than a loyal friend during the Cinq-Mars conspiracy. The bond between these two men was fascinatingly perverse.

Would it be far-fetched to suggest, given all this, that art, spectacular, wondrous art, was for Richelieu the sublimation of the awesome sovereign power he supported, in a large measure created, and lived? Jean Desmarets de Saint-Sorlin, the cardinal's favorite impresario who helped him create elaborate political festivals on his private stage at the Palais-Cardinal, and celebrated the marvels of his château and gardens at Richelieu, left an intriguing description of his patron's leisure time: "The matters of state settled, [Richelieu] would meet in private with a theologian, to tackle the loftiest religious questions. His mind seemed to gain in strength with this change of topic. After that I would be ushered into his study, alone with him, to share his enjoyment of gayer and more delicate artistic matters. His pleasure was then extraordinary."[11] Therein might be the cardinal's most enduring legacy.

ACKNOWLEDGMENTS

I heartily thank Will Lippincott, agent extraordinaire and surely the most dapper in New York. George Gibson, who welcomed this book at Walker and set high standards for it, Margaret Maloney, who smartly edited the manuscript and allowed me see the baroque hero in Richelieu, and the entire team at Bloomsbury USA are the objects of my sincere appreciation. Special thanks also to my former classmate at Yale, Caroline Weber.

Let me acknowledge a *grand monsieur* of French seventeenth-century studies, Orest Ranum. M. Ranum read the manuscript carefully, showed support, and expressed his good advice diplomatically. Also most valuable was input from my colleagues and friends Benoit Bolduc, Michelle Hartel, Trenholme Junghans, Robin Wagner-Pacifici, and Carina Yervasi. Swarthmore's Anna Levine, Dennis Hogan, Andrew Petzinger, and Matthew Thurm read the manuscript at several stages. Getting a thumbs-up from these bright students was some of the best encouragement I could receive.

I want to salute my Parisian gang: Paul Salas, Stéphane Carcillo, Anne Durez, Hortense Creizer, Bertrand Creizer, and Véronique Salaün. Not only have these friends been generous hosts during my research trips to Paris, but their interest fueled many a dinner conversation on Richelieu, to my great benefit.

Finally, I acknowledge an enormous debt of gratitude to Bruce Grant, for his ever available and patient presence. But most important, he gave me the confidence that I needed to publish these pages.

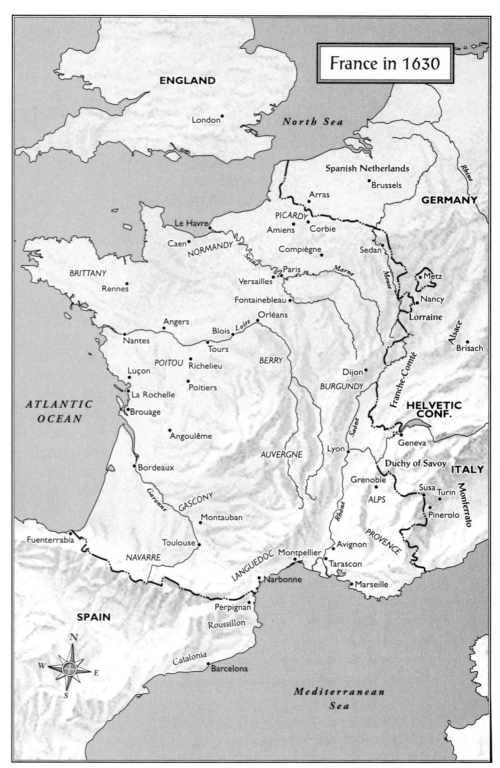

France in 1630

ENGLAND

London

North Sea

Spanish Netherlands

Brussels

Rhine

GERMANY

Arras

PICARDY

Le Havre

Amiens

Corbie

Caen

NORMANDY

Sedan

Compiègne

Seine

Metz

BRITTANY

Paris

Marne

Meuse

Nancy

Rennes

Versailles

Lorraine

Fontainebleau

Orléans

Alsace

Angers

Loire

Blois

Brisach

Nantes

Tours

Franche-Comté

POITOU

Richelieu

BERRY

Dijon

Luçon

Poitiers

BURGUNDY

La Rochelle

HELVETIC
CONF.

Brouage

ATLANTIC
OCEAN

Angoulême

Saône

Geneva

AUVERGNE

Lyon

Duchy of Savoy

ITALY

Bordeaux

Grenoble

Susa

Turin

Garonne

GASCONY

ALPS

Montferrato

Montauban

Rhône

Pinerolo

Fuenterrabía

Toulouse

PROVENCE

Avignon

NAVARRE

LANGUEDOC

Montpellier

Tarascon

Narbonne

Marseille

Perpignan

SPAIN

Roussillon

N

W   E

S

Catalonia

Barcelona

Mediterranean
Sea

(Gary Antonetti/Ortelius Design)

September 9, 1585: Birth of Armand-Jean du Plessis (Richelieu)
September 27, 1601: Birth of Louis XIII

1607: Richelieu becomes Bishop of Luçon
May 14, 1610: Assassination of Henri IV and regency of Marie de' Medici
October 1614–February 1615: Estates General
November 1615: Marriage of Louis XIII and Anne of Austria
September 24, 1616: Richelieu becomes secretary of state
April 24, 1617: Assassination of Concini

1618
April: Richelieu exiled in Avignon
May 23: Defenestration of Prague

1619
February 22: Flight of Marie de' Medici from Blois
April 30: Peace of Angoulême between Louis XIII and Marie de' Medici
August 28: Ferdinand II becomes Holy Roman Emperor

1620
Summer: War between Louis XIII and Marie de' Medici
July: Spanish invasion of the Valtellina
August 10: Peace of Angers between Louis XIII and Marie de' Medici
November 8: Battle of the White Mountain near Prague

1621

March 31: Philip IV becomes King of Spain
August–November: Siege of Montauban
December 15, 1621: Death of Luynes

1622

August–October: Siege of Montpellier
September 5: Richelieu becomes cardinal

1623

Government of Brûlart de Sillery

1624

Government of La Vieuville
April 29: Richelieu at the king's council

1625

March 27: Charles I becomes King of England
May 11: Marriage of Henriette Marie with Charles I of England (by proxy)
September 18: Montmorency chases the Huguenots of Soubise

1626

February 5: Treaty with the Huguenots
May 5: Treaty of Monzón with Spain
April–August: Conspiracies of the Dames and of Chalais
July 1: Charles I of England dismisses the French house of Henriette Marie
October 20: Richelieu becomes Grand Maître de la Navigation
December–February 1627: Assembly of Notables

1627

July 20: Buckingham and his English fleet in view of the island of Ré
September: Siege of La Rochelle begins
December 26: Death of Vincent II of Mantua

1628

August 23: Death of Buckingham
October 28: Surrender of La Rochelle

1629

March 6: Ferdinand II's Edict of Restitution
March 6: French victory at the Susa Pass against Charles Emmanuel I of Savoy
June 28: Grace of Alais with the Protestants
November: Richelieu becomes Principal Minister of State

1630
March: Campaign in the Alps and capture of Pinerolo
Summer: Invasion of Savoy
July 26: Death of Charles Emmanuel I of Savoy
September: Critical illness of Louis XIII
November 11: Day of the Dupes

1631
January 23: Treaty of Berwäld with King of Sweden Gustavus Adolphus
March–April: Flight of Gaston to Lorraine
June 19: Treaty of Cherasco with Spain
July 18: Flight of Marie de' Medici to the Spanish Netherlands
August 13: Richelieu becomes Duc and Pair de France
Works begin at Richelieu, in the Poitou
September 17: Swedish victory at Breitenfeld

1632
January 6: Treaty of Vic with Charles IV de Lorraine
May 10: Execution of Louis de Marillac
September 1: Battle of Castelnaudary against Montmorency
November: Gaston flees to the Spanish Netherlands
November 16: Death of Gustavus Adolphus at the Battle of Lützen

1633
April 13: League of Heilbronn

1634
February 25: Death of Albert of Wallenstein
September 5–6: Swedish defeat at the Battle of Nördlingen
October: Gaston returns to France

1635
April 28: Treaty of Compiègne with Sweden
May 22: French victory at the Battle of Avein
July 11: Treaty of Rivoli with the Italian dukes
Fall: Campaign of Louis XIII in Lorraine

1636
July–August: Spanish invasion of France
October: Conspiracy of Gaston and Soissons at Amiens
November 10: Corbie reconquered

1637
February 15: Ferdinand III becomes Holy Roman Emperor
August: Val-de-Grâce affair
December: Disgrace of Nicolas Caussin

1638
April: The siege of Brisach begins
September 5: Birth of the Dauphin Louis
September 7: French rout at the siege of Fuenterrabía
November: Marie de' Medici in England
December 18: Capitulation of Brisach
December 18: Death of Father Joseph

1639
June 29: Surrender of Hesdin
July–November: Revolt of the Nu-Pieds in Normandy
Early fall: Meeting of Louis XIII and Christine of Savoy;
Cinq-Mars becomes the king's favorite

1640
June 7: Uprising in Catalonia
June–August: Siege of Arras

1641
January 14: Premiere of *Mirame* at the Palais-Cardinal
February: The King of France limits the powers of the Paris Parlement
July 6: Battle of La Marfée and death of Soissons
November: The conspiracy of Gaston, Cinq-Mars, and Bouillon begins

1642
April–August: Siege of Perpignan
July 3: Death of Marie de' Medici
September 12: Execution of Cinq-Mars and de Thou
December 4: Death of Richelieu

1643
May 14: Death of Louis XIII

PRINCIPAL CHARACTERS

RICHELIEU, HIS CIRCLES AND ARTISTS

Richelieu, Armand-Jean du Plessis, Cardinal-Duc de. Principal Minister of State

du Plessis, Henri
du Plessis, Alphonse. Archbishop of Lyon. Cardinal
Combalet, Marie-Madeleine de Vignerot, de. Duchesse d'Aiguillon
Maillé-Bréȝé, Urbain, Marquis de. Maréchal
Maillé-Bréȝe, Jean-Armand, Duc de
La Meilleraye, Charles de La Porte, Duc de. Maréchal

Father Joseph. François-Joseph Le Clerc du Tremblay, known as. Capuchin

Charpentier, Denis
Le Masle, Michel

Boisrobert, François Le Métel de
Champaigne, Philippe de
Desmarets de Saint-Sorlin, Jean
Lemercier, Jacques

ROYAL FAMILY OF FRANCE

Marie de' Medici, Queen Mother of France

Louis XIII, King of France, father of the Dauphin, future Louis XIV
Anne of Austria, Queen of France

Christine, Duchess of Savoy
Élisabeth, Queen of Spain
Gaston, Duc d'Orléans
Henriette Marie, Queen of England

LOUIS XIII's FAVORITES

Luynes, Charles d'Albert, Duc de. Connétable de France. Minister of justice (Garde des sceaux)
Barradas, François de
Saint-Simon, Claude de Rouvroy, Duc de
de Hautefort, Marie
La Fayette, Louise-Angélique Motier de
Cinq-Mars, Henri Coiffier de Ruzé, Marquis de

HIGH NOBILITY AND MILITARY MEN

Bassompierre, François, Marquis de. Maréchal
Bouillon, Henri de La Tour-d'Auvergne, Duc de
Chalais, Henri de Talleyrand-Périgord, Comte de
Chevreuse, Marie de Rohan, Duchesse de
Épernon, Jean-Louis de Nogaret de La Valette, Duc d'. Colonel Général
Montmorency, Henri, Duc de. Maréchal
Nevers, Charles III de Gonzague, Duc de
Rohan, Henri, Duc de
Soissons, Louis de Bourbon, Comte de
Soubise, Benjamin de Rohan, Seigneur de

Châtillon, Gaspard III de Coligny, Seigneur de. Maréchal
La Force, Jacques-Nompar de Caumont, Duc de. Maréchal
La Mothe-Houdancourt, Philippe, Comte de. Maréchal
La Valette. Bernard de Nogaret de
La Valette, Louis de Nogaret de. Cardinal
Schomberg, Henri de. Maréchal
Sourdis, Henri d'Escoubleau, de. Archbishop of Bordeaux
Toiras, Jean du Caylar, de Saint-Bonnet, Seigneur de. Maréchal

GOVERNMENT OFFICERS, ECCLESIASTICS, AND OTHER COURTIERS

Bérulle, Pierre de. Cardinal
Bouthillier, Claude. Superintendant
Brûlart de Sillery, Nicolas. Chancellor
Caussin, Nicolas. Jesuit
Chavigny, Léon Bouthillier, Comte de. Secretary of State
Concini, Concino. Marquis d'Ancre. Maréchal
Galigaï, Leonora
La Vieuville, Charles, Marquis de. Superintendant

Marillac, Michel de. Minister of justice (Garde des sceaux)
Mazarini, Giulio. Nuncio. Cardinal
Ornano, Jean-Baptiste d'. Maréchal
Puylaurens, Antoine de l'Age, Duc de
Séguier, Pierre. Chancellor
Thou, François-Auguste de

FOREIGN RULERS, LEADERS, AND MILITARY MEN

Charles I, King of England
Charles IV, Duc de Lorraine
Charles Emmanuel I, Duke of Savoy
Christian IV, King of Denmark
Ferdinand II, Holy Roman Emperor
Ferdinand III, Holy Roman Emperor
Frederick V, Elector Palatine
Gregory XV, Pope
Gustavus Adolphus II, King of Sweden
Isabella, Governor of the Spanish Netherlands
John George I, Elector of Saxony
Maximilian I, Duke of Bavaria
Paul V, Pope
Philip III, King of Spain
Philip IV, King of Spain
Urban VIII, Pope

Buckingham, George Villiers, Duke of
Olivares, Gaspar de Guzmán y Pimentel, Count-Duke of
Oxenstierna, Axel. Lord High Chancellor

Cardinal-Infant, Juan of Austria, known as
Gallas, Matthias
Horn, Gustav Karlsson
Lamboy, Guillaume de
Mansfeld, Ernest of
Piccolomini, Octave
Saxe-Weimar, Bernard, Duke of
Spinola, Ambrose
Thomas of Savoy. Prince of Carignano
Tilly, Jean Tserclaes, Count de
Wallenstein, Albert, Count. Duke of Friedland

Werth, Jean de

LOUIS XIII'S FAMILY TREE

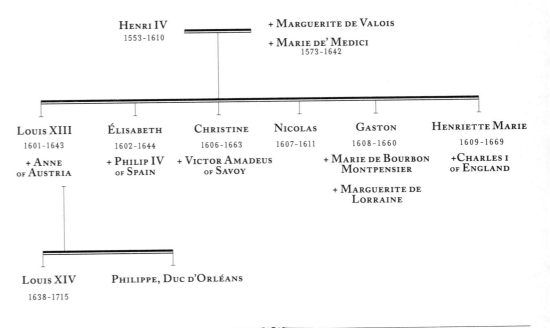

HENRI IV
1553-1610

\+ **MARGUERITE DE VALOIS**

\+ **MARIE DE' MEDICI**
1573-1642

LOUIS XIII	**ÉLISABETH**	**CHRISTINE**	**NICOLAS**	**GASTON**	**HENRIETTE MARIE**
1601-1643	1602-1644	1606-1663	1607-1611	1608-1660	1609-1669
\+ **ANNE** OF **AUSTRIA**	\+ **PHILIP IV** OF **SPAIN**	\+ **VICTOR AMADEUS** OF **SAVOY**		\+ **MARIE DE BOURBON MONTPENSIER**	\+**CHARLES I** OF **ENGLAND**
				\+ **MARGUERITE DE LORRAINE**	

LOUIS XIV
1638-1715

PHILIPPE, DUC D'ORLÉANS

RICHELIEU'S FAMILY TREE

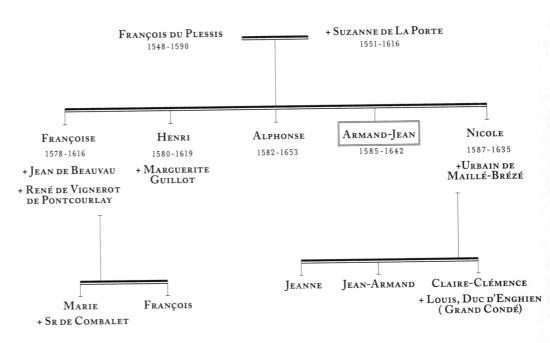

FRANÇOIS DU PLESSIS
1548-1590

\+ **SUZANNE DE LA PORTE**
1551-1616

FRANÇOISE	**HENRI**	**ALPHONSE**	**ARMAND-JEAN**	**NICOLE**
1578-1616	1580-1619	1582-1653	1585-1642	1587-1635
\+ **JEAN DE BEAUVAU**	\+ **MARGUERITE GUILLOT**			\+**URBAIN DE MAILLÉ-BRÉZÉ**
\+ **RENÉ DE VIGNEROT DE PONTCOURLAY**				

MARIE
\+ **SR DE COMBALET**

FRANÇOIS

JEANNE

JEAN-ARMAND

CLAIRE-CLÉMENCE
\+ **LOUIS, DUC D'ENGHIEN**
(**GRAND CONDÉ**)

NOTES

All translations from the French and Italian to the English are the author's.

INTRODUCTION

1. Kissinger, *Diplomacy*, p. 58.

2. Richelieu, *Testament politique*, p. 245. See J. Wollenberg, *Trois Richelieu*, and F. Hilde-seimer, *Relectures de Richelieu* for useful information on this question.

3. Richelieu, *Testament politique*, p. 241.

4. Goulas, *Mémoires*, 1879, p. 283.

5. Richelieu's portrait was on a French banknote not so long ago, and his name on a navy warship. A famous scholar, Louis Batiffol, once published an article that explained why Richelieu never sought to make Alsace, the region that lies on the west bank of the Rhine, a part of the French kingdom. By acquiring citadels in what was at the time a fiefdom of the Holy Roman Empire, Richelieu merely wanted to have posts to help his German allies. This clearly contradicted a certain view that Richelieu expanded French territory to "natural" borders, so much so that the editors of the august *Revue historique* who published Batiffol's "Richelieu et la question d'Alsace" took the unusual step to declare their disagreement with the author. The year of the publication was 1921.

6. Retz, *Mémoires*, p. 51.

7. Richelieu, *Testament politique*, p. 43.

8. "Richelieu," in *Dictionnaire universel du XIXe siècle*, 13.2 (1866–1879; Slatkine Reprints, 1982) pp. 1187–88.

9. Montrésor, *Mémoires*, p. 202.

10. Aubery, *Histoire*, p. 589.

11. Richelieu's correspondence designates a vast ensemble of writings. The cardinal was a man in control. He often provided outlines and drafts for the letters of the king or for those of his closest collaborators in the administration. As far as his "own" signed letters are concerned, they are usually not from his hand. He dictated (fast!) and then his secretaries—the most famous one was called Denis Charpentier—provided clean, formalized copies, in a calligraphy that imitated Richelieu's own. Complicating the matter is that Richelieu used

different calligraphies for different types of people. In a sea of documents, there are actually very few that can be said with certainty to be from Cardinal Richelieu's "hand." The impossible task of sorting this out caused headaches for nineteenth-century paleographers. Nowadays, historians tend to agree that the question of direct authorship, as it concerns the papers of Richelieu, is less pressing.

12. This history of Louis XIII's reign can be called "memoirs" of Richelieu in the sense of "memorandum," and not as if it were an autobiography. It was actually compiled, composed, and written by the cardinal's secretaries, under his supervision for the larger part. Historians of all ages have considered that these "memoirs" relay accurately the cardinal's thoughts and his own version of events. In essence, these so-called memoirs raise the same problems of authorship as the correspondence.

1: TOWARD A COUP D'ÉTAT (1617)

1. Bentivoglio, *Nunziatura*, vol. 1, p. 202.
2. Richelieu, *Mémoires*, vol. 1, p. 428.
3. The house of du Plessis stood on the rue du Bouloi, a street stretching between the Louvre and Les Halles, the former central market. There is considerable ambiguity surrounding the birthplace of Richelieu. Chroniclers of his time, such as Tallemant des Réaux, claim that he was born in the town of Richelieu. Joseph Bergin's careful examination of the documents and circumstances surrounding the birth of the cardinal shows that he was a true Parisian, as he later claimed. See Bergin's *Rise of Richelieu*, pp. 86–87.
4. See ibid., pp. 32–45.
5. Tallemant des Réaux, *Historiettes*, vol. 1, p. 233.
6. Bergin, *Rise*, p. 53.
7. See Batiffol, *Autour de Richelieu*, p. 145.
8. The Abbé de Pure states in his biography that Armand-Jean was so weak as an infant that many thought he would not survive.
9. We also owe the most extensive account of these early years to Bergin's *Rise*.
10. The famed physician Théodore de Mayerne treated him for a "*gonorrhoea inveterata.*" See Trevor Roper, *Europe's Physician*, p. 66.
11. Richelieu, *Lettres*, vol. 1, p. 24.
12. Richelieu, *Instructions du chrétien*, 15. Françoise Hildesheimer notes this judiciously in her biography, *Richelieu*, p. 39.
13. Richelieu, *Sermon*.
14. Richelieu, *Lettres*, vol. 1, p. 56.
15. A popular misconception designates Richelieu as the "Éminence grise," but this moniker actually refers to Father Joseph.
16. Fontenay-Mareuil, *Mémoires*, p. 49.
17. By law, women could not access the French throne. Marie de' Medici had six children: Louis, born in 1601, Élisabeth (1602), Christine (1606), Nicolas (1607; he was always very weak and died in 1611), Gaston (1608), and Henriette Marie (1609).
18. The Dutch Republic was originally part of the Spanish Netherlands and had been inherited from Charles V. In 1566 the republic affirmed its autonomy, to finally declare itself independent

from the Spanish Crown in 1581. After years of war between Spain and the republic, a truce had been declared in 1609; it lasted twelve years.

19. *Conjuration de Conchine*, p. 11.

20. Concini was Count de la Pena, although he did not use the title to better blend in with French society.

21. Henri Concini was born in 1603, and Marie in 1607.

22. Bibliothèque Nationale de France (hereafter cited as BN), Ms français 23200 (Sorbonne 1135), folio 266, or Richelieu, *Lettres*, vol. 1, p. 121.

23. James H. Kitchens, in "Judicial Commissions and the Parlement of Paris," gives an excellent definition of the French parlement on p. 324: "The Parlement's ancient conciliar derivation made it the court of peers, endowed it with supreme jurisdiction in ordinary litigation, and most importantly, generated its extensive political functions as legal counsel to the monarchy. By Louis XIII's reign, the Parlement was acting as the principal guardian of the kingdom's constitution and was, through its procedure of legislative review, registration, and remonstrance, the national institution most capable of defending the traditional principles of limited government."

24. For an additional tax known as *paulette*, holders could secure the permission to bequeath their offices to their next of kin. This annual tax was nicknamed after the first officer who benefited from it, Charles Paulet.

25. It did not help the Jesuits' reputation that in the last two decades three members of the Society of Jesus, Juan de Mariana, Cardinal Bellarmine, and Francisco Suárez, had published works that took a benign view of tyrannicide. In the wake of Henri IV's assassination, this position caused much outrage.

26. Hildesheimer, *Richelieu*, p. 57.

27. Henri IV, in contrast to his predecessors, had not called clergymen to his high council.

28. Richelieu, *Harangue . . . du Petit-Bourbon*, pp. 34–35.

29. The dual royal weddings were celebrated on October 18. Both French and Spanish consorts were not in the presence of each other when the ceremonies were performed, thus requiring a proxy person in Bordeaux for the marriage of Élisabeth, and in Burgos for Louis. Both princesses traveled to be formally exchanged over the river Bidassoa, which separated the two kingdoms. Anne of Austria arrived in Bordeaux, and the royal union was blessed in the town's cathedral on November 28.

30. Fontenay-Mareuil, *Mémoires*, p. 35.

31. Richelieu, *Lettres*, vol. 1, p. 122 (February 12, 1614); see also the testimony of Nuncio Bentivoglio, in his letters dated January 17 and March 28, 1617.

32. The information in Héroard's *Journal* concerns first the hygiene of the Dauphin, his diet, his health, and his bodily functions. Then there are the daily, hour-by-hour activities: playing, hunting, and ballet rehearsals. Pets are important in these descriptions of everyday life at the French court: there are dogs, of course, but also parrots and monkeys, and later birds of prey in an aviary. What is so striking about the first years of the *Journal* is that Héroard transcribes Louis's baby talk, evokes his behavior, his mood, giving us a unique intimacy with a historical figure of another time. Madame de Montglat, the governess, is "mamanga"; Gaston-Henri, the half brother, is "féfé Verneuil." Sometimes the margins of

the manuscript feature images drawn by the unsteady hand of the little Dauphin: calligraphy exercises, cranes on the Pont-Neuf, a monkey riding a pigeon. See Héroard, *Journal*, vol. 1, pp. 166–79.

33. See Dubost's biography on this matter, pp. 146–51.

34. Héroard, *Journal*, vol. 1, p. 430.

35. Ambassador Cioli, quoted in Chevallier, *Louis XIII*, p. 35. Héroard points out that on the day of Louis's coronation, once the ceremonies were over and he could rest in his bedroom, the king played with tin soldiers and made war engines out of paper.

36. Pietro Contarini, May 17, 1615; or Gussoni and Bon, March 17, 1615.

37. Nicolas Pasquier, *Lettres*, p. 556.

38. On this self-distrust of Louis XIII, see, for example, Goulas, *Mémoires*, p. 16.

39. Moote, *Louis XIII*, p. 59. On Louis's talent for dissimulation, see Déageant, *Mémoires*, p. 57.

40. Pontchartrain, *Mémoires*, p. 305. Leonora Galigaï called Marie de' Medici thick and clumsy (*la balorda*), and Marie's son, the king, an "idiot."

41. Richelieu had also recently lost his sister Françoise, who had died a widow and leaving two orphans. The letter he wrote to his brother Alphonse shows heartfelt pain at the passing of his mother, Suzanne de La Porte: "My brother, I have much regret that you should learn with this letter of the common loss of our poor mother . . . her life and death should be taken as proofs that you shall find her in heaven." *Lettres*, vol. 1, p. 170.

42. Pontchartrain, *Mémoires*, p. 377.

43. Richelieu, *Lettres*, vol. 1, p. 183.

44. Technically, Villeroy was still a minister, but a scheme to get him away from power without having to buy back his charge had been devised during the earlier change of personnel.

45. See dispatch of the Venetian ambassadors Bon and Gussoni on November 26, 1616. BN, Ms italiens 1770, folio 140.

46. Emphasis added. See Richelieu, *Lettres*, vol. 1, pp. 208–39, and vol. 8, p. 12.

47. *Relation exacte*, p. 463.

48. Pontchartrain, *Mémoires*, p. 250.

2: Wars of a Mother and a Son (1617–1620)

1. Arnaud d'Andilly, *Journal*, p. 293.

2. *Relation exacte*, p. 461.

3. Pontchartrain, *Mémoires*, p. 300.

4. Notably, the Duc de Longueville hosted a legendary reception on May 11, a week after the departure of the queen mother.

5. Richelieu, *Lettres*, vol. 7, p. 384.

6. Richelieu, *Mémoires*, vol. 1, p. 243.

7. *Les Principaux points de la religion catholique défendus contre l'écrit au roi par les quatre ministres de Charenton*, 1618. Françoise Hildesheimer points out interestingly how this book elaborates on the theme of submission that subjects must have before the king and the Church (*Richelieu*, p. 89).

8. Many wondered whether Concini's killing was an act of self-defense, a necessity, or a murder: "Why not give d'Ancre to a court of justice? Why this blood?" asked Fontenay-Mareuil, *Mémoires*, p. 119. Naturally, then, polemicists and memoirists favorable to the king

explained that Louis had only wanted to have him arrested, and that the other plotters had taken advantage of the king's innocence. Other, less favorably inclined writers surmised that Louis had given his tacit accord to the Italian's killing should he resist, and that was a convenient way to suggest the necessity of the execution. Finally, there are those, such as the court writer Robert Arnaud d'Andilly, who bluntly stated that the king just ordered the killing. Specific circumstances, in the end, did not matter much. The monarch was thought to have acted with prudence and magnanimity (*L'Enterrement*, p. 3). After careful deliberation, the "Messieurs" of the parlement came to the conclusion that "since the king himself had decided the death, this sole recognition covers any lack in [judicial] formality, even for such an extraordinary matter; otherwise, it would cast doubt on the powers of the king." *Relation exacte*, p. 29. See also the *Mémoires* of Molé, vol. 1, pp. 145–47.

9. The historian Hélène Duccini asserts that an envoy, the Duc de Bellegarde, visited the judges to explain the wishes of the government, while Sharon Kettering, Luynes's most recent biographer, denies that Luynes ever caused the woman's death. See Duccini, *Concini*, p. 380; Kettering, *Power and Reputation*, p. 82.

10. Much was made that Leonora Galigaï had used the services of a Jewish doctor, astrologists, and exorcists. The papers of the trial, however, clearly show that Leonora did not practice sorcery. See BN, 500 Colbert 221, folio 406, 411, testimony of Andrea de Lizza.

11. On her way to the Place de Grève, the place of execution, the frail Leonora marveled at how many people were gathered to see her die. "So many people to watch a poor afflicted woman pass by," she exclaimed. She died bravely, so bravely that the crowd who watched the execution had a change of heart, even for her, the presumed cause of France's ills. Fortunately, an Italian expatriate took care of Leonora's twelve-year-old son Henri and eventually sent the child to Florence, where he died in 1631.

12. According to Maréchal de Bassompierre, Luynes and his clients had convinced Louis that his mother wanted to imitate Catherine de' Medici, who was thought to have poisoned her son Charles IX. *Mémoires*, p. 128.

13. Motteville, *Mémoires*, p. 17. Less kindred spirits said that her attractiveness was marred by too much makeup and a shrill voice.

14. While these developments only spelled potential threat for the French monarchy, the Habsburg menace had proved much more tangible when Spanish troops attacked French ally the Duke of Savoy, even necessitating the intervention of a French army to retake the town of Vercelli.

15. Richelieu, *Lettres*, vol. 1, p. 419.

16. Ibid., vol. 7, pp. 424–25.

17. Claude Barbin was eventually tried and banished from the kingdom.

18. Richelieu, *Mémoires*, vol. 2, pp. 306–7; Griselle, *Profils de Jésuites*, pp. 251–52.

19. The secretary who composed the duke's letter was Jean-Louis Guez de Balzac.

20. Girard, the secretary of d'Épernon who left us a description of the scene, specifies that frantic shouts stopped the vehicle right away. A valet bolted from the carriage and ran back two hundred feet to fetch a case of precious jewels that had fallen behind. One hundred thousand *écus* worth of jewels were in this case.

21. *Relazioni*, p. 120.

22. Louis XIII, "Louis," pp. 308–9.

23. Ibid., p. 315; *Négociation commencée*, p. 147.

24. Richelieu, *Mémoires*, vol. 2, p. 364.

25. The duke's secretary, Girard, writes: "This ring had a heart-shaped diamond which passes today as one of the most beautiful, and purest—considering its size—gems in France. That is the only reward he got for the services he performed for the queen, and for the expense of two hundred thousand *écus* he incurred while performing that service. But it was a greater reward than what he expected, considering the sorry financial state of that princess at the time, and that the honor of having served her with success was the worthiest prize he had ever considered." *Histoire*, vol. 3, p. 422.

26. Ambassador Contarini, dispatch of September 10, 1619, in *Relazioni*, p. 125.

27. See Louis's letter to Marie de' Medici sent right before the meeting in Couzières: "You could not have made me happier before your arrival than by sending the Bishop of Luçon, having given to him a trust that I have not given to anyone that you have sent me." In Louis XIII, "Louis," p. 331; see also Contarini's dispatch sent September 3, 1619, in *Relazioni*, p. 124: "[Luçon], ben veduto dal rè e da Luynes."

28. Fontenay-Mareuil, *Mémoires*, p. 140.

29. Louis XIII, "Louis," pp. 97–98.

30. Bentivoglio, *Nunziatura*, vol. 3, p. 202.

31. The emperor thus ignored the rights of a 1609 declaration called the Letter of Majesty, which granted all Bohemians civil liberties and freedom of religious exercise; it was the linchpin of religious coexistence in Bohemia until Ferdinand came to power.

32. Frederick V was elected King of Bohemia on November 5, 1619. At the same time, Ferdinand had to face an insurrection led by the Prince of Transylvania, Gabriel Bethlen, in his kingdom of Hungary.

33. The Béarn was a kingdom of its own, a possession of the French Crown where Louis's father, Henri IV, was born and where his grandmother the Calvinist queen Jeanne d'Albret had routed the Catholics decades before. To accede to the French throne, Henri had converted to Catholicism. Other conditions to his elevation included the restitution of possessions seized from the Catholics in the Béarn. The matter was never settled. Demands for restitution then went ignored by the Protestants. The Crown sent a commissar in charge of enacting Paris's resolution after the coup d'état. He was publicly ridiculed. In a final provocation, the obstinate Protestants officially declined to ratify the Edict of Restitution, in their capital, Pau (June 29, 1618). From the Béarn, discontent ended up spreading to other Protestant populations in France, making them more sympathetic toward the queen and her allies.

34. Ministère des Affaires Étrangères, Archives diplomatiques (hereafter cited as AAE), Mémoires et documents, France 773, folio 173.

35. Richelieu, *Mémoires*, vol. 3, p. 81.

36. Fontenay-Mareuil, *Mémoires*, p. 146.

37. See a letter from Louis in Molé, *Mémoires*, vol. 1, p. 241, where the king declared that the Bishop of Luçon was seizing state revenues on the queen's behalf.

38. *Harangue à la reine mère du roi sur les troubles et divisions de ce temps.*

39. Louis wrote on this subject: "The duty of kings who want to reign as legitimate rulers in their fatherland is to favor the general good over their own private interests. Royalty stands above human laws, and it takes its rights and reasons following the needs and necessities of

kingdoms. Much as the salvation of people is the object of legitimate sovereignty, all that guarantees quiet must be considered regardless of human matters. Think of it, Madam." Louis XIII, "Louis," pp. 295–96. This is possibly a response to the 1620 pamphlet *Vérités chrétiennes*, which was written by a man from the queen's entourage, Mathieu de Morgues. J. Bergin attributes the pamphlet to Richelieu in *The Rise*, p. 208.

40. *Mercure François*, 1620, p. 327.

41. "Madame: I have been, it seems, without some news for a longer time than usual. That brought me sadness, because my content is to get news from you often. I like to see what comes from you, be assured, and the scarf you sent makes me happy as well. Thank you, I shall wear it on Tuesday for the general showing of my army. I hope to wear it in a good place and to testify that I am the only one in the world worthy of carrying a sign of your favor." In *Lettres de la main de Louis XIII*, pp. 60–61. Eugène Griselle mistakenly attributes this letter to Marie, whereas, if one considers the reference to the army parade on a Tuesday and the goings of Louis as recorded by Héroard, it can only have been written before the battle and thus has to be addressed to Anne of Austria. Why would Louis write like that to his mother, before the battle? Perhaps some of the letters presented in the third part of Griselle's edition of "Louis XIII et sa mère" and also attributed to Marie were actually to his wife, given the likeness in tone with the one quoted above.

42. See the *Méditations de l'hermite Valérian*, p. 17, for a use of the term *drôlerie*.

43. Richelieu, *Mémoires*, vol. 3, p. 81.

44. Louis XIII, "Louis," p. 304; *Mercure françois*, 1620, p. 337.

45. Rohan, *Mémoires*, p. 516.

46. See AAE, Mémoires et documents, France 773, folio 211.

47. See, for example, Luynes's exasperated missive to Richelieu on June 1: "We have up until now thought of you what one ought to think from a good man." Ibid., folio 54.

48. See Degert, "Le Chapeau," pp. 235–36, based notably on Bentivoglio's correspondence.

3: Jupiter's Favor (1621–1624)

1. Elizabeth was the daughter of King James I and sister of Charles I. Historians of philosophy will recall that Tilly's army at the White Mountain battle counted a very smart soldier in its ranks, René Descartes, and that by a strange coincidence Frederick V's daughter, also named Elizabeth, is the woman with whom Descartes shared a brilliant philosophical correspondence.

2. See the papal nuncio's detailed exposé on these geopolitical matters in Zeller, *Richelieu*, pp. 312–14.

3. Mousnier, *Homme rouge*, p. 203.

4. See G. Priuli's dispatch on June 12, 1621, printed in Zeller, *Connétable*, p. 305.

5. Castelnau, *Mémoires*, in La Force, *Mémoires*, vol. 4, p. 197.

6. In August 1621, the minister of justice, Guillaume du Vair, had died, so Luynes took on his duties. It was quite scandalous to see this man of such mediocre talent snatching two of France's highest offices. Condé, who during the war kept the Bourbonnais region in check, bitingly commented on the constable that "if one distinguishes the times, he is fit for both charges: a good keeper of the seals in times of war, and an equally good constable in peacetimes."

7. Fancan, *Chronique*, p. 29.

8. Castelnau, in La Force, *Mémoires*, vol. 4, p. 293: "The reasons of those who opposed the treaty were that for the sake of keeping their liberty and their religion, they had lost fathers and mothers, children, brothers and sisters. It would be a heartbreak and chagrin, if, after that, they were forced to ask for forgiveness."

9. There is a historian's debate on the merits of Luynes's role as a member of the government from 1617 to 1621. I am referring to the conversation initiated in the nineteenth century by Victor Cousin's article "Le Connétable de Luynes." Cousin's positive assessment was accepted, to a certain extent, by Berthold Zeller in his *Connétable* book. Tapié's book on the French role at the beginnings of the Thirty Years' War seems to settle the matter as far as foreign policy was concerned: it was the ministers' role to oversee French policy, and not Luynes's. S. Kettering recently provided an account that is more favorable to Luynes.

10. Bassompierre, *Mémoires*, p. 148.

11. Richelieu, *Mémoires*, vol. 3, p. 183.

12. Héroard, *Journal*, vol. 2, p. 2821.

13. Luynes had secret communications with the leaders of Monheur and thought that the rendition of the city would come quickly. See Bassompierre, *Mémoires*, p. 185.

14. When he learned of his coming death, Luynes wrote letters to Louis, but the king could not touch them for fear of contagion. In these letters, Luynes asked for protection of his family, to which the king responded that he would care for his relatives as he had cared for him. The constable's body was carried to Tours, where dignified ceremonies saluted his passing. During the trip, however, Luynes's body was the object of less respect: at one point the memoirist Fontenay-Mareuil witnessed soldiers of the guard playing cards on his coffin.

15. Pesaro, dispatch of December 24, in Zeller, *Connétable*, p. 333, or BN, Ms Italiens 1777, p. 193.

16. AAE, Mémoires et documents, France 775, folio 84v.

17. Corsini, dispatch of January 10, 1622; Archive Nationales, 129MI/58, folio 6.

18. Richelieu, *Mémoires*, vol. 3, p. 213.

19. This place should not be confused with the island of Ré.

20. See Molé, *Mémoires*, vol. 1, pp. 262–66 for a useful account.

21. *Mercure françois*, 1621, p. 637.

22. Another source of concern for the king as he was preparing to lay siege in Montpellier was a menace that stood at the border of the Champagne region. Frederick V, the deposed King of Bohemia, had hired an army to defend the Palatinate, but the imperial army had defeated it, and now the general of the Protestant army, Ernst von Mansfeld, was looking to employ eight thousand horsemen and an infantry of fifteen thousand. Standing at the border of Champagne, he could create a welcome diversion and help Montpellier resist the king's attack. Fortunately, Mansfeld's plan did not go through, and this foreign army left for Holland on August 25, taking its ravages to other unfortunate lands.

23. Héroard, *Journal*, vol. 2, p. 2859.

24. Richelieu, *Lettres*, vol. 1, p. 732.

25. Richelieu, *Mémoires* (Paléo), vol. 4, p. 9.

26. Gaspar de Guzmán y Pimentel, Count Olivares and Duke of San Lúcar la Mayor.

27. Fancan, *Voix publique*, p. xii.

28. Dispatch of October 2, 1623, in *Relazioni*, p. 175.

29. The Palais du Luxembourg was named after the estate that the queen bought to allow for the building of Brosse's construction. Since 1612, plantings had already begun. The first stone was set on April 2, 1615.

30. Fontenay-Mareuil, *Mémoires*, p. 175.

31. Dispatch of May 10, 1624, quoted in Zeller, *Richelieu*, pp. 316–18.

32. Richelieu, *Mémoires*, vol. 4, p. 36.

33. It was harder to follow Fancan's *Le Mot* when it described the brainy cardinal as "young" and "vigorous"!

34. Fancan, *Voix publique*, p. xvi.

35. Gaston, the king's brother, held a grudge against La Vieuville because he had fired the prince's beloved tutor, Colonel d'Ornano. Gaston's revenge was a prank by which his cooks beat their pots and pans in the middle of the night to wake d'Ornano up. The minister was so terrorized that Richelieu had to get out of bed and calm him down.

36. The cardinal resigned as bishop, while managing to keep a hefty revenue from religious holdings in Luçon. The notarized act concerning this resignation from Luçon's bishopric was signed on May 19, 1623.

37. In Fancan's pamphlet *La France en convalescence*, p. 3, the writer asked the king this rhetorical question: "How is it that I see you all grey, all hunched, and as worn out as you should be in thirty years?"

38. Saavedra Fajardo, *Le Prince*, p. 538: IOVI, ET FULMINI, next to a mountain. The author gives the example of Concini to illustrate his maxim.

39. Malherbe, "Lettre à Racan," September 10, 1625, in *Œuvres*, p. 259.

4: Angel or Demon? (1624–1626)

1. Richelieu, *Lettres*, vol. 3, p. 78.

2. A papal legate, Urban VIII's own nephew, had come to Paris to complain and to solve the Valtellina situation, but his efforts turned out to be useless. On the Ligurian coast, French armies, led in collaboration with the Duke of Savoy, were pushing hard against Genoa.

3. Well-known titles published against Richelieu's anti-Spanish policies in 1625 are the *Mysteria Politica* and the *Admonitio ad Regem Galliae*. In response to this wave of pro-Habsburg propaganda, the cardinal could get his own pamphleteers to write well-argued defenses, or get the parlement to burn these tracts at the stake.

4. See: BN, NA françaises 7020 (Brienne 49), folio 327; *Mercure François*, 1625, p. 366; Garasse, *Mémoires*, 1860, pp. 69–71. Garasse says that the gardens and orchards surrounding Paris had been laid waste to prepare food for the party, with neither fruits nor flowers remaining, as if springtime had not come that year.

5. Richelieu's proactive anti-Spanish policy was reaffirmed a few months later, on September 29, 1625, when Chancellier d'Aligre pronounced one of the opening discourses at the Assemblée des Notables.

6. The Duke of Buckingham had had a direct testimony of how charming the Queen of France could be. At the time when the Prince of Wales fancied a marriage with the daughter of Philip IV, the prince and Buckingham had decided to travel to Spain incognito. Free from protocol and diplomacy's burdens, the Prince of Wales thought that he would have a better chance of obtaining the hand of the Infanta. His father, James I, was very reluctant to approve

of this sophomoric enterprise, but he had a soft side and he finally let the two go. The two adventurers, as they journeyed through France in 1623 under fake names and with false beards, stopped in Paris for a few days. "Tom and Jack Smith" were lucky. One night, a co-operative usher allowed them into the Louvre. Later, once the two companions were back in their inn, an excited Prince of Wales was writing the following lines to his father: "We saw the young queen, little Monsieur, and Madame, at the practicing of a masque that is intended by the queen to be presented to the king, and in it there danced the queen with Madame with as many as made up nineteen fair dancing ladies, amongst which the queen is the handsom-est, which had me a greater desire to see her sister." In *Original Letters Illustrative of English History*, vol. 3, pp. 121–22. Spelling modernized. Anne rehearsed the ballet dressed up as the mythological goddess Juno. Her sister is the Spanish princess that Charles wanted to marry.

7. Leisurely freedom may have been pushed even a little farther by the Duchesse de Chevreuse, when she brought a copy of the infamous *Cabinet Satyrique* to the queen's gatherings. This collection of poems included pieces that can best be described as lewd.

8. Motteville, *Mémoires*, p. 20.

9. Poisson, *Duchesse*, p. 89.

10. Leveneur de Tillières, *Mémoires*, p. 65.

11. Motteville, *Mémoires*, p. 20.

12. La Porte, *Mémoires*, p. 7.

13. The editor of Richelieu's correspondence, Avenel, denies that personal enmity between the two men could have had any influence on politics; see a note in the *Lettres*, vol. 2, pp. 44–45.

14. Brienne, *Mémoires*, p. 36.

15. La Porte, *Mémoires* p. 7.

16. Motteville, *Mémoires*, p. 19.

17. The Queen of England arrived in her adoptive country with one bishop and twenty-eight clerics. It was agreed by the terms of a secret contract that English subjects would have liberty of conscience, that Henriette and her entourage would be able to celebrate Catholic mass, and that English subjects would be allowed into her chapel.

18. See the letter of John Pory, in *Original letters*, vol. 3, p. 241: "This French bishop [the Bishop of Mende, François du Plessis, who was a relative of Richelieu], who when he was last in France suing to be a secretary of state, fell short of that and so took instructions from the Pope's nuncio, which in case he could bring to effect, he was promised a cardinal's hat, which now lies in the dust. The rest of that clergy were the most superstitious, turbulent, and Jesu-ited priests that could be found in all France; very fit to make firebrands of sedition in a for-eign state." Spelling modernized.

19. As extraordinary at it may sound, Chevreuse gave birth to a baby girl in Holland's house, over the summer, after having concealed her pregnancy from the general public.

20. See Batiffol, *Duchesse*, p. 72. The correspondent was kindly asked, at the end of the note, to remain discreet on this attempt at being facetious: "This letter, if you don't mind, will only be read by you."

21. Leveneur de Tillières, *Mémoires*, p. 68.

22. Imperial military movement in the Valtellina prompted Richelieu to send Maréchal de Bassompierre to Switzerland on November 18, 1625, in the hopes of shoring up support from both Catholic and Protestant Swiss so that the terms of the Treaty of Madrid might finally be

observed by the Spanish. Success was also proving to be elusive on a diversionary front opened against the Genoese, ever since the Spanish had augmented their forces and pushed the French army corps back into Savoy territory.

23. On Richelieu's knowledge that Spain and the French Protestants had shared designs, see J. de Bouffard-Madiane, *Mémoires*, p. 101.

24. Peace with the city of La Rochelle was negotiated later, on April 17, 1626.

25. Bassompierre, *Mémoires*, p. 248.

26. For evidence that Richelieu's real intent was to conclude a peace treaty with Spain because Protestant internal pressure was too strong, see the testimony of the Venetian ambassador Simeone Contarini, quoted in Malvezzi, "Papa Urbano VIII," pp. 49–50. Romolo Quazza, always well informed, supports the thesis that Richelieu double-crossed his allies, in "Politica Europea," pp. 139 and 149.

27. Gaston d'Orléans, *Mémoires*, p. 569; Vittorio Siri recounts the same anecdote in *Memorie recondite*, vol. 5, pp. 137–38. It is likely that he took it from the first source quoted.

28. Richelieu, *Lettres*, vol. 7, pp. 588–89.

29. Batiffol, *Duchesse*, pp. 78–79.

30. In 1624, the minister La Vieuville had removed Colonel d'Ornano from his charge, but then Richelieu reinstated him in August of 1624 when Gaston began to live a dissolute life.

31. These are the very words Vittorio Siri employs in his *Memorie*, vol. 5, p. 131.

32. Some contemporaries thought that the scheming hand of Richelieu was responsible for this proposal by d'Ornano. According to this theory, Father Joseph suggested to d'Ornano that Gaston should request a place at the council, thus leading d'Ornano into further dissent when the request was denied; this would have eventually allowed Richelieu to dismiss him. See Siri, *Memorie*, vol. 5, p. 131.

33. Bois d'Annemetz, *Mémoires*, p. 301, in *Archives curieuses*, 2nd series, vol. 3.

34. Letter of the Venetian ambassador, in *Relazioni degli stati europei*, p. 205.

35. *Pièces du procès de Henri de Talleyrand*, pp. 7–8.

36. Griffet, *Histoire*, p. 496.

37. Siri, *Memorie*, vol. 6, p. 155.

38. See Vittorio Siri's account of the interesting conversation Richelieu had with Nuncio Spada after a long evening spent interrogating Chalais, in ibid., pp. 147–48.

39. Quoted in Griffet, *Histoire*, p. 500.

40. César, Duc de Vendôme, had been raising troops in Brittany. His brother Alexandre had also been one of the conspirators, having been kept abreast of the failed plot at Fleury, but he thought that his role had remained secret. So when the king asked his two half brothers to come to court to discuss possible promotions, Alexandre asked if César would be safe. Louis responded, "I give you my word that he will not be harmed any more than you will." Shortly after their arrival in Blois, César and Alexandre were *both* arrested in the middle of the night and taken to prison.

41. See a letter from the Sieur de Blainville to Richelieu, dated July 4, 1626, and quoted in Cousin, *Madame de Chevreuse*, p. 351.

42. How exciting it would be to know who these observers were. Unfortunately, Richelieu used code names in the letter where he reveals the existence of agents who were betraying Anne of Austria (in Richelieu, *Lettres*, vol. 2, pp. 258–59).

43. The guards duly observed and took note of all of Chalais's actions and words. Their depositions became evidence in the file that Richelieu assembled for the grand jury that was to judge Chalais.

44. *Pièces du procès*, p. 110; also quoted in Batiffol, *Duchesse*, p. 98. In this passage, Chalais invokes Greek mythology and compares the duchess to Diana, the goddess of the hunt whom Actaeon was able to see at the price of being turned into a stag and devoured by his own dogs.

45. Bois d'Annemetz, *Mémoires*, in *Archives Curieuses*, vol. 3, p. 329.

46. Details of the execution come from the *Mercure François*, 1626, p. 409, and from pages of Robert Arnauld d'Andilly's *Journal*, in *Lettres de la main de Louis XIII*, p. 525.

47. Bois d'Annemetz, *Mémoires*, in *Archives Curieuses*, vol. 3, p. 341.

5: Wonder by the Sea (1627–1628)

1. See Goulas, *Mémoires*, vol. 1, pp. 18–19; Fagniez, *Père Joseph*, vol. 1, p. 379. As Bishop of Luçon, it seems that Richelieu had discussed with Father Joseph the necessity of tackling the proud and rebellious Atlantic city of merchants. On Gaston's contacts with La Rochelle, see Cousin, *Madame de Chevreuse*, p. 366.

2. One witness left us a vivid description of the chaotic scene that took place on the day of this expulsion. The King of England took his wife into a room of his palace, while his officers told the members of the queen's entourage that they had to leave the palace immediately: "The women howled and lamented as if they had been going to execution, but all in vain, for the Yeomen of the guard . . . thrust them and all their country folks out of the queen's lodgings, and locked the doors after them. It is said also the queen, when she understood the design, grew very impatient, and broke the glass windows with her fists." John Pory to Joseph Mead, July 5, 1626, in *Original letters*, p. 239. Spelling modernized. As it turns out, Henriette Marie quickly recovered from the shock. She even began to get along with her husband, proving that, indeed, the Catholic clergy in her household exerted a pernicious influence on her.

3. These measures included razing the military forts that had become useless and buying back parts of the royal domain that had been alienated, so as to provide a new flow of income to the treasury. See Ardier, *Assemblée*, 1652.

4. The cardinal founded the Compagnie des Cents Associés on March 31, 1626. Later the company dissolved because of its lack of organization and general success. For the same purpose, a more successful venture, the Compagnie de la Nouvelle-France, was founded on May 6, 1628.

5. There had been sporadic English raids on French merchant fleets, especially now that Buckingham understood how the cardinal's response to his threat aimed at more than just countering attacks: it was a military and economic challenge to England's entire dominion over the seas.

6. La Rochelle was a maritime power of its own, a rich city of traders who had sent the first Frenchmen to Canada, as far as the Saint Lawrence River. From this perspective, it seemed imperative to act with force before being caught in the cardinal's stranglehold.

7. Richelieu, *Lettres*, vol. 2, p. 564.

8. Mademoiselle de Montpensier died on June 4 after giving birth to a daughter. Since France did not allow women on the throne, the sad event was also a political setback for Gaston and his claims to power. The child would grow up to be the famous Grande Mademoi-

selle, who was destined to play a lively role in the civil disturbances of the Fronde and at the court of Louis XIV.

9. It seems that the historians working for Cardinal Richelieu took pains to erase Gaston's contribution from history books. Whatever the extent of Gaston's role, he did participate actively in the preparations leading to the French supplying of the citadel at Saint-Martin. See the prince's *Mémoires*, 1879, p. 575, those of Goulas, pp. 34–35, and Richelieu, *Lettres* vol. 2, pp. 504–5.

10. Brienne, *Mémoires*, p. 46. Legend has it that Buckingham had a shrine on his flagship where he could worship Anne of Austria's picture. But whatever the queen knew of these romantic details must have been far away from her mind when Montague—the English envoy who had tried to create a diversion in tandem with other powers—was arrested. Anne suddenly lived in fear that her knowledge of the Chevreuse plot would come out. For such treason, it was quite likely that she would be repudiated and sent back to Spain. The queen lost sleep and stopped eating. Finally, unable to withstand the tension anymore, she dispatched her man La Porte to see Montague. If we are to believe his own testimony, Anne's valet ingeniously approached the prisoner during his transfer to the Bastille and received assurances that the queen was not named in his papers and that the Englishman would not divulge her secret either. All this took quite a long time, so much so that La Porte found the queen deeply depressed when he finally was able to meet with her back in Paris. Anne of Austria could not contain her joy when she heard of Montague's assurances.

11. *Mercure françois*, 1627, p. 635.

12. This episode of ancient history can be found in Quintus Qurcius.

13. Richelieu, *Lettres*, vol. 3, p. 26.

14. Ibid., pp. 47–48.

15. See Fagniez, *Père Joseph*, vol. 1, p. 398.

16. Richelieu, *Lettres*, vol. 3, p. 30.

17. Goulas, *Mémoires*, 1879, p. 23.

18. Guillaudeau, *Diaire*, p. 362. Mervault, *Histoire*, p. 37, recounts a similar divine intervention.

19. Louis XIII, *Lettres inédites*, ed. La Caille, p. 8.

20. See Rodocanachi, *Derniers Temps*, p. viii.

21. Richelieu, *Lettres*, vol. 2, p. 95.

22. In the vocabulary of the time, a "machine" refers to any man-made assemblage of parts, not necessarily a moving one, requiring human genius.

23. The beauty of the machine's design lay as much in its resilience as in its destructive force. By using an interwoven pattern of beams inspired by roof-building technique, du Plessis-Besançon made sure that the entire structure could absorb shocks by distributing the force of impact. Du Plessis-Besançon had set up a building shop close to wood-supplying forests, near the city of Saintes. From there, the machines were sent on barges down the river Charente and then delivered by sea. Eventually, once the first two rows of machines were added, a third one was installed. This time, the machines were placed on floating rafts, all tied together with iron rings. Finally, two other systems of defense were added. A first blockade of boats, which stood before the bulwark and the machines, formed a triangle pointing toward the ocean. A second stockade of boats was put in the bay, behind the bulwark, to prevent La Rochelle's ships from

mounting an attack. The ships had hatches at their bottom, so that they could be sunk at will and used to create an even tighter barrier.

24. Guiton had been elected on May 2, 1628.

25. See *Mercure françois*, 1628, p. 619.

26. This letter from a contemporary described the death of Buckingham in graphic details: "Madam, I am to trouble your Grace with a most lamentable relation. This day between nine and ten o'clock in the morning, the Duke of Buckingham then coming out of a parlor, into a hall, to go to his coach and so to the king . . . was by one Felton (once a lieutenant of this our army) slain at one blow, with a dagger-knife. In his staggering he turned about, uttering only this word, 'Villain!', and never spoke word more, but presently plucking out the knife for himself, before he fell to the ground, he made towards the traitor, two or three paces, and then fell against a table although he were upheld by diverse that were near him, that . . . could not perceive him hurt at all, but guessed him to be overswayed by some apoplexy, till they saw the blood gushing from his mouth and the wound, so fast, that life, and breath, at once left his begored body." Dudley Lord Carleton to the Queen, in *Original Letters*, vol. 3, pp. 256–57. Spelling modernized. Madame de Chevreuse, upon hearing the news, fainted and had to be bled three times to come back to her senses.

27. Mervault, *Histoire*, p. 214.

28. Richelieu even considered a plan to place a net before the port, to prevent any fish from reaching the waters near the wharfs.

29. Mervault, *Histoire*, pp. 183–84.

30. Other painful details on the Rocheloises's suffering can be found in ibid., p. 196: "Many women and young girls of the ordinary people proceeded in the midst of the vineyards where they were raped and beaten with pitchforks and halberd poles, then stripped. So it was all naked and without their shirt, just like the day they came out of their mothers' wombs, that they would come back to the city. I saw a few of them returning like that, while some other women coming from inside came towards them with clothes to offer them cover."

31. Madame de Rohan's cook walked out of La Rochelle and told the soldiers who caught him that he would rather be hanged than go back and die from hunger. See Richelieu, *Mémoires*, vol. 8, p. 49.

32. Ibid., p. 208. See also a passage in the same spirit, quoted by Batiffol in *Richelieu et le roi Louis XIII*, p. 30: "It is much better for men to remain in their duty by their own volition, than by force."

33. Richelieu, *Mémoires*, vol. 8, p. 190. Fontenay-Mareuil says the same, in his *Mémoires*, p. 207.

34. *Mercure françois*, 1628, p. 618. For other signs of this sort, see Sieur de Pontis, *Mémoires*, p. 546. To understand how the bulwark was taken as a sign in a system of apocalyptic predictions, see Gauffreteau, *La Digue*.

35. It is worth noting that the English weaponry featured what were probably the first torpedoes. See *Le Siège de La Rochelle*, in *Archives Curieuses*, vol. 3, p. 103; Sainte-Marthe, *Histoire de la rebellion des Rochelois*, p. 121.

36. See Richelieu's own memoirs for this episode, and those of Bassompierre, p. 280.

37. It took a few days to distribute food and make a minimum of preparations for the cardinal and Louis's entrance into the miserable city. For a testimony on the situation, see this letter

written from the English fleet on October 30, in *Original Letters*, vol. 3, pp. 274–75: "The famine was such that the poor people would cut off the buttocks of the dead that lay in the church yard unburied, to feed upon. All the English that came out thence, looked like anatomies." Richelieu notes that given the amount of corpses found lying all over the city, it was surprising how little infection there was. It was because the dead bodies had been so malnourished that they dried out instead of decomposing. *Mémoires*, vol. 8, p. 205. I would consider some even more ghoulish tales that the Sieur de Pontis recounts in his own memoirs as implausible. *Mémoires*, p. 546.

6: GREAT STORM (1629–1630)

1. Sieur de Matel, *Les Louanges guerrières de Monseigneur le cardinal de Richelieu*, p. 3.

2. Nowadays, the Medici name evokes much more prestige than the Gonzague, but there was something to Nevers's tactless remark. The Medicis were wealthy bankers who had been elevated to nobility just a century before, and their name had something of a parvenu quality when put next to that of the age-old and prestigious Mantuan dynasty.

3. The historian Georges Pagès delineated this political context of the late 1620s in a landmark essay titled "Autour du Grand Orage."

4. Before the siege of La Rochelle, Louis had ordered the polemicist who had stimulated public opinion so well on the cardinal's behalf, Fancan, thrown into the Bastille, accusing him of collaborating with foreign Protestant potentates and of fomenting general sedition. "Writing political tracts was his usual means of decrying the government, to make the person of the king and its counsels the object of hatred," explained Richelieu. But had the cardinal not pursued alliances with Protestant powers until very recently, and with the help of Fancan's quill? Historians suggest that jailing Fancan was mostly the price to pay for obtaining the Devouts's support against La Rochelle, and, if true, clearly this had been a useless gesture. The historian Françoise Hildesheimer notices that the memoir pages where Richelieu attacked the unfortunate Fancan—the man ended up dying in his prison cell—have the fury of someone who is trying to convince himself of his own innocence. In any case, Richelieu gave himself the good role when he recounted the story: "since [the cardinal's] manner was always to reward good service and diminish the punishment of faulty actions, he humbly begged His Majesty to be content with putting [Fancan] in a prison."

5. See Goulas, *Mémoires*, 1879, p. 65.

6. Richelieu, *Mémoires*, vol. 10, pp. 7–9.

7. See Fontenay-Mareuil, *Mémoires*, p. 216.

8. Bassompierre, *Mémoires*, p. 293.

9. In courtly society, relations of power and subordination were expressed in many ways. Space and distance, among other things, were highly significant. How much space was left between the address of a letter and the message itself, how far one would accompany a guest after a visit, these were ways to signify varying degrees of respect and social consideration. A fine and rather comical example of this behavior can be found in the *Mémoires* of Souvigny, pp. 204–5, when the author describes the awkward encounter between Louis XIII, Richelieu, and the Duke of Savoy, after the signing of the treaty at Susa: "Once Susa's citadel was in the hands of the king, the Duke of Savoy came to see him. His Majesty took the pretext of a promenade and met him at a short distance from the citadel. As soon as he saw the king, who

was mounting a big white horse, he stepped down and walked towards him, while the king remained on his horse until he came up close. Then, seeing that the duke was about to bow very low, the king held him up, embraced him, and climbed back on his horse. The duke did the same, went to the king's left, and spoke amiably while holding his hat in his hand. The king kept inviting him to put back his hat: 'Monsieur, cover yourself.' He had to repeat his invitation at least four or five times. Upon arriving near Susa they met the cardinal. Both the cardinal and the duke saluted each other without stepping down."

10. Hushed voices suggested that the entire love story between Gaston and Marie was an intrigue set up by Gaston and his mother, Marie de' Medici, to bring discord on purpose and ruin Richelieu's reputation. The author of Gaston's memoirs, Lasséré, proposes the theory on p. 578: "The queen mother and Monsieur agreed on the stratagem, that Monsieur would often visit princess Marie, would pretend to be madly in love, and that the queen mother would act as if she was angry and against his marriage."

11. Richelieu, Lettres, vol. 3, p. 317.

12. There are two versions of what happened in Privas. On the one hand, the king, Richelieu, and their various propaganda outlets argued that one last Protestant holdout thought that he would be executed, and chose to commit suicide by blowing up a barrel of gunpowder. That would have triggered the uncontrolled wave of destruction. On the other hand, the Duc de Rohan argued that it was the king's men who put fire to the barrel and used the incident as an excuse to destroy the city. Mémoires, p. 597.

13. The treaty between Rohan and the Spanish was agreed upon in May of 1629. It was an unlikely alliance between mortal enemies. But after consulting with theologians, Olivares had decided that the greater interest of his Very Catholic Majesty the King of Spain was at stake. To Rohan's chagrin, the envoy who was carrying the treaty back from Madrid was caught. Under torture, he revealed to the cardinal's police all the details of the negotiation. For Rohan, the unsavory move of seeking Spanish subsidies appeared to be the only way to prevent the final sinking of the French Protestant political cause. See his memoirs' awkward justification, p. 607.

14. Before the Grace of Alais Father Joseph practiced some even less savory tactics to persuade the Protestants to convert. They included taking away children from their families and extorting money. For details, see Fagniez, Père Joseph, vol. 1, pp. 416, 423–24.

15. de Morgues, Vérité défendue, p. 16, in Recueil. See also BN, Ms français 17486, folio 189r.

16. Gaston received two hundred thousand pounds to settle his debts and added the government of Orléans and the Duchy of Valois—together with their revenues—to his already large landholdings.

17. See Sieur de Pontis, Mémoires, pp. 559–60.

18. Jacques de Chastenet, Seigneur de Puységur and an officer of the army, describes these harsh conditions of the campaign and narrates an amusing anecdote that highlights once again how the cardinal was mindful of his standing but also quite realistic about what one could expect from his men: "Soldiers were so extraordinarily wet that they kept cursing the cardinal and his people. As I was passing before him the cardinal called upon me to say that he found those soldiers of the guard quite insolent, and wondered if I was hearing them too. I responded that yes, I did hear them, and that this is how soldiers tended to react when they were suffering. I added that, when they were at ease, they always praised their general, got

drunk and wished him the best with many toasts. Still, the cardinal said, it would be better if they refrained from that kind of language . . .The army arrived in Rivoli where the cardinal and the guard took their quarters at the château, which was well supplied. Then the cardinal heard the men chant and toast that great Cardinal Richelieu. That night when I went to fetch my orders . . . , he remarked that the soldiers had changed their tune, and wondered if it was because I had warned them about their language. I replied that I had not yet, and the cardinal found it suitable that I did not press on the matter." (*Guerres*, pp. 90–91.)

19. Quoted in Pagès, "Autour du Grand Orage," p. 85.

20. BN, Ms français 3826 (Béthune 9320), folio 27. See also Richelieu, *Lettres*, vol. 3, pp. 745–46.

21. Bassompierre, *Mémoires*, p. 319 or BN, Ms français 3826.

22. Father Joseph's official mandate in Regensburg was technically that of an adviser to Brûlart, but all in Regensburg knew that no decisions would be taken without consulting with this closest adviser and friend of the cardinal. Actually, not being an officially mandated ambassador allowed him to free himself from many fastidious diplomatic servitudes and to be more efficient. The two men thus formed a tandem.

23. On how Richelieu contemplated resignation, see AAE, Mémoires et documents, France 254, folio 237.

24. *Mercure françois*, 1630, p. 789.

25. Ibid., p. 792. The text of this account, which is a letter sent by Suffren, can also be found in *Archives curieuses*, vol. 3, pp. 369–70.

26. Brienne, *Mémoires*, p. 52.

27. Richelieu, *Lettres*, vol. 3, pp. 912 and 917.

28. In fairness to the French ambassadors present in Regensburg, one must say that Richelieu's original order of mission did not give any specifics concerning the conditions for a peace, and that after the king fell ill, it became impossible to obtain information from the French government.

29. See Richelieu, *Papiers*, vol. 5, p. 606, for an amazing description of these symptoms by the queen's physician.

30. See, for example, Fontenay-Mareuil, *Mémoires*, p. 229.

31. Contemporaries often thought that Richelieu kept waging wars to secure his position with the king. In this perspective, and with regard to the dismissal of the treaty signed at Regensburg, see Siri, *Memorie*, vol. 6, pp. 246–47.

32. Brienne, *Mémoires*, p. 52.

33. Fontenay-Mareuil explains that given how well Marie de' Medici concealed her feelings on the way back from Lyon, Richelieu thought that she had changed her mind about ousting him. See *Mémoires*, p. 229.

34. Goulas, *Mémoires*, vol. 1, p. 93.

35. Louis XIII, *Lettres à Richelieu*, pp. 9–10.

36. Richelieu, *Lettres*, vol. 3, p. 942.

37. See Bassompierre, *Mémoires*, p. 319.

38. Richelieu, *Mémoires* (Paléo), vol. 11, p. 190.

39. See Richelieu, *Lettres*, vol. 3, pp. 436–38. Avenel situates this note in the follow-up of the first breakdown at Fontainebleau, but admits that it could also have been written on the Day

of the Dupes. I would opt for the latter proposition, given how desperate and confused the letter sounds. Besides, the author alludes to the "colère naissante de son roi," as if Louis XIII was present when the event that motivated the letter happened.

40. Richelieu, *Lettres*, vol. 4, p. 12.

7: RESTLESS DRAGON (1631–1634)

1. Richelieu drew his arguments in favor of his alliances with Protestants from late Scholastic commentators of Thomas Aquinas such as Francisco de Vitoria, whose works he kept in his own library. See Wollenberg, *Trois Richelieu*.

2. Richelieu, *Lettres*, vol. 4, p. 48.

3. Aubery, *Histoire*, p. 148.

4. Motteville, *Mémoires*, p. 29.

5. See AAE, Mémoires et documents, France 795bis, folio 355–58.

6. Richelieu, *Testament politique*, p. 261. Bassompierre narrates in his own memoirs that he burned more than four thousand love letters before heading for prison.

7. The royal declaration was dated March 30, and the parlement declined to register the text on April 26. Louis was so irate that he summoned the delegates of the parlement to the Louvre on May 13 and tore up the April response before them.

8. *Lettre écrite au roi par Monsieur*, p. 54.

9. Griffet, in his *Histoire*, vol. 2, p. 84, remarks that against the queen, Richelieu's "cold and tranquil hatred never leaped but out of the most exact circumspection."

10. After holding this post in Champagne Marillac was sent to fight in Italy, the place where he was arrested in November 1631. Richelieu first brought Marillac before an extraordinary commission, instead of having him judged by the parlement in Paris, the normal procedure for such a high-ranking officer. Richelieu liked quick action, and ever since Chalais's trial he found the traditional ways of French justice too slow and unreliable. The commission was filled with judges chosen from the Burgundy court, where by judicial tradition the burden of proof was less stringent. Richelieu then chose Isaac de Laffemas to gather the evidence and instruct the case, a task the man carried out with flawed procedures and pressures on the witnesses. The scandal was great, especially because at the same time, another extraordinary chamber of justice was operating at the Arsenal to judge cases such as accusations of counterfeiting. Death sentences pronounced by this chamber were carried out in the middle in the night. The parlement protested, but it was rebuked repeatedly by the royal council. Vittorio Siri notes, to the cardinal's benefit, that a common perception at the time found that the parlement had been too lenient in the past when judging high nobles and officers. *Memorie*, vol. 7, p. 496.

11. Principal actors and contemporaries of this drama between Marie and her son were extremely conscious of how history seemed to be repeating itself. First, take this letter from Marie de' Medici to Louis, written toward the end of May in 1631: "Everyone knows that my staying here has nothing to do with the safeguard of your [state], and that these are nothing but the same pretexts that were used during your first separation with others, pretexts that gave you so many regrets, once you came back to your senses after the Connétable de Luynes passed away." Aubery, *Mémoires*, vol. 1, pp. 362–63. Or consider this declaration of Father Suffren: "What happened in Blois, fifteen years ago, is nothing compared to what is happening today." June 24, 1631; quoted in Fouqueray, *Le Père Jean de Suffren*, p. 63. Craftily, the cardinal's pam-

phleteer Sirmond, in *La Défense du roi*, turned this rhetoric inside out and used it to discredit the queen herself. How could she be credible if she spoke from the past? Sirmond asked. In other words, if history was repeating itself, it was only as a farce: "These [accusatory] accents are studied, and represented as comedies, which originate not from the heart, but from custom." *Mercure françois*, 1631, p. 272. See also Fontenay-Mareuil, *Mémoires*, p. 234.

12. AAE, Mémoires et documents, France 799, folio 123.

13. The erudite Maximin Deloche estimates that on average the cardinal fed between 160 to 180 mouths per day. See *Maison*, p. 287.

14. Louis XIII authorized Richelieu to have a company of guards as early as 1626, following the Conspiracy of the Dames. This company numbered up to one hundred recruits. The cardinal formed the company of musketeers in 1634, and it was actually less prestigious than that of the guards. They went on foot and served for three years, whereas the guards served the cardinal for as long as they could.

15. The entirety of Richelieu's income is not accounted for in this steady stream of money. As the historian Joseph Bergin tells us in his authoritative work on the cardinal's revenues, *Cardinal Richelieu*, p. 256: "Not the least of his achievements was to take secrets of this [financial] nature with him to the grave and to ensure that they would remain there."

16. See Richelieu, *Lettres*, vol. 3, p. 181. Incidentally, France had signed in the town of Cherasco (Italy) a treaty with Spain, on June 19, 1631, to confirm its hold on the strongholds of Susa. Another secret agreement with the Duke of Savoy kept Pinerolo under French control.

17. The sack of Magdeburg took place on May 20, 1631, and it is thought to have caused at least twenty thousand deaths.

18. AAE, Correspondance politique, Allemagne 8, folio 149.

19. Goulas, *Mémoires*, 1879, p. 169.

20. See Elliott, *Richelieu*, pp. 118–19.

21. Thus relations between the Crown and the Paris parlement were still very much strained. One low point came in January 1632, while the court was still in northeast France. Louis XIII, who was so prickly on matters of his sovereign authority that he lost sleep over the parlement's claims, again summoned the delegates to express his discontent. The men traveled for eleven days before reaching Metz, where the king made them wait three weeks before giving them an audience. The parlement respectfully signaled that the practice of extraordinary commissions was causing great scandal. Louis's response was mean: "You have been established only to judge between *maître* Pierre and *maître* Jean, and I will bring you down to what is your true duty. Should you keep on with your pretenses, I will trim your nails so close that you will suffer." Molé, *Mémoires*, vol. 2, pp. 143–44.

22. Richelieu, *Lettres*, vol. 4, p. 270.

23. Rumors were that Richelieu had solicited all judges one by one before they went into deliberation. See Siri, *Memorie*, vol. 7, p. 498.

24. See Vaissières, *Un grand procès*, p. 197.

25. M. de Montmaur, *Relation véritable*.

26. Claude Courtin, *Mémoires curieux*, BN Arsenal, Ms 4661, folio 283.

27. Hay du Chastelet, *Observations*, 1633.

28. *Histoire de Henry II*, 1699.

29. Goulas, *Mémoires*, 1879, p. 175.

30. Treaty of Liverdun, signed June 21, 1632.

31. Richelieu, *Testament politique*, p. 260. From the same perspective, Richelieu is also known to have said, "Indulgence is the vice of people with good nature" (Aubery, *Histoire*, p. 594).

32. It is remarkable that not long before these unfortunate events, a man like Montmorency would have had good hopes of getting away with his revolt. As the behavior of the high nobles during the regency of Marie de' Medici amply illustrates, it was part of their sense of self-worth to be able to contest royal power in the name of justice, and for this reason the regent showed extraordinary patience with these nobles. Even with the implacable Richelieu in power, pleas for mercy for Montmorency poured in from all corners of the kingdom. Condé wrote for him, though this former rebel was now completely subservient to Louis and his principal minister.

33. See *Mémoires de Henry, dernier duc de Montmorency*, in *Archives curieuses*, vol. 4, p. 85; *Relazioni*, p. 291.

34. Girard, the secretary of d'Épernon, gives an interesting list of the petty motives that contributed to the two men's enmity: when the duke wrote to congratulate the cardinal for his promotion in 1624, he did not leave enough space between the address of the letter and the text itself, an important mark of consideration; in the same letter he only referred to himself as his "humble servant." Richelieu replied likewise. See Girard, *Histoire*, vol. 3, p. 30. Another motive of resentment for the duke was his absence in Rubens's painting representing the 1619 flight from Blois in the Palais du Luxembourg gallery.

35. La Porte, *Mémoires*, p. 15.

36. Richelieu, *Lettres*, vol. 5, p. 402 (November 13, 1632).

37. Anne's solemn entry into La Rochelle was a splendid show of unambiguous royal power, quite different in essence from the recognition of mutual prerogatives that this kind of municipal ceremony used to be. Take this harsh description of La Rochelle in the harangue the local representative of the monarchy pronounced to greet the queen: "This city (if it can still be referred as such), this remnant of the scourge of the gods and of the king's indignation, the skeleton and ghost of La Rochelle, resuscitated upon your Majesty's arrival to throw itself at her feet." In all likelihood the entire program had been approved by Richelieu, if not drawn up by him.

38. The Swedish army actually had won the battle.

39. *Gazette de France*, January 8, 1633.

40. Respite was short for Richelieu, since at that time he again had to tackle his enemy Madame de Chevreuse. In an attempt to win back the trust of Anne of Austria, the cardinal had taken the bold step of allowing the duchess back at court. But once again, the duchess caused trouble: she seduced the minister who had replaced Michel de Marillac as chief of justice, Monsieur de Châteauneuf, and used him to obtain state secrets. Madame de Chevreuse had been helping the cardinal in his dealings with her former lover Charles de Lorraine, notably by writing letters to the duke that were dictated by the cardinal himself (see Richelieu, *Lettres*, vol. 4, pp. 308–9). She ended up double-crossing Richelieu by providing secret information to both Lorraine and England. Then she relentlessly mocked the cardinal in private for his continuing attempts at being gallant and his ailments, a mockery which he eventually learned about when the duchess's correspondence with Châteauneuf ended up in his hands. Thus Richelieu discovered that Chevreuse called him *cul pourri* (rotten ass). Châteauneuf ended up

in prison, and Madame de Chevreuse in her château of Couzières, near Tours. The duchess, before leaving court, promised the queen that she would keep writing to her in secret. In replacement of Châteauneuf, Pierre Séguier was nominated as keeper of the seals on February 25, 1633.

41. Feuquières, *Lettres et négociations*, vol. 2, p. 215, to Bouthillier: "[Wallenstein] wants to become King of Bohemia, bring the news himself to the emperor, and follow him wherever he shall retreat, should it be in Hell." See also AAE, Correspondance politique, Allemagne 9, folio 27, 148, or Fagniez, *Père Joseph*, vol. 2, p. 165, n. 2.

42. With the Treaty of Charmes, Charles abdicated in favor of his brother, Cardinal Nicolas-François. Signed on January 19, 1634, this was the third treaty that the French extracted from Lorraine's sovereigns in two years.

43. The royal army, led by Maréchal de La Force, took the citadel of Bitche on May 18 and that of La Mothe on July 28.

44. Maximin Deloche speaks of this nurse in his *La Maison du cardinal de Richelieu*, p. 131. Adding to Richelieu's woes was the very publicity that surrounded them. From Brussels, Marie de' Medici's most virulent pamphletist, Mathieu de Morgues, harangued him: "You do not need a valet who shouts at you every morning, in the likes of those kings of Persia: 'Remember that you are a man!' The migraines, the ardors of your blood, the fevers worthy of a lion that constantly plague your life, the syringes, the surgeon's knives, and the basins, all this tells you not only that you are mortal, but that you live your days at great expense." Mathieu de Morgues, *Charitable remonstrance du Caton chrétien*, p. 5 in *Recueil*. This admonition, admittedly, was still quite elliptical on the nature of Richelieu's ailments. But when the relics of Saint Fiacre were brought from Meaux to Paris, in a grand procession, to alleviate Richelieu's condition, little was left to the imagination. Saint Fiacre was invoked by persons suffering from hemorrhoids. Pilgrims who traveled to Meaux to ask for the saint's intercession recited their prayers while sitting on the tombstone that covered his resting place. The following days, Parisians were reading a hilarious and very clandestine mock heroic pamphlet, titled *On the Removal of the Relics of Saint-Fiacre, for the Healing of Monseigneur Cardinal Richelieu's Ass*. This is why his code name with Anne and Madame de Chevreuse was *cul pourri* (rotten ass). The matter might seem distasteful, but one cannot ignore it given the role it has in the life of the cardinal and in his correspondence. See, for example, the following letter to Secretary of State Bouthillier: "I can't conceal anymore that I fear so much a new episode of the illness I have suffered from in the past. I was bled abundantly yesterday, which had not prevented the fire from burning in that place you know, where it is either a fire of internal hemorrhoids that one can't see, or the new beginning of what I fear. . . . The apprehension of having to leave for Paris on a stretcher, should my condition worsen, leads me to depart today." Richelieu, *Lettres*, vol. 4, p. 557.

45. See Fagniez, *Père Joseph*, vol. 2, p. 239.

46. *La Vie de Marie de Hautefort*, p. 17.

47. The following anecdote gives a good idea of the atmosphere that reigned at court. One day, Louis entered his wife's apartment as Mademoiselle de Hautefort was reading a note in which someone playfully mocked her for attracting the king's passion. She hid the letter in her bosom as soon as she saw the king, who then asked her what it was about. Eventually, he ordered her to read the note. Anne, who was sitting nearby at her toilette, told him that he should

take it and read it himself. Seeing how this request left her prudish husband confounded, the queen stood up, took both of his hands, and again urged him to take the note. Louis's response was abrupt. "He took some silver tongs by the fireplace to try to catch the note, but could not since she had placed it too deeply in her corset." The queen let him go after laughing at the embarrassment of Mademoiselle de Hautefort and that of her husband. La Rochefoucauld, *Mémoires*, p. 384.

48. Louis also sent affectionate notes. See, for example, the letter sent by the king in AAE, Mémoires et documents, France 244, folio 41: "The fire at Versailles is even livelier than the one in Rueil."

49. On February 21, 1634, Wallenstein learned that he had been deposed as commander of his army. Four days later, around midnight, he lay dead in a room at Eagra's citadel, his gored body in a puddle of blood. The evening had started with a massacre. Three of Wallenstein's officers who had defected to the emperor set up a trap by inviting the general's closest supporters to a dinner. All of these were murdered at dessert time with cries of "Viva Ferdinand and the House of Austria!" After, it was Wallenstein's turn to meet his fate.

50. Richelieu, *Mémoires* (Paléo), vol. 14, p. 90.

51. This Alpheston arose suspicions because he traveled with two men who were known to be from the queen mother's guards. Then, the would-be assassin was riding a beautiful gray horse known as Le Polacre, or Le Grand Hongre. This horse was identified as belonging to the queen, too. Richelieu, after the execution, sent back the horse, "out of respect for her." See AAE, Mémoires et documents, France 253 and 808 for documents concerning Alpheston and other killing attempts.

52. Carmona, *Marie de Médicis*, p. 509.

53. Elliott, *Olivares*, p. 482.

54. The terms of the Treaty of Paris were settled on November 1, 1634. The Swedish chancellor later rejected the accord because he found it too favorable to the French. The envoy who then kept the talks going was the famed jurist Hugo Grotius.

55. For a while Chanteloube had persisted in trying to get rid of the cardinal. See AAE, Mémoires et documents, France 810. This time, two assassins arrived from Cadix disguised as pilgrims.

56. On May 3, 1634, Gaston's favorite courtier, Puylaurens, narrowly escaped being shot to death while he was climbing the stairs of the prince's residence. It could well have been the work of Marie's priest, Jacques Chanteloube, who resented that talks for the prince's return went along without any concern for the mother and her own entourage. In any case, the point of the coup was to sow dissent between Gaston's court and Paris by raising suspicions that the cardinal had ordered it to derail the negotiations and double-cross Gaston by keeping him at bay. In the end, it only produced further enmity between the mother and her youngest son.

57. La Capelle was that stronghold before which, in July of 1631, Marie de' Medici had made the decision to flee to Brussels.

58. There was not much to do, however, for the many children the French were leaving behind. Goulas estimates those to have been a few hundreds. See his *Mémoires*, 1879, p. 256.

59. The cause of Gaston's marriage was officially presented before parlement on January 4, 1634. Days later Richelieu reiterated the Crown's rejection of the marriage in an hour-long

speech that left his august audience once again impressed with his rhetorical talents. On September 5, the parlement declared the marriage null because it believed Charles had kidnapped the French prince and forced him into a marriage without his brother's consent.

60. *Récit véritable*, 1634.

61. Richelieu ordered that only Gaston be given an armchair at the table and that he should be provided ample space to mark his special quality. A select group of nobles waited on him. The cardinal himself ceremoniously washed his hands. The night ended with fierce gaming that left Cardinal La Valette much poorer. These details are to be found in V. Siri, *Memorie*, vol. 8, pp. 103–4. Siri specifies that Richelieu abstained from the gambling.

62. It was not the first time that Puylaurens had betrayed Richelieu: in violation of the contract signed in the aftermath of Montmorency's capture, he had failed to inform the king of Gaston's second marriage. See Richelieu, *Lettres*, vol. 4, pp. 376, 382, and 383. Gaston had also taken public initiatives to secure his marriage. While he was in the Spanish Netherlands, theologians from Louvain had examined the validity of the union to certify it, and the Bishop of Malines had then blessed the union for a second time. Pope Urban VIII was indignant when he heard of the parlement's decision to annul the marriage, and how Richelieu's intent was to eventually get a religious annulment as well. In the pope's view, these actions had the double effect of submitting matters of dogma to the politics of lay powers and of fostering French religious independence from Rome.

63. See Richelieu, *Lettres*, vol. 4, p. 650. See BN, Ms italiens 1808, folio 285 for proof of the Venetian ambassadors' surprise. The king's letter might have been dictated by Richelieu.

64. *Ballets*, vol. 5, p. 58.

65. The challenge was to arrest Puylaurens. First and foremost, another panic from Gaston had to be avoided. Furthermore, catching Puylaurens meant the arrest of other underlings, that is, a great risk of mayhem and scandal. Clearly the coup demanded meticulous preparation, and Richelieu decided to have a bit of fun with it. What better partner could he find in this enterprise than the king, that consummate hunter who liked to trap with cruel refinement those who had crossed him?

On February 14, 1635, the fateful day of Puylaurens's arrest, Richelieu was at the house of Séguier, the minister of justice, in the company of Condé and two of Gaston's closest confidants, du Fargis and Coudray-Montpensier. See the dispatch of Nuncio Bolognetti, February 15 and 20, 1634; AN 129MI/77. At the same time, the king was hosting Gaston and Puylaurens at the Louvre. A meticulously choreographed setup began. The cardinal spoke amiably with the favorites on several business matters. Then he asked them to stay for lunch, and later to gamble a bit. The papal envoy, who describes the night in his dispatch to the Vatican, reports that the two were given very poor seats. The point, obviously, was not to honor them, but to keep them away from the Louvre. Messages kept arriving from the palace. The king wanted the cardinal to come and see the rehearsal. Richelieu sent back the messenger to excuse himself. The messenger came back to insist. These were all codes that Louis was using to keep Richelieu informed of preparations on his side. Upon leaving Séguier's *hôtel*, the cardinal kindly asked some financiers who were present to hear a request for money from Coudray-Montpensier while he took the other man with him. Later on, a messenger sent by the cardinal came to ask Séguier to prepare a comedy for him. This impromptu request seemed odd, but Coudray did not suspect anything. When the messenger came a second time to assure that only two portable screens would suffice for the set, the man was arrested on the spot and taken to the Bastille.

At the Louvre, things proceeded with the same chilling artifice. When Richelieu arrived, he sent du Fargis to fetch a group of nobles in a particular room. What the confidant found was the captain of the guards ready to arrest him. The cardinal then met the king, who was in the company of Gaston. Puylaurens was still not there. Finally, the main actor in this cruel comedy arrived. As all three were heading to the dance hall, Louis asked his brother to come with him to visit the queen, leaving Puylaurens with the cardinal. Puylaurens was a man of few words and of rather cold temperament. Richelieu sarcastically asked him when his icy demeanor would melt. Then he left. The guards appeared to capture Puylaurens.

66. Rambouillet's words are hyperbolic. More to the point is that the air of Vincennes was reputed to be deadly. See Richelieu, *Papiers*, ed. Grillon, vol. 6, p. 367.

67. Richelieu, *Lettres*, vol. 4, p. 634.

68. Notably, the cardinal sent the courtiers La Rivière and d'Elbène to the Bastille in 1636.

69. Richelieu appreciated all literatures and thought they were one of the greatest ornaments of states. Richelieu, *Testament politique*, p. 137.

70. The concept of a learned academy, of course, was nothing new. Italian princes, for example, often patronized such assemblies of erudite and learned men. The Académie Française had its origin when, in 1629, a few men of letters held weekly and private gatherings at the house of one of them, Valentin Conrart. It was, in the words of H. G. Hall, more like a "dining club with cultural interests." *Richelieu's Desmarets*, p. 119. Richelieu heard of it through Boisrobert and offered to sponsor the group. The original academicians feared that they were about to lose the casual ease that gave so much charm to their meetings, but they did not have much choice. The desires of the cardinal were orders.

71. The treaty was signed with Frederick Henry of Nassau, the brother of the famous warrior Maurice. The prince had been raised in Paris and spoke French. His relations with the cardinal were cordial, in spite of the ever-enduring suspicion that existed on both sides.

72. The negotiations led to the May 30, 1635, Peace of Prague.

73. According to J. Stradling, in "Olivares and the Origins of the Franco-Spanish War," p. 82, the Spanish minister was resolved in his plans to attack France.

74. See Louis XIII's letter to the cardinal in Richelieu, *Lettres*, vol. 7, pp. 718–24.

75. Parrott, *Richelieu's Army*, 2001.

76. C. Wedgwood, *Thirty Years' War*, p. 131.

77. Richelieu, *Testament politique*, p. 85. So many of the cardinal's officers were useless buffoons, and not the least his own "creatures." For example, one of these men asked to leave the front because he did not want to miss the melon season in his property in Anjou. See Montglat, *Mémoires*, pp. 68–69. Another one left ship so as not to miss a comedy.

78. The cardinal, after renting this property in Rueil for many years, finally bought it in July 1633. Large-scale work to enhance the gardens and the waterworks occurred in 1635–1636.

79. See Girard, *Mémoires*, vol. 3, p. 123: "Already, on account of the great number of affairs which occupied the cardinal, or because the less persons he saw, the more venerable and authorized he appeared, he had adopted a way of life, by which one saw him quite rarely."

8: WAR (1635–1637)

1. Richelieu, *Lettres*, vol. 4, p. 761. This was the declaration of war: "I have come to find you on behalf of the King my master, my one and only Lord, to tell you that: since you have refused to free Monsieur the Archbishop of Trier, an Elector of the Holy Empire who had placed himself under his protection because he could not get any security from the emperor and from any other prince; since against the dignity of the empire and the right of people, you retain prisoner a sovereign prince, with whom you are not at war, His Majesty declares that it is by means of arms that he is resolved to settle a matter that is of concern to all princes of Christianity."

2. History textbooks often refer to this conflict as the "French phase" of the Thirty Years' War.

3. Louis XIII, *Lettres inédites*, ed. La Caille, p. 11.

4. Richelieu, *Lettres*, vol. 5, pp. 54–55.

5. Ibid., p. 158.

6. AAE, Mémoires et documents, France 808, folio 106.

7. Chavigny, October 6, 1635, AAE, Correspondance politique, Lorraine 26, folio 424–25; see also Mémoires et documents, France 815, folio 232.

8. The deal signed with Saxe-Weimar on October 27 guaranteed a subsidy of four million pounds to Sweden. In exchange, Saxe-Weimar was to keep an army of confederate Protestant forces. Fortunately, this arrangement left a great measure of autonomy to what was one of the best men of war of his time.

9. Richelieu asked Mazarini to reply to Marie de' Medici that she should have saved her display of sentiments for when she would really have the interests of France at heart. Mischievously, the nuncio's response was signed and dated from Rueil.

10. Siri, *Memorie*, vol. 8, p. 360.

11. AN, 129MI/78, folio 162.

12. Richelieu, *Lettres*, vol. 5, p. 514.

13. See AAE, Mémoires et documents, Picardie 1678, for documents concerning this period.

14. Lepré-Balain, *Père Joseph*, quoted in Fagniez, *Père Joseph*, vol. 2, p. 309.

15. Fontenay-Mareuil, *Mémoires*, p. 256.

16. One of the pleasures of Gaston's return at court had to be when he was reunited with his daughter, the perky seven-year-old Anne Marie Louise.

17. Richelieu, *Lettres*, vol. 5, p. 622.

18. Soyécourt was condemned to death by order of Louis during a session of the royal council. The sentence had to be carried out in effigy, however, because Soyécourt had fled the kingdom soon after his surrender, like the governors of La Capelle and Le Catelet before him. Louis's former favorite Saint-Simon, a relative of Soyécourt, had warned the man of his impending arrest. Richelieu eventually heard of this warning. Thus the fall of Corbie and the punishment of its governor also caused the disgrace of a longtime, albeit already declining, companion to the king.

19. Maréchal de Châtillon had originally proposed the idea.

20. Since the death of Henri IV, state revenues had ballooned by a staggering sixfold increase to match the spending, and the war against Spain demanded even more money.

21. I am referring here to the man whose tragic story is told by A. Huxley in his book *The Devils*.

22. Richelieu, *Lettres*, vol. 5, p. 696.

23. Richelieu, *Traité*, chap. 44.

24. Of course, this is not the only reason why the year remains in the annals of the theater. In 1637 the, the author Pierre Corneille produced a play titled *Le Cid*, in which a Spanish woman named Chimène confronts the fact that the man she loves, Rodrigue, is also the one who killed her father in a duel of honor. *Le Cid* enjoyed an enormous success among the public. The Académie Française, however, found many aspects of this piece extravagant and openly criticized Corneille for it on doctrinal grounds. Richelieu was kept abreast of all the details of the long literary quarrel.

25. The triumph of *La Grande Pastorale* demanded that the play be printed for posterity to enjoy. Just before making the decision, however, Richelieu decided to consult the secretary of his recently founded Académie Française for an opinion on his talents as a bard. The man was Jean Chapelain, and he faced a difficult task when he came back with his colleagues' opinions. No matter how delicately he proceeded, there was no way around the fact that he needed to tell the cardinal that his verses were bad. Richelieu read the observations of the Académie. Suddenly, anger overwhelmed him, and he tore the sheet in small pieces. Chapelain left not a little worried. In the middle of the night, the cardinal thought of his own reaction, asked for the pieces of paper to be collected, and glued them back together. He then read the observations in their entirety and decided he should abandon the project of publishing the play, and, most likely, had all the manuscript copies destroyed. It is the only play sponsored by Richelieu of which text we have lost all traces. Pellisson-Fontanier, *Histoire*, vol. 1, p. 83.

26. The catalog of the Biblothèque Nationale attributes La Miliade to Jacques Favereau.

27. BN, Ms français 25054, folio 10.

28. Louis XIII, *Lettres inédites*, ed. Beauchamps, p. 300.

29. Richelieu, *Lettres*, vol. 5, p. 773.

30. Motteville, *Mémoires*, p. 34.

31. After the British invasion, Richelieu had asked for a detailed report of the state of the fleet and its installations. They were still very poor. Equipment was old and damaged; ports were falling in disrepair, personnel was scarce and poorly trained. The fleet was still wanting boats. By 1636, this sorry picture was changing rapidly. Notably, the fleet had increased by a substantial number of vessels. The "Ponant" fleet, which operated on the Atlantic, now had almost forty ships. The "Levant" fleet, which operated in the Mediterranean, had about twelve galleys. Improvements in the Mediterranean fleet did not mean that the wretched men who rowed on these galleys lived better. They worked in hair-raising conditions and fell in large number to disease and ill-treatment. Being sent to the galleys was still a commonly used punishment for all sorts of crimes. It was Saint Vincent de Paul who demanded from the cardinal that the living conditions of the galley men be improved.

32. The beautiful buildings that one can presently admire at the Val-de-Grâce were built by Anne of Austria, but at a much later date.

33. Anne's letter was written in Spanish on May 28, 1637, BN, Ms français 9241, folio 41v.

34. The queen was aware of this surveillance. One day, as she was writing a letter, she realized that one of her ladies who was reading nearby held her book upside down. She still thought that the precaution of writing from the safe haven of the Val-de-Grâce was enough to guard her from the cardinal's spies and secret police. How vain a presumption that was.

35. Kleinman, *Anne of Austria*, pp. 96–97.

36. BN, Ms français 10215.

37. Richelieu, *Mémoires* (Paléo), vol. 17, p. 342.

38. La Porte, *Mémoires*, p. 28.

39. De Hautefort contacted the valet of another prisoner jailed by Richelieu, De Jars. This valet had access to the terrace of the tower in which La Porte's cell was located. He dug a hole into the ground, which allowed him to reach the cell of some "Croquants" who had been jailed after their revolt in the southwest. These men did the same to communicate with a man who belonged to the late Maréchal de Marillac. This one finally reached La Porte through the floor of his own cell. La Porte was left to conclude that "all prisoners show a charity towards each other that is hard to fathom, and that I could have hardly believed, had I not experienced it myself." La Porte, *Mémoires*, p. 31.

40. Richelieu, *Lettres*, vol. 5, pp. 17–18.

41. Louis XIII, *Lettres inédites*, ed. Beauchamp, p. 328.

42. Caussin, quoted in Rochemonteix, *Nicolas Caussin*, p. 185. This quote leaves little doubt that Caussin thought the cardinal was accomplishing the works of the devil.

43. AAE, Mémoires et documents, France 830, folio 24.

44. Richelieu, *Mémoires* (Paléo), vol. 17, p. 353.

45. Caussin, "Lettre à Richelieu" in *Documents inédits*, p. 453.

46. On the political significance of this theological quarrel, see Monique Cottret's comments on Jean Delumeau's study *L'Aveu et le Pardon*, 1990, pp. 526–27 of her article "Raison d'État."

47. Quoted in Jean Orcibal, *Jean Duvergier de Hauranne*, p. 401.

48. Richelieu had given Madame de Combalet the title Duchesse d'Aiguillon, after throwing Puylaurens in jail and stripping him of his duchy. For convenience and clarity, we shall keep using her former name.

9: TURNING POINTS (1638–1640)

1. With a vow to honor the Virgin Mary, Louis resolved to rebuild the grand altar at Notre-Dame Cathedral and to have a mass sung every year and everywhere in the kingdom, on the day of the Assumption.

2. The memoirs of Monglat or de Chizay, which Louis XIII's biographer P. Chevallier adopts as his sources, propose an interesting account of Louis XIV's conception. On the afternoon of December 5, 1637, as this story goes, Louis bid farewell to Mademoiselle de La Fayette at the Convent of the Visitation, just when a terrible storm broke out and plunged Paris into darkness. The king was on his way from Versailles to another country house. His baggage—meaning not only the king's clothes but also his furniture, tableware, and bedding—was already at his destination. The captain of his guards suggested he ask for the queen's hospitality at the Louvre. Louis immediately rejected the idea. The storm still battered Paris, and the captain renewed his proposition. Louis objected that the queen held her supper and retired much too late for him. Guitaut—that was the name of this man to whom France may have owed so much—assured the king that the queen would gladly adjust her schedule for him. He sent out a messenger. Indeed, Anne obliged, and she welcomed Louis at the Louvre that night. The anecdote, indeed, is dramatic, but as the historian Ruth Kleinman

noticed, there are other documents that make it unacceptable. See her *Anne of Austria*, pp. 106–7.

3. Parrott, *Richelieu's Army*, p. 127.

4. After he gave his word of honor that he would not escape, the king allowed de Werth to go about freely in the capital. Soon enough this general found himself the object of Parisians' insatiable appetite for novelty. The dames paid him visits. Richelieu offered a banquet in his honor. Common people were less worldly with de Werth: they spent the summer singing burlesque songs about the general, or reading pamphlets that mocked him, including one title that explained how the military man who had once sown terror in their capital now happily enjoyed French wine instead of German beer. Jean de Werth was liberated in 1642 in exchange for General Horn, who had been captured at the Battle of Nördlingen in 1634.

5. Noailles, *Bernard de Saxe-Weimar*, vol. 2 of *Épisodes*, p. 349.

6. Montglat, *Mémoires*, p. 66.

7. Richelieu, *Lettres*, vol. 6, p. 105.

8. Ibid., p. 116 and 128.

9. Louis XIII, *Lettres inédites*, ed. La Caille, p. 21.

10. Motteville, *Mémoires*, p. 32.

11. Richelieu, *Lettres*, vol. 6, p. 116.

12. Let us remember that infant mortality remained high in early modern Europe.

13. Goulas, *Mémoires*, 1879, p. 329.

14. Richelieu, *Mémoires* (Paléo), vol. 18, p. 261.

15. The cardinal personally chose a governess for the child from among his partisans. Anne's preference went to Madame de Saint-Georges, who was the daughter of Madame de Montglat, the woman who had raised Louis, Gaston, and his band of brothers and sisters. Later, in November, Anne's lady-in-waiting, whom Richelieu had also picked, turned out to be less than a devoted ally. The cardinal promptly replaced her.

16. Louis XIII, *Lettres inédites*, ed. La Caille, p. 22.

17. Quoted in Whitaker, *Royal Passion*, p. 159.

18. Elliott, *Olivares*, p. 540.

19. Richelieu, *Lettres*, vol. 6, pp. 182, 183. Once he recovered his spirits, Richelieu gave orders so that the *Gazette*'s editor would know how to present this bad news. "One must tell Renaudot that when he speaks in his gazettes of how the siege of Fontarabie was lifted, he should declare about five or six hundred dead, and the same number of wounded, with ten cannons. Then Renaudot will not forget to add that we took five or six hundred as well this year, and as many on the seas." Ibid., p. 189.

20. Bernard of Saxe-Weimar died of illness on July 18, 1639.

21. In spite of repeated attempts, Richelieu had never succeeded in having Father Joseph named a cardinal. The role he played in forming alliances with the Protestants, and then the deteriorating relations with the pope on the matter of Gaston's marriage, made this request unacceptable in Rome.

22. Early modern warfare was a curious mix of savagery and civility: when the Spanish commander at Hesdin realized that the king himself was present at the siege, he sent out an envoy to learn the location of the august visitor, so as not to inconvenience him with a barrage of cannon shots. Montglat, *Mémoires*, p. 77.

23. Richelieu, *Lettres*, vol. 6, p. 391.

24. Ibid., p. 81.

25. Ibid., p. 539.

26. Chavigny to Mazarin, October 26, 1639, in ibid., p. 643.

27. Richelieu, *Lettres*, vol. 6, p. 501.

28. Tallemant des Réaux's *Historiettes* recount savory anecdotes to suggest that Louis's relationship with Cinq-Mars was more than platonic. Historians, however, generally handle these stories with caution, especially given the unreliable nature of Tallemant's own sources. In view of Louis's prudish nature and the fact that no one else alluded to this physical aspect, it seems best to ignore Tallemant's testimony. See *Historiettes*, vol. 1, pp. 346–47.

29. Richelieu, *Testament politique*, pp. 204–5, 207.

30. Saumières, *Mémoires*, p. 102.

31. Richelieu, *Lettres*, vol. 6, p. 644.

32. Ibid., pp. 641–42.

33. I take the details of this scene from the memoirs of Montglat, p. 91.

34. Richelieu, *Lettres*, vol. 6, p. 712.

35. Ibid., p. 713.

36. Letter of H. Arnauld, July 22, 1640, BN, Ms français 20634.

37. Vittorio Siri gives curious details on François du Hallier's departure for Arras. He says that Louis did not believe in the success of this rescue and feared that an attack on the convoy would be so catastrophic that it would forever destroy the reputation of his reign. The king would have rather lost the army in Arras than suffer this kind of setback. Thus, if we follow Siri, he gave secret orders to du Hallier to ignore his minister's instructions and not to leave. When du Hallier received Richelieu's order to depart for Arras, it did not take much for him to figure out that he would rather obey the minister—how telling, if true.

38. Montglat, *Mémoires*, p. 94.

39. For Châtillon's description of this day, see AAE, Mémoires et documents, Picardie 1679, folio 182.

40. Montrésor concluded that "those who mingle in the affairs of princes, must put limits to their own designs with a thorough knowledge of the ones they serve, and never measure those designs as if they were acting instead of those princes." Montrésor, *Mémoires*, 1879 p. 205. Let us note that Goulas considers the entire plot story "a bit fabulous." *Mémoires*, p. 300.

41. AAE, Mémoires et documents, France 836, folio 80.

42. Richelieu, *Lettres*, vol. 6, pp. 728 and 729. Also in Louis XIII, *Lettres inédites*, ed. Beauchamps, p. 375.

43. Louis XIII, *Lettres inédites*, ed. Beauchamps, p. 379.

44. Arnauld, *Mémoires*, p. 504.

45. See Siri, *Memorie*, vol. 8, p. 808.

46. Richelieu, *Lettres*, vol. 6, p. 646.

47. "Mémoire inédit de Richelieu contre Cinq-Mars," p. 249.

48. See Scotti, *Correspondance*, p. 434, or a letter from the Venetian ambassador A. Correr, August 5, 1640.

49. Goulas, *Mémoires*, 1879, pp. 347–48.

10: THE FINAL SCENE (1641–1642)

1. "Lettres de Vineuil," in *Variétés historiques et littéraires*, vol. 8, p. 120.

2. Claire-Clémence was the daughter of Richelieu's sister Nicole, who passed away in 1635.

3. Last but not least, Louis also showed reluctance to the marriage project. See Scotti, *Correspondance*, p. 276.

4. Richelieu was keenly aware of how far he was reaching with the marriage of his niece with a Condé. His vanity led him to include a special clause in the marriage contract, by which he stated that he would not include Claire-Clémence in his succession. The point was that the Condés might have been one of the most prominent families in the kingdom, but the Duc d'Enghien was not marrying for money but for sheer prestige. This arrangement led to a lawsuit after the cardinal's death.

5. Quoted in Murray, "Richelieu's Theater," p. 295.

6. Marolles, *Mémoires*, quoted in H. G. Hall, *Richelieu's Desmarets*, p. 186.

7. Some courtiers confessed puzzlement at the awkward analogy between Mirame's story and Anne's own romance with Buckingham, especially when the princess's character said:

I feel I am criminal,
To be in love with a foreigner
Who puts this state in danger,
For the sake of my love.

Could it have been a mischievous trick by the cardinal? Others thought it hard to believe that the play was malicious considering how the master of the house honored the queen that night. According to Nuncio Scotti, Louis had refused to see another play at Rueil, just a few days before the premiere of *Mirame*, because he frowned upon the extravagant spending at a time when France was under such fiscal pressure.

8. This suspicion was fueled by the publishing, in 1638, of a large treatise titled *Traité des libertés de l'Église gallicane*. The book was censored by Roman religious authorities in 1640. Many thought that Richelieu was behind the book's publishing, although this appears untrue. In June of 1641, Pope Urban VIII emitted a bull that forbid him to unduly take control of the Church's rights and possessions.

9. On June 8, a royal declaration condemned the rebels. Soissons replied with a manifesto that ripped Louis's principal minister apart. The text alluded to "a bad scheme" of 1636, most probably the attempt to kill the principal minister. See Richelieu, *Lettres*, vol. 6, p. 810.

10. Dispatch of G. Giustinian, July 16, 1641, in *Relazioni*, pp. 369–71.

11. Saumières, *Mémoires*, p. 71.

12. Montglat, *Mémoires*, p. 126.

13. "My first peril during this trip was to be killed in Lyon, without any chance for me to escape, and it would have happened if God had not stopped a few who were in this conspiracy and who had an authority that was necessary to execute the resolution. I say, without any chance for me to escape, because the design was to assassinate me in the king's lodging, which is a place where one goes unarmed, and where respect prohibits the use of force in reply." Pierre de Vaissière, *Conjuration*, p. 45.

14. Richelieu, *Lettres*, vol. 6, p. 900.

15. In exchange for armed reinforcements, Gaston had to cede Sedan to the Spanish king, give back any territorial gains made in the Roussillon, and nullify all treaties signed by the French Crown with the Habsburgs' enemies.

16. Chouppes, *Mémoires*, pp. 14–15.

17. Richelieu, *Lettres*, vol. 6, p. 906

18. Avenel, the editor of the cardinal's correspondence, makes cryptic remarks on the cardinal's condition, vol. 6, p. 920. He writes that the wounds were only the symptoms of another illness that remained profoundly hidden. We do know that a physician treated Richelieu for gonorrhea when he was a student in Paris. See chapter 1, n. 10.

19. AAE, Mémoires et documents, France 842, folio 208.

20. Molé, *Mémoires*, vol. 4, p. 157.

21. The historian Vassal-Reig analyzed this rationale in his thorough account of the Roussillon campaign, *Prise de Perpignan*, p. 213.

22. Richelieu, *Lettres*, vol. 6, p. 921.

23. Montglat, *Mémoires*, p. 128.

24. Fortunately, the Spanish general de Melo had to pull back when the more successful troops of the Franco-Weimerian army caused a timely diversion.

25. Montglat, *Mémoires*, p. 128.

26. Richelieu, *Lettres*, vol. 6, p. 926.

27. At the end of April, Louis had ordered his wife to go to live alone in Fontainebleau and to leave her two children in the hands of their governess and a captain of the guards. The king was in great fear that something could happen to the heir to the throne while he was away. Before leaving Paris, Louis had given the captain a gold coin, and the man was to obey an order from the king only if it came with the same kind of coin. Anne, naturally, was devastated by the order to leave her children behind. Raising her children and spending time in prayers had been her only activities ever since the Val-de-Grâce affair. In a bid to keep her children, she wrote and asked Richelieu for his intercession. Suspiciously, the queen received permission to stay with little Louis and Philippe right after the "marvelous discovery." This is why many have considered giving her a role in the discovery of the treaty. A close examination of the dates makes this theory, as tantalizing as it is, impossible. On this matter, see C. Dulong's clarifications.

28. Tallemant des Réaux, *Historiettes*, vol. 1, pp. 282–83.

29. Richelieu, *Lettres*, vol. 6, p. 935.

30. Ibid., pp. 937–38.

31. Griffet, *Histoire*, vol. 3, p. 479.

32. BN, Ms français 18431, folio 400. This volume contains Chancellier Séguier's papers concerning conspiracies and crimes of state. Louis's letter, which is in the king's own writing, bears a crossed S, an esoteric sign called "fermesse." Louis used this sign only in difficult times—one can see it in certain letters sent to Marie de' Medici before the Day of the Dupes—to signify heartfelt truth. I thank Orest Ranum for pointing out the existence of this letter and explaining the nature of this "fermesse."

33. Quoted in Dubost, *Marie de Médicis*, p. 854. It took a while for the queen mother's body to come back to France. On March 3, 1643, she was buried next to her husband, Henri IV, in the royal sanctuary at the basilica of Saint-Denis.

34. In Richelieu's view, the kind of man who was worthy of this responsibility had to be "capable of speculating and remain fixated on the means he could use to achieve his ends." Vaissières, *Conjuration*, p. 71.

35. This is a ruse that Richelieu had already used during the detention of Chalais in 1626.

36. Letters of H. Arnaud, BN, Ms français 20635, folio 50.

37. "Passage du Cardinal de Richelieu à Viviers," in *Variétés historiques et littéraires*, vol. 7, pp. 342–43.

38. According to Fontrailles, de Thou already knew of the treaty when he told him in Carcassonne that the conspirators had betrayed their country; still according to Fontrailles, de Thou had obtained this secret from Queen Anne. *Relations*, p. 254. This raises the question whether de Thou lied during his trial to protect the queen's reputation.

39. Condemning de Thou required the judges to invoke an obscure ordinance of 1477 which had not been used in more than seventy years. The text stated that people who hear of conspiracies and fail to reveal them are considered as guilty as the conspirators themselves. The verdict also called for Cinq-Mars to be interrogated one last time, under torture. While the death sentence left Cinq-Mars quite unmoved, he appeared to be shocked by this part of the judgment, as much for the horror of it as for the infamy that it represented for a noble. It was Laubardemont who took him to the chamber, attached him to the bench, and once again asked him to reveal everything he knew. But, as it turns out, this demonstration was only a subterfuge to incite Cinq-Mars to reveal the last secrets he might have kept. A clause in the verdict indicated that the young man would only be threatened with the torture, not that it needed to be carried out.

40. After hearing the news, Richelieu asked for the names of those two judges who had voted against the death sentence for de Thou. See Avenel, "Richelieu, Louis XIII et Cinq-Mars," p. 163. The two judges were one Sautereau, from the parlement of Grenoble, and Miromesnil, a councillor from Paris.

41. *Relation de tout ce qui s'est passé depuis la détention de MM. le Grand et de Thou*, in Fontrailles, *Relations*, p. 265.

42. King James version, verses 17–18.

43. Both bodies were taken away in the same carriage that had taken them to their place of execution. De Thou's remains were embalmed and given to his sister. Monsieur le Grand was buried in Lyon, at the Feuillants' convent.

44. "Documents relatifs au procès de Cinq-Mars," p. 320.

45. Richelieu, *Lettres*, vol. 7, pp. 219–20. Also printed in Aubery, *Mémoires*, vol. 2, p. 842. "Cinq-Mars offered to get rid of the cardinal for me, and said that he could do it himself," Louis would write on another occasion. Griffet, *Histoire*, vol. 3, p. 422. For another proof of the king's involvement, see Avenel, "Richelieu, Louis XIII et Cinq-Mars," p. 121, n. 1.

46. Montglat, *Mémoires*, p. 126.

47. For example, see Motteville, *Mémoires*, p. 36.

48. Richelieu, *Lettres*, vol. 7, p. 169.

49. Desmarets, *Europe*, p. 80. Paris: H. Le Gras, 1643; also in *Théâtre complet*, p. 929, verses 1639–1644.

50. See Pintard, "Pastorale," p. 450. The printed edition of the play omitted these crude references to current events.

51. Louis made these dismissals of Tréville and the three other men less harsh with compensations.

52. Richelieu, *Lettres*, vol. 7, p. 177.

53. Historians dismiss this anecdote on the grounds that it can be found in the memoirs of Montrésor, who was politically opposed to the cardinal. But Montrésor specifies (*Mémoires*, p. 242) that his source is the account that can be found in "Un Récit inédit de la mort du cardinal de Richelieu." An anonymous author who seemed to have been an eyewitness wrote this description of Richelieu's last moments. His account, then, is actually much more credible than the hagiographic one provided by Father Leon's acolyte (in *Archives Curieuses*, vol. 5).

54. Letters of H. Arnaud, BN, Ms français 20635, folio 184, 194.

CONCLUSION

1. *Le Trésor des épitaphes pour et contre le cardinal de Richelieu.*

2. Richelieu, *Testament politique*, p. 241.

3. On this relation between justice and absolute authority, see the fine pages of Orest Ranum in *Richelieu: l'Art et le Pouvoir*, pp. 59–60.

4. Richelieu commissioned many theoretical treatises on the subject, such as Cardin Le Bret's 1632 opus, *De la souveraineté du roi*.

5. Richelieu, *Testament politique*, p. 212.

6. *Relazioni*, p. 333.

7. Montchal, *Mémoires*, vol. 2, pp. 707–11.

8. Richelieu, *Mémoires*, vol. 4, p. 13. On this self-distrust of Louis XIII, see Goulas, *Mémoires*, 1879, p. 16.

9. Saumières, *Mémoires*, p. 35. The story of Wallenstein's death, as Richelieu's memoirs represent it, is also telling in this regard.

10. De Morgues, *La Vérité défendue*, p. 40, in *Recueil*.

11. Desmarets de Saint-Sorlin, *Délices de l'esprit*, quoted in *Théâtre complet*, p. 19.

BIBLIOGRAPHY

MANUSCRIPTS

Archives Nationales de France
L397; 129MI/53 to 82

Bibliothèque Nationale de France, Département des Manuscrits
Ms français: 3708, 3722, 3811, 3817, 3825, 3826, 9241, 9354, 10215, 16156, 17486–87, 18431,
    20632–35, 23200, 25054
NA françaises: 7020, 17544
500 Colbert: 97, 98, 221
Ms italiens: 1762–1820

Bibliothèque Nationale de France, Bibliothèque de l'Arsenal
Ms 4661, 5181

Ministère des Affaires Étrangères, Archives diplomatiques

Mémoires et documents
France: 19, 78, 244, 252–57, 286–88, 406, 772–80, 795, 795bis, 799–806, 808, 810, 815, 820–
    22, 828, 830, 836, 842–45
Petites séries: Île-de-France 1475, 1476, Languedoc 1628, 1632–34, Picardie 1678, Roussillon
    1744, 1745

Correspondance politique
Allemagne: 8, 9
Angleterre: 20, 21.
Espagne: 5, 6, 275.
Suède: 1–3

PRINTED SOURCES

Primary Sources

Allégresse publique pour le jour de l'arrivée de Monseigneur le duc de Buckingham. 1625.

Ambassade extraordinaire de Messieurs le duc d'Angoulême, comte de Bethune et de Preaux Chasteau-Neuf. Paris: F. Preuveray, 1667.

Andilly, Arnaud d', Robert. *Journal.* Paris: Techener, 1857.

————. *Mémoires.* Nouvelle Collection des mémoires relatifs à l'histoire de France, vol. 23. Paris: Didier, 1854.

Archives curieuses de l'histoire de France. 2nd series. 12 vols. Paris: Beauvais, 1837.

Ardier, Paul. *L'Assemblée des notables tenue à Paris ès années 1626 et 1627.* Paris: Cardin Besongne, 1652.

Arnauld, Abbé. *Mémoires.* Nouvelle Collection des mémoires relatifs à l'histoire de France, vol. 23. Paris: Didier, 1854.

L'Arrivée du grand convoi au camp devant Arras et la prise de deux demi-lunes. 1640.

L'Arrivée du grand convoi au siège devant Arras. 1640.

Artigny, Abbé. *Nouveaux mémoires d'histoire, de critique et de littérature.* Vol. 4. Paris: Debure, 1751.

L'Attaque faite contre les Espagnols contre le camp du roi devant Arras. 1640.

Aubery, Antoine. *L'Histoire du cardinal duc de Richelieu:* Paris: A. Bertier, 1660.

————. *Mémoires pour l'histoire du cardinal duc de Richelieu.* Paris: A. Bertier, 1660.

Ballet de la merlaison. Paris: J. Martin, 1635.

Ballets et mascarades de cour de Henri III à Louis XIV. Ed. P. Lacroix. 6 vols. Geneva: Gay, 1868–1870.

Banne, Jean de. "Passage du cardinal de Richelieu à Viviers. Anecdote extraite du journal manuscrit." In *Variétés historiques et littéraires,* ed. É. Fournier, vol. 7, pp. 339–45. Paris: P. Jannet, 1858.

Bassompierre, François de. *Mémoires.* Nouvelle Collection des mémoires relatifs à l'histoire de France, vol. 20. Paris: Didier, 1854.

Baudier, Michel. *Histoire du maréchal de Toiras.* Paris: F. Mauger, 1666.

————. *Le Soldat piémontois.* Paris: P. Rocolet, 1641.

Beaulieu-Persac, Philippe Prévost de. *Mémoires.* Paris: Renouard, 1913.

Beauvais-Nangis, Nicolas de Brichanteau de. *Mémoires.* Paris: Renouard, 1862.

Bentivoglio, Guido. *La Nunziatura di Francia.* 4 vols. Florence: Le Monneur, 1863.

Bernard, Charles. *Histoire de Louis XIII.* Paris: A. Courbé, 1646.

Boisrobert, François Le Métel de. *Le Sacrifice des Muses.* 1633.

Botel, sieur de Gaubertin, Pierre. *Histoire des guerres et choses mémorables arrivées sous le règne très glorieux de Louis le Juste.* Rouen: J. Besongne, 1624.

Bouffard-Madiane, Jean de. *Mémoires. Archives historiques de l'Albigeois,* vol. 5. Paris and Toulouse: Picard and Privat, 1897.

Brienne, Louis-Henri de Loménie de. *Mémoires.* Nouvelle Collection des mémoires relatifs à l'histoire de France, vol. 27. Paris: Didier, 1854.

Canault, Jean. *Vie du maréchal J.-B. d'Ornano.* Grenoble: Éd. Des Quatre Seigneurs, 1971.

Cardin Le Bret. *De la souveraineté du Roi.* Paris, 1632.

Catalogue of the Collection of Autograph Letters and Historical Documents Formed Between 1865 and 1882 by Alfred Morrison. 6 vols. London: Strangeways and Sons, 1883–1892.

Chapelain, Jean. *Lettres.* Ed. P. Tamizey de Larroque. 2 vols. Paris: Imprimerie Nationale, 1880.

——. *Ode à Monseigneur le cardinal duc de Richelieu.* Paris: J. Camusat, 1633.

Chizay, Louis Favreau de. *Mémoires.* Paris: Plon, 1914.

Chorier, Nicolas. *Histoire de la vie de Charles de Créquy de Blanchefort, duc de Lesdiguières.* 2 vols. Paris: J. Collombat, 1695.

Chouppes, Aymar de. *Mémoires.* Paris: J. Techener, 1861.

Cinq-Auteurs, Les. *La Comédie des Tuileries et L'Aveugle de Smyrne.* Paris: Champion, 2008.

Commission du Roi donnée . . . pour faire et parfaire le procès au comte de Chalais. Lyon: C. Armand dit Alphonse, 1626.

La Conjuration de Conchine. c. 1617

Déageant, Claude Guichard. *Mémoires.* Grenoble: P. Charvys, 1668.

Déclaration du roi, sur la réduction de la ville de La Rochelle en son obéissance. Paris: A. Étienne, 1629.

Déclaration du roi, sur la sortie de la reine sa mère et de Monseigneur son frère, hors le royaume. Paris: A. Estienne et al., 1631.

La Défaite de l'armée espagnole venant au secours de Colioure. Beziers: J. Pech, 1642.

La Défaite des Castillans devant Tarragone, par les armes du roi. Paris, 1641.

La Défaite des Croquans par Mr le duc de La Valette. Paris: G. Petit, 1637.

De Gellerain. *L'Espagne dépouillée ou Discours politique et militaire sur la prise de Perpignan.* Paris: J. Paslé, 1642.

De l'autorité royale. 1615.

Delort, André. *Mémoires de ce qui s'est passé de plus remarquable dans Montpellier depuis 1622 jusqu'en 1691.* Montpellier: C. Coulet, 1876.

Desmarets de Saint-Sorlin, Jean. *Les Promenades de Richelieu ou les Vertus chrétiennes.* Paris: H. Le Gras, 1653.

——. *Théâtre complet (1636–1643).* Paris: H. Champion, 2005.

De Ville, Antoine. *Obsidio Corbeiensis dicata Regi.* Paris: N. Buon, 1637.

——. *Le Siège de Hesdin.* Lyon: J. Caflin and F. Plaignard, 1639.

Discours au roi touchant les libelles faits contre le gouvernement de son État. 1631.

Discours au vray du ballet dansé par le Roy le dimanche XXIXᵉ jour de janvier MDCXVII. Paris: P. Ballard, 1617.

Divers mémoires concernant les guerres d'Italie. 2 vols. Paris: S. Mabre-Carmoisy, 1669.

Documents inédits. Ed. A. Carayon. Vol. 223. Paris: 1886.

"Documents relatifs au procès de Cinq-Mars." *Bulletin de la Société de l'histoire de France,* 2nd series, 3 (1861–1862): 319–22.

L'Enterrement obsèques et funérailles de Conchine maréchal d'Ancre. Paris: B. Hameau, 1617.

L'Entrevue du roi et de Monsieur son frère à Saint-Germain-en-Laye. Rouen: C. Le Villain, 1634.

Estrées, François Annibal, d'. *Mémoires.* Nouvelle Collection des mémoires relatifs à l'histoire de France, vol. 20. Paris: Didier, 1854.

Fancan, François Dorval-Langlois de. *La Chronique des favoris.* 1622.

————. *La France en convalescence*. 1624.

————. *Le Mot à l'oreille de Monsieur le marquis de La Vieuville*. 1624.

————. *La Voix publique au Roy*. 1624.

Favereau, Jacques. *La Miliade*. c.1637.

Feuquières, Manassès de Pas de. *Lettres et négociations*. Ed. Abbé Perau. 2 vols. Amsterdam: J. Neaulme, 1753.

————. *Lettres inédites*. Ed. É. Gallois. 5 vols. Paris: Leleux, 1845–1846.

Fontenay-Mareuil, François Duval de. *Mémoires*. Nouvelle Collection des mémoires relatifs à l'histoire de France, vol. 19. Paris: Didier, 1854.

Fontrailles, Louis d'Astarac de. *Relations des choses particulières de la cour arrivées pendant la faveur de M. de Cinq-Mars, grand écuyer, avec sa mort et celle de M. de Thou*. Nouvelle collection des mémoires relatifs à l'histoire de France, vol. 27. Paris: Didier, 1854.

Fortin de la Hoguette, Philippe. "Lettre au roi Louis XIII." In *Notices et documents publiés pour la Société de l'histoire de France*, pp. 375–86. Paris: Renouard, 1884.

Garasse, François. *Mémoires*. Paris: Amyot, 1860.

Gaston, duc d'Orléans. *Mémoires*. Nouvelle Collection des mémoires relatifs à l'histoire de France, vol. 23. Paris: Didier, 1854.

Gaufreteau, Jean de. *La Digue*. Bordeaux: P. de La Court, 1629.

Girard, Guillaume. *Histoire de la vie du duc d'Épernon*. 3 vols. Paris: T. Joly, 1663.

Godefroy, Théodore. *Le Cérémonial françois*. 2 vols. Paris: Cramoisy, 1649.

Goulas, Nicolas. *Mémoires*. Vol. 1. Paris: Renouard, 1879.

————. *Mémoires et autres inédits*. Ed. N. Hepp. Paris: Champion, 1995.

Le Grand et Juste Châtiment des rebelles de Nègrepelisse. 1622.

Griffet, Henri. *Histoire du règne de Louis XIII, roi de France et de Navarre*. 3 vols. Paris: Librai-res Associés, 1758.

Guez de Balzac, Jean-Louis. *Le Prince*. Paris: La Table Ronde, 1996.

Guillaudeau, Joseph. *Diaire*. Archives historiques de la Saintonge et de l'Aunis 38 (1908).

Hay du Chastelet, Paul. *Observations sur la vie et la condamnation du maréchal de Marillac*. Paris, 1633.

Héroard, Jean. *Journal*. Ed. M. Foisil. 2 vols. Paris: Fayard, 1989.

Histoire de Henry II, dernier duc de Montmorency. Paris: J. Guignard, 1699.

Histoire journalière de ce qui s'est passé dans le Montferrat. Paris: J. de la Tourette, 1631.

Histoire véritable de tout ce qui s'est fait et passé dans la ville de Toulouse, en la mort de Monsieur de Montmorency. 1633.

Hyacinthe de Reims. *Remarques sur les vertus et la mort du TRP Joseph Le Clerc du Tremblay*. Calais: Imp. des Orphelins, 1888.

L'Innocence justifiée en l'administration des affaires. 1631.

Joly, Hector. *Histoire particulière des plus mémorables choses qui se sont passées au siège de Montauban, et de l'acheminement d'icelui*. Leiden: T. Basson, 1622.

Journal au vrai de ce qui s'est passé dans l'île de Ré. Toulouse: R. Colomiez, 1628.

Journal de ce qui s'est passé à l'arrivée de l'armée du roi près Sedan, commandée par le maréchal de Châtillon. Paris: Isle du Palais, 1641.

La Force, Jacques Nompar de Caumont de. *Mémoires authentiques*. 4 vols. Paris: Charpentier, 1843.

Lancre, Pierre de. *Le Livre des princes*. Paris: N. Buon, 1617.

La Porte, Pierre de. *Mémoires*. Nouvelle Collection des mémoires relatifs à l'histoire de France, vol. 32. Paris: Didier, 1854.

La Rochefoucauld, François de. *Mémoires*. Nouvelle Collection des mémoires relatifs à l'histoire de France, vol. 29. Paris: Didier, 1854.

Le Bret, Henry. *Histoire de la ville de Montauban*. Montauban: S. Dubois, 1668.

Lettre au roi par Monseigneur. Paris: A. Vitray, 1631.

Lettre de Cléophon à Polemandre sur les affaires de ce temps. 1619.

Lettre de la reine mère au roi avec la réponse de Sa Majesté. Paris: S. Cramoisy, 1631.

"Lettres de Vineuil à M. d'Humières, sur la conspiration de Cinq-Mars." In *Variétés historiques et littéraires*, ed. É. Fournier, vol. 7, pp. 119–29. Paris: P. Jannet, 1857.

Lettre du père Caussin jésuite, confesseur de Louis XIII, à Monseigneur le cardinal de Richelieu. c. 1773.

Lettre du roi envoyée au provinces. Paris: J. Martin, 1631.

Lettre du roi . . . sur la détention du duc de Puylaurent. 1635.

Lettre écrite au roi par Monsieur. Paris: A. Vitray, 1631.

Lettres et mémoires adressés au chancellier Séguier. 2 vols. Paris: Presses Universitaires de France, 1964.

Le Vassor, Michel. *Histoire de Louis XIII, roi de France et de Navarre*. 6 vols. Amsterdam: au dépens des Associés, 1757.

Leveneur de Tillières, Tanneguy. *Mémoires inédits*. Paris: Poulet-Malassis, 1862.

Lezeau, Nicolas Lefèvre de. *La Vie de Michel de Marillac (1560–1632)*. Sainte-Foy: Presses de l'Université Laval, 2007.

Louis XIII. "Lettres (1619–1626)." *Annuaire-Bulletin de la Société de l'histoire de France* (1873): 182–92, 197–208, 213–24, 228–58.

———. *Lettres de la main de Louis XIII*. Ed. E. Griselle. Paris: Société des bibliophiles français, 1914.

———. *Lettres inédites*. Ed. G. La Caille. Paris: N. Charavay, 1901.

———. *Lettres inédites de Louis XIII à Richelieu*. Ed. M. Topin. Paris: Didier, 1876.

———. *Louis XIII d'après sa correspondance avec le cardinal de Richelieu*. Ed. comte de Beauchamp. Paris: H. Laurens, 1902.

———. "Louis XIII et sa mère." Ed. E. Griselle. *Revue historique* 105 (1910): 302–31; 106 (1911): 82–100, 295–308.

La Maladie et guérison de la reine très-chrétienne Anne d'Autriche. Paris: P. Ramier, 1620.

Malherbe, François de. *Œuvres*. Paris: Gallimard, 1971.

Marguerite de Valois. *Mémoires suivis des anecdotes inédites de l'histoire de France pendant les XVIᵉ et XVIIᵉ siècles tirées de la bouche de M. le garde des sceaux du Vair et autres*. Paris: Jeannet, 1858.

Matel, sieur de. *Les Louanges guerrières de Monseigneur le cardinal de Richelieu*, Paris: J. Martin, 1629.

Matthieu, Jean-Baptiste. *Histoire de Louis XIII, roi de France et de Navarre*. In Pierre Matthieu, *Histoire de France*, vol. 2. Paris: P. Baillet, 1631.

Méditations de l'hermite Valerian. 1621.

Mercure françois. 1613–.

Mervault, Pierre. *Histoire du dernier siège de La Rochelle*. Rouen: J. Berthelin and J. Cailloue, 1648.

La Merveille royale de Louis XIII roi de France. Paris: Guerreau, 1617.

Les Merveilles et coup d'essai de Louis le Juste. Paris: J. Berjon, 1617.

Molé, Matthieu. *Mémoires*. 4 vols. Paris: Renouard, 1855.

Montchal, archevêque de Toulouse. *Mémoires*. 2 vols. Rotterdam: G. Fritsch, 1718.

Montglat, Charles de. *Mémoires*. Nouvelle Collection des mémoires relatifs à l'histoire de France, vol. 29. Paris: Didier, 1854.

Montmaur, Pierre de. *Relation véritable de ce qui s'est passé au jugement du procès du maréchal de Marillac*. 1632.

Montpensier, Anne-Marie-Louise d'Orléans de. *Mémoires, 1627–1686*. Vol. 1. Paris: Paléo, 2007.

Montrésor, Claude de Bourdeille de. *Mémoires*. Nouvelle Collection des mémoires relatifs à l'histoire de France, vol. 27. Paris: Didier, 1854.

Morgues, Mathieu de. *Recueil de diverses pièces pour servir à l'histoire de France sous le règne de Louis XIII, roy de France et de Navarre*. Antwerp, 1644.

———. *Vérités chrétiennes*. 1620.

Motteville, Françoise Bertaut de. *Mémoires*. Nouvelle Collection des mémoires relatifs à l'histoire de France, vol. 24. Paris: Didier, 1854.

Négociation commencée au mois de mars de l'année 1619 avec la reine. Paris: A. Vitré, 1673.

Négociations, lettres et pièces relatives à la conférence de Loudun. Collection de documents inédits sur l'histoire de France, 1st series, Histoire politique, vol. 52. Paris: Imprimerie Impériale, 1862.

Original Letters Illustrative of English History. 3 vols. London: Harding, Triphook, and Lepard, 1824.

Pasquier, Nicolas. *Lettres*. Paris, 1623.

Patin, Guy. *Lettres*. Paris: J.-B. Baillière, 1846.

Pellisson-Fontanier, Paul. *Histoire de l'Académie Française*. 2 vols. Paris: Didier, 1858.

Pièces du procès de Henri de Talleyrand, comte de Chalais, décapité en 1626. London, 1781.

Plessis-Besançon, Bernard du. *Mémoires*. Paris: Renouard, 1892.

Pontchartrain, Paul Phelypeaux de. *Mémoires concernant les affaires de France sous la régence de Marie de Médicis*. Nouvelle Collection des mémoires relatifs à l'histoire de France, vol. 19. Paris: Didier, 1854.

Pontis, Sieur de. *Mémoires*. Nouvelle Collection des mémoires relatifs à l'histoire de France, vol. 20. Paris: Didier, 1854.

La Prise de la ville de Bergerac et entière dissipation des Croquans par le duc de La Valette. Paris, 1637.

La Prise par force et brûlement de la ville et château de Privas. Paris: A. Vitray, 1629.

Puget de la Serre, Jean. *Histoire curieuse de tout ce qui s'est passé à l'entrée de la reine*. Antwerp: B. Moret, 1632.

Pure, Michel de. *Vita Alphonsi Ludovici Plessaei Richelii*. Paris, A. Vitré, 1663.

Puységur, Jacques de Chastenet de. *Les Guerres de Louis XIII et de la minorité de Louis XIV*. 2 vols. Paris: Librairie de la société bibliographique, 1883.

Rapine, Florimont. *Recueil très exact et curieux de tout ce qui s'est fait . . . en l'assemblée générale des États.* Paris: A. de Sommaville et al., 1651.

Récit de ce qui s'est passé aux environs de la ville d'Arras par les armes du Roi. Paris, 1640.

Récit de la mort de Monsieur le duc de Montmorency et de ce qui s'est passé lors en cour. Paris: Bureau d'adresse, 1632.

"Récit particulier de ce qui s'est passé un peu avant la mort de Monsr. le cardinal de Richelieu." *Revue Historique* 55 (1894): 302–8.

Récit véritable de ce qui s'est fait et passé en l'armée du Roi, depuis le trentième de juillet 1620 jusqu'au traité fait avec la reine mère Sa Majesté. Paris: F. Bourriquant, 1620.

Récit véritable de ce qui s'est nouvellement fait et passé à Montauban. Paris: A. Saugrain, 1621.

Récit véritable de ce qui s'est passé à Blavet. Lyon: C. Armand dit Alphonse, 1624.

Récit véritable de ce qui s'est passé au Louvre depuis le 24 avril jusqu'au départ de la reine mère du roi. 1617.

Récit véritable de l'exécution du comte de Chalais. Paris: J. Bessin, 1626.

Récit véritable de tout ce qui s'est passé au château de Saint-Germain-en-Laye, au retour de Monseigneur frère unique du roi. Paris: P. Targa, 1634.

Récit véritable du furieux combat donné devant Arras. 1640.

Recueil de diverses pièces pour servir à l'histoire. Ed. P. Hay du Chastelet. 1643.

Recueil de diverses relations des guerres d'Italie, ès années 1629, 1630 et 1631. Bourg en Bresse: J. Bristot, 1632.

Recueil de pièces concernant l'histoire de Louis XIII. 4 vols. Paris: Montalant, 1716.

Recueil de plusieurs pièces pour servir à l'histoire de Port-Royal. Utrecht, 1740.

Recueil des pièces les plus curieuses qui ont été faites pendant le règne du connétable jusqu'à présent. 1622.

Relation de ce qui s'est naguère passé dans Perpignan après l'entrée de l'armée du roi en ladite ville. Orléans: R. Fremont, 1642.

Relation de ce qui s'est passé en la bataille gagnée contre l'armée du roi, contre celle d'Espagne, commandée par le prince Thomas. Lyon: C. Larjot et J. Juilleron, 1635.

Relation de la descente des Anglais en l'île de Ré. Paris: E. Martin, 1628.

Relation du combat donné par l'armée navale du Roi. 1640.

Relation du siège de Saint-Affrique. 1628.

Relation envoyée au roi par Monsieur le maréchal de Schomberg du combat fait entre les armes qu'il commande et l'armée de Monsieur près de Castelnaudary. Paris: Bureau d'adresse, 1632.

Relation exacte de tout ce qui s'est passé à la mort du maréchal d'Ancre. Nouvelle Collection des mémoires relatifs à l'histoire de France, vol. 19. Paris: Didier, 1854.

Relation succinte du siège et reddition d'Arras, envoyée d'Amiens. Paris: S. Cramoisy, 1640.

Relazioni degli stati europei lette al senato dagli ambasciatori veneti nel secolo decimosettimo. Ser. 2 (France), vol. 2. Venice: P. Naratovich, 1859.

Remontrance du maréchal de Marillac au roi. 1631.

Remontrance du maréchal de Marillac aux commissaires pour servir de justification, et montrer qu'ils ne peuvent être ses juges. 1631.

Requêtes présentées à la cour du parlement de Paris. 1631.

Requêtes présentées à Messieurs les commissaires de la chambre souveraine établie par le roi au lieu de Ruei par le m. de Marillac. Paris, 1632.

Retz, François de Gondi, cardinal de. *Mémoires.* Paris: Gallimard, 1956.

Richelieu, Armand-Jean du Plessis de. *Harangue à la reine mère du roi sur les troubles et divisions de ce temps.* 1620.

——. *Harangue prononcée en la salle du Petit-Bourbon, le 23 février 1615, à la clôture des États tenus à Paris.* Paris: S. Carmoisy, 1615.

——. *Instruction du chrétien.* Paris: N. de la Vigne, 1626.

——. *Lettres, instructions diplomatiques et papiers d'État.* Ed. M. Avenel. 8 vols. Paris: Imprimerie Impériale, 1853.

——. "Un Mémoire inédit de Richelieu contre Cinq-Mars." *Revue des questions historiques* 43 (1818): 234–50.

——. *Mémoires.* Société de l'Histoire de France. 10 vols. Paris: Renouard, 1912.

——. *Mémoires.* 18 vols. Paris: Paléo, 2000–.

——. *Les Papiers de Richelieu. Empire allemand.* Ed. A. Wild and A. V. Hartmann. 3 vols. 1982–1999.

——. *Les Papiers de Richelieu. Section politique intérieure.* Ed. P. Grillon. 6 vols. 1975–1997.

——. *Les Principaux points de la religion catholique défendus contre l'écrit au roi par les quatre ministres de Charenton.* Poitiers: A. Mesnier, 1617.

——. *Un sermon inédit de Richelieu.* Ed. A. M. P. Ingold. Luçon: M. Bideaux, 1889.

——. *Testament Politique.* Ed. F. Hildesheimer. Paris: Société de l'Histoire de France, 1995.

——. *Traité de la perfection du chrétien.* Ed. F. Hildesheimer and S. Morgain. Paris: H. Champion, 2002.

Rohan, Henri de. *Mémoires.* Nouvelle Collection des mémoires relatifs à l'histoire de France, vol. 19. Paris: Didier, 1854.

Saavedra Fajardo, Diego. *Le Prince chrétien et politique.* Paris: Cie des libraires, 1668.

Sainte-Marthe, sieur de. *Histoire de la rebellion des Rochelois et de leur réduction à l'obéissance.* Paris: J. Villery, 1629.

Saint-Simon, Louis de Rouvroy de. *Mémoires.* Vol. 1. Paris: Hachette, 1879.

Saumières, Jacques de Langlade, Bon de. *Mémoires de la vie de Frédéric Maurice de La Tour-d'Auvergne duc de Bouillon.* Paris: P. Trabouillet, 1691.

Scotti, Ranuccio. *Correspondance (1639–1641).* Rome and Paris: Presses de l'Université Grégorienne and E. de Boccard, 1965.

Siège de La Rochelle, journal contemporain (20 juillet 1627–4 juillet 1630). La Rochelle and Paris: A. Thoreux and J.-B. Dumoulin, 1872.

Le Siège et la bataille de Leucate. Toulouse: A. Colomiez, 1637.

Siri, Vittorio. *Memorie recondite.* 8 vols. Paris: S. Cramoisy, 1677–1679.

Sirmond, Jean. *Le Coup d'État de Louis XIII, au roi.* 1631.

Le Soleil au signe du lion. Lyon: J. Juilleron, 1623.

Sourdis, Henri d'Escoubleau de. *Correspondance.* Ed. E. Sue. 3 vols. Paris: Imprimerie du Crapelet, 1839.

Souvigny, Jean Gangnières de. *Mémoires.* Paris: Renouard, 1906.

Sur l'enlèvement des reliques de saint Fiacre, apportées de la ville de Meaux, pour la guérison du cul de Mr le cardinal de Richelieu. Antwerp, 1643.

Tallemant des Réaux, Gédéon. *Historiettes.* 2 vols. Paris: Gallimard, 1960.

Talon, Jean. *Mémoires de Louis de Nogaret cardinal de La Valette.* Paris: Ph. D. Pierres, 1772.

Thou, Jacques-Auguste de. *Histoire universelle.* Vol. 10. The Hague: Scheurleer, 1740.

Le Trésor des épitaphes pour et contre le cardinal. Antwerp.

La Véritable Représentation de tous les triomphes, magnificences et feux d'artifice faits à Lyon. Paris: J. Martin, 1622.

La Vie de Marie de Hautefort, Duchesse de Schomberg. 1799.

Vignier, M. *Le Château de Richelieu, ou l'Histoire des dieux et des héros de l'antiquité, avec des réflexions morales.* Saumur: I. et H. Desbordes, 1676.

Le Voyage de Mr de Bullion à Beziers, vers Monseigneur le duc d'Orléans frère unique du roi. Paris: Bureau d'adresse, 1632.

Wotton, Henry. *A Short View of the Life and Death of George Villiers, Duke of Buckingham.* London: W. Sheares.

Secondary Sources

Anquez, Léonce. *Histoire des assemblées politiques des réformés de France (1573–1622).* Paris: A. Durand, 1859.

Anselme, Père. *Histoire généalogique.* 9 vols. Paris: Compagnie des Libraires, 1726–1733.

Antier, Jean-Jacques. *Les Grandes Heures des îles de Lérins.* Paris: Perrin, 1975.

Aronson, Nicole. *Madame de Rambouillet ou la Magicienne de la chambre bleue.* Paris: Fayard, 1988.

Aumale, duc d'. *Histoire des princes de Condé pendant les XVIe et XVIIe siècles.* 8 vols. Paris: Calmann-Lévy, 1886.

Avenel, Georges d'. "L'Évêque de Luçon et le connétable de Luynes." *Revue des questions historiques* 6 (1869): 77–131.

———. "La Jeunesse de Richelieu jusqu'à l'ouverture des États de 1614." *Revue des questions historiques* 6 (1869): 146–224.

———. "Richelieu, Louis XIII et Cinq-Mars." *Revue des questions historiques* 4 (1868): 92–180.

Avezou, Laurent. "Richelieu vu par Mathieu de Morgues et Paul Hay du Chastelet: le Double miroir de Janus." *Travaux de Littérature* 28 (2005): 167–78.

Bailey, Donald A. "Anti-Richelieu Propaganda and the Dévots: A Reinterpretation of Mathieu de Morgues." In *Proceedings of the Second Meeting of the Western Society for French History*, ed. B. D. Gooch, pp. 94–103. Santa Barbara: Western Society for French History, 1975.

———. "The Family and Early Career of Michel de Marillac (1560–1632)." In *Society and Institutions in Early Modern France*, ed. M. P. Holt, pp. 170–89. Athens: University of Georgia Press, 1991.

Bailly, Christian. *Théophraste Renaudot: Un homme d'influence au temps de Louis XIII et de la Fronde.* Paris: Pré aux Clercs, 1987.

Baschet, Armand. *Le Roi chez la Reine.* Paris: Plon, 1866.

Batiffol, Louis. "Anne d'Autriche et Buckingham." *Revue de Paris* 2 (1913): 539–62.

———. *Autour de Richelieu.* Paris: Calmann-Lévy, 1937.

————. "Le Cardinal de Richelieu et la Sorbonne." *Revue de Paris* 4 (1935): 92–117.

————. "Le Coup d'État du 24 avril 1617." *Revue historique* 95 (1907): 292–308; 97 (1908): 27–77, 264–286.

————. *La Duchesse de Chevreuse*. Paris: Hachette, 1924.

————. "Un jeune ménage royal." *Revue de Paris* 6 (1909): 105–32.

————. "Louis XIII et le duc de Luynes." *Revue historique* 102 (1909): 241–64; 103 (1910): 32–62, 248–77.

————. *Le Louvre sous Henri IV et Louis XIII*. Paris: Calmann-Lévy, 1930.

————. "Richelieu et la question d'Alsace." *Revue historique* 138 (1921): 161–200.

————. *Richelieu et le roi Louis XIII: les Véritables Rapports du souverain et de son ministre.* Paris: Calmann-Lévy, 1934.

————. *Le Roi Louis XIII a vingt ans*. Paris: Calmann-Lévy, 1910.

————. *Au Temps de Louis XIII*. Paris: Calmann-Lévy, 1907.

————. "Au Temps du siège de La Rochelle." *Revue de Paris* 5 (1902): 118–55.

————. "Le Trésor de la Bastille de 1605 à 1611." *Revue Henri IV* 3 (1909–1912): 200–209.

————. "La Véritable Figure du cardinal de Richelieu." *Revue hebdomadaire* 7 (1921): 509–26.

————. *La Vie intime d'une reine de France au XVIIe siècle*. Paris: Calmann-Lévy, 1906.

Baudoin-Matuzek, Marie-Noëlle. *Marie de Médicis et le palais du Luxembourg*. Paris: Délégation à l'action artistique, 1991.

Baudson, Émile. *Charles de Gonzague, duc de Nevers, de Rethel et de Mantoue, 1580–1637.* Paris: Perrin, 1947.

————. *Un Urbaniste au XVIIe siècle: Clément Metezeau, architecte du roi*. Mézières: Éd. de la Société des études ardennaises, 1956.

Bayard, Françoise. *Le Monde des financiers*. Paris: Flammarion, 1988.

Beijer, Agne. "Une Maquette de décor récemment retrouvée pour le "Ballet de la prospérité des armes de France." In *Le Lieu théâtral à la Renaissance*, ed. J. Jacquot, pp. 377–403. Paris: Éd. du Centre National de la Recherche Scientifique, 1964.

Belvederi, Raffaele. *Guido Bentivoglio e la politica europea del suo tempo, 1607–1621*. Padova: Leviana, 1962.

Benoist, Pierre. *Le Père Joseph: l'Éminence grise de Richelieu*. Paris: Perrin, 2007.

Béranger, Jean. "Relations internationales et subversion: Essai de typologie." In *La France, l'Alsace et l'Europe: Problèmes intérieurs et relations internationales à l'époque moderne*. pp. 245–55. Colmar: Éd. d'Alsace, 1986.

Bercé, Yves-Marie. "Richelieu: la Maîtrise de l'histoire et le conformisme historique." In *Idéologie et propagande en France*, ed. M. Yardeni, pp. 99–106 Paris: Picard, 1987.

————. "Rohan et la Valtelline." In *Guerre et paix dans l'Europe du XVIIe siècle*, ed. L. Bély et al., pp. 321–35. Paris: Sedes, 1991.

Bergin, Joseph. *Cardinal Richelieu and the Pursuit of Wealth*. New Haven: Yale University Press, 1985.

————. *The Making of the French Episcopate (1589–1661)*. New Haven: Yale University Press, 1996.

————. *The Rise of Richelieu*. New Haven: Yale University Press, 1991.

Betton, Félicien. "Louis XIII et Richelieu à Montfrin et à Tarascon en 1642." *Bulletin de la société d'histoire et d'archéologie de Beaucaire* 69 (1981): 3–10; 70 (1981): 3–11.

Bigot, P.-H. "Le Procès de Cinq-Mars et de Thou à Tarascon." *Revue historique de Provence* (1901): 526–36, 608–18.

Bitton, Davis. *The French Nobility in Crisis, 1560–1640*. Stanford: Stanford University Press, 1969.

Blanchet, Andrien. "Un récit inédit de la mort du maréchal d'Ancre." *Bulletin de la Société de l'histoire de Paris et de l'Île-de-France* 27 (1900): 135–41.

Blet, Pierre. *Le Clergé de France et la monarchie*. Rome: Librairie éditrice de l'Université Grégorienne, 1954.

——. *Richelieu et l'Église*. Versailles: Via Romana, 2007.

Bonneau-Avenant, Alfred. *La Duchesse d'Aiguillon*. Paris: Didier, 1879.

Bonnet, Jules. "Le Siège de Saint-Affrique." *Bulletin historique et littéraire* 25 (1876): 49–60.

Bonney, Richard. *The King's Debts: Finance and Politics in France, 1589–1661*. Oxford: Clarendon Press, 1981.

——. *Political Change in France under Richelieu and Mazarin, 1624–1661*. Oxford: Oxford University Press, 1978.

Bossebeuf, Louis-Auguste. *Richelieu et ses environs*. Paris: Res Universis, 1990.

Bouyer, Christian. *Gaston d'Orléans (1608–1660)*. Paris: Albin Michel, 1999.

Bretaudeau, A. *Histoire des Ponts-de-Cé*. Angers: Germain et G. Grassin, 1904.

Callot, P.-S. *Jean Guiton, Dernier Maire de l'ancienne commmune de La Rochelle, 1628*. La Rochelle and Paris: A. Caillaud, 1898.

Canova Green, Marie-Claude. "Créatures et créateurs: les Écrivains patronnés et le ballet de cour sous Louis XIII." *Papers on French Seventeenth Century Literature* 15 (1988): 101–13.

Careri, Giovanni. "An Ambiguous Portrait: Louis XIII Dances the Jerusalem Delivered." *Acta ad archaeologiam et artium historiam pertinentia*, Series altera, 12 (2001): 110–16, 210–15.

Carmona, Michel. *Les Diables de Loudun: Sorcellerie et politique sous Richelieu*. Paris: Fayard, 1988.

——. *Le Louvre et les Tuileries: Huit Siècles d'histoire*. Paris: Éd. La Martinière, 2004.

——. *Marie de Médicis*. Paris: Fayard, 1981.

——. *Richelieu: l'Ambition et le Pouvoir*. Paris: Fayard, 1983.

Carroll, Stuart. *Blood and Violence in Early Modern France*. Oxford: Oxford University Press, 2006.

Carutti, Domenico. *Storia della diplomazia della corte di Savoia*. Vol. 2. Rome: Fratelli Bocca, 1876.

Castagnos, Paul. *Richelieu face à la mer*. Rennes: Éd. Ouest-France, 1989.

Champier, Victor, and G.-Roger Sandoz. *Le Palais-Royal d'après des documents inédits (1629–1900)*. Vol. 1. Paris: Société de propagation des livres d'art, 1900.

Charnacé, Guy de. *Un ambassadeur de Louis XIII*. Paris: Éd. de la Nouvelle Revue, 1903.

Chartier, Roger. "À propos des États Généraux de 1614." *Revue d'histoire moderne et contemporaine* 23 (1976): 68–79.

——. "La Noblesse française et les États Généraux de 1614: Une réaction aristocratique?" *Acta Poloniae Historica* 36 (1977): 65–81.

Chevallier, Pierre. "Heurs et malheurs d'un favori de Louis XIII, Claude de Saint-Simon." *Cahiers Saint-Simon* 21 (1993): 3–12.

——. *Louis XIII: Roi cornélien*. Paris: Fayard, 1979.

————. "La Véritable Journée des Dupes (11 novembre 1630)." *Mémoires de la Société académique de l'Aube* 108 (1974–1977): 193–253.

Church, William F. *Richelieu and Reason of State.* Princeton: Princeton University Press, 1972.

Claretta, Gaudenzio. *Storia della Reggenza di Cristina di Francia.* 3 vols. Turin: Stabilimento Civelli, 1868.

Clarke, Jack A. *Huguenot Warrior: The Life and Times of Henri de Rohan, 1579–1638.* The Hague: Nijhoff, 1966.

Coniglio, Giuseppe. *I Gonzaga.* Milan: Dall'Ogio, 1967.

Constant, Jean-Marie. *Les Conjurateurs: le Premier libéralisme politique sous Richelieu.* Paris: Hachette, 1987.

Cottret, Monique. "Raison d'État et politique chrétienne entre Richelieu et Bossuet." *Bulletin de la Société de l'Histoire du protestantisme français* 138 (1992): 515–36.

Cousin, Victor. "Le Duc et connétable de Luynes." *Journal des Savants* (1861–1863).

————. *Madame de Chevreuse.* Paris: Didier, 1876.

————. *Madame de Hautefort.* Paris: Didier, 1886.

Couton, Georges. *Richelieu et le théâtre.* Lyon: Presses Universitaires de Lyon, 1986.

Cramail, Alfred. *Le Château de Rueil et ses jardins sous le cardinal de Richelieu et sous la duchesse d'Aiguillon.* Fontainebleau: E. Bourges, 1888.

Cristianesimo e Ragion di Stato. Ed. E. Castelli. Rome: Bocca, 1953.

Degert, Antoine. "Le Chapeau du cardinal de Richelieu." *Revue historique* 118 (1915): 223–88.

————. "Le Mariage de Gaston d'Orléans et de Marguerite de Lorraine." *Revue historique* 143 (1923): 161–80;144 (1923): 1–57.

Delavaud, Louis. "Au Siège de La Rochelle (1627–1628): Lettres inédites de Raymond Phélypeaux d'Herbault." *Archives historiques de la Saintonge et de l'Aunis* 43 (1912): 114–76.

Delhommeau, Louis. *Documents pour l'histoire de l'évêché de Luçon, 1317–1801.* Luçon: chez l'auteur, 1971.

Deloche, Maximin. *Autour de la plume du cardinal de Richelieu.* Paris: Société française d'imprimerie et de librairie, 1920.

————. *Le Cardinal de Richelieu et les femmes.* Paris: Émile-Paul frères, 1931.

————. *Un frère de Richelieu inconnu.* Paris: Desclée de Brouwer, 1935.

————. *La Maison du cardinal de Richelieu.* Paris: H. Champion, 1912.

————. *Les Richelieu: le Père du cardinal François du Plessis, grand Prévost de France.* Paris: Perrin, 1923.

De Mun, Gabriel. "Un frère de Richelieu: le Cardinal de Lyon (1582–1653)." *Revue d'histoire diplomatique* 18 (1904): 161–99.

Desjonquères, Léon. *Le Garde des sceaux Michel de Marillac et son œuvre législative.* Paris: Bonvalot-Jouve, 1908.

Desprat, Jean-Paul. *Les Bâtards d'Henri IV: l'Épopée des Vendômes (1594–1727).* Paris: Perrin, 1994.

Des Robert, Ferdinand. *Campagnes de Charles IV duc de Lorraine et de Bar en Allemagne, en Lorraine et en Franche-Comté.* Paris and Nancy: H. Champion and Sidot frères, 1883.

Dethan, Georges. *Gaston d'Orléans: Conspirateur et prince charmant.* Paris: Fayard, 1959.

————. "Mazarin avant le ministère." *Revue historique* 227 (1962): 33-66.

————. *La Vie de Gaston d'Orléans*. Paris: De Fallois, 1992.

Deyan, Pierre and Solange. *Henri de Rohan: Huguenot de plume et d'épée*. Paris: Perrin, 2000.

Dictionnaire du Grand Siècle. Ed. F. Bluche. Paris: Fayard, 2005.

Dorival, Bernard. "Art et politique en France au XVIIᵉ siècle: la Galerie des hommes illustres du Palais-Cardinal." *Bulletin de la Société de l'histoire de l'art français* (1973): 43–60.

Dubost, Jean-François. *Marie de Médicis: la Reine dévoilée*. Paris: Payot, 2009.

Duccini, Hélène. *Concini, grandeur et misère du favori de Marie de Médicis*. Paris: Albin Michel, 1991.

————. *Faire voir, faire croire: l'Opinion publique sous Louis XIII*. Seyssel: Champ Vallon, 2003.

Ducéré, M. *Recherches historiques sur le siège de Fontarabie*. Bayonne: Société des sciences et des arts de Bayonne, 1880.

Duchein, Michel. *Le Duc de Buckingham*. Paris: Fayard, 2001.

Dufourg, Robert. *Un prélat amiral sous Louis XIII, Henri de Sourdis*. Bordeaux: R. Picquot, 1944.

Dulong, Claude. *Anne d'Autriche: Mère de Louis XIV*. Paris: Hachette, 1980.

————. "Les Signes cryptiques dans la correspondance d'Anne d'Autriche avec Mazarin." *Bibliothèque de l'École des Chartes* 140 (1982): 61–83.

Durand, Yves. "Je n'ai jamais eu d'autres ennemis que ceux de l'État: la Mort de Richelieu et le carme Léon de Saint-Jean." In *Études sur l'ancienne France*, ed. B. Barbiche and Y.-M. Bercé, pp. 129–52. Paris: École des Chartes, 2003.

Elliott, John H. *The Count-Duke of Olivares*. New Haven: Yale University Press, 1986.

————. *Richelieu and Olivares*. Cambridge: Cambridge University Press, 1984.

Europa Triumphans: Court and Civic Festivals in Early Modern Europe. Ed. J. R. Mulryne et al. Vol. 2. Aldershot and London: Ashgate and the Modern Humanities Research Association, 2004.

Everat, Edouard. *Michel de Marillac: sa vie, ses œuvres*. Paris: Hachette, 1889.

Externbrink, Sven. "Le Cœur du monde et la liberté de l'Italie: Aspects de la politique italienne de Richelieu, 1624–1642." *Revue d'histoire diplomatique* 114 (2000): 181–208.

Fagniez, Gustave. "Fancan et Richelieu." *Revue historique* 107 (1911): 59–78, 310–22; 108 (1911): 75–87.

————. "Mathieu de Morgues et le procès de Richelieu." *Revue des Deux Mondes* 162 (1900): 530–86.

————. "L'Opinion publique et la presse politique sous Louis XIII, 1624–1626." *Revue d'histoire diplomatique* 14 (1900): 352–401.

————. *Le Père Joseph et Richelieu (1577–1638)*. 2 vols. Paris: Hachette, 1894.

Foisil, Madeleine. *L'Enfant Louis XIII: l'Éducation d'un roi (1601–1617)*. Paris: Perrin, 1996.

————. *La Révolte des Nu-Pieds et les révoltes de Normandie de 1639*. Paris: Presses Universitaires de France, 1970.

Fontenelle de Vaudoré, A.-D. de la. *Histoire du monastère et des évêques de Luçon*. 2 vols. Fontenay-le-Comte: Audin, 1847.

————. *Le Maréchal de La Meilleraye*. Paris: Derache, 1839.

Fouqueray, Henri. *Histoire de La Compagnie de Jésus en France des origines à la suppression (1528–1762)*. 5 vols. Paris: Bureau des études, 1925.

————. *Le Père Jean de Suffren à la cour de Marie de Médicis et de Louis XIII*. Paris: Aux Bureaux de la Revue, 1900.

Franklin, Alfred. *La Cour de France et l'assassinat du maréchal d'Ancre*. Paris: Émile-Paul Frères, 1913.

French Political Pamphlets, 1547–1648. Ed. R. O. Lindsay et al. Madison: University of Wisconsin Press, 1969.

Garde, Henry de la. *Le Duc de Rohan et les protestants sous Louis XIII*. Paris: Plon and Nourrit, 1884.

Gardiner, Samuel Rawson. *History of England from the Accession of James I to the Outbreak of the Civil War*. 10 vols. London, 1883–1884.

———. *Prince Charles and the Spanish Marriages, 1617–1623*. London: Hurst and Blackett, 1869.

Garrison, Charles. "Une erreur historique: les Deux Massacres de Nègrepelisse en 1621 et 1622." *Bulletin de la Société de l'Histoire du Protestantisme français* 43 (1894): 113–21.

Geley, Léon. *Fancan et la politique de Richelieu de 1617 à 1627*. Paris: Cerf, 1884.

Griselle, Eugène. "Un cardinalat différé." *Documents d'histoire* 2 (1911): 527–43.

———. *Profils de Jésuites au XVIIᵉ siècle*. Lille: Société Saint-Augustin and Desclée de Brouwers, c. 1911.

Guervin, M.-H. "En 'L'Année de Corbie.' Maximilien de Belleforière, Marquis de Soyécourt." *Dix-Septième Siècle* 24 (1953): 641–85.

Haehl, Madeleine. *Les Affaires étrangères au temps de Richelieu: le Secrétariat d'état, les agents diplomatiques (1624–1642)*. Brussels: PIE-Peter Lang, 2006.

Hall, Hugh Gaston. *Richelieu's Desmarets and the Century of Louis XIV*. Oxford: Clarendon Press, 1990

Hanotaux, Gabriel. *Histoire du cardinal de Richelieu*. 6 vols. Paris: Firmin-Didot, 1896–1947.

Hauser, Henri. *La Pensée et l'action économique du cardinal de Richelieu*. Paris: Presses Universitaires de France, 1944.

Hayden, J. Michael. "Continuity in the France of Henry IV and Louis XIII: French Foreign Policy, 1598–1615." *Journal of Modern History* 45 (1973): 1–21.

———. *France and the Estates General of 1614*. Cambridge: Cambridge University Press, 1974.

———. "The Uses of Political Pamphlets: The Example of 1614–1615 in France." *Canadian Journal of History* 21 (1986): 143–66.

Hayem, Fernand. *Le Maréchal d'Ancre et Leonora Galigaï*. Paris: Plon and Nourrit, 1910.

Henrard, Paul. *Marie de Médicis dans les Pays-Bas*. Paris: J. Baudry, 1876.

Herman, Arthur. "The Huguenot Republic and Anti-Republicanism in Seventeenth-Century France." *Journal of the History of Ideas* 53 (1992): 249–69.

Hermann de Franceschi, Sylvio. "La Genèse française du catholicisme d'état et son aboutissement au début du ministériat de Richelieu." *Annuaire-bulletin de la Société de l'histoire de France* (2001): 19–63.

Herr, Richard. "Honor versus Absolutism: Richelieu's Fight Against Dueling." *Journal of Modern History* 27 (1955): 281–85.

Hildesheimer, Françoise. "Une créature de Richelieu: Alphonse Lopez, le seigneur Hebreo." In *Les Juifs au regard de l'histoire*, ed. G. Dahan, pp. 293–99. Paris: Picard, 1985.

———. *Relectures de Richelieu*. Paris: Publisud, 2000.

———. *Richelieu*. Paris: Flammarion, 2004.

————. "Richelieu et Séguier ou l'Invention d'une créature." In *Études sur l'ancienne France*, ed. B. Barbiche and Y.-M. Bercé, pp. 209–26. Paris: École des Chartes, 2003.

————. "Les Scrupules de Richelieu." *Journal des Savants* (2000): 99–122.

Histoire de Montauban. Ed. D. Ligou. Toulouse: Privat, 1992.

Horric de Beaucaire, Charles-Prosper-Maurice. "Les Machines du Plessis-Besançon au siège de La Rochelle." *Archives historiques de la Saintonge et de l'Aunis* 18 (1887): 368–88.

Houssaye, Michel. *Le Cardinal de Bérulle et le cardinal de Richelieu, 1625–1629*. Paris: Plon, 1875.

Hugon, Alain. *Au service du Roi Catholique: "Honorables ambassadeurs" et "divins espions."* Madrid: Casa Velásquez, 2004.

Humbert, Jacques. *Les Français en Savoie sous Louis XIII*. Paris: Hachette, 1960.

————. *Le Maréchal de Créquy: Gendre de Lesdiguières (1573–1638)*. Paris: Hachette, 1962.

Jacquart, Jean. "Le Marquis d'Effiat, lieutenant général à l'armée d'Italie (été 1630)." *Dix-Septième Siècle* 45 (1959): 298–313.

Jadart, Henri. *Louis XIII et Richelieu à Reims du 13 juin au 26 juillet 1641*. Reims: F. Michaud, 1885.

James, Alan. "The Development of French Naval Policy in the Seventeenth-Century: Richelieu's Early Aims and Ambitions." *French History* 12 (1998): 384–402.

Jouanna, Arlette. *Le Devoir de révolte: La noblesse française et la gestation de l'État moderne, 1559–1661*. Paris: Fayard, 1989.

Jouhaud, Christian. *La Main de Richelieu ou le Pouvoir cardinal*. Paris: Gallimard, 1991.

Jubert, Gérard. "Michel Le Masle: Chanoine de Notre-Dame-de-Paris, secrétaire de Richelieu (1587–1662)." *Bulletin de la Société de l'histoire de Paris et de l'Île-de-France* (1991): 103–40.

Kerviler, René. *Le Chancellier Pierre Séguier*. Paris: Didier, 1874.

————. *Guillaume Bautru*. Paris: Librairie Menu, 1876.

————. *La Presse politique sous Richelieu et l'académicien Jean de Sirmond (1589–1649)*. Paris: J. Baur, 1876.

Kettering, Sharon. *Power and Reputation at the Court of Louis XIII: The Career of Charles d'Albert, Duc de Luynes (1578–1621)*. Manchester: Manchester University Press, 2008.

Kissinger, Henry. *Diplomacy*. New York: Simon and Shuster, 1994.

Kitchens, III, James H. "Judicial Commissions and the Parlement of Paris: The Case of the Chambre de l'Arsenal." *French Historical Studies* 12 (1982): 323–50.

Kleinman, Ruth. *Anne of Austria, Queen of France*. Columbus: Ohio State University Press, 1985.

Knecht, Robert J. "The Reputation of Cardinal Richelieu: Classical Hero or Romantic Villain." *Papers on French Seventeenth-Century Literature* 15 (1993): 5–24.

Labatut, Jean-Pierre. *Les Ducs et pairs au XVIIᵉ siècle*. Paris: Presses Universitaires de France, 1972.

La Bruyère, René. *La Marine de Richelieu: Maillé-Brézé général des galères, grand amiral (1619–1646)*. Paris: Plon, 1945.

Lacour-Gayet, G. *La Marine militaire de la France*. Vol. 1. Paris: H. Champion, 1911.

Lacroix, Lucien. *Richelieu à Luçon: sa Jeunesse, son épiscopat*. Paris: Letouzay et Ané, 1890.

La Force, Duc de. *Le Maréchal de La Force: le Serviteur de sept rois (1558–1652)*. Paris: Éd. de la Table Ronde, 1950.

Larcade, Véronique. "L'Affaire de Fontarabie (1638–1639): L'Exploitation d'une défaite." In *La Défaite*, ed. M. Vaïsse, pp. 29–42. Reims: Presses Universitaires de Reims, 1994.

Laurain-Portemer, Madeleine. *Une Tête à gouverner quatre empires. Études mazarines*, vol. 2. Paris: chez l'auteur, 1997.

Lecestre, L. "Un mémoire inédit de Richelieu." *Revue des questions historiques* 43 (1888): 234–50.

La Légende de Richelieu. Paris and La Roche-sur-Yon: Somogy and Conseil général de la Vendée, 2008.

Legné, Gabriel. *Urbain Grandier et les possédées de Loudun*. Paris: Charpentier, 1884.

Le Pas de Sécheval, Anne. "Le Cardinal de Richelieu, le théâtre et les décorateurs italiens." *Dix-Septième Siècle* 186 (1995): 135–45.

Lockyer, Roger. *Buckingham*. London and New York: Longman, 1981.

Lonchay, Henri. *La Rivalité de la France et de l'Espagne aux Pays-Bas (1635–1700)*. Brussels: Imprimerie De Hayez, 1896.

Louis, Gérard. *La Guerre de Dix Ans, 1634–1644*. Besançon: Presses de l'Université de Franche-Comté, 2005.

Magne, Émile. *Voiture et les origines de l'hôtel de Rambouillet, 1597–1635*. Paris: Mercure de France, 1911.

Major, J. Russell. *Representative Government in Early Modern France*. New Haven: Yale University Press, 1980.

Malettke, Klaus. "Le Concept de sécurité collective de Richelieu et les traités de paix de Westphalie." In *L'Europe des traités de Westphalie*, ed. L. Bély, pp. 55–61. Paris: Presses Universitaires de France, 2000.

———. *Les Relations entre la France et le Saint-Empire au XVIIᵉ siècle*. Paris: H. Champion, 2001.

Malvezzi, Aldobrandino. "Papa Urbano VIII e la questione della Valtellina." *Archivio storico lombardo* 7 (1958): 5–113.

Mann, Golo. *Wallenstein*. New York: Holt, Rinehart, and Winston, 1976.

Marie de Médicis: Un gouvernement par les arts. Blois and Paris: Château de Blois and Somogy éditions d'art, 2003.

Mariéjol, J. H. *Henri IV et Louis XIII (1598–1643)*. Vol. 6, part 2 of *Histoire de France illustrée*, ed. E. Lavisse. Paris: Hachette, 1891.

Marvick, Elizabeth W. "Favorites in Early Modern Europe: A Recurring Psychopolitical Role." *Journal of Psychohistory* 10 (1983): 463–89.

———. *Louis XIII: The Making of a King*. New Haven: Yale University Press, 1986.

———. *The Young Richelieu: A Psychoanalytic Approach to Leadership*. Chicago: University of Chicago Press, 1983.

Mastellone, Silvio. *La Reggenza di Maria de' Medici*. Messina: d'Anna, 1962.

Michaud, Claude. "François Sublet de Noyers superintendant des bâtiments de France." *Revue historique* 241 (1969): 327–64.

Mieck, Ilja. "L'Assassinat de Wallenstein." In *Complots et conjurations dans l'Europe moderne*, ed. Y.-M. Bercé and E. Fasano Guarini, pp. 507–34. Rome: École française de Rome, 1996.

Minot, Pierre. *Sur quelques cas de psychopathie dans la famille du cardinal de Richelieu*. Paris: Imprimerie de la faculté de médecine, 1927.

Mongrédien, Georges. *Le Bourreau du cardinal de Richelieu: Isaac de Laffemas (1584-1657)*. Paris: Bossard, 1929.

———. *La Journée des Dupes*. Paris: Gallimard, 1961.

———. *Leonora Galigaï: Un procès de sorcellerie sous Louis XIII*. Paris: Hachette, 1968.

———. *Marion de Lorme à la Place-Royale. Les Œuvres libres*. Paris: Fayard, 1939.

Moote, A. Lloyd. *Louis XIII, the Just*. Berkeley: University of California Press, 1989.

Morgain, Stéphane-Marie. "L'Église est-elle dans l'État ou l'État est-il dans l'église?" *Pierre d'Angle* 5 (1999): 73–86.

Mousnier, Roland. *L'Homme rouge ou la Vie du cardinal de Richelieu (1585–1642)*. Paris: Laffont, 1992.

Murray, Timothy C. "Richelieu's Theater: The Mirror of a Prince." *Renaissancy Drama* 8 (1977): pp. 275–98.

Noailles, Vicomte de. *Épisodes de la guerre de Trente Ans*. 3 vols. Paris: Perrin, 1906–1913.

Nosjean, Madeleine. "Le Siège de La Rochelle et les poètes du temps." *Dix-Septième Siècle* 42 (1990): 433–45.

Orcibal, Jean. *Jean Duvergier de Hauranne, Abbé de Saint-Cyran et son temps (1581–1638)*. Vol. 2, *Les Origines du Jansénisme*. Louvain and Paris: Bureaux de la revue and J. Vrin, 1947.

Pace, Claire. "Le Plus Illustre des Amateurs: Aspects of Richelieu's Patronage of the Visual Arts." *Seventeenth-Century French Studies* 15 (1993): 33–54.

Pagès, Georges. "Autour du Grand Orage. Richelieu et Marillac: Deux Politiques." *Revue historique* 179 (1937): 63–97.

———. *La Guerre de Trente Ans*. Paris: Payot, 1939.

Pange, Jean de. *Charnacé et l'alliance franco-hollandaise (1633–1637)*. Paris: A. Picard et fils, 1905.

Parker, David. *La Rochelle and the French Monarchy: Conflict and Order in Seventeenth-Century France*. London: Royal Historical Society, 1980.

Parker, Geoffrey. *The Army of Flanders and the Spanish Road, 1567–1659*. Cambridge: Cambridge University Press, 1972.

Parrott, David. "The Causes of the Franco-Spanish War of 1635–1659." In *The Origins of War in Early Modern Europe*, ed. J. Black, pp. 72–111. Edinburgh: J. Donald, 1987.

———. "The Mantuan Succession, 1627–1631: A Sovereignty Dispute in Early Modern Europe." *English Historical Review* 112 (1997): 20–65.

———. "A Prince Souverain and the French Crown: Charles de Nevers, 1580–1637." In *Royal and Republican Sovereignty in Early Modern Europe*, ed. R. Oresko et al., pp. 149–87. Cambridge: Cambridge University Press, 1997.

———. *Richelieu's Army*. Cambridge: Cambridge University Press, 2001.

Pavie, Eusèbe. *La Guerre entre Louis XIII et Marie de Médicis*. Angers: Germain and Grassin, 1899.

Pépin, Eugène. "Une ville créée au XVIIᵉ siècle: Richelieu, cité du cardinal." *La Vie urbaine*, new series, 4 (1966): 241–54.

Perrens, François-Tommy. *L'Église et l'État sous le règne de Henri IV et la régence de Marie de Médicis*. 2 vols. Paris: Durand and Pedone-Launiel, 1872.

———. *Les Mariages espagnols sous le règne de Henri IV et la régence de Marie de Médicis*. Paris: Didier, n.d.

Petitfils, Jean-Christian. *Louis XIII*. Paris: Perrin, 2008.

Pintard, René. "Pastorale et comédie héroïque chez Richelieu." *Revue d'histoire du théâtre* 64 (1964): 447–51.

Pithon, Rémy. "Les Débuts difficiles du ministère de Richelieu et la crise de la Valteline." *Revue d'histoire diplomatique* 74 (1960): 298–322.

————. "La Suisse, théâtre de la guerre froide entre la France et l'Espagne pendant la crise de la Valteline (1621–1626)." *Schweizerische Zeitschrift für Geschichte* 13 (1963): 33–53.

Poisson, Georges. *La Duchesse de Chevreuse*. Paris: Perrin, 1999.

Prat, J. M. *Recherches historiques et critiques sur la Compagnie de Jésus au temps du P. Coton, 1564–1626*. 4 vols. Lyon: Briday, 1876.

Prunières, Henry. *Le Ballet de cour en France avant Benserade et Lully*. Paris: H. Laurens, 1914.

Puyol, abbé. *Louis XIII et le Béarn*. Paris: de Soye et fils, 1872.

Quazza, Romolo. *La Guerra per la Successione di Mantova e del Monferrato (1628–1631)*. 2 vols. Mantua: G. Mondovi, 1926.

————. "La Politica di Carlo Emanuele I durante la guerra dei Trent'Anni." In *Carlo Emanuele I miscellanea*, vol. 2, pp. 3–45. Turin: Biblioteca della Società storica subalpina, 1930.

————. "Politica Europea nella questione valtellinica." *Nuovo archivio veneto* 42 (1921): 50–151.

————. *Tommaso di Savoia-Carignano nelle campagne di Fiandra e di Francia, 1635–1638*. Turin: Società Editrice Internazionale, 1941.

Quelques procès criminels des XVIIe et XVIIIe siècles. Ed. J. Imbert. Paris: Presses Universitaires de France, 1964.

Ranum, Orest. *Artisans of Glory: Writers and Historical Thought in Seventeenth-Century France*. Chapel Hill: University of North Carolina Press, c. 1980.

————. *Paris in the Age of Absolutism*. University Park: Penn State University Press, 2002.

————. *Richelieu and the Councillors of Louis XIII*. Oxford: Clarendon Press, 1963.

Rapports et notices sur l'édition des Mémoires du cardinal de Richelieu. 3 vols. Paris: Renouard, 1907–1914.

Représentation et vouloir politique. Ed. R. Chartier and D. Richet. Paris: Éditions de l'École des hautes études en sciences sociales. 1982.

Richelieu and His Age. Ed. J. Bergin and L. Brockliss. Oxford: Clarendon Press, 1992.

Richelieu et la culture. Ed. R. Mousnier. Paris: Centre National de la Recherche Scientifique, 1987.

Richelieu et le monde de l'esprit. Paris: Imprimerie nationale, 1985.

Richelieu: l'Art et le Pouvoir. Ed. H. T. Goldfarb. Montréal: Musée des Beaux Arts, 2002.

Richet, Denis. *La France Moderne: l'Esprit des institutions*. Paris: Flammarion, 1973.

Roberts, Michael. *Gustavus Adolphus and the Rise of Sweden*. London: English Universities Presses, 1973.

Rochemonteix, Camille de. *Nicolas Caussin: Confesseur de Louis XIII*. Paris: A. Picard et fils, 1911.

Rodocanachi, E. *Les Derniers Temps du siège de La Rochelle (1628): Relation du nonce apostolique*. Paris: A. Picard et fils, 1899.

Rott, Édouard. "Rohan et Richelieu." *Revue d'histoire diplomatique* 27 (1913): 161–204.

Russell Major, J. "The Revolt of 1620: A Study in the Ties of Fidelity." *French Historical Studies* 14 (1986): 391–408.

Sawyer, Jeffrey K. *Printed Poison: Pamphlet Propaganda, Faction Politics, and the Public Sphere in Early Seventeenth-Century France.* Berkeley: University of California Press, 1990.

Schalk, Ellery. *From Valor to Pedigree: Ideas of Nobility in France in the Sixteenth and Seventeenth Century.* Princeton: Princeton University Press, 1986.

Schloder, John E. "Un artiste oublié: Nicolas Prévost, peintre de Richelieu." *Bulletin de la Société de l'histoire de l'art français* (1980): 59–69.

Schmidt, J.-A. *Les Campagnes de Louis XIII en Lorraine.* Nancy: L. Wiener, 1868.

Solomon, Howard M. *Public Welfare, Science, and Propaganda in Seventeenth-Century France.* Princeton: Princeton University Press, 1972.

Stradling, Robert A. "Catastrophe and Recovery: The Defeat of Spain, 1639–1643." *History, the Journal of the Historical Association* 64 (1979): 205–19.

―――. "Olivares and the Origins of the Franco-Spanish War, 1627–1635." *English Historical Review* 101 (1986): 68–94.

Tapié, Victor-L. *La France de Louis XIII et de Richelieu.* Paris: Flammarion, 1967.

―――. *La Politique étrangère de la France et le début de la guerre de Trente Ans (1616–1621).* Paris: Leroux, 1934.

The Thirty Years' War. Ed. G. Parker. London and New York: Routledge, 1984.

Thuillier, Jacques. *Rubens: la Galerie Médicis au Palais du Luxembourg.* Paris and Milan: Laffont and Rizzoli, 1969.

Toulier, Christine. "Richelieu: La Ville du cardinal." *Bulletin de la Société des amis du vieux Chinon* 9 (1993): 785–816.

Trevor-Roper, Hugh. *Europe's Physician: The Various Life of Sir Theodore de Mayerne.* New Haven: Yale University Press, 2006.

Trudel, Marcel. *The Beginnings of New France, 1524–1663.* Toronto: McLelland and Stewart, 1973.

Vaissières, Pierre de. *La Conjuration de Cinq-Mars.* Paris: Hachette, 1928.

―――. *Un grand procès sous Richelieu: l'Affaire du maréchal de Marillac (1630–1632).* Paris: Denin, 1924.

Valone, James S. *Huguenot Politics, 1601–1622.* Lewiston: E. Mellen, 1994.

Variétés historiques et littéraires. 10 vols. Paris: P. Jannet, 1855–1863.

Vassal-Reig, Charles. *La Guerre en Roussillon sous Louis XIII (1635–1639).* Paris: Occitania, 1934.

―――. *La Prise de Perpignan (1641–1642).* Paris: Caffin, 1939.

―――. *Richelieu et la Catalogne.* Paris: Occitania, 1935.

Vaux de Foletier, François de. *Le Siège de La Rochelle.* Paris and La Rochelle: Quartier Latin and Rupella, 1978.

Vigier, Octave. "Une invasion en France sous Louis XIII." *Revue des questions historiques* 56, new series, 12 (1894): 440–92.

Vignal Souleyreau, Marie-Catherine. *Richelieu et la Lorraine.* Paris: L'Harmattan, 2004.

―――. *Richelieu ou la Quête d'Europe.* Paris: Pygmalion, 2008.

Waddington, A. *La République des Provinces-Unies, la France et les Pays-Bas espagnols de 1630 à 1650.* Vol. 1. Paris: G. Masson, 1895.

Weber, Hermann. "Richelieu et le Rhin." *Revue historique* 239 (1968): 265–80.

Wedgwood, Cicely V. *The Thirty Years' War*. New York: New York Review of Books, 2005.

Weibull, Lauritz. "Gustave-Adolphe et Richelieu." *Revue historique* 174 (1934): 216–29.

Whitaker, Katie. *A Royal Passion: The Turbulent Marriage of King Charles I of England and Henrietta Maria of France*. New York: W. W. Norton, 2010.

Wilson, Peter H. *The Thirty Years' War: Europe's Tragedy*. Cambridge: Belknap Press, 2009.

Wollenberg, Jörg. *Les Trois Richelieu: Servir dieu, le roi et la raison*. Paris: F. X. de Guibert, 1995.

Zeller, Berthold. *Le Connétable de Luynes, Montauban et la Valteline*. Paris: Didier, 1879.

———. *Louis XIII, Marie de Médicis chef de conseil*. Paris: Hachette, 1898.

———. *Louis XIII, Marie de Médicis, Richelieu ministre*. Paris: Hachette, 1899.

———. *Richelieu et les ministres de Louis XIII*. Paris: Hachette, 1880.

IMAGE CREDITS

1. *Armand-Jean du Plessis, Cardinal Richelieu* by Philippe de Champaigne. La Sorbonne, Paris. © Archives Charmet/The Bridgeman Art Library.

2. *Louis XIII as a Boy* by Frans Pourbus the Younger. Galleria Palatina, Palazzo Pitti, Florence. © Nimatallah/Art Resource, New York.

3. *Louis XIII* by Philippe de Champaigne. Museo del Prado, Madrid. © The Bridgeman Art Library.

4. *Marie de' Medici* by Peter Paul Rubens. Museo del Prado, Madrid. © Boltin Picture Library/The Bridgeman Art Library.

5. *Gaston d'Orléans* by Anthony van Dyck. Musée Condé, Chantilly. © Giraudon/The Bridgeman Art Library.

6. *Anne of Austria* by Peter Paul Rubens. Musée du Louvre, Paris. © Erich Lessing/Art Resource, New York.

7. *View of the Château and Gardens of Richelieu* by Jean Marot. Bibliothèque Nationale, Paris. © Giraudon/The Bridgeman Art Library.

8. *Louis XIII, Anne of Austria, and Cardinal Richelieu at the Theater of the Palais-Cardinal in 1641 (Ballet de la Prospérité des armes de France)* by Juste d'Egmont. Bibliothèque des Arts Décoratifs, Paris. © Archives Charmet/The Bridgeman Art Library.

9. *Marquis de Cinq-Mars* by an unknown artist. Musée Mandet, Riom. © Scala/White Images/Art Resource, New York.

Jean-Vincent Blanchard is associate professor of French Studies at Swarthmore College, Pennsylvania. Born in Canada and raised in Europe, he earned his Ph.D. from Yale University in 1997. He is a specialist on pre-revolutionary France, with particular emphasis on the seventeenth century, and has published on a broad range of subjects in politics, history, religion, philosophy, and the arts. *Éminence* is his first book in English.